What Your Colleague

I love the book! It was a quick read and super useful. As an educational leader on the ground, I found the clarity of the spoken feedback chapter a "for sure we need to study" at my site. Teachers love to give verbal feedback, but meaningful feedback that acknowledges the work, gives specifics, and pushes for students to continue to grow is a hard balance. I also find the chapter on nonverbal feedback extremely useful, especially when we think of students new to the country where English may be a second or third language. When I think about newcomers, they are on constant overload. They are listening to a language they do not fully understand, reading a language that may be very odd, and trying to understand what someone is saying. The combinations of spoken, nonverbal, and written feedback suggested in this book can make a tangible difference. Regardless of what levels of language learners are in your classroom, everyone wants to be better and grow. Can't wait to grab *Feedback for Continuous Improvement in the Classroom* for my staff when it comes out!

Amber Andrade
Principal
Paradise Valley Engineering Academy
Morgan Hill Unified School District

I enjoyed this book, and if you are an educator keen to provide feedback that is effective and equitable for your students, so will you. The book covers some territory that may initially be familiar, with formative assessment practices as its backdrop, but it does so from new vantage points and with connections to a slew of different strategies that can deepen those practices so teachers provide feedback to advance student learning or to facilitate their students in providing feedback to one another or engaging in self-driven formative feedback. The power of this book stems from the different ways the authors support the reader's own learning—they use some of the very techniques they are promoting with our students. Using guiding questions and the SOLO taxonomy, the reader is invited to gauge their own learning about formative assessment and feedback along the way. "Scaffolds and Guided Practice" sections, discussion starters, and activities for lesson study and professional learning communities as well as "Try It Tomorrow" ideas that include useful tips for using technology to efficiently record and share feedback provide opportunities for educators to try out suggestions. A "Ticket Out the Door" section at the close of each chapter prompts both further practice and reflection. All this adds up to skillfully answering the central question of the book: How can we use feedback effectively and equitably to ensure all of our students are ready for college and the workplace because they know how to and are able to use feedback for continuous improvement?

Alison Bailey
Professor, UCLA Graduate School of Education & Information Studies
Former Project Director for Assessing English Language Proficiency at the Center for The Study of Evaluation & National Center for Research on Evaluation, Standards, and Student Testing (CRESST)

This book couldn't be more timely. As the world heals from a pandemic and school leaders and teachers are expected to accelerate student learning and address their social-emotional needs, the commitment to feedback for all can help us feel and be more connected. I appreciate the focus on equity and excellence that lies at the heart of each chapter. Duckor and Holmberg understand that formative assessment and continuous feedback are critical to engaging, eliciting, and extending student learning. This book provides concrete research-based tools with videos, reflective questions, vignettes, and self-assessments to help us engage students in their learning through formative feedback. If your staff engage in these practices, your students are sure to benefit!

Blanca Baltazar-Sabbah
Former Associate Superintendent
Salinas Unified High School District

Feedback for Continuous Improvement in the Classroom: New Perspectives, Practices, and Possibilities is an absolute must-have for educators energized to close existing opportunity gaps by putting student work back at the center of learning. By using formative feedback as a tool to create schools that "work for all students," Duckor and Holmberg weave authentic stories, practical strategies, and evidence-based practices that capitalize on their extensive partnerships with TK–12 schools. Targeted for pre-service and in-service teachers, school administrators, and teacher educators, this book is essential for any educator searching for how to enact transformational practices. I loved it and I am confident my teacher candidates will, too!

Nicole Barnes
Professor, Department of Educational Foundations
Montclair State University

Brent Duckor and Carrie Holmberg's *Feedback for Continuous Improvement in the Classroom: New Perspectives, Practices, and Possibilities* is a "must-read" for educators at every level. It is chock-full of practical examples and guiding questions and is the perfect guide for improving assessment practices in classrooms. I intend to use it in a book study with educators in my work this year.

Carrie Bosco
Assistant Superintendent, Curriculum & Instruction
Los Altos School District

The authors' commitment to every child having the right to learn as part of democratic education shines through the book, as does their commitment to feedback as the exchange of information that serves as the link between equity and excellence. Throughout the text, research evidence is interleaved with practical examples and prompts for reflection and self-assessment. The classroom examples in particular resonated with me. Throughout, the nature of and possibilities for student participation are outlined with sensitivity and respect for student ideas and agency. I can readily imagine that *Feedback for Continuous Improvement in the Classroom* could anchor productive and provocative individual and collective learning aligned with the authors' vision of education as an opportunity for students and teachers to learn, care, and experience joy.

Bronwen Cowie
Professor and Associate Dean of Research
University of Waikato
New Zealand

Feedback for Continuous Improvement in the Classroom is a deft, accomplished guide to an important but seldom examined feature of teaching. While reforms come and go, feedback will remain an enduring feature of teachers' work in our schools. Both novice and mid-career teachers will benefit from this book.

Larry Cuban
Professor Emeritus, Graduate School of Education
Stanford University

In *Feedback for Continuous Improvement in the Classroom*, Brent Duckor and Carrie Holmberg combine important scholarly insights from past and current reforms with deep knowledge from their work as expert educators to produce a blueprint for building equitable schools that enable all students to learn and grow continuously. The book's focus on classroom teaching with rich tasks and real-world projects aptly re-centers the need for authentic assessment in the 21st century. By bringing forth a vision of the future that builds firmly on past reform, Brent and Carrie's work offers policymakers and practitioners a solid foundation for progress in supporting success for all.

Linda Darling-Hammond
President
California State Board of Education

There are many books on feedback, but hardly any have sticking power. Brent Duckor and Carrie Holmberg's *Feedback for Continuous Improvement in the Classroom* is a deep winner. It is comprehensive yet specific and powerful in all respects. The chapter formats are well-designed for garnering author insights, using guiding questions, identifying purpose-driven feedback goals, and accessing a plethora of tools, organizers, videos, and touchpoints to advance schools and systems from inside the classroom. The core of their action-oriented formative feedback framework is crystal clear and well-aligned with other reform efforts across California and beyond. The book is based on the premise of teacher-driven, teacher-led change that enables leaders in the building as well as peers to join as guides on the side in the promise of effective feedback for all children. I especially liked the chapter on peer-driven feedback with its guiding questions and other tools to promote focused collaboration in the classroom. The authors provide very clear distinctions about what peer-driven formative feedback is and isn't, and they consistently offer practical tips and to-do's to bring everyone toward deeper learning and consensus on what matters. All in all, Duckor and Holmberg's latest book is a treasure trove of ideas, insights, and schemas that benefit individuals as well as teams and groups of teachers. It covers the gamut of feedback exchanges from individuals to small groups to the whole class and back to oneself. This is a true accomplishment, in large part, based on their deep experiences with middle and high school assessment reform for many decades.

Michael Fullan
Global Leadership Director
New Pedagogies for Deep Learning

Busy practitioners want to know what to do tomorrow. Duckor and Holmberg's *Feedback for Continuous Improvement in the Classroom* delivers the "Try It Tomorrow" and tech tips to get feedback happening *now* in your classroom. Putting aside the dysfunctional detail and stale ideas about the role of rubrics, the authors open up new possibilities with progress guides for student, peer, and teacher-led assessment that deepen learning. All teacher educators can use this book as a resource to teach the *how* and the *why* while getting new feedback processes and routines up and running with novices and more seasoned instructors at your school. Both practical and philosophically grounded, this book is a worthy addition to the playbook of any progressive, equity-minded educator.

Ben Daley
President
High Tech High Graduate School of Education

Duckor and Holmberg's latest book, *Feedback for Continuous Improvement in the Classroom*, challenges society's obsession with grades, turning our attention toward ways in which specific, timely formative feedback invites TK–12 students to reflect upon, deepen, and stretch their thinking, shedding light on understanding and possibilities. This is the real work of teaching and learning. Going beyond the research findings, this book proposes actionable ways teachers might better embed formative feedback into their curriculum, creating a feedback-rich school culture—one classroom, one student at a time.

Annamarie M. Francois
Executive Director, UCLA Center X
UC Representative, California Commission on Teacher Credentialing
UCLA School of Education & Information Studies

Duckor and Holmberg's *Feedback for Continuous Improvement in the Classroom* fills an important gap between the general knowledge that formative feedback is critical for supporting student learning and the knowledge of how to actually provide students the feedback that will support them best. The power of the book lies in the balance between a framework that provides a comprehensive view of the different contexts and types of feedback and the specific details of how those factors shape what the most effective feedback structures and approaches look like in practice. This work will be critical to policymakers looking to better connect systems of support to the daily work of equity-driven teaching and learning in California schools.

H. Alix Gallagher
Director of Strategic Partnerships
Policy Analysis for California Education (PACE)

In their compelling book, Duckor and Holmberg make a powerful, nuanced case for the necessity of feedback for a democratic education. They spell out why and how both teacher-driven and student-driven feedback works, offer lots of practical advice (including many examples of feedback as well as advice from teachers), and provide structured opportunities for readers' reflection and self-assessment. Anyone who wants to understand the value of feedback and how to put it into practice to benefit learning should definitely read this book.

Margaret Heritage
Educational Consultant and Author

Teachers in different types of schools, regions, and cultural contexts will all find this book very relevant and helpful to their work. As formative assessment has become an important ingredient in classroom instruction, the question of how to give formative feedback follows naturally. Yet, limited resources are available on feedback. This book provides a framework to understand formative feedback as well as many concrete suggestions on how to take action in various classroom settings. With guiding questions, definition boxes, and well-selected examples, the chapters are easy to read and the tips from the authors are easy to implement. In summary, Duckor and Holmberg's *Feedback for Continuous Improvement in the Classroom* is a wonderful reference on formative feedback. It will be worthwhile to have different language versions of this book so that teachers in other countries and regions can benefit from it, too.

Xiaoting Huang
Graduate School of Education
Peking University, China

Feedback has been argued to be an important and powerful tool in a teacher's pedagogical repertoire, and yet it often remains fleeting and practiced without deep considerations of the complex suite of curricular ideas and instructional and assessment strategies that can empower learners and learning. Duckor and Holmberg's *Feedback for Continuous Improvement in the Classroom* is a research-informed, authentic, and easy-to-read book that provides practitioners with a comprehensive understanding of formative feedback that can improve their practices and increase student engagement and learning. The book beautifully weaves together theory, research, evidence, examples, and practical ideas in a highly accessible manner to help teachers effectively mobilize feedback in constructive and powerful ways in their classrooms. Through their formative feedback framework, Duckor and Holmberg have produced a fantastic resource for teachers in any educational setting to reflect on their own practice; engage deeply with fundamental ideas on feedback, rich tasks, learning goals, learning contexts, configurations, modalities, and directionalities of feedback; and ultimately bring their feedback practices to the next level.

Dennis Kwek
Director, Centre for Research in Pedagogy and Practice
Associate Dean Strategic Engagement
National Institute of Education, Singapore

Huge kudos to Brent Duckor and Carrie Holmberg for offering our communities *Feedback for Continuous Improvement in the Classroom: New Perspectives, Practices, and Possibilities*. The depth, breadth, and practicality of this book will be a great tool for teachers and those who support teachers in improving teaching, learning, and assessment. Our own gold standards for project-based learning design and teaching elements are highly aligned with the tools and processes detailed in Duckor and Holmberg's book. Their unique focus on long-cycle projects, utilizing different lenses on feedback with shared progress guides, is a welcome innovation. There are many synergies, including elements of reflection, critique, and revision and student voice and choice in our design elements, and assessment and scaffolding of student learning in our teaching elements at PBL Works. Our curriculum and teacher consulting teams at the Buck Institute for Education (PBL Works and PBL Now) look forward to sharing *Feedback for Continuous Improvement in the Classroom: New Perspectives, Practices, and Possibilities* and its strategies with the teachers and education leaders we work with across the United States and the world.

Bob Lenz
President
PBL Works

There is a general consensus in the field that instructional feedback has great potential to improve a range of student outcomes. However, questions of how it works, for whom, and under what instructional circumstances still stand. *Feedback for Continuous Improvement in the Classroom: New Perspectives, Practices, and Possibilities* will help you to get answers to these—and many other—questions. If you want to understand the nature, purpose, applications, processing, and caveats of feedback, this book is for you. It is a terrific resource for teacher candidates, in-service teachers, and researchers who want a quick yet thorough introduction to the field of feedback. Thank you for this terrific volume!

Anastasiya Lipnevich
Professor
Queens College & the Graduate Center, City University of New York

Duckor and Holmberg have given us a roadmap to deepen feedback with concrete tools to deepen assessment for learning in our district. The introduction of progress guides to our teachers' classroom assessment repertoire led to a shift in a group of educators, immediately appearing in math and science classrooms of participating teachers. These guides opened up new possibilities for self and peer-led assessments; we'd been waiting to provide that purposeful feedback that moves student learning forward. The teachers, staff, and instructional coaches jumped on board. Practical and innovative, this book is different. It is equity in action for all our kids.

Elida MacArthur
Superintendent
Mount Pleasant Elementary School District

This impressive, scholarly book is destined to become a seminal text on formative feedback, primarily because it puts myriad feedback practices at the epicenter of student achievement in a systematic way. In ten clearly written chapters, the authors present feedback practices that are based on contemporary research as well as classroom constraints and realities, with an emphasis on how feedback connects with ambitious teaching and equity. It is unique in providing an in-depth, comprehensive, engaging, and research-based treatment of all aspects of providing formative feedback that enhances student learning, including spoken, nonverbal, written, peer-based, individual, and small-group feedback. Notably, each chapter contains numerous learning aides, including teacher reflections and quotes, videos, author insights, guiding questions, examples, templates, and chapter recaps that will enhance practitioner applications to unique contexts.

James McMillan
Professor Emeritus
Virginia Commonwealth University

Every part of this book points at the purpose of public investment in education in any democracy. Feedback is not a luxury or afterthought. It must be practiced in every classroom and experienced in our schools. The power of formative feedback in the classroom—by all and with all—is on display in Duckor and Holmberg's work. This timely book focuses on the habits of feedback that true democracy—with a small *d*—requires of us all!

Deborah Meier
Founder
Central Park East Schools, NYC

Providing students with effective feedback is an important aspect of teaching, as it can significantly contribute to their learning and, ultimately, their achievement. By providing frequent, constructive, and instructive feedback to students, teachers can begin to bridge the gap between a student's current state and the desired student outcomes. Duckor and Holmberg's *Feedback for Continuous Improvement in the Classroom: New Perspectives, Practices, and Possibilities* provides a well-conceived and accessible framework for teachers, instructional coaches, and professional developers for considering how to better incorporate student feedback on a more consistent basis throughout the learning cycle. The text will be a useful resource for all educators.

Tonya R. Moon
Professor and Director of Education and Human Development Institutes
on Academic Diversity
University of Virginia

It is no secret that improving student learning requires deep collaboration and problem solving, which requires specific purpose-driven feedback guided by the desire to improve. *Feedback for Continuous Improvement in the Classroom* provides educators a road map with specific processes and structures that enhance effective feedback for the purposes of improving learning goals that are supported by rich learning tasks.

Matt Navo
Executive Director
California Collaborative for Educational Excellence (CCEE)

Acclaimed African American educator and civil rights activist who was a national advisor to Franklin D. Roosevelt, Mary McCloud Bethune, had a motto for school: Enter to learn, depart to serve. Highly skilled, equity-minded teachers are vital to the success of all students and the future of our country. To reach every child, we need teachers who see formative feedback as one of the core missions of school. Duckor and Holmberg's latest book, *Feedback for Continuous Improvement in the Classroom*, equips the reader with a dynamic repertoire of teacher moves and strategies necessary to serve students effectively so that they will not only learn but thrive. It's something the profession has needed for a long time and it's well worth the read.

Jacquelyn Ollison
Co-director
California Teacher Residency Lab

Duckor and Holmberg's newest book lays out an important challenge for policymakers, one that is worth taking up as we rethink systems of support to address inequity. They start with the subtle yet obvious idea: Feedback for our students is the foundation of public education in a democracy. Then with the hard-earned wisdom of practice, they show how accessible this vision is.

State accountability frameworks and support systems need to find room for the formative feedback framework presented here; this is our future. In the meantime, teachers, staff, and administrative leaders can use this book to initiate change for how students and educators experience education today.

Glen Price
Founder, GPG
Former Chief Deputy Superintendent, California Department of Education

In China, we have a long history with the concept of feedback. Every master and apprentice relied on feedback to communicate. Sadly, in modern Chinese culture, "face is bigger than sky;" therefore, too often, it is not as easy to receive sincere and constructive feedback. We refrain from giving honest feedback not because we don't want to but because we don't know how. That's why I was so excited when I found out that Duckor and Holmberg are putting together a book on such a crucial but neglected topic. With innovative insights and practical tips like this, I hope feedback in China may evolve to become the upgrade and substitute of "traditional" assessment, as it is more effective and more useful to the apprentice, especially in student-centered and project-based learning environments.

Terry Qian
Founder
UNSCHOOL

New teachers want resources to help them build relationships with children and young people—from day one. Advice and support from expert educators can help them grow their capacity to connect their passion for subject matter with good feedback practices to support student learning. Brent and Carrie's latest book, *Feedback for Continuous Improvement in the Classroom*, is a remarkable resource for our new teachers and their mentors. Every chapter captures a dimension of formative feedback in the classroom and provides strategies to use and reflect upon. Rooted in research on what works, the book provides a blueprint for building teacher capacity to lead equitable and equity-focused classrooms and schools. It empowers all of us who support the teaching profession to envision what a focus on growth, care, and connection with our students truly means. Teachers are deeply respected in these pages and all are invited to improve continuously.

Mary Vixie Sandy
Executive Director
California Commission on Teacher Credentialing

This is a major piece of work on feedback, one that is teacher-friendly and caring. Teachers and teacher educators will have a major source of information on formative feedback in all its variations at their fingertips.

Rich Shavelson
Professor Emeritus and Former Dean, Graduate School of Education
Stanford University

In their latest book, *Feedback for Continuous Improvement in the Classroom*, Duckor and Holmberg have done a beautiful job of attending to the relational and collaborative aspects of meaningful feedback. Once again, ambitious teaching is seamlessly interwoven with research-based formative assessment strategies. By emphasizing a focus on long-cycle projects, rich tasks, and other meaningful assignments—those that offer opportunities for deeper feedback exchanges in the classroom—they successfully demonstrate why feedback is what makes the difference in supporting and improving student learning. I appreciate that the book offers practical prompts, tools, and routines that help students internalize criteria for quality work and supports them in developing agency as they engage with teachers and peers to learn and improve. There are lots of examples that bring to life research on what makes feedback essential to deeper learning, and it is clear these authors speak from hard-won experience in assessment reform.

Lorrie A. Shepard
Distinguished Professor
Former Dean, School of Education
University of Colorado Boulder

Like a chocolate lava cake, this book is rich with new insights and can be consumed slowly, but in the end, you'll be fully satisfied with a new perspective on feedback. Duckor and Holmberg have done a great job making their formative feedback framework accessible to a wide range of readers, but most importantly, it is written with teachers in mind. I enjoyed the logical array of the chapters, each one containing advance organizers, periodic calls for self-reflection, practical examples provided by real teachers, and takeaways at the end. As noted in the opening, it is "formative feedback that matters most to continuous improvement." Duckor and Holmberg's book has delivered a recipe to help students and teachers achieve this goal in today's classrooms.

Valerie Shute
Professor Emerita
Florida State University

Feedback for Continuous Improvement in the Classroom: New Perspectives, Practices, and Possibilities is the perfect book for educators at all levels who want to be absolutely current with the research, thinking, and practice on instructional feedback. Duckor and Holmberg present readers with a thorough and accessible introduction to the field and bring them right up to the minute on current thinking in this rapidly evolving and increasingly complex field. It would be great as a text for teacher education, or individual chapters could be "starters" for in-service workshops. My feedback is simple: Congratulations on an excellent job!

Jeffrey K. Smith
Former Dean, College of Education
Otago University
New Zealand

We can argue whether or not humans are the only teachers in the animal kingdom, but there is no question that our species alone provides feedback on performance. We might therefore consider feedback on learning as the pinnacle of pedagogy. Do we gain our capacity for assessing learners and offering guidance by instinct or extensive practice? This outstanding book obviates the question because it shows in careful detail and in the use of extensive examples how to learn what learners know (and have yet to learn) and offer directions for the next steps. I can think of no educator, at any level of expertise, who would not benefit from reading this book and using the ideas herein.

Kip Téllez
Professor, Education Department
University of California Santa Cruz

What Duckor and Holmberg have accomplished is to craft a reading experience that, while grounded in solid scholarship, feels very much like a learning journey. The combination of the big ideas with the very practical "Try It Tomorrow" recommendations and authentic "Teacher Reflections" center practice in a way that feels deeply respectful and not overwhelming. I also appreciate explicit guidance to the individual adult learner as well as scaffolding for collective learning by grade-level teams or whole schools. This is a book that delivers on one of those rarest of promises—translating research knowledge into practicable knowledge. Quality feedback is key to accelerating learning; this book will accelerate your learning about feedback.

Christopher Thorn
Chief of Program and Partnerships, Partners in School Innovation
Former Associate Scientist at University of Wisconsin-Madison and
Senior Associate and
Director at the Carnegie Foundation for the Advancement of Teaching

Our university focuses on teaching college-level students 21st century skills with a focus on entrepreneurial thinking and design. Duckor and Holmberg's latest book, *Feedback for Continuous Improvement in the Classroom: New Perspectives, Practices, and Possibilities* is a total winner. By unpacking the practical skills needed to develop entrepreneurial thinking (which is project-based, collaborative, and communication driven), our undergraduates will be ready to give and take feedback to the next level. Well researched and full of hands-on examples, global-minded business schools will benefit from this comprehensive handbook.

Diah Wihardini
Director, BINUS Global University
Indonesia

Duckor and Holmberg provide a passionate yet realistic approach to providing feedback to students to fulfill their civil right to learn. It is unconscionable to teach students without providing daily and in-the-moment feedback and leveraging students' own voices in the process of their learning. These authors lay out a framework and a series of action steps to help all teachers, novice through expert, reflect on their classroom practice and consider their own professional growth through the lens of understanding how students are thinking and developing while they are teaching them. This is a must-read for all soon-to-be-teachers who seek real engagement with the next generation of students in our public schools. Reading this user-friendly book, teachers will feel empowered to guide students and learn with them as they each grow to better understand students' cognitive processes and as students grow in their understanding of the learning standards.

Diana Wilmot
Director, Program Evaluation and Research
Sequoia Union High School District

This book is a wonderful resource for teachers and other educational professionals who want to know more about formative feedback. The chapters capture all the most important aspects, and some you probably did not know about. Each chapter has a useful general orientation to one aspect of formative feedback, including guiding questions, definitions, and a very clarifying "What It Is and What It Isn't" table. The chapter helps the individual reader understand what they can readily learn through a self-assessment that also defines for the reader the different levels of sophistication in that aspect of formative feedback. This is followed by brief and very readable sections on planning, the research background, personal reflections from teachers who are well-accomplished at formative feedback, and practice tips. This is all woven together with brief summaries of important concepts and instructional tactics; together, these provide the reader with a masterly overview of the topic. Altogether, this is the authoritative account of formative feedback available today—and a great resource for the practicing teacher.

Mark R. Wilson
Distinguished Professor, Berkeley School of Education
Director, Berkeley Evaluation and Assessment Research (BEAR) Center
University of California, Berkeley

Duckor and Holmberg's latest book, *Feedback for Continuous Improvement in the Classroom: New Perspectives, Practices, and Possibilities*, is an important resource for teachers, school leaders, teacher educators, and curriculum developers alike. This well-written book explores formative feedback in secondary school contexts through a new, innovative framework by looking at its directionalities, configurations, and modalities. This book brings together research-based evidence from across the globe, real-life examples in U.S. schools, and practical suggestions and tips for teachers across the world. With this book, readers from different contexts and countries will find much to stimulate their thinking about formative feedback and improve their feedback practices in the classrooms.

Hwei-Ming Wong
Senior Education Research Scientist
Centre for Research in Pedagogy and Practice
National Institute of Education, Singapore

Brent Duckor and Carrie Holmberg's new book seamlessly weaves together research on formative feedback with issues of equity and pedagogical content knowledge, all while illustrating key ideas with student and teacher voices. There are so many practical tools embedded throughout the chapters that this book will be a go-to resource to support teacher learning communities find meaningful entry points into this critical work. It is a book that I know I will return to repeatedly.

Caroline E. Wylie
Principal Research Scientist/Research Director
K–12 Teaching, Learning and Assessment Division
ETS

If you are looking for a comprehensive resource for maximizing the depth and effectiveness of feedback in your setting, this is it. Duckor and Holmberg have written a well-researched and highly practical book that will become a cornerstone for improving the overall learning and growth of all students in your classroom and school. The concern for differentiated feedback and academic language support is timely and needed for the field.

Jeff Zwiers
Director, Understanding Language Initiative
Center to Support Excellence in Teaching
Stanford University

Feedback for Continuous Improvement in the Classroom

To Barbara Nakakihara, who has traveled
the long road and continues to bring
love, laughter, and wisdom along the way
—Brent Duckor

To Dur Seible, a public school teacher who
embodied the best of formative feedback
at a critical juncture in my life
and in the lives of so, so many others
—Carrie Holmberg

Feedback for Continuous Improvement in the Classroom

New Perspectives, Practices, and Possibilities

Brent Duckor
Carrie Holmberg

For information:

Corwin
A SAGE Company
2455 Teller Road
Thousand Oaks, California 91320
(800) 233-9936
www.corwin.com

SAGE Publications Ltd.
1 Oliver's Yard
55 City Road
London EC1Y 1SP
United Kingdom

SAGE Publications India Pvt. Ltd.
B 1/I 1 Mohan Cooperative Industrial Area
Mathura Road, New Delhi 110 044
India

SAGE Publications Asia-Pacific Pte. Ltd.
18 Cross Street #10-10/11/12
China Square Central
Singapore 048423

President: Mike Soules
Vice President and Editorial Director: Monica Eckman
Publisher: Jessica Allan
Senior Content Development Editor: Lucas Schleicher
Content Development Editor: Mia Rodriguez
Editorial Assistant: Natalie Delpino
Production Editor: Tori Mirsadjadi
Copy Editor: Erin Livingston
Typesetter: Integra
Proofreader: Annie Lubinsky
Indexer: Maria Sosnowski
Cover Designer: Rose Storey
Marketing Manager: Olivia Bartlett

Copyright © 2023 by Corwin Press, Inc.

All rights reserved. Except as permitted by U.S. copyright law, no part of this work may be reproduced or distributed in any form or by any means, or stored in a database or retrieval system, without permission in writing from the publisher.

When forms and sample documents appearing in this work are intended for reproduction, they will be marked as such. Reproduction of their use is authorized for educational use by educators, local school sites, and/or noncommercial or nonprofit entities that have purchased the book.

All third-party trademarks referenced or depicted herein are included solely for the purpose of illustration and are the property of their respective owners. Reference to these trademarks in no way indicates any relationship with, or endorsement by, the trademark owner.

Printed in the United States of America

Library of Congress Cataloging-in-Publication Data
Names: Duckor, Brent, author. | Holmberg, Carrie, author.
Title: Feedback for continuous improvement in the classroom : new perspectives, practices, and possibilities / Brent Duckor, Carrie Holmberg.
Description: Thousand Oaks, California : Corwin Press, Inc., 2023. | Includes bibliographical references and index.
Identifiers: LCCN 2022049404 | ISBN 9781544361574 (paperback) | ISBN 9781544361567 (epub) | ISBN 9781544361550 (epub) | ISBN 9781544361543 (pdf)
Subjects: LCSH: Teachers--Rating of. | Effective teaching. | Reflective teaching. | Observation (Educational method) | Feedback (Psychology)
Classification: LCC LB2838 .D83 2023 | DDC 371.14/4--dc23/eng/20221207
LC record available at https://lccn.loc.gov/2022049404

This book is printed on acid-free paper.

23 24 25 26 27 10 9 8 7 6 5 4 3 2 1

DISCLAIMER: This book may direct you to access third-party content via web links, QR codes, or other scannable technologies, which are provided for your reference by the author(s). Corwin makes no guarantee that such third-party content will be available for your use and encourages you to review the terms and conditions of such third-party content. Corwin takes no responsibility and assumes no liability for your use of any third-party content, nor does Corwin approve, sponsor, endorse, verify, or certify such third-party content.

Contents

What Readers Can Download and Print	xxi
List of Videos	xxii
Preface	xxiii
Acknowledgments	xxviii
About the Authors	xxxv
How to Use This Book	xxxvii

Learning Goals, Tasks, and Cycles of Feedback for Continuous Improvement

Chapter 1: On the Role of Learning Goals, Tasks, and Cycles of Feedback for Continuous Improvement	**2**

Directionality

Chapter 2: Teacher-Driven Feedback	**36**
Chapter 3: Peer-to-Peer-Driven Feedback	**60**
Chapter 4: Self-Driven Feedback	**80**

Configuration

Chapter 5: Feedback With the Whole Class	**118**
Chapter 6: Feedback With Small Groups	**144**
Chapter 7: Feedback With Individuals	**176**

Modality

Chapter 8: Written Feedback   **212**

Chapter 9: Spoken Feedback   **250**

Chapter 10: Nonverbal Feedback   **274**

Self-Study Checklist   299
Glossary   306
References   323
Index   334

Visit the companion website at
resources.corwin.com/ContinuousImprovement
for downloadable resources.

What Readers Can Download and Print

CHAPTER	TYPE	TITLE
1	Figure 1.1	Formative Feedback Framework
1	Figure 1.3	Progress Guide: Using Evidence to Support My Claim
1	Figure 1.4	Formative Feedback Process Model
1	Matrix, p. 29	Self-Assessment + Instructions
4	Figure 4.3	Progress Guide for Students to Self-Assess and Generate Next Steps for Causes of the Dust Bowl: Understanding and Weighing Evidence
5	Figure 5.1	Progress Guide for Teacher Use: Using Evidence to Examine Causes of the Dust Bowl
7	Figure 7.1	Formative Assessment (FA) Moves
End Matter	Checklist, p. 299	Self-Study Checklist

List of Videos

VIDEO NAME	PAGE(S)
Graduation by Portfolio from Vimeo	11, 95, 105, 286
FA Moves: Module 1 Introduction from CCEE series	260, 313
FA Moves: Module 2 on Priming from CCEE series	318
FA Moves: Module 3 on Posing from CCEE series	12, 317
FA Moves: Module 4 on Pausing from CCEE series	316
FA Moves: Module 5 on Probing from CCEE series	318
FA Moves: Module 6 on Bouncing from CCEE series	307
FA Moves: Module 7 on Tagging from CCEE series	321
FA Moves: Module 8 on Binning from CCEE series	307
FA Moves: Module 9 on Closing Opportunity Gaps from CCEE series	316
All Things in Moderation on YouTube Formative Feedback For All	72
Introducing Self-Assessment Using a Progress Guide on YouTube Formative Feedback For All	134

Note From the Publisher: The authors have provided video and web content throughout the book that is available to you through QR (quick response) codes. To read a QR code, you must have a smartphone or tablet with a camera. We recommend that you download a QR code reader app that is made specifically for your phone or tablet brand.

Links may also be accessed at **resources.corwin.com/ContinuousImprovement**

Preface

Many people have asked us in the course of writing this book: Why feedback? And in particular, why now? What motivated you to tell this story, together?

A Shared Passion for Assessment for Learning

When Brent and I first met over a decade ago, we were both teacher educators at a large public university in California, where we still teach today. Despite our differences in age, gender, and where we grew up—in my case on the East Coast and in Brent's on the West Coast, we had a lot in common. Most significantly, we were both products of having taught in promising high schools that believed deeply in the sacred right of all students to learn.

I taught my first English classes at Wilcox High School, a Title I school in the Bay Area. I was passionate about writing, literature, and mentoring young people in their journeys to express their voices. My time at the Stanford Teacher Education Program (STEP) with esteemed faculty and practitioner-scholars such as Larry Cuban, Lee Shulman, and Linda Darling-Hammond made me aware that school reform was never easy but was always necessary to achieve what is best for kids at the margins whose voices need to be heard.

When I found out from the department chair at San José State University (SJSU) that I had an office mate, Dr. Duckor, I didn't think much about it. I thought it might be nice to talk shop about working with pre-service teachers in the credential program with him. From that first day, however, as Brent and I started talking, it became clear we shared the same core values in teacher education and the teaching profession: Strive to teach teachers to find the power of their ideas in the work of activating and honoring the habits of heart, mind, and work of the young people they serve. There was a strange familiarity to the way Brent talked about what he called "the work." We also discovered we shared a vision about the power of formative assessment, the importance of formative feedback, and fostering curiosity with learning to learn. Key to it all was a passion for authentic classroom projects, tasks, and activities. It was uncanny to share so much in common with a colleague I had just met.

And then Brent shared with me that he taught at Central Park East Secondary School in New York City—a school that literally formed the core curriculum of our teacher education program at Stanford. My jaw dropped. I got it! Brent and I spoke a similar language because we shared a similar experience of progressive democratic education. We both connected to the promise of education to make a difference for children who've been marginalized and, too often, left behind by those seeking more accountability and results but not always real, authentic improvement in the lives of actual children and young people.

It was clear from the start that Brent and I both believed strongly in authentic assessment and the crucial role of using meaningful tasks to bring school to life for all children. Our conversations moved quickly in those days. We believe today, as much as we did in those days, in new ways of working and thinking about schools and schooling. We believe at our core in growth, change, and development—what today some call *continuous improvement*. We hold these beliefs and values today because of the mentors who guided us in the past. In the buildings where we began our careers, we saw and learned from professionals in every department. Faculty, staff, and parents helped to form us. We now recognize that because we were supported as beginning teachers—at Wilcox and at Central Park East Secondary—by phenomenal colleagues, staff, parents/guardians, and administrators, we became better teachers over the years.

Looking back on our service to the teacher education program at San José State University, we realized we had met for a reason. We had stories to share about our deepest convictions about what the purpose of schooling is. Then and now we maintain: Feedback is a purpose—perhaps *the* purpose—of why we teach.

Connection Through a Special School: Central Park East Secondary School

I didn't meet Brent until 2011. As it turns out, when I was a graduate student at Stanford in the mid-1990s, I was introduced to Central Park East Secondary School (CPESS), the acclaimed small school in East Harlem founded by Deborah Meier, in our "Foundations of Learning" course. The instructor was none other than Lee Shulman. He spoke reverently of CPESS, a school centered around helping young Black and Hispanic teens use their hearts and minds well. By embodying and exercising five habits of mind (connection, perspective, evidence, supposition, and relevance), these young people were accomplishing tremendous things in a world that seemed to (and at times, did) stand in their way.

In Dr. Shulman's class, we watched the documentaries, read the books, and discussed the implications of reforms in this small school in East Harlem that captivated the world. How did these public school teachers do it? Who were they? Why were they successful? These questions burned as we discussed them in our seminar that featured *The Power of Their Ideas* (1995) by Debbie Meier.

We decided that everything came back to the ways students were positioned to question the world they lived in. These students were invited daily, even pushed at times, to ask in every classroom

- How is this event or idea connected to others? What causes what? (Connection)
- From whose point of view is this being presented? (Perspective)
- How do we know what we know? (Evidence)
- What if things were different? (Supposition)
- Who cares? So what? Why is this important? (Relevance)

As an organizing principle and anchor for all formal and informal assessments, the habits of mind fascinated me. I had never been to such a school nor was my experience of any curriculum quite like theirs. Was this part of the secret of deeper learning in places like the Coalition of Essential Schools, a movement we learned started with Ted Sizer and Debbie Meier as they advocated for the deeper educational purposes of private and public schools in a thriving democracy? Dewey started making more sense in these school examples than much of the content of my own—quite honestly—privileged, comprehensive, mainstream, traditional education.

Teachers at CPESS, Professor Shulman told us, cultivated a culture of revision with their students, an ethos that was schoolwide. Teachers knew all their students well; they worked tirelessly on cultivating relationships built upon foundations of trust, respect, and resilience. Every teacher had a number of advisees they were responsible for mentoring and with whom they forged deep connections over the years. One of those former advisees reached out to Brent recently and we remarked how everyone's lives were *still* being changed by their experience at CPESS!

Assessment was by portfolio in these high schools, and students defended their work publicly—in front of other faculty, adults, parent/guardians, and peers. Revision was a key to the students' and therefore these schools' success. That much became clear as we read about what students at CPESS were expected to know and be able to do with their middle and high school work. Hearing all this while I was student teaching at Wilcox—a large, traditional, comprehensive high school in Northern California—I wondered, "What would it be like to teach young people using these five habits of mind in different circumstances?"

By the time I joined SJSU's department of secondary education (now the department of teacher education), I had already had half a dozen student teachers and had been coaching beginning teachers for years after having left Wilcox High School. While working as a coach with beginning teachers as part of a nationally recognized induction program, I noticed that assessment for learning was as important as content knowledge or what some called classroom management skills. In fact, it was utterly clear to me that the practice of formative assessment was the way to improve, as Lee Shulman calls it, the development of teachers' pedagogical content knowledge.

Teaching pre-service teachers in a single-subject credential program across eight academic disciplines forced me to step outside of my own subject matter expertise (English language arts) and start coaching others in science, math, art, music, history, world languages, and physical education to engage their students with authentic assessment practices. We talk a lot about the meaning of engagement in my courses and field supervision seminars at SJSU. I found that real engagement starts when we begin learning how to learn from our students—the power of their ideas as they exhibit their habits of mind and heart. Again, giving and taking up feedback is indispensable to authentic engagement with the content and processes of learning.

After many years of working as a teacher educator and mentor, several questions emerged in my own professional practice: How can I help novice teachers become better at differentiating feedback with their students than I had been with my own students when starting out? What tools and scaffolds do my credential candidates need to know and be able to do to lean into the art of feedback without becoming overwhelmed or exhausted? Can teachers' learning processes with formative feedback be accelerated? Can teachers feel more connected with their students by experiencing the processes and cycles of feedback?

Working with all sorts of teachers from a multiplicity of backgrounds and orientations in our diverse dynamic communities, I soon realized we needed to work together as a teaching profession to answer these questions. Importantly, we also bring different perspectives and expertise on what makes feedback so powerful. We need to dialogue about feedback as educators in our communities with policymakers and leaders. It is time to put feedback at the center of policy talk about what matters. Achieving our dreams of equity and excellence requires that we start getting real about feedback—its importance to students' growth and lives—and that we are given spaces and time to do the work, both individually and in teams.

Connecting With Every Student

Brent and I write together because we hope to achieve a balance: part provocation and part invitation. You will notice that we take risks. We are co-authors because we believe in shared voices born from different experiences and dispositions. We want you to understand that we understand we are making claims that are subject to dispute.

Even as you may argue with—and potentially reject—some of the ideas or suggestions in this book, I want you to trust that what we've put forth here is offered in the spirit of continuous improvement in the classroom *for all*—not only students we may connect with easily, not only students who may be like us in one way or another, not only students we may find especially interesting, not only students who may be easygoing or make our lives easier—but for *all* students. Each student is a unique, precious human being. And everyone has something to teach their teacher.

Feedback is, in point of fact, for all. Feedback can open up new possibilities for children, adolescents, and young adults. And it can be just as satisfying for us, their guides, as it is for the next generation of students who teach us. In public schools in democratic nations especially, feedback for all (skillfully practiced) can play a critical role for the common good. Feedback for all can also change the trajectories of the lives of individuals for the better. This, too, drives our passion for feedback as we press everyone in these pages to leave the world a better place than we found it.

Our Wish for You

May the new things you try with feedback—whether inspired by this book, your colleagues, or something else altogether—be imbued with curiosity, care, creativity, and new possibilities. May you connect with young people over projects, performances, and authentic learning experiences in ways you had not yet imagined. May feedback help you influence lives in positive and profound ways.

—Carrie

Acknowledgments

In our last book, *Mastering Formative Assessment Moves* (2017, p. xiii), we wrote: "Every book is the culmination of years of struggle to broaden the horizon of a topic." Little did we know then that our next book would be written during a global pandemic, a massive shift to remote online learning, and a realignment of values that now call into question the role of standardized testing, assessment, and evaluation in serving the aims of democratic education. This book, *Feedback for Continuous Improvement in the Classroom: New Perspectives, Practices, and Possibilities,* is the culmination of many, many lessons learned over the past several years about what still makes a good education, and it stakes a claim on who must carry forth the promise of equity and excellence in our schools if we are to achieve it together.

Our aim in writing this book is to broaden the horizon on the topic of feedback. Feedback, as one reviewer has put it, may be "the pinnacle of pedagogy." Feedback is also more. It lays the foundation of democracy in education. We wrote this book on feedback to deepen everyone's appreciation for feedback's fundamental role in rethinking *how* and *why* we learn and teach in schools. Feedback is not only something that people do in K–12 classrooms. Feedback is something we all do for each other in many contexts, in many places, and in many ways. The book itself is the product of feedback and we wish to honor those who've provided it and engaged us in cycles of feedback on this journey. By their offering us feedback on our thinking about feedback, we've learned in the company of many, many others. We wish to thank our students, colleagues, family, and friends for their insights and perspectives to bring "the work" forward, as we put it. This book/project is the culmination of those conversations.

First, we have to acknowledge and thank the teacher candidates and graduates from our summer 2020 cohort at San José State University's college of education. EDTE 282 was fully online for the first time as the university and the California State University system moved to implement remote instruction during the pandemic. We redesigned our signature 282-course "Assessment and Evaluation in Secondary Schools" to test out new assessment-for-learning processes and projects that promote collaboration and rely on explicit feedback protocols and strategies to model walking the walk. This meant centering our course performance assessments (e.g., lesson planning, task and progress guide design, and a micro teaching event) on cycles of sustained feedback in different configurations, modalities, and directionalities. The implementation of these long- and short-cycle feedback exchanges taught us all new ways to advance student work online at a distance.

We are grateful to have experimented with and learned from our students (the next generation of teachers in California!) on how to effectively use tech platforms such as Google Docs, Slides, and Sheets, while making use of Zoom during student team teaching events to explore the use of just-in-time peer-driven and self-driven feedback so everyone could improve their projects before the end-of-course grading period. A special thanks to Laura Amador, Karen Arias, Rene Cantoadams, Davy Cao, Lacey Coenen, Julia Duggs, Emese Erdos, Leo Fernandez, Ervine Flores, Kelly Heuschkel, Yangling Hua, David Knight, Jennavieve Kunz, Jia Ying Lin, Angelica Lopez, Caity Maerzluft, Sumeet Naidu, Josh Parees, Dalton Pizzuti, Margarita Ramirez, John Riffle, Stephanie Rodriguez, Shreya Saha, Judy Schulze, Portia Sharma, Natasha Singha, Greg Stefani, Stephanie Todd, and Camila Torres. We also wish to acknowledge the subsequent students who have made contributions to our perspective on what works in deepening how to teach teachers to see feedback as essential to effective classroom assessment. These former students include Kazi Ayeni-Watley, Hector Cornejo, Kristi Hlaing, Johnny Khuu, Roberta Love, Vaishnavi Murugesan, Stacey Olson, Brandon Rulloda, Pia Satana, and David Soriano.

Prior to the pandemic, we also tested out new ideas and strategies about structured feedback with our teacher candidates in EDSC 184X, a faculty-led seminar that constitutes Phase I teaching and supports the California Teacher Performance Assessment (TPA) cycles at SJSU. We taught the seminar on campus in-person in the evenings and went to our candidates' placement sites to observe our student teachers in a diverse range of middle and high schools across our Santa Clara County service territory. As we worked to coach these beginners, we also ensured they were prepared for the assessment portions of the California Teacher Performance Assessment (CalTPA) Cycles 1 and 2. In university seminars and at the school sites, we focused our candidates on designing progress guides aligned with rubrics to sharpen their skills with one-on-one feedback (for supporting their students' assignments during the 15 days of teaching!) in their art, science, physical education, and language arts classrooms. We were astounded to learn that these Phase 1 student teachers not only began collaborating more deeply with their mentor teachers, but also, our students were soon leading conversations on how to improve communication and engagement using these progress guides in their placements. A special thanks to Justin Choi, Allyson Dudzinski, Lewis Duong, Tiffany Garcia, Marty LeMoine, Norine Nakamura, and Josh Parees, who worked with us in this seminar.

Our interviews with newly minted and seasoned teachers also deepened the voices of educators, highlighting the wisdom of practice in cross-sectional settings from middle and high schools in the San Francisco Bay Area. By listening to science, world language, language arts, music, history, art, math, and physical education teachers as part of our research for this book, we better grounded the (at times) abstract feedback literature in lived experiences of our practitioner peers. A note of deep appreciation to all of them and especially Greg Brown, Alisa Burmeister, Christina Courtney, Anne Dumontier, Marisa Fruzza, Christina Masuda, Tanveer Mann, Alice McNally, Stacey Olson, Erica

Pon, Leim Tran-Zwijsen, Dustin Tao, Niloofar Vakili, Kim Vinh, and Roy Walton.

Our commitment to school districts, school administrators, instructional coaches, and teachers during the pandemic; the massive social and economic dislocations; and the all-too-real daily crises facing school children never wavered. Because of our strong ties to the amazing people we've come to know over the years, we asked, "How can we support assessment for learning with a focus on feedback for every child?" The answer came in fall 2021, when we launched a collaborative action research project with Mount Pleasant Elementary School District (MPESD). Under the guidance of superintendent Dr. Elida McArthur and leadership from her team at August Boeger Middle School, we put the focus on developing customized visible scaffolds for self-assessment, a topic of deep interest to the district. Through online meetings, we laid out a plan to design, create, and put progress guides in a unit for the math and science teachers. As guides on the side, we provided feedback in shared Docs, Zoom calls, and other distributed platforms to help everyone build up confidence and understanding in how to use these new tools with the kids. Video exemplars, vignettes, and real-world examples of feedback practice are woven across this book because of this collaboration. We remain ever grateful to Principal Shannon Soza and Instructional Coach Amanda Faulkner (who works as a senior improvement partner at Partners in School Innovation with the district) and we remain in awe of the August Boeger Middle School teachers Gideon Cheng, Neha Kapil, George MacArthur, and Augustin Rodriguez, who never flinched at the opportunity to try out new ideas, tools, and procedures in the classroom—masks and all. Gideon, Neha, George, and Augustin: Thank you for being partners in extraordinary times!

In addition to teaching courses in the department of teacher education at SJSU, we also have close ties with SJSU's education doctoral program. The EdD Leadership program has offered new opportunities to try out feedback for graduate students, many of whom are superintendents, principals, instructional coaches, teachers, school counselors, and other K–12 providers. In our courses EDD 530 "Assessment, Testing and Evaluation: Contexts and Implications for School Reform"; EDD 501 "Quantitative Methods: Logic, Perspectives, and Procedures"; and EDD 511 "Leadership for Learner-Centered Organizations," we have garnered many insights into the generalizability and relevance of the formative feedback framework for those learning to learn about feedback in various learning environments and school ecosystems. It turns out that the principles and practices we offer in this book for K–12 educators and those who prepare them have similar benefits for masters- and doctoral-level studies. In graduate courses that use performance tasks, projects, and long-term assignments as their focal point, we found that students in higher education benefit from deeper exchanges of feedback before grades are due. For these insights, we thank Cohort 5 (Edgar Alcaraz, Carrie Bosco, Joseph Bosco, Tram Dang, Jennifer Izant Gonzales, Taunya

Jaco, Michael Mansfield, Father Gerald Nwafor, Michelle Poirier, Richard Ruiz, Tricia Ryan, Anne Tran, Mara Williams, and Rafael Zavala), Cohort 6 (Gigi Carunungan, Janet Gutierrez, Vladimir Ivanovic, Amna Jaffer, Yolanda Jimenez, Charlene Lee, Arthur Maldonado, Renee Paquier, Roberto Portillo, Noah Price, Candice Nance, Marcella McCullum, Furwa Rizvi, Blanca Tavera, Lesyle Tinson, Hanh Tran, and Parinaz Zartoshty), and Cohort 7 (Jeremy Adams, Hanna Asrat, Christina Ballantyne, Kevina Brown, Ryan Carter, Katherine Chang, Carrie Cisneros, Padmavathy Desikachari, Genvieve Dorsey, Isaac Escoto, Kristina Grasty, Angela Guzman, Diana Huang, Willy Kwong, Jaclynne Medina, Marisol Quevedo, and Tijan White). Most recently, we experimented with whole-class, small-group, and one-on-one configurations of *drafting* (embedding timely, specific, focused feedback using cycles of peer-driven and instructor-led rounds). A special thanks to Cohort 8 (Anthony Alvarado, Ashley Busby, Joe Fessehaye, Sofia Fojas, Drew Giles, Martin Gutierrez, Tim Harper, Kelly Mack, Selene Munoz, Harshdeep Nanda, Mylinn Pham, Lauren Reagan, Nannette Regua, Keri Toma, and Diana Valle) for helping us see the value of deep assessment for learning for our doctoral candidates.

There are many critical friends and colleagues from professional organizations, research groups, and associations that have heard our argument for continuous improvement in the classroom represented in this book. Part of our process in writing the book has been to present with peers who can inform our views of formative feedback as part of the larger commitment to classroom assessment. Thanks to our colleagues at University of California (UC) Santa Cruz (Kip Téllez and Adria Patthoff) for working together on the California Teacher Education Research and Improvement Network (CTERIN) project to better understand how novice teachers' formative assessment moves provide the foundations for deepening short-cycle feedback processes in diverse classrooms. Thank you to George Harrison of the University of Hawaiʻi at Mānoa and his colleagues in the Curriculum Research and Development Group for inviting us to share at the College of Education what we were discovering in the project's early days. The discourse that emerged set the tone for much of our subsequent exploration of feedback. We also appreciate our colleagues at UC Berkeley's graduate school of education and the Berkeley Evaluation and Assessment Research (BEAR) Center, who've offered us multiple opportunities to share what the role of feedback in the formative assessment literature looks like from historical, psychometric, testing, and evaluation perspectives. Mark Wilson, Karen Draney, William Fisher, Linda Morell, Josh Sussman, Yidan Zhang, Shruti Bathia, Weeraphat Suksiri, Aubrey Condor, Mingfeng Xue, and Himilcon Inciarte have ensured the conversations were lively, and we benefited from their research perspectives. Our connection to the National Council on Measurement in Education (NCME) and American Educational Research Association (AERA) classroom assessment special interest groups continues to provide a collaborative space and we've appreciated folks from the leadership teams, including Nicole Barnes, Bethany Brunsman, Chris DeLuca, Chad Gotch, Michael Holden, Dustin Van Orman, Erin Riley-Lepo, Mary Yakimowski, and Tonya Moon. A special thanks to Caroline Wylie at Educational Testing Service, who invited us to the last official FAST/SCASS (Formative Assessment for Student and Teachers/State Collaborative on Assessment and Student Standards) for a keynote and for always opening the door to East and West Coast perspectives on assessment for learning. We deeply appreciate dynamic conversations with multiple lenses with those who share our passion for formative assessment.

We have also grown from the deep, ongoing conversations with leaders of California's education reforms in state-led accountability. Countless discussions over the past years with distinguished policy leaders and directors of systems of support in California have allowed us to find a complementary voice in the promise of continuous improvement rooted in teachers' work in the classroom. We wish to thank in particular Glen Price, former deputy director of the California Department of Education, and Michael Kirst, former president of the California Board of Education, for their unwavering support for our commitment to continuous improvement—as we put it, "one project, one child, one 'draft' at a time." Mike and Glen got it when we said teacher and student feedback *is* continuous improvement daily, from the ground up. Similar conversations over the years with the amazing team at the California Collaborative for Educational Excellence (CCEE) has accelerated the need for this book. CCEE shares our vision for school improvement and has offered us several opportunities to share the power of assessment for learning in extraordinary times with stakeholders across the state. Through the creation of learning pathways/modules, webinars, and conversations with countries and districts, CCEE allowed us to lay the formative assessment (FA) foundation upon which this book is built. Thanks, Matt Navo, Tom Armelino, Sujie Shin, Stephanie Gregson, Michelle Magyar, Roni Jones, and James McKenna for the opportunity to learn from and work with you all.

Our deeper dive into scholarship on feedback has intersected different departments, colleges, and programs at SJSU. We thank our Dean, Heather Lattimer, for timely Research Scholarship and Creative Activity (RSCA) support and for her continued trust in our contributions to the field. We are grateful for colleagues who have offered different perspectives based on their unique disciplinary expertise. We wish to thank those faculty who have supported our courses over the years. These colleagues include, from the department of teacher education and single subject credential program, Katya Aguliar, Kara Ireland D'Ambrosio, Lara Ervin-Kassab, Mark Felton, David Goulette, Eduardo Muñoz-Muñoz, Luis Poza, Roxana Marachi, Paula Oakes, Cheryl Roddick, and our chair, David Whitenack.

Special thanks are also due to the outstanding faculty and dissertation advisors in the EdD Leadership program, who have continued to offer suggestions and ideas about how research on feedback must be a core principle of any continuous improvement plan for educational systems. We have taught side by side with these accomplished EdD faculty at SJSU and want to recognize their collegial contributions to this work in the context of higher education doctoral studies preparation: Thank you, Lorri Capizzi, Pam Cheng, Arnie Danzig, Bob Gliner, Roxana Marachi, Nikos Mourtos, Eduardo Muñoz-Muñoz, Brad Porfilio, and Noni Reis. A special thanks to SJSU staff members Jean Shiota, Maria Muñoz, Ana Paz-Rangel, and Sarah Arreola for all the years of steady support and care.

We also owe an enduring debt of gratitude to those colleagues from Central Park East Secondary School (CPESS) and Wilcox High School who changed the trajectories of our lives as teachers and later as teacher educators. From a small school in District 4 East Harlem, this book represents the living memory of democratic education for all and lessons learned about deep feedback for learning from colleagues at CPESS: Lenny Alexander, Bridgit Belletierre, Angelo Campanile, Lorraine Chanon, Julian Cohen, Laura Deigen-Ayala, Dave Feldman, John Gunn, Joel Handorff, Rahsaan Harris, Shirley Hawkinson, Jo Ho-Rolle, Richard Miller, Anne Purdy, Todd Rolle, Paul Schwarz, David Smith, Mardi Tuminaro, Pat Wagner, Pat Walter, and Joe Walter. The memory and wisdom of colleagues at Wilcox High School in the Bay Area are alive in the pages and include Rod Adams, Jeannette Brunton, Dane Caldwell-Holden, Meredith Dodd, Ophny Escalante, Mariama Gray, Cliff Harris, Craig Hedlund, Kristin Kapasi, Beth Lincoln, Anand Marri, Crystal Matsuoka, Maria Messina, Jeff Muralt, Dani Salzer, Misa Sugiura, Kelly Villareal, and the late Joan Owen.

Our families continue to inspire, support, and challenge us to move ahead with communicating our vision for schools and schooling. In our last book, we wrote: "Family, friends, and colleagues are ultimately the unsung heroes of any long-term project" (2017, p. xv). Suffice it to say, this long-term project was impossible to carry forth during these extraordinary times without the love, hope, and faith of those who have stood by our commitment to serving public education institutions. Bob Holmberg, Hazel Holmberg, and VivIan Holmberg have stood by, solid as a rock and with loving words of encouragement, as have Dan and Regina Sakols, pandemic pod neighbors extraordinaire. Barbara Nakakihara, Sydney Ellyn Duckor, and Ildiko Duckor have offered a firm foundation of love and much wisdom about work/life balance, as has neighbor Mitch Ikuta, who always had the right words—at the right time—to help us persevere. We are grateful to our children who moved into a new high school, entered college at Oberlin, and graduated from George Washington University's Elliott School of International Affairs—all during the making of this book! Indeed, time passes. And we stand in awe of how everyone made a difference in what has landed in these pages.

A final note to our editors: We cannot say enough to thank our publisher, Jessica Allan at Corwin. Jessica stood by every iteration of this text, offering care and insight along the way, and always trusted our process. She has been a patient steward and expert guide on the side during this pandemic. Jessica, thank you for having the confidence that what we *really* had to say was worth waiting for. Bringing Lucas Schleicher, senior content development editor, aboard at just the right time made all the difference. Luke wrestled with our prose, challenged our philosophical musings, and sharpened our thinking about the core message across the whole book. Mostly, Luke offered timely, concrete, and focused next steps—in multiple modalities and configurations—which epitomized the use of expert feedback to advance the work. We thank Jessica and Luke for their commitment to enacting the principles and practices embedded in this book. Their long-cycle formative feedback was instrumental at every step of the way. All errors and omissions contained in this work, of course, remain our own, but we appreciate the extra pair of eyes and gentle nudges from Corwin and the team.

Publisher's Acknowledgments

Corwin gratefully acknowledges the contributions of the following reviewers:

Natalie Bernasconi
Educator
UC Santa Cruz
Santa Cruz, CA

Andrew Harries
Head Teacher, Science and Agriculture
Quirindi High School
New South Wales, Australia

Renee J. Nealon
Teacher
McDowell Elementary
Petaluma, CA

Venessa Powell
Senior Curriculum Developer
Northern Caribbean University
Mandeville, Manchester, Jamaica

Amy Tepper
Author, Consultant
Tepper & Flynn, LLC
Avon, CT

About the Authors

Brent Duckor, PhD, is professor in the department of teacher education at San José State University. Dr. Duckor also serves as a core faculty member in the EdD Educational Leadership program at the Lurie College of Education. He taught government, economics, and history at Central Park East Secondary School in New York City in the 1990s. With the passage of No Child Left Behind, Brent returned to earn a doctorate at the University of California, Berkeley and study educational measurement, testing, and assessment in the quantitative methods and evaluation program at the graduate school of education.

Brent's research on formative assessment and teachers' understanding and use of classroom assessment is informed by his work as a former high school teacher at a nationally renowned urban high school. He has worked to support innovation in teacher licensure exams in state and national contexts. Both his scholarship and teaching seek to integrate a developmental perspective on teachers' growth and empowerment in the teaching profession. His scholarship has appeared in *Teachers College Record, Journal of Teacher Education, Educational Leadership, Phi Delta Kappan, Mathematics Teaching in the Middle School, Journal of Educational Measurement,* and most recently, the *4th International Encyclopedia of Education*. He is also co-author of *Mastering Formative Assessment Moves: 7 High-Leverage Practices to Advance Student Learning* (ACSD, 2017) with Dr. Carrie Holmberg.

Once an avid windsurfer, Brent now enjoys long walks and exploring the Pacific Northwest and the Columbia River Gorge with his wife, Barbara.

He can be reached at brent.duckor@sjsu.edu.

Carrie Holmberg, EdD, is a lecturer in the department of teacher education and a pre-service teacher educator at San José State University. She taught at a Title I comprehensive high school in Silicon Valley for nearly a decade and has extensive experience mentoring new teachers. Carrie has twice earned her National Board Certification. She also worked with the Stanford Partner School Induction Program and the Santa Cruz/Silicon Valley New Teacher Program for many years.

Carrie obtained her EdD in educational leadership in 2017 from SJSU. Her scholarship has appeared in *The English Journal, California English, Mathematics Teaching in the Middle School, Educational Leadership, Phi*

Delta Kappan, Journal of Educational Measurement, and most recently, the *4th International Encyclopedia of Education.* Carrie has served as chair of the Classroom Assessment Special Interest Group (SIG) for the American Educational Research Association (AERA).

In addition to exploring the Sierras with her husband, Bob, and family, Carrie enjoys playing water polo competitively and surfing in the Pacific.

She can be reached at carrie.holmberg@sjsu.edu.

How to Use This Book

This book gives teachers, instructional coaches, professional developers, teacher educators, and educational leaders a new way of looking at feedback for continuous improvement in today's schools. Whether you are working with students online or in blended or traditional classroom settings, the book is designed to help everyone implement classroom-based formative feedback practices rooted in research on what works.

We have organized this book for multiple users and purposes while maintaining a consistent structure and approach to each chapter. These purposes include

- using the book as a study guide for unit and lesson planning,
- offering a mentoring/coaching framework for goal setting,
- assisting in department-level collaboration to build cohesion,
- developing school-level conversation starters to help professional learning communities (PLCs) examine current practices, and
- providing district-level decision makers with a quick survey to better identify the tools, resources, and materials needed for success.

Each chapter also offers concrete tools and suggestions that make feedback for continuous improvement easier. Among them are

- self-assessments for determining how and where current practice resides in the big picture
- graphic organizers and scaffolds for creating customized progress guides,
- objectives and recaps for summarizing key learnings and takeaways,
- guiding questions for opening and leading conversations on feedback for all,
- "Try It Tomorrow" suggestions with tech tips and recommendations for broadening the menu of feedback options, and
- video exemplars to show feedback moves in action.

A list of QR codes for all videos, along with template and exemplar documents for download, is available at the front of the book.

An extensive up-to-date glossary is available in the back of the book to ensure clarity of key concepts and offer a working knowledge of terminology within the field. References for every chapter are also available at the end of the book.

One Coherent Framework

Our formative feedback (FF) framework provides the reader with three main focal points and corresponding lenses for making feedback practices visible to all. The FF framework ensures that one can see how contexts for learning, educational goals, and content standards are embedded in continuous improvement of instruction and assessment. Whether the reader chooses to dive deeper into the various directionalities, configurations, or modalities of feedback, each focal point is interconnected with the other, and we offer solutions on how to connect and weave each of them together in practice.

Contexts for Learning		
Face-to-Face	Blended	Distance Learning
Focal Point		
Directionality	Configuration	Modality
Lenses		
Teacher-driven	Whole class	Written
Peer-to-peer-driven	Small groups (2–4)	Spoken
Self-driven	Individual (1:1)	Nonverbal
Tasks, Projects, Activities	Learning Goals, Standards, Skills Rubrics, Progress Guides, "Next Steps" Organizers	

Our FF framework serves to guide the reader through possibilities for diving deeper into any focal point while maintaining a systematic, integrated, and holistic view of the power of feedback to change the trajectory of outcomes.

Individual But Related Chapters

This book is written with multiple entry points in mind. Some may wish to pick one chapter to focus on, while others may want to read several chapters connected to a main theme in order to improve, for example, how to balance the directionalities of feedback their students experience during a unit of instruction. Or one could dive deep into the lens of nonverbal feedback as a primary modality (Chapter 10), for instance, while connecting those feedback practices to written and spoken modalities (Chapters 8 and 9 respectively). Similarly, one might carefully examine individual (one-on-one) feedback practices (Chapter 7) while situating them within whole-class and small-group configurations at the lesson or unit level (Chapters 5 and 6 respectively).

In this sense, each chapter can be treated as a separate module for quick access and focused action. Before you begin a chapter, take a moment to decide whether you want to focus on a particular set of objectives. The "Self-Study Checklist" has learning objectives and goals for each chapter and can be used to ensure you meet your personal and professional goals at your own pace. Whether you are looking for ideas to promote feedback during a specific lesson, over several units, or throughout a yearlong planning cycle, each chapter can be put to use immediately.

The Organization of the Book

For consistency and ease of use, each chapter is formatted as follows:

- An opening/epigraph
- Guiding Questions
- Planning for . . . What to Consider and Why It Matters (offering guidance for successful implementation)
- What the Research Tells Us
- Focus on Practice (providing concrete examples of implementation)
- Scaffolds and Guided Practice for Individual Teachers
- Setting Goals and Monitoring Progress
- Recap/Review
- Ticket Out the Door

We have designed this book based on our experiences with teachers over the last several decades. We know from experience in pre- and in-service settings that teachers are familiar with feedback yet have many unanswered questions about its most effective uses. Questions around the efficacy, effectiveness, and equity of traditional feedback practices abound. Many wonder if these practices can provide soft data for immediate use in a way that hard data (numbers, points, grades) can not. We tackle these important questions by asking along with teachers and students:

- Who is feedback for?
- Who provides feedback?
- Who benefits from feedback?
- What good does feedback serve?
- How can feedback make a difference?

To set the stage and begin this conversation, we review how to situate feedback in educational purposes, taxonomical objectives, rich tasks, authentic projects, and (perhaps most importantly) cycles of information exchange that attend to what it means to use formative feedback well. Chapter 1, "On the Role of Learning Goals, Tasks, and Cycles of Feedback for Continuous Improvement," delves into the necessity of establishing meaningful learning goals that are connected to performance tasks, projects, and long-term assignments that allow teachers and students to work through cycles of formative feedback. We introduce the SOLO taxonomy and other tools for seeing how to differentiate outcomes while reminding ourselves that feedback on proverbial "first drafts" is the real work of continuous improvement. No matter whether we are in the classroom, lab, theater, studio, or on the playing field, everyone is learning how to improve.

The rest of the book is organized by focal points integral to our exploration of classroom formative feedback practices. There are three focal points: directionality, configuration, and modality. Within each focal point, there are three lenses we use to look closely at what occurs—or could occur—with formative feedback in secondary school contexts and ambitious learning communities more broadly.

We begin with the focal point of *directionality* because it best addresses the question, "Who is most responsible for the actions that occur during a set of formative feedback practices and who is the primary driver of the formative feedback process?" Directionality of feedback centers our inquiry on questions of responsibility, leadership, and agency. In Chapter 2, we begin with teacher-driven feedback because there can be no doubt about it—a teacher, as the responsible adult, leader of the classroom, and subject area expert, is responsible for the timing and quality of the cycles of formative feedback in which students engage. We then move to peer-to-peer-driven and self-driven feedback in Chapters 3 and 4.

The middle chapters (Chapters 5–7) explore classroom-based formative feedback practices through the focal point of *configuration*. Configurations of feedback center our inquiry on questions of spatial arrangements, interpersonal dynamics, collaboration skills and routines, and other necessary features of working smart with students in differing contexts. Chapter 5 examines what is most salient regarding whole-class feedback; Chapter 6 addresses what's important to consider about formative feedback with small groups of students; and Chapter 7 focuses on situations where the formative feedback is configured with individual students in one-on-one settings.

The closing chapters (Chapters 8–10) explore the role of *modality* in feedback, whether written, spoken, or nonverbal. Chapter 8 emphasizes that written feedback (to oneself, from or to a peer, or from or to the teacher) cannot stand alone. Chapter 9 addresses the challenges and myriad potential benefits of routines and scaffolds that support formative feedback that occurs through verbal exchanges and turns of talk while speaking. Chapter 10 digs into how formative feedback conversations can benefit from paying attention to nonverbal communication and skills and cues related to body-kinesthetic routines.

We hope that you will find this customizable approach to unpacking feedback for all helpful and inspirational. Each chapter emphasizes innovation and creativity while offering concrete advice for improved practice, so let your interests and curiosity lead the way.

LEARNING GOALS, TASKS, AND CYCLES OF FEEDBACK FOR CONTINUOUS IMPROVEMENT

CHAPTER 1

On the Role of Learning Goals, Tasks, and Cycles of Feedback for Continuous Improvement

> If we want the next generation to truly be better educated . . . then they need a setting in which they can practice, get feedback, and try again as new ideas gradually begin to make sense.
>
> —Meier (1995, p. 148)

We open this first chapter with a set of claims. These claims derive from our deepest convictions about the purposes of schooling. Any book on what is to be done in education today needs to situate the values, the beliefs, and the proposed work for schools by its authors with clarity and transparency. Like Deborah Meier (1995), we believe that students need spaces where they "can practice, get feedback, and try again" (p. 148) as new ideas come into their lives.

To draw on lessons from past assessment reforms, ones that have at times promised more than they yielded, we have begun the book with an exploration of learning goals—for our schools, for our teachers, and for our students. Good **feedback** will always be rooted in important, enduring educational goals.

In this chapter, we offer a larger framework for the ingredients, concepts, and tools that matter in making feedback *formative*. Setting learning goals out on the table for everyone to see matters in our experience. Therefore, each chapter will unpack the argument for enduring educational goals and will better articulate the core elements of what we mean by "feedback for all"—with a purpose.

In the meantime, to engage more deeply about the larger aims of feedback, before we start the journey, let's agree: Feedback only matters in a world where we grow, where we learn, and where we expect everyone to change for the better. To move ahead in any endeavor in life, we need help understanding where we are going, what is on the horizon, and which steps will lead us there. Feedback literally shows us the way.

Without purpose, feedback loses its power. For feedback to be effective, we must ask:

- Who is feedback for?
- Who provides feedback?
- Who benefits from feedback?
- What good does feedback serve?
- How can feedback make a difference?

In the chapters ahead, we outline a framework for establishing, as Dr. Linda Darling-Hammond puts it in *The Right to Learn* (1997), what it looks and feels like to engage students in democratic education. To this charge of creating schools that work for all students, we add a corollary: **Formative feedback** *must be a living, breathing part of every child's education.*

Feedback is not a luxury; it is a necessity. Feedback serves the most sacred purposes of democratic education. Feedback both enlightens and advances us toward **lifelong learning** goals, in part by caring for the educational process as much as educational outcomes. Put simply, feedback is not a mere means to an end—it is an end in itself. No one learns without feedback on how they are doing and where they can go next with support.

In today's schools, we must take the purposes of schooling and the need for formative feedback more seriously than ever.

Author Insight

W.E.B. DuBois

Of all the civil rights for which the world has struggled and fought for 5,000 years, the right to learn is undoubtedly the most fundamental. . . . The freedom to learn . . . has been bought by bitter sacrifice. And whatever we may think of the curtailment of other civil rights, we should fight to the last ditch to keep open the right to learn, the right to have examined in our schools not only what we believe but what we do not believe; not only what our leaders say, but what the leaders of other groups and nations, and the leaders of other centuries have said. We must insist upon this to give our children the fairness of a start which will equip them with such an array of facts and such an attitude toward truth that they can have a real chance to judge what the world is, and what its greater minds have thought it might be.

Source: Foner (1949) pp. 230–231.

Every young person has the right to learn (Darling-Hammond, 1997). At reformed middle and high schools in the U.S., **performance assessments**, portfolios, and projects have served as beacons of assessment reform for decades. Nationally recognized examples of assessment reform from schools such as Central Park East Secondary School, Fannie Lou Hamer Freedom High School, International High School, and the Urban Academy demonstrate that the pursuit of academic excellence and equity are obtainable and mutually reinforce one another. At these schools, the success of classroom and schoolwide assessment reform is not a distant aspiration of policymakers or advocates for change. Assessment reform visibly appears in students' work (Palladino & Shepard, 2022). Student projects, performance tasks, and assignments exemplify the values of **assessment for learning** for all.

Darling-Hammond (1997) writes:

> At Central Park East Secondary School (CPESS), students' intellectual development is guided by five "habits of mind": the abilities to weigh and use evidence, to see and understand differing viewpoints, to see connections and relationships, to imagine alternatives, and to assess implications and effects. These intellectual habits permeate the entire curriculum and evaluations of student work. They are incorporated in the assessment criteria. . . . (pp. 156–157)
>
> [Performance assessments] are rigorously evaluated and often sent back for more work; students learn what it takes to develop a piece of work that meets the standards of inquiry in a field and the standards of written and oral discourse demanded by committee members. They get feedback and revise and revise and revise; they internalize standards; they develop the capacity for sustained effort and ambitious work. (p. 157)
>
> An alternative approach to [accountability] reform [in these schools] uses standards and assessments as means of giving feedback to educators and tools for organizing student and teacher learning, rather than as a sledgehammer to beat schools into change. (p. 241)

Darling-Hammond and colleagues' observations ring true today as much as they did at the end of the last century. It is time to embrace our most vulnerable and **at-promise** learners by providing the feedback practices they need to advance and grow. We know that students seek and appreciate true mentorship, an exchange of ideas, and opportunities to engage in authentic conversation about meaningful topics. But to reach these places of learning, caring, and joy (Newmann, 1996; Sizer, 2013; Yeager et al., 2013), we must recommit to feedback for and by all.

Embracing Educational Purposes and Values

Schools have always had multiple goals and purposes (Apple, 2011; Dewey, 1923; Kliebard, 2004; Ravitch, 2001), but how do these goals and purposes look and feel from the perspective of classroom learning and assessment as the proverbial rubber hits the road? Do these myriad purposes bring us closer to academic excellence day by day, lesson by lesson, draft by draft? Do they bring us closer to equity task by task, project by project, assignment by assignment? Can we have both equity and excellence in the work our students produce in our schools in the pursuit of a more informed, educated, and just society?

We believe we can. Like those of you reading this book, we believe schools still matter in shaping values and unleashing the power of young people's ideas (Meier, 1995). **Habits of mind,** heart, and work matter. Schools are places where young people learn to try out, challenge, and make a go of these and other habits. The habits of mind are critical to democracy (Dewey, 1903). To acquire them, one needs feedback.

Educators have always had a special role in society. Teachers set specific and general educational goals to realize a broad range of educational purposes. In middle and secondary school contexts, subject content and disciplinary knowledge is key. Teachers work to weave good instruction with positive assessment experiences to foster engagement in science, music, computing, art, mathematics, history, economics, civics, ethnic studies, world languages, and physical education of all kinds, including sports. Each of these contexts offers us purpose and direction as we work to answer the question: What makes a good school and what does it mean to assess well?

Yet, if reform has taught us anything, it is that knowing what makes a good education must be clear to all stakeholders (Cuban, 1990; Tyack, 1974; Tyack & Cuban, 1995). Parents, children, and teachers must be working from similar goals and assumptions. We've noticed that getting on the same page takes communication about what matters: In this book, we will show that it is formative feedback that matters most to **continuous improvement.**

If assessment reform has taught us anything, it is that everyone benefits from signposts and roadmaps that tell us where we are and what we can expect down the road. Accountability over the last decades has promoted a data-driven mindset: Numbers, points, and scores have occupied many. A focus on formative feedback is different; it re-centers our work. It says that interim assessments that track yearly progress are not enough. We need better resourced and more nimble feedback strategies that work for all—each day in every learning space. The real, daily work of improvement comes from looking closely at student work, not at grades and test scores. Each teacher has the power to make a difference and to help others to improve when feedback is valued by the school and the community as a means to that end.

Schools are places where children can be invited to grow intellectually, emotionally, and socially. We shepherd our students daily along different paths toward different educational goals, sometimes with specific purposes in mind and other times with more general hopes and aspirations. But without clear, consistent feedback practices, procedures, and signals, it is unlikely our students will be able to share our vision. To correct course and get back on track or dive deeper, students and teachers need feedback cycles and routines.

Educational goals that bring feedback to life—in every classroom—can and should orient us. An authentic commitment to these goals rooted in student work allows teachers and students to reflect on first and final drafts. These feedback-driven goals remind us to look at next steps and support students as they develop their habits of work. True accountability will guide our educational priorities toward student work—on rich tasks, real-world projects, and longer-term assignments that honor our students' individual progress and growth.

We will say it as teachers, researchers, and educators again and again: Feedback practices will always do the heavy lifting in any continuous improvement plan. To move us beyond laudable aspirations and good intentions of assessment reforms, we must put feedback to work, minute by minute, day by day.

Guiding Questions

1. How can we think about feedback more *effectively*? Can feedback affect how students advance toward specific goals?

2. How can we use feedback more *equitably*? Can feedback create conditions for success that advance students' work on projects, assignments, and tasks to fulfill these goals?

3. How can we use feedback *effectively* and *equitably* to ensure all of our students are ready for college and the workplace because they know how to and are able to use feedback for continuous improvement?

We have organized this book around our formative feedback (FF) framework to provide everyone with three main lenses and corresponding focal points for making feedback practices visible to all. The FF framework (Figure 1.1) ensures that one can see how contexts for learning, educational goals, and content **standards** are embedded in continuous improvement of instruction and assessment. Whether one chooses to dive deeper into ***directionality***, ***configurations***, or ***modalities*** of feedback, each lens is interconnected with the others, and we offer solutions on how to connect and weave each of them together in practice in the chapters ahead.

Figure 1.1 Formative Feedback Framework

Contexts for Learning		
Face-to-Face	Blended	Distance Learning
Focal Point		
Directionality	**Configuration**	**Modality**
Lenses		
Teacher-driven	Whole class	Written
Peer-to-peer-driven	Small groups (2–4)	Spoken
Self-driven	Individual (1:1)	Nonverbal
Tasks, Projects, Activities	Learning Goals, Standards, Skills Rubrics, Progress Guides, "Next Steps" Organizers	

online resources Available for download at **resources.corwin.com/ContinuousImprovement**

As we have written in the How to Use This Book section, our FF framework also serves to guide the reader through possibilities for diving deeper into any focal point while maintaining a systematic, integrated, and holistic view of the power of feedback to change the trajectory of outcomes.

These guiding questions and the FF framework (Figure 1.1) will anchor our exploration of the role of learning goals, rich tasks, and the need for cycles of feedback. For now, let's define more concretely what we mean by *purpose-driven* formative feedback, which is tied to learning goals.

Purpose-Driven Feedback Is Tied to Learning Goals

If there is one thing we know as teachers, it's that purposes for feedback matter. No one wants to waste time on feedback that does not aim at improvement or change. We have chosen the term *purpose-driven feedback* for two reasons. First, feedback must be tied to learning goals (LGs) in the subject discipline, curriculum, and **unit of instruction**. Second, we recognize that teachers are responsible for ensuring their students receive the purposeful feedback everyone needs

- to advance learning toward a set of LGs and
- to use LGs to gauge current levels of performance with tasks, projects, and other work products.

Purpose-driven feedback led by teachers is anchored by well-defined competencies, skills, and dispositions (i.e., learning goals in an academic subject). It is also fundamentally student centered. The purpose of feedback is to support student growth and development with a task. The aim of purpose-driven feedback is to assist in bringing students to the next step. But that cannot be done without care, respect, and attention for where the student currently is, nor without the knowledge and expertise of the teacher to establish LGs for the class.

Establishing Goals to Guide Feedback Practices

Learning Goals Matter and Can Shift Over Time

Formative assessment practices must be tied to the curriculum in a unit of instruction and over a sequence of coursework rooted in subject disciplines (Heritage & Wylie, 2020).

We know that as students advance through the system of schooling, the demands for disciplinary practice and expertise increase. Reading, writing, and speaking and listening skills are important as our students progress from elementary grade levels toward high school. But demands, for example, for more complex mathematics coursework or sports programs increase as we prepare young people for college and work.

Everyone wants a good, engaging general education for their children, but we expect schools to prepare young adults to specialize eventually. To specialize in science, math, or art, for example, purpose-driven feedback is required to maximize impact; your purpose-driven feedback will be anchored in the subject discipline practices and skills themselves. Feedback for algebra may look different than feedback for physics or portraiture or Spanish or global history. But there will also be commonalities and places we agree to set aside subject matter differences.

It's difficult turning complex educational and learning goals into tangible, developmentally appropriate avenues for authentic exchanges of ideas. And yet it is key to making feedback work. We must know where we are going today, next week, and over the course of a semester. The table below outlines what purpose-driven feedback goals are and how they differ from other kinds of assessment goals.

PURPOSE-DRIVEN FEEDBACK GOALS	
Typically	**Typically are not**
▸ are connected to larger frameworks (e.g., standards, taxonomies, LGs).	▸ tied to a single objective(s) at end of each lesson.
▸ are focused on prioritizing core expectations/success criteria for student success.	▸ checklists for an assignment.

PURPOSE-DRIVEN FEEDBACK GOALS	
Typically	**Typically are not**
• are accompanied by graphic organizers and visual aids such as progress guides for unpacking a task or project. • are rich with exemplars of first drafts and finished products that emphasize incremental steps. • involve well-defined processes during class time to gauge where we are now and the next possible step(s). • use feedback-friendly tools (e.g., Universal Design for Learning [UDL] accessibility to all learners). • emphasize opportunities to grow through a process of revision, rethinking, and redoing. • center assessment relationships between teacher and student(s) on exchanges of information.	• aimed at positive reinforcement for behaviors (e.g., classroom management). • points driven. • part of a quiz, review, or test corrections event. • used for making summative judgments. • rooted in grading practices that assign *A*, *B*, *C*, *D*, or *F*.

We noted that purpose-driven feedback goals are always connected to larger frameworks (e.g., standards, taxonomies, LGs). Let's now discuss how to develop assessment activities based on clear, well-defined, and meaningful LGs. With this brief review, we will show how to use different schematic representations of LGs while reminding ourselves that it is essential to map pathways of feedback with visible tools, processes, and practices.

In contrast to static checklists that merely enumerate all the possible destinations of subject competence, purpose-driven feedback practices and routines set goals that are achievable for students. Too many standards documents, especially those provided by the policymakers, miss this mark. They offer a vaguely visible distant horizon but contain no directions for how to get there.

Whether they are known as *core competencies*, *essential knowledge*, or *power standards*, these conceptualizations of education standards attempt to describe what students should know and be able to do at key junctures in their educational journey. They offer lists of proficiencies designed to identify markers of success for college and the workplace. These education standards promise to show us where to prepare students to engage in deep, lifelong learning (National Research Council, 2012). In other words, they represent aspirations for adults who have set learning goals for students.

Key to all the policy talk around educational standards and purposes is—or should be—the possibility of assessing a thinking, living curriculum that serves children well (Brown et al., 1992; Resnick & Resnick,

1992; Rothman, 1995; Shepard, 2000; Torrance, 1995a, 1995b; Wiggins, 1993a, 1993b).

The new 21st century approach to standards includes notions such as crosscutting concepts and skills-based practices that represent a commitment to student growth and development. Ideally, such LGs and skills-based practices link different domains of knowledge and help students make connections within and across subject disciplines.

For example, in science and engineering curricula at reform-based high schools, we can see how crosscutting concepts such as understanding patterns, stability and change, systems and system models, and structure and function help students develop a coherent and scientifically grounded view of the world. In schools that embody curricula that emphasize crosscutting practices, students are

- asking questions,
- developing and using models,
- planning and carrying out investigations,
- analyzing and interpreting data,
- using mathematics and computational thinking,
- constructing explanations,
- engaging in argument from evidence, and
- obtaining, evaluating, and communicating information.

It's important to recognize that the "new standards" aren't so new. Many are borrowed from schools like CPESS that are committed to the *habits of mind*, an outcomes-based framework that emphasizes authentic portfolio and performance assessment reforms in the decades prior to No Child Left Behind (2000). Other approaches to anchoring educational goals in the curriculum draw from well-established taxonomies, including Bloom's taxonomy of educational objectives, Webb's **depth of knowledge (DOK)**, and Biggs and Collis's structure of observed learning outcomes (SOLO).

Some readers may be very familiar with these educational goals and standards-based frameworks; others may appreciate a quick refresher. We have seen school districts and state authorities grapple with different frameworks over the years. We know they matter to policymakers and school leaders, so we will take the time to revisit and review how these frameworks can (in theory) advance all the purpose-driven feedback approaches to classroom and school-based assessment presented in our book.

The questions before us include the following:

- How do these various "big picture" frameworks used to define LGs advance and support the work of formative feedback for students?

CHAPTER 1. On the Role of Learning Goals, Tasks, and Cycles of Feedback

- Can these various frameworks serve as guideposts to better define the purposes of feedback in our lessons, units, and larger curricular aims?

- What can be done with standards-based frameworks in particular to better ground them in concrete feedback practices that make an actual difference in our students' work product in our classrooms and places of learning?

The Habits of Mind Framework

The habits of mind at CPESS (Darling-Hammond, 1996; Duckor & Perlstein, 2014; Meier, 1995) refer to learning goals that educators at the school expect students to engage in and eventually internalize to accomplish complex, real-world tasks and activities aimed at preparation for college. These habits are necessarily cognitive, social, psychological, and practical. The goal of a CPESS education was to habituate every young person, as school founder Deborah Meier says, with the passion "to use one's mind well" (Gold & Lanzoni, 1993).

In keeping with the student-centered focus of CPESS and its commitment to **project-based learning (PBL)**, a mini-documentary—*Graduation by Portfolio*—was created by staff, teachers, and students in 1993. This documentary was part of a PBL activity that a group of students engaged in over a year. The student-created documentary now serves as a record of assessment reform that shows the power of school-based accountability systems centered on enduring LGs. These LGs—the five habits of mind—were interwoven into a teacher-developed curriculum that focused on rich tasks, PBL, and long-term assignments called **exhibitions** and investigations; formative feedback was essential to success for all.

Following John Dewey's notion that education is a process of practicing what we learn to better understand it, these social and cognitive habits of mind describe how students can experience a living curriculum and transform their own understanding of the world through real-world practice.

The habits of mind, cast by the faculty at CPESS as **essential questions (EQs)**, formed the cornerstone of the curriculum and schoolwide LGs. Through the cognitive lens of the five habits of mind, all the teachers at CPESS sought to develop interdisciplinary curricula to better foster

> **WATCH THIS**
>
> *Graduation by Portfolio*
>
> Please use the QR code above and watch the entire video.
>
> To read a QR code, you must have a smartphone or tablet with a camera. We recommend that you download a QR code reader app that is made specifically for your phone or tablet brand.

their students' curiosity, intellectual engagement, and academic mastery in preparation for college.

The five habits of mind demand that everyone ask:

- *Evidence*: How do we know what we know? What is the source? Is it credible?

- *Perspective*: From whose point of view is this being presented? Are there other viewpoints on this topic?

- *Connection*: How is this event or work connected to others? What causes what?

- *Supposition*: What if things were different?

- *Relevance*: Who cares? Why is this important?

Using questions that frame cognitive learning goals, the habits of mind are demonstrated through *exhibitions*, which are sets of performance tasks (labs, essays, art installations, research papers, videos, etc.). These artifacts lead to portfolios that serve as examples of achievement. Each assignment, exhibition, and portfolio is developed, revised, and transformed by formative feedback from classroom teachers, advisors, paraprofessionals, and the resource room staff.

It is the inquiry-driven, performance task-based learning approach of schools such as CPESS that brings feedback practices to the foreground. Each question for students is grounded in a **rubric**, which outlines a set of learning outcomes shared by all. The **learning criteria** and EQs are schoolwide. Students, parents, and staff can examine the evidence for reaching a particular level of performance while committing themselves to working on current drafts of student work to ensure progress is being made.

> **WATCH THIS**
>
> *FA Moves: Module 3 on Posing from CCEE series*
>
> Please use the QR code above.

The approach to continuous improvement embodied at schools such as CPESS puts formative feedback on equal footing with summative or benchmark assessment. A common thread in these feedback-driven reforms is the focus on *process* and *product*. There is a consensus: Having standards is necessary but not sufficient for coaching children and young people in how to use their minds well. At these places of learning, feedback—in short and long cycles—ensures that students know what next steps are within their reach on a daily basis.

The Bloom's Taxonomy of Educational Objectives Framework

Today's standards are typically guided by the more familiar attempt to describe what students should know and be able to do using Benjamin Bloom's taxonomy. Very often, we see unit and **lesson plans** borrowing the language of Bloom's **schema**. The original and later revised versions of Bloom's taxonomy are a schema (or **mental model**) for classifying educational goals, objectives, and skills that employ a cumulative hierarchical framework. Bloom's (1956) original version of the taxonomy delineated six levels:

- Knowledge
- Comprehension
- Application
- Analysis
- Synthesis
- Evaluation

Each level of Bloom's taxonomy is intended to differentiate higher-order thinking from lower-order thinking in a curriculum and has been used for the purpose of differentiating questions and tasks.

Bloom's revised version (Anderson et al., 2001) describes two "dimensions" of LGs: a knowledge dimension, of which there are four categories—factual, conceptual, procedural, and metacognitive—and a dimension encompassing cognitive processes. Both are important to defining learning goals within and across curricula. In the revised version, the six categories of the cognitive process dimension (Anderson et al., 2001) are remember, understand, apply, analyze, evaluate, and create.

While conceptually useful for planning curricula and classifying assessments, these two dimensions operate without any reference to content-specific learning trajectories or progressions. Because Bloom's taxonomy lacks traceable progress levels, it is difficult for teachers and students to figure out what feedback is necessary along a continuum of practice and when to apply feedback in the learning cycle. It is also difficult to determine what next steps should be pursued, in part because Bloom's taxonomy was never designed to address feedback practices.

The Webb's Depth of Knowledge Framework

Similar to Bloom, Norman Webb introduced the concept of DOK in 1997 in the context of defining criteria for judging the alignment between expectations and assessments in math and science. He later extended his thinking to other content areas. Unlike Bloom's taxonomy, which focuses on the type of thinking students are expected to demonstrate, Webb's

DOK focuses on the context, scenario, setting, or situation in which students express the extent of their thinking.

The DOK taxonomy is a general theoretical framework used in assessment contexts to describe, characterize, or hierarchically organize student responses to cognition-related tasks. The model designates how deeply students must know, understand, and be aware of what they are learning to attain and explain answers, outcomes, results, and solutions. There are four DOK levels:

- *Level 1* focuses on recall and reproduction of data, definitions, details, facts, information, and procedures (knowledge acquisition).

- *Level 2* involves the use of academic concepts and cognitive skills to answer questions, address problems, accomplish tasks, and analyze texts and topics (knowledge application).

- *Level 3* requires students to think strategically and reasonably about how and why concepts, ideas, operations, and procedures can be used to attain and explain answers, conclusions, decisions, outcomes, reasons, and results (knowledge analysis).

- When demonstrating *Level 4* cognition, students think extensively about what else can be done, how else learning can be used, and how the student could use what they have learned in different academic and real-world contexts (knowledge augmentation).

While Webb's DOK taxonomy designates how extensively students are expected to transfer and use what they have learned in different academic and real-world contexts, there is a knowing–doing gap similar to the one found in Bloom's taxonomy. We are presented with important learning goals but little idea of how to embed them within processes, procedures, and **scaffolds** that support feedback.

These taxonomies describe a destination, but they lack suggestions for how teachers and students can bring formative feedback to life on actual projects and tasks that aim to demonstrate what students know and can do.

The SOLO Taxonomy Framework

The limits of Bloom's and Webb's taxonomies become apparent when we refocus attention on trajectories of feedback. The abstract learning goals that help define higher-order thinking skills are laudable and, in principle, useful for planning or reviewing curriculum and assessment targets across large educational and testing systems. But feedback for, with, and by students is difficult when we only describe *levels* and *types* of knowledge.

A more useful taxonomy for feedback-driven goal setting is found in John Biggs and Kevin Collis's structure of observed learning outcomes (SOLO). The **SOLO taxonomy** tracks the development of knowledge and skills across a generic but emerging learning trajectory. The five levels of progress are

- pre-structural,
- unistructural,
- multi-structural,
- relational, and
- extended abstract.

These levels (or *ramps* as we call them) can be and often are adapted to the SOLO design when used in the classroom. In our work as teacher educators and former high school teachers, we have adapted SOLO for the design of rubrics, **progress guides**, and other visual scaffolds to assist student learning. We have also found it useful to add nuance to some SOLO levels (for example, levels prior to pre-structural) to better represent and support students who are struggling to get on task. We have found that some students are not yet ready to start the task and it helps to map our specific feedback strategies in these equally important **zones of proximal development (ZPDs)**. Similarly, we have modified SOLO-type guides when students are in different places within the same level. Key to any representation of students' work on a continuum is that it be developmentally sensitive and sufficiently nuanced to uncover the next steps within and between levels (Wilson, 2005, 2009; Wilson & Sloane, 2000).

Following Vygotsky's (1978) insight that education is a process of discovering and learning to close the gap on ZPDs, the levels of the SOLO taxonomy allow us to see junctures, pathways, and on-ramps. These sorts of taxonomies move us closer to dynamic pathways for multiple learning goals that evolve over time.

The SOLO taxonomy (Figure 1.2) is a general theoretical framework used in assessment contexts to describe, characterize, or hierarchically organize student responses to cognition-related performance tasks. As learning progresses, performances become more complex, as do feedback opportunities and demands in terms of directionality, configuration, and modality. We discuss these three major focal points of feedback more in later chapters. For now, it is important to note that feedback can and must be differentiated by its directionality (Chapters 2–4), configuration (Chapters 5–7), and modality (Chapters 8–10) and that one size does not fit all.

Figure 1.2 SOLO Taxonomy

| Pre-structural | Uni-structural | Multi-structural | Relational | Extended Abstract |

Source: Graphic based on model first described in Biggs, J. B., & Collis, K. F. (1982). Evaluating the quality of learning: The SOLO taxonomy (structure of the observed learning outcome). *Educational psychology series*. Academic Press.

Of its many useful features, the SOLO taxonomy allows us to set learning goals and develop concrete feedback tools, processes, and practices during and across lessons. When coupled with **graphic organizers** such as rubrics and progress guides, it operates at a grain size that students, teachers, and paraprofessionals can use and make sense of during instruction. Popham (2007, p. 80) writes,

> Grain size refers to the breadth or scope of something. For instance, in the case of a curricular aim, a large grain size would be a significant, long-term goal that might take a full school year for students to reach. A curricular aim with a smaller grain size would be an instructional objective that students can achieve during a single classroom session.

The modified SOLO taxonomy operates at a grain size that makes it adaptable to rubrics, progress guides, and other means for assessing where students currently are and where they can go next (with assistance). Using SOLO-type taxonomies with well-designed progress guides can serve as a means of classifying larger learning outcomes in terms of their complexity while enabling us to offer meaningful specific feedback on students' work. Whether we are teaching and learning on the playing field, in the science lab, at the theater, or in the classroom, these approaches focus us all on progress and the process of growth.

Author Insight

On Feedback Parameters and Systems Thinking

Ramaprasad (1983) is known for identifying three essential questions about feedback: "Where am I headed? Where am I now? How do I close the gap?"

But he also focuses us on feedback systems and key parameters:

1. The focus of feedback may be any system parameter: input, process, or output.

2. The necessary conditions for feedback are the existence of data on the reference level of the parameter, data on the actual level of the parameter, and a mechanism for comparing the two to generate information about the gap between the two levels. There cannot be any feedback if one of the three (data on the reference level, data on the actual level, mechanism for comparing) is absent.

3. The information on the gap between the actual level and the reference level is feedback only when it is used to alter the gap. If the information is stored in memory, it is not feedback.

While Ramaprasad's theory looks at feedback systems largely in terms of inputs, processes, and outputs, we see implications for next steps rooted in progress guides, visible scaffolds, and other tools that can be used to support differentiated, feedback-rich ecosystems in the classroom.

Source: Ramaprasad (1983), p. 5.

For feedback to matter, it must include artifacts, scaffolds, and mechanisms in the classroom learning experience that are anchored in learning criteria. These learning criteria must move beyond abstraction or aspirations and lean into the work of making **feedback loops** and pathways visible to our students. Ramaprasad's (1983) work reminds us to consider feedback in terms of inputs, outputs, and processes. We follow this insight throughout this book.

Identifying Meaningful Activities, Rich Tasks, and Authentic Projects to Enrich Feedback Practices

Rich, Authentic, Complex Tasks Matter

Purpose-driven feedback goals must be mapped with a set of tasks, projects, and other work products that allow students to grow, progress, and find their ZPDs in the subject content matter. Whether we adopt an elaborate standards-based curriculum or use carefully chosen elements of Webb's DOK taxonomy, identifying meaningful activities will form the foundation for authentic learning. Without rich, meaningful tasks in a lesson and unit, we will know the destination but miss the mark.

Rich, meaningful tasks are complex to design and sometimes difficult to enact. These tasks require sustained effort by our students, opportunities for revision of **first drafts**, and a set of collaborative skills that call upon the whole learning community (Darling-Hammond & Adamson, 2014; Guha et al., 2018). We know from years of experience in schools that emphasize real-world immersion and learning by doing that these richer, more complex tasks require many exchanges of, as Ramaprasad (1983) calls it, "information." Feedback is, at its heart, the exchange and production of such information.

Rich tasks embedded in the curriculum may include science labs, persuasive essays, electronic art installations, propaganda posters, travel log webpages, research papers, choral performances, track and field events, software programs, videos, and so forth. No matter the design or format, each task requires that our students practice feedback—for themselves and for others—in our company as educators.

Many standards-based professional associations have embraced the move toward authentic assessment across a variety of subject disciplines. The National Science Teaching Association, quoting experts in performance task design (Stoll & Schultz, 2019, p. 40), notes that

> Performance tasks enable teachers to gather evidence not just about what a student knows, but also what he or she can do with that knowledge. . . . Rather than asking students to recall facts, performance tasks measure whether a student can apply his or her knowledge to make sense of a new phenomenon or design a solution to a new problem. In this way, assessment becomes phenomenon-based and multidimensional as it assesses both scientific practices and content within a new context.
>
> As we move away from traditional testing, the purpose of assessment begins to shift. Instead of only measuring students' performance, we also strive to create an opportunity for students to learn throughout the process. Not only are students learning more as they are being assessed, but the feedback you gain as a teacher is far richer than traditional assessment. . . . This allows teachers to gather more information about what students do and do not know in order to better inform meaningful next steps in their teaching.

Similarly, those committed to PBL have consistently argued for the role of meaningful, long-cycle assessments that engage children and young adults in real-world, authentic learning. Students working on a project that engages them in solving a real-world problem or answering a complex question over an extended period—from a week up to a semester—is key (Dewey, 1900/1990, 1902, 1916; Kilpatrick, 1918; Knoll, 1995; Waks, 1997). These authentic projects often lead to the creation of a public product or presentation for an audience. This engagement with adults outside the school allows students to not only demonstrate subject matter competence but also to put their critical thinking, collaboration, creativity, and communication skills on display.

> ## Author Insight
> ### John Dewey
>
> The logic which commits [one] to the idea that the management of the school system must be in the hands of an expert commits [one] also to the idea that every member of the school system, from the first-grade teacher to the principal of the high school, must have some share in the exercise of educational power. *The remedy is not to have one expert dictating educational methods and subject-matter to a body of passive, recipient teachers, but the adoption of intellectual initiative, discussion, and decision throughout the entire school* corps. The remedy of the partial evils of democracy, the implication of the school system in municipal politics, is in appeal to a more thoroughgoing democracy.

Source: Dewey (1903), p. 196, italics added.

Experts have noted that while PBL has become more widely used in schools and other educational settings, there are key characteristics that differentiate "doing a project" from engaging in rigorous PBL. The PBL Works (2022) website, sponsored by the Buck Institute for Education, states:

> We find it helpful to distinguish a "dessert project"—a short, intellectually-light project served up after the teacher covers the content of a unit in the usual way—from a "main course" project, in which the project *is* the unit. In Project Based Learning, the project is the vehicle for teaching the important knowledge and skills students need to learn. The project contains and frames curriculum and instruction.
>
> In contrast to dessert projects, PBL requires critical thinking, problem solving, collaboration, and various forms of communication. To answer a driving question and create high-quality work, students need to do much more than remember information. They need to use higher-order thinking skills and learn to work as a team.

Backward design, also called *backward planning* or *backward mapping*, is a process that educators use to design learning experiences and instructional techniques to achieve specific learning goals. Backward-mapping curriculum is a critical step in planning a rich set of tasks for an instructor's course or department. Whether using state standards mapping or well-vetted design principles laid out by experts in performance-based assessment, PBL, or real-world immersion activities, we see feedback mechanisms and processes as the place where the proverbial rubber hits the road.

Wiggins and McTighe (1998) have laid out the fundamental rationale and principles for teachers who think through their curriculum. Because they encourage intentionality during the instructional and assessment design process, lesson and unit planning requires a continual revisiting of the purpose of teaching something *before* implementing it into the curriculum. They write:

> Deliberate and focused instructional design requires us as teachers and curriculum writers to make an important shift in our thinking about the nature of our job. The shift involves thinking a great deal, first, about the specific learnings sought, and the evidence of such learnings, before thinking about what we, as the teacher, will do or provide in teaching and learning activities. (2005, p. 15)

How we design, plan, execute, and monitor our formative feedback practices is essential for deeper equity in today's classrooms. To engage and support our students through complex, long-cycle tasks, projects, and assignments requires focused and sustained effort from everyone. We as teachers must design many opportunities for revision and conversation about progress and plan for ways to uncover and make sense of feedback skills, disposition, and habits.

These sorts of richer, more complex performance-based tasks require frequent exchanges of information between teachers, peers, and self. Performance tasks embedded in the curriculum may include projects, social media blogs, installations, posters, software code, research papers, art and music performances, videos, and so forth. But in each case, these instructional and assessment products must be supported by feedback processes if there is to be any hope for formative assessment playing a role in our students' development and growth.

Evidence of **deeper learning** depends on an array of rich tasks (Darling-Hammond et al., 2020), but such evidence cannot be discovered without a feedback-rich learning environment in which information flows freely and consistently. Feedback practices are the link to equity and excellence.

Right-Sized Feedback With a Progress Guide: Between Rubrics and a Hard Spot

Advocates for performance assessment and PBL often point to rubrics for evidence of learning goals and success criteria. But too frequently, rubrics are flawed—sometimes by design, other times from a failure to implement. When the goal of one's assessment practice is the generation of right-sized formative feedback for students to use to improve their work, rubrics can be especially problematic. This is because rubrics often contain "dysfunctional detail" (Popham, 1997). Dysfunctional detail makes rubrics awkward and difficult to use for both teachers (when looking at drafts of student work) and students (when self-assessing their work).

Students and teachers can only juggle so many elements at once and therefore need a streamlined, focused document when they are formatively assessing work. Processing power consumed by the dysfunctional detail of a rubric drains brain power and distracts teachers who would be better served by figuring out and articulating appropriate next steps for their students. Too often, rubrics get in the way of timely, specific, flexible feedback.

In the chapters ahead, we will introduce an innovation called the *progress guide* that we have used to build a bridge between rubrics and other tools for making sense of next steps. The **big idea** that animates the progress guide is that it allows students (and teachers) to focus on next steps along a strand of the current work-in-progress to make just-in-time adjustments before summative judgment (i.e., marking and **grading** periods). We will share many examples from different projects, but here is one to help visualize the structure and function of progress guides. Figure 1.3 depicts a "Using Evidence" **exemplar** of a progress guide connected to an argumentation rubric.

Figure 1.3 Progress Guide: Using Evidence to Support My Claim

Current Level (Circle)	MY PROGRESS GUIDE	
	I Can	Next Steps to Revise My Draft
****	Weigh evidence	Now I need to . . .
***	Add some evidence	Now I need to . . .
**	Take a position	Now I need to . . .
*	Restate	Now I need to . . .

Source: Courtesy of Validity Partners LLC © Do Not Circulate without Permission.

Available for download at **resources.corwin.com/ContinuousImprovement**

A progress guide is an excellent supplement to a well-designed analytic rubric since a progress guide, by definition, has already prioritized what is most important to focus on in a piece of student work or a performance. This is the case whether it is the teacher using the progress guide to give feedback to the student or the student using the progress guide to generate next steps feedback for a classmate (or for themselves). We introduce the notion of the progress guide in Chapter 4 with several examples of its uses in the remaining chapters.

In many cases, **English learners** (ELs) and students with special needs can benefit from a "less is more" approach. Rubrics can pose unnecessary barriers to learning how to learn; a progress guide offers a supportive on-ramp to help students gauge where the draft is and what may be next to improve it. Less extraneous verbiage means ELs and students with special needs can dedicate more time and resources to understanding next steps, the essence of formative feedback for all. Tools such as the progress guide focus on drafting, revising, and rethinking "the current work" rather than gaming "the system" for points.

Our solution to the problem of right-sized feedback—the use of progress guides—is simple without being simplistic. We will discuss how to utilize progress guides for PBL and performance task design to keep the focus on feedback loops rather than grades and points. And we will invite everyone to design their own progress guides in places it makes sense for their own curriculum and classrooms.

For now, we note that a set of progress guides that align with a well-designed analytic rubric rooted in standards/learning criteria is a crucial feature of feedback-rich assessment and instructional design. We know formative feedback works when students are invited into the flow of the learning with footholds, checkpoints, and scaffolded processes that reveal both what is ahead and how far we've come. As we will discuss in the next chapter, teachers, peers, and students themselves can mark progress and identify next steps in the learning trajectory. Progress guides must play a role in the process of defining what's next and how to get there.

But first, a word about cycles of feedback, which are too often taken for granted. Yes, it is essential to use well-defined frameworks, standards, and criteria for purpose-driven feedback. It is equally essential that students engage in rich tasks, authentic performances, and meaningful assignments so they can exercise the habits of mind and work required for 21st century learning. To do this well, though, we must set everyone up for success in long and short cycles of feedback that weave across units of instruction.

Ensuring Long and Short Cycles for Feedback Practices

The timing of feedback matters. We all know this. The cycles and rhythms of feedback must occur frequently to mark and support progress on a continuum of practice. We tell our students, "Everything in due time" as they struggle to reach the next level in an activity. We tell them, "Be patient" with this project or task. "Trust the process." We remind them again and again in the flow of learning, "You don't know how to do that—yet."

But we must also use time to everyone's advantage. The art of formative feedback is in its timing. And time is limited.

Our feedback practices must reflect the rhythms of performance task creation and project-based work as each evolves and unfolds over time. This respect for process (and product) allows us to examine and embrace the distinct and intersecting sets of shorter and longer feedback loops that occur in places where information flows. We've come to realize that it's all about information flows. The question is, how do we make space and time for these exchanges?

Short-Turn Cycles of Feedback

The time available to offer, process, and incorporate feedback can be brief. The information transfer rate is short and often informal. It can occur in "short turns" of talk, accompanied by verbal and nonverbal communication. We see teachers leaning in, dropping by, huddling with their students to offer quick suggestions and comments. Teachers engaged in short-turn cycles of feedback do it because they see they can make a difference.

These flows of information are essential to sizing up where we are and where we are going next with the work. No matter the academic subject, students rely on our just-in-time interventions to advance their progress. They appreciate the time and care it takes to attend to their work-in-progress. Experts outside of education also note:

> "Just-in-time" is a management philosophy and not a technique. It originally referred to the production of goods to meet customer demand exactly, in time, quality and quantity, whether the "customer" is the final purchaser of the product or another process further along the production line. It has now come to mean producing with minimum waste. "Waste" is taken in its most general sense and includes time and resources as well as materials. (Institute for Manufacturing, 2016)

No matter what we produce, make, or create, virtually every working adult knows that effective teamwork is essential. To be effective, we try to use our time efficiently and productively. The idea of wasted time or resources is not foreign to feedback. People become frustrated and disparaged when they feel that their feedback is useless or too little too late.

To move forward, we all require guidance (both individually and in smaller groups). As we work on projects, assignments, and performance tasks together in a classroom, time must be on our side. From the first draft to the final product, there is an expectation that we can get this done in the time that remains before the deadline. We must have some degree of hope that the proverbial mountain can be climbed. One needs faith in the guide on the side as well, which is why we have written this book.

To get things done in the work world, we need feedback, often in the moment and at multiple times in the life of the project. Why should it be different for students in our schools who are engaged in authentic real-world projects and complex tasks? As teachers who are leading our students, we need to anticipate, be ready for, and expect to provide quick taps and gentle nudges to keep everyone moving forward. These may happen with a **pause** in the lesson, an unexpected but teachable moment, or a pivot of "turn and talk to your partner" to see what the students think is next. Just-in-time feedback **moves** from all directions are essential to supporting our students engaged in the work of deeper learning.

Long-Turn Cycles of Feedback

In other cases, what we will call *long-turn cycles of feedback* are part of the menu. The time to offer, process, and incorporate particular types of information (such as teacher-driven, peer-to-peer-driven, or self-driven feedback) takes longer. These feedback loops can extend over days, weeks, or even months depending on the task, project, or assignment.

These long-turn exchanges are usually written as comments, suggestions, and notes; they may also be supported by verbal and nonverbal feedback routines, which take time. In these cases, our students will rely on clear protocols for engagement (and re-engagement) with these long-turn cycles on a visible, mutually agreed-upon timeline. They will also need to know the destination and the various on-ramps and routes to success. As we've said, learning goals matter for purpose-driven feedback to work over time.

As guides on the side facilitating longer-term projects, performance tasks, and assignments, our students need to know our expectations and how these are aligned with well-defined learning goals and outcomes. Our students also need to receive consistent messages about success criteria. The message of "Where are we now and where are we going next?" must be connected to a visible workflow where feedback is produced, acknowledged, and resolved.

Why? Because the world of work and higher education also moves to the rhythms of long-turn feedback cycles and exchanges of information. People are expected to track, monitor, and fully incorporate information as they produce together as a team and against real deadlines. Teachers, much like team leaders in the workplace, are in a unique position to lead and support their students. Today more than ever, teachers must anticipate "production" bottlenecks, be ready for proverbial "supply chain" disruptions, and know how and when to apply gentle but persistent pressure to keep everyone moving forward.

Each of these cycles—long and short turn—has its place in weaving a coherent set of feedback practices. By thinking through our feedback practices and protocols through a backward-design process in the curriculum, we can ensure that we use everyone's time well. Experts and seasoned practitioners know that deeper learning only occurs when timely and persistent feedback occurs with such cycles and exchanges of information.

Intersecting Feedback Loops With a Shared Project

Long- and short-cycle feedback loops intersect over the life of any school-based, department-based, or classroom-based project and extended performance task. These loops represent a production process, one that we can articulate to others within and outside of our schools. At the center of the commitment to feedback-for-all is the notion of a shared project, one that we plan for with our students. Students and teachers must join together in these shared projects, tasks, and assignments so that both can feel the power of authentic learning as a team. Feedback loops are key to the success of these efforts. But we have to make them visible first.

One way to envision an effective, robust feedback loop is to consider how it evolves as a process that gains purchase over time. We want to get traction on the shared project. Thinking through the work process and project cycle with our students as partners is key. Figure 1.4 shows the five major components or phases that students should be aware of before embarking on a performance task, project, or assignment. Each phase can serve as a checkpoint and, if necessary, as a stopping point to discuss norms, adjust as needed, and evaluate what's next for the class.

We use the example of "evaluating a project" to delineate the markers and goals for the cycle of a feedback loop, but there will likely be many iterations and subroutines within and between components/phases. That is why we say classroom assessment is an art as much as a science (National Research Council, 2001). This schema helps students, teachers, and paraprofessionals alike to see the big picture.

Phase 1. Setting a Purpose

To open the **formative feedback loop**, we must first define the purpose of a shared project. Students are invited into the project as partners in its resolution. They have a stake in the project and can see their own work as essential to the success of the unit.

Figure 1.4 Formative Feedback Process Model

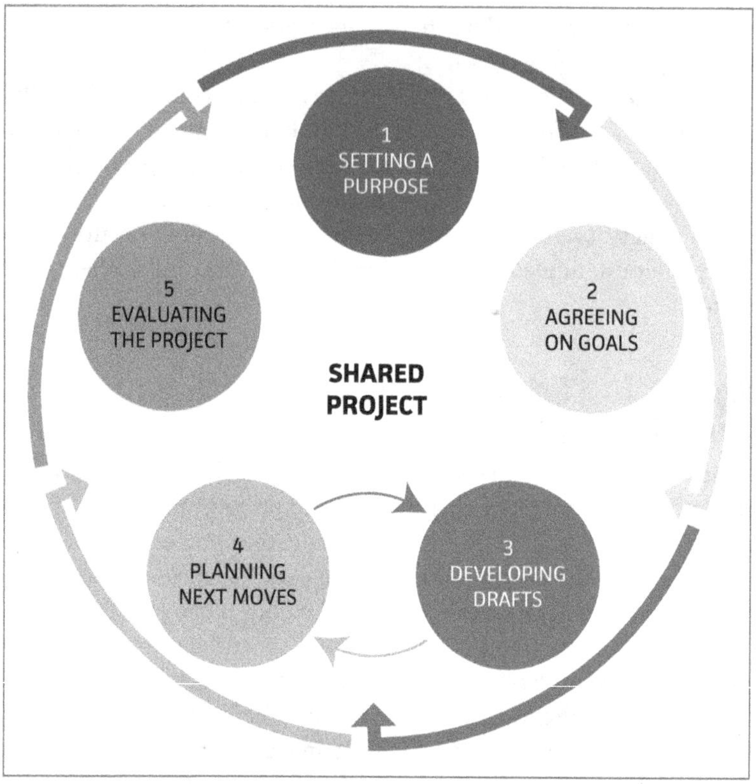

Circular diagram titled "SHARED PROJECT" with five phases: 1. Setting a Purpose, 2. Agreeing on Goals, 3. Developing Drafts, 4. Planning Next Moves, 5. Evaluating the Project.

Available for download at **resources.corwin.com/ContinuousImprovement**

Phase 2. Agreeing on Goals

Every project must have an end goal that is known from the outset. Teachers will often show exemplars and/or samples of exemplary student work to help students visualize the destination. The exemplars are polished but the samples can be rough. Whatever the case, each student in the class must see how the work-in-progress will become the final project.

Phase 3. Developing First Drafts

Once the parameters for the shared project have been agreed upon and the course set in terms of time, resources, and materials, we begin the process of testing our ideas (what we call *first drafts*). At this point, the feedback loop is open; it includes our first drafts and all our attempts to get started with the project. We can break down components of the project, differentiate the skills required for it, and put in place the required supports and scaffolds. But getting everyone started is essential to equity-driven work in today's learning environments.

Key to monitoring, uptake, and momentum is the iterative cycle of drafting with all our students, however incomplete or nascent the drafts may be at the outset of the project. If students cannot or have not yet iterated a response with themselves, with others, or with us as mentors, then the feedback loop stalls or collapses into familiar expressions of frustration: "I am stuck" or "This is stupid" or "She never pays attention." These expressions are normal, even healthy, from a developmental perspective. Our students are novices, not experts. But these are not signs of a doomed project. They are evidence of students learning to draft and revise. Authentic assessment and projects are messy work; everyone needs to pause, honor, and acknowledge: "It's okay. We are learning by doing—together."

The disposition to test one's ideas in front of others is a risky thing. Students are not always eager to take risks. Their experience of making a mistake, failing, or producing less-than-perfect results are often anchored in entirely negative contexts. Some may ask us, if all that matters are the points on a rubric (which lead to the final grade), then why iterate at all?

Too often at this stage, the project loses its intrinsic value and the students lose their internal momentum: They stop seeing their work as "in progress" and instead prepare themselves for a final judgment. Focusing on a graded outcome short-circuits our students' motivation to use feedback to grow, stretch, and change.

Any authentic project that involves kids generating their personal best over a period of time for a complex assignment is going to involve communication. With communication comes breakdowns. But there is hope. This is part of a cycle—Phase 3 to be exact. It is important to **prime** everyone: When we provide feedback, we respond to what we see at this moment. There will be several iterations, from first draft to the final project.

Phase 4. Planning Next Moves

We need robust information exchanges to check for mutual understanding. They are characterized by phrases such as:

- "What I see is . . ."
- "What we are working on is . . ."
- "A next step might be . . ."
- "If I try this, then . . ."

Each of these **sentence starters** brings us a step closer to the "plan forwarding" aspect of **assessment for learning.** In this context, a progress guide is an anchor: It allows us to visualize, discuss, and break down next steps.

In one-on-one conversations with our students, we will look at initial writing samples, spreadsheet results, research findings, video clips, drawings, media objects, physical movements on the court or field, and warm-up routines. We must ask ourselves, as guides on the side, what we will use to guide our comments, suggestions, and questions (that is, feedback!) about those drafts as they emerge over the project cycle.

Teachers' formative feedback, similar to peer-to-peer or self-directed feedback, is effective when it is broken down into manageable chunks of information. That information must be anchored in a continuum: at the proper grain size and with the appropriate **academic language** for students.

Planning next steps on a project or performance task is impossible if we don't know where we were in the last draft and where we plan to be in the next one. Moreover, without exemplars and progress guides to serve as signposts, it will be difficult to evaluate progress and next steps.

Phase 5. Evaluating the Project

Closing the formative feedback cycle is as important as opening it. We need routines for reflection. In some instances, we will use a formal rubric, **scoring guide**, or some other evaluative tool to assess the quality of the student work. In other instances, a simple debrief or informal self-reflection on the project helps everyone learn how they did, where they got stuck, and how to improve stewardship of the next cycle.

The right amount of feedback at the appropriate time, in an accessible academic language **register** rooted in progress guides, matters. The Formative Feedback Process Model represented in Figure 1.4 draws everyone's attention to how they will work together while each person produces their own project for the unit or semester. Phases 3 and 4 of any authentic performance task, project, or assignment are where the action is. But Phases 1 and 2 are where it starts. Effective feedback is purpose-driven and anchored on LGs and well-articulated progressions.

Check for Understanding/Self-Assessment

Well-articulated on-ramps—when anchored in purposeful feedback tools, artifacts, and processes—are as important as the destination. The roadmaps and on-ramps that form our educational goals and purposes are many. Some researchers have turned to the concept of **learning progressions** in subject disciplines to understand pathways to success (Alonzo & Gotwals, 2012; Claesgens et al., 2009; Duncan & Hmelo-Silver, 2009; Heritage, 2008). We note that whatever theory of student learning accompanies our educational goals, identifying footholds, bottlenecks, and just-in-time feedback that moves everyone forward is the next step for ensuring continuous improvement in our classrooms. We must design so-called embedded assessment experiences that engage critical thinking, ensure revision, and work across the curriculum to elicit students' habits of mind. This is the ongoing educational journey toward excellence and equity that DuBois calls the "freedom to learn" (Foner, 1949). It requires us all to work to advance all students with respect and care.

Take a moment to consider the reasons why you have adopted other people's standards, objectives, and learning goals in the past. (Maybe you've used Webb's DOK or state standards or learning progressions.) Did you borrow or adapt others' ideas to fit your classroom or department's values? How do these choices promote your educational goals for students in your daily care?

Reflect

Which standards, course objectives, and learning goals currently matter the most to you? Are particular documents (e.g., curriculum frameworks, taxonomies, syllabi) useful to you? What about the educational goals in these documents appeals most to you? How do these educational goals connect to the kinds of purpose-driven formative feedback we've discussed in this chapter?

Self-Assess

Instructions: Put a check mark by the level that best describes the current state of your instructional and assessment practices as a teacher responsible for providing students with clear, well-defined learning goals.

SOLO LEVEL	DESCRIPTION	PUT A ✓ MARK
Extended Abstract	I have research-informed, clear, visible, and consistent learning goals (LGs) embedded in my class for all performance tasks, projects, and long-term assignments.	
	I can differentiate my feedback tools and feedback processes within and across lessons and adapt to kids, contexts, and subject-based demands.	
Relational	I have a set of coherent learning goals (LGs) that incorporate practices, tools, and procedures across each part of my curriculum.	
	I can refer my students to a system (e.g., Figure 1.4) for producing and evaluating drafts using different configurations, modalities, and directionalities of feedback.	
	I use a combination of long- and short-cycle feedback protocols to ensure students are processing, incorporating, and owning next steps.	
Multi-structural	I have many different learning goals (LGs) and use feedback (e.g., various practices, tools, or procedures) as regularly as possible.	
	I activate students as owners of feedback to position them to take next steps before accepting final work.	
Unistructural	I try to give feedback before major assignments are due.	
	I typically use the same feedback tool format (e.g., rubric).	
Pre-structural	I don't usually give feedback *before* I grade.	
	My grades are feedback on how students are doing.	

Available for download at **resources.corwin.com/ContinuousImprovement**

Learning goals founded in purpose-driven feedback routines and processes must be visible, tangible, and actionable for all. When you observe a classroom and see students working in schools immersed in feedback-rich environments, they can tell you what specific tools and procedures are guiding them. They can orient you to where they are now in the cycle. These students in reform-driven schools give and take feedback; it's part of the learning process as they build up their understanding of the task or project.

Because these orientations and habits are articulated in the work of student learning, during lessons and across units of instruction, there is alignment between adult aspirations (also called *habits of mind*, *content standards*, and *21st century skills*) and the students' experiences. We must remember: Students from myriad linguistic, cultural, and socio-economic backgrounds are working with us as apprentices to make sense of our aspirations. Our goals and purposes for schooling may not (yet) be theirs.

Purpose-driven feedback is fundamentally a form of student-centered assessment that treats the learning and assessment experience as positive and mutually reinforcing. When our students are given information about progress through an array of feedback practices, they can communicate with us *when* they experience setbacks and feel stuck. Together, we can then rethink what it takes to move forward. Progress is made as a team in a community of learners.

The wisdom of a former co-principal of CPESS guides us today as much as yesterday: David Smith was fond of saying "You may not know that—yet" (Wulf, 1997). That is, our students' right to learn goes hand in hand with our duty to make feedback essential to what makes a good education—for them and for us. It is the collaborative, **dialogic** nature of feedback when centered on rich tasks and authentic activities that places students on an equal footing with each other, with us, and with their mentors (Lieberman et al., 2007).

Our book is written to inspire the current and next generation of educators to take the feedback challenge—together.

Recap/Review

- Equity and excellence in education demand we place feedback practices, strategies, and moves at the center of learning and teaching experiences.
- Having a formative feedback framework (Figure 1.1) allows us to focus on intersecting dimensions of practice and to plan for combinations of feedback practices more systematically.
- Clear, well-defined, and meaningful learning goals can be drawn from various taxonomies such as Bloom's, Webb's, or SOLO, but the focus must remain on progress.
- Rich tasks, complex projects, and extended assignments require deep feedback processes and cycles to support student achievement.
- Success criteria and learning goals must operate at a grain size that focuses on growth and development during the feedback cycle (short or long).
- Feedback that is timely and relevant can provide useful information about the gap between the actual level and the reference level (next steps) of performance.
- Progress guides, aligned with analytic rubrics, allow all stakeholders (students, parents, staff) to know where a student is, where they are going with assistance, and what is to be done at the task/project level to move ahead.
- A mental model such as the Formative Feedback Process Model (Figure 1.4) of the process for supporting and sustaining formative feedback loops helps the teacher and students work together to improve performance.

Ticket Out the Door: What Are Your Goals?

For some, the purpose of schooling is to help students prepare for a career in the 21st century. In a competitive global economy, with shifting priorities and ever-changing demands, learning to work collaboratively, to offer and receive feedback, and to sustain effort across multiple projects will be essential for a good education.

For others, the purpose of schooling is related to higher education. In that case, helping students do their best in college is the daily goal of our academic work. We value deeper learning because it instills a lifelong commitment to personal and professional development.

Professional advancement for our students requires subject matter competency in everything from science, math, and art to music, history, economics, civics, and world languages. We believe that a willingness to engage and re-engage in lifelong learning in a particular field of inquiry or subject discipline while acquiring habits of mind, heart, and work (Meier, 1995) are what make a good education. Feedback is key to all of these aspirations for our children and young adults.

Luckily, for most of us today, some combination of these fundamental goals and purposes will define our work in the classroom. As we prepare students for work and college, feedback will play a critical role. To make the promise of feedback work, we will need feedback to be personally fulfilling and culturally responsive for everyone.

Good formative assessment practice, which has always included feedback practices, routines, and moves, is a fundamental purpose of schooling. No matter how much policy chatter we hear or posturing we witness, we can never ignore and must never forget that children deserve the right to learn. Feedback is a sacred duty that helps fulfill that right.

As you go ahead with us on this journey, take a moment to reflect:

1. Why do excellence and equity in education matter for you and your classroom?

2. How does feedback play a role in making these two core educational purposes visible to administrators, to parents, to other teachers, and, most importantly, to all our students—particularly those who are fighting daily for the right to learn?

3. How will deepening your feedback practices in your classroom and school bring equity and excellence to life? For whom in particular?

These EQs will accompany us as we move ahead. Now that you have a big-picture view of how to think about the features of learning goals, tasks, timing of feedback, and feedback cycles/loops, we will move into the work of understanding how feedback directionality, configurations, and modalities make a difference in student achievement.

DIRECTIONALITY

CHAPTER 2

Teacher-Driven Feedback

> The process of evaluating and revising and re-evaluating makes the assessment process fundamentally a learning process, one that promotes both self-evaluation capabilities and habits of work—the internalization of standards—for students as well as staff.
>
> —Darling-Hammond et al. (1995, p. 54)

No matter the subject, each of us recognizes that it is essential to our work as teachers to provide **formative feedback** that improves student learning and performance. It's one of our core responsibilities. Equity and excellence live in the depth and breadth of feedback for learners.

Yet it's difficult to provide **feedback** to everyone and do it well. It's also time-consuming and requires planning. Even with the potentially time-saving boosts that myriad apps and new technological functions offer—such as voice typing, audio memos, or assigning a comment on a shared electronic document to a particular student—we struggle to offer quality feedback while teaching a set of fast-paced lessons and complex unit topics.

Today, education technology is everywhere. The array of choices available for providing formative feedback to students can be dizzying—for us and for them. These choices lead to inevitable trade-offs. Do we offer feedback in real time with shorter cycles of feedback, even within one day? Or do we move to asynchronous suggestions/comments with longer feedback cycles so students have time to digest next steps?

But access to such options only necessitates more important questions, perhaps *the* most important questions: How do we know whether students have used our feedback (whether it is spoken, written, or an audio comment)? And how do we know whether it was useful? For whom was it useful? If it was useful, how was it used?

As teachers responsible for improving the learning and performances of a diverse set of students, we want to know how we can get better at differentiating our feedback. Perhaps most relevant for teachers accustomed to reflecting as a method for improving is the question, what aspects of teacher-driven formative feedback are most important for us to consider as we plan, enact, and reflect on our practices with our students?

This chapter launches our exploration of what we're calling *teacher-driven formative feedback*, by far the most ubiquitous approach. Teacher-driven feedback practices are situated closely with peer-to-peer-driven and self-driven feedback **directionalities** in our book.

The four guiding questions below anchor our explorations on the power of teacher-driven feedback. Taken as a whole, each of the three chapters on feedback directionality (teacher-driven, peer-to-peer-driven, and self-driven) points to the challenges and opportunities with separating and connecting different angles of information exchange and to the need for weaving well-defined, consistent, and reflective teacher-based feedback practices into your **units of instruction** and lessons.

Guiding Questions

1. Why plan, enact, and reflect on teacher-driven formative feedback? For whose good is this type of feedback most useful? Which educational goals or purposes can this feedback best serve?

2. What are the conditions necessary to support students in gaining habits and skills using teacher-driven formative feedback?

3. How do we support teacher-driven feedback activities in ways that get *everyone* better at giving and receiving feedback?

4. How can I help students get better at generating and following through on teacher-driven formative feedback exchanges that move current performances forward *and* concretely show how to achieve the next levels with a task, project, or long-term assignment?

The modifier *teacher-driven* comes from the organizing principle we're using to categorize the different lenses through which we look at formative feedback. The three main focal points are **directionality**, **configuration**, and **modality**.

Figure 2.1 depicts three main focal points and their lenses. This chapter is about directionality and the first of the three lenses associated with directionality. We will interchangeably refer to this lens as *teacher directionality* or a *teacher-driven formative feedback approach*. Teachers who engage students in formative feedback practices, protocols, and experiences will always be instructional leaders. Their subject expertise, pedagogical content knowledge (PCK), and curricular duties as adults—as guides on the side—will drive what feedback looks like and what it can be for students in their care.

Figure 2.1 Formative Feedback Framework

Contexts for Learning		
Face-to-Face	Blended	Distance Learning
Focal Point		
Directionality	**Configuration**	**Modality**
Lenses		
Teacher-driven	Whole class	Written
Peer-to-peer-driven	Small groups (2–4)	Spoken
Self-driven	Individual (1:1)	Nonverbal
Learning Goals, Standards, Skills Tasks, Projects, Activities Rubrics, Progress Guides, "Next Steps" Organizers		

Defining Teacher-Driven Feedback

Directionality refers to the agent or player most responsible for the feedback process: the teacher, the peer (as in peer-to-peer or student-to-student formative feedback), or the self (as in **self-assessment** or *self-driven formative feedback*, as we refer to it in Chapter 4). One way to think about directionality is "Who is the primary driver of the formative feedback process?" Is it teacher-driven, peer-driven, or self-driven?

The directionality of formative feedback practices offers multiple ways to engage students, elicit important information, and extend student work/performance. For now, let's define what we mean by *teacher-driven feedback*. The term *teacher-driven formative feedback* recognizes that teachers are responsible for ensuring their students receive the feedback they need to move learning forward and to improve performances and work products.

Teacher-driven stands in contrast to *peer-driven* and *self-driven* formative feedback processes, even though, of course, teachers hold significant responsibility for planning and facilitating peer- and self-driven feedback activities with students.

What makes feedback teacher-driven is that it issues from a teacher's mouth, keyboard, hand gesture, and so forth. It is received, processed, and interpreted by a student or group of students by listening, reading, or watching. Teacher-driven feedback, however, may or may not be initiated by the teacher. For example, when a student seeks feedback from a teacher (e.g., by asking, "Did I do this part correctly?" or "How would you rate my jump?" or "Where have I gone wrong in trying to solve this problem?"), we still consider this teacher-driven feedback because the term *self-driven* is reserved for the feedback students generate "by themselves" and for themselves (we put "by themselves" in quotation marks because we know the important role teachers play as guides on the side in the process of helping students generate feedback to themselves).

Teacher-driven feedback does not take away a student's power to decide for themselves nor does it carry out the student's next steps. Significantly, teacher-driven feedback always expects the student to carry out the next steps and improvements recommended for their performance. So, this feedback is *not* synonymous with the feedback of a line editor, fact checker, or proofreader, who makes changes to a draft immediately before it's completed and published. Teacher-driven feedback draws from the power of coaching whether we observe it on the playing field, in the lab, in the theater, or in the traditional classroom setting.

TEACHER-DRIVEN FEEDBACK

What It Is	What It Isn't
• from a teacher to a student(s)	• a grading exercise
• spoken, written, visual, haptic/body-kinesthetic	• a time in which teachers do the work to improve the draft/performance
• in real time (e.g., online chat, phone) or asynchronous (e.g., digital comment, audio-recorded memo)	• a guarantee that students will learn from suggestions, comments, and/or advice
• in person (e.g., sitting side-by-side) or via communication technology (e.g., via Zoom, Google Meet)	• always a valuable use of a teacher's time (e.g., when students are at the very beginning phases of learning or work on a project, they generally need guidance, not feedback)
• intentional, purposeful, dialogic	
• can be in direct response to a student's request or wholly initiated by teacher	• a way to convey instructions on how to complete the assignment
• values students doing the heavy lifting (e.g., the decision making) while providing scaffolds	• a one-off solution
• an opportunity to grow the depth and quality of relationships between teacher and students	

Self-Assessment for Directionality Chapters Ahead

As you read these next few chapters on directionalities, we'd like you to reflect and self-assess. Take a moment to consider the conditions that contributed to your uptake of feedback from teachers, peers, and even yourself in the past. Then determine where you feel you are in terms of thinking about and delivering on formative feedback with your current students.

Reflect

When did feedback matter the most to you? Who gave it to you and why do you think you received it so well?

Think about a time in which feedback was critical to your growth and development. List three to five reasons it worked. Explain.

Self-Assess

Instructions: In the following table, place a check mark beside the **SOLO** (structure of observed learning outcomes) **taxonomy** level that best describes the current state of your instructional practices as a teacher responsible for providing students with helpful formative feedback.

SOLO LEVEL	DESCRIPTION	PUT A ✓ MARK
Extended Abstract	I have a research-informed schema for differentiating my feedback/feedback processes; it values students' metacognition, learning to learn, agency/autonomy, self-regulation, and individuality.	
Relational	I have a system (e.g., engage, elicit, extend) for evaluating my feedback to/processes with students.	
Multi-structural	I know that the kinds of formative feedback moves I make matter to students' uptake and next steps.	
Unistructural	I regularly give feedback before major assignments are due.	
Pre-structural	"I need to give feedback *before* I grade?"	

> Distance learning, interestingly, has given me the distance I needed to reflect on why, when, and how I give feedback to students. I used to move around the room a lot and connect with students that way. So much of the feedback I gave counted on that. But now it's about engaging and re-engaging students with new feedback routines.
>
> —Fergus, chemistry teacher

Planning for Teacher-Driven Feedback

Dwight Eisenhower famously said, "Plans are nothing; planning is everything." When we plan a formative feedback-rich lesson, it helps to be intentional and to prioritize some aspects of what we plan to do at each turn of the lesson. In work with the California Collaborative for Educational Excellence (CCEE, 2019) Statewide Leading Forward Learning Pathways Series, we've explored different **lesson plan** formats to support informal feedback routines/**formative assessment (FA) moves** (Module 9). Our goal in this book is to help everyone dive deeper in long-cycle feedback routines that are directly tied to performance tasks, projects, and long-term assignments.

Table 2.1 presents five aspects to consider when planning for teacher-driven feedback across a unit or several units. The table communicates why these planning aspects matter and provides tips and questions to guide your decision-making processes. In addition to purpose and timing, we focus on the three *E*s of formative feedback. No matter what approach to teacher-driven feedback you take, it is essential to consider student *engagement*, *eliciting* information, and *extending* performance.

One of the most important ideas to take away from Table 2.1 is that you are responsible for deciding what is most important for students to attend to as they strive to revise their work and performances. What you plan for a lesson or unit should build upon essential understandings and goals within your learning environment.

Table 2.1 Planning for Teacher-Driven Feedback: What to Consider and Why It Matters

ASPECT	ASK YOURSELF	WHY IT MATTERS	TIPS AND TO-DO'S
Purpose: **Why and What Is the Goal**	What will I gain? How will students benefit? (Name two outcomes.) What's most important for students to attend to at this point? How is the focus of this feedback related to previous instructional units or tasks?	Formative feedback moves should reflect aims. Students can't learn everything at once; focus on what matters. Formative feedback processes/protocols should inform your future instruction and build off previous skills/assets.	• Know that you will learn from the feedback process and keep track of "takeaways." • Have a system for noting what you learn to carry forward into the next unit. • Frame feedback in subject-related, real-world terms: "Feedback is what [professionals] do to get better at [XYZ skill]." • Prioritize feedback purposes: Less really is more.

(Continued)

(Continued)

ASPECT	ASK YOURSELF	WHY IT MATTERS	TIPS AND TO-DO'S
Timing: **When and Where to Offer Feedback**	Given where students are in their learning/project, what feedback will best help them? When is the best time to intervene in the task/project cycle?	See "What the Research Tells Us" later in this chapter.	▶ Discover where (in what phase) students are (e.g., with a progress guide). ▶ Meet them where they are before you delve into giving feedback.
Engaging in the Work: **Keeping the Connection Going**	How does each formative feedback move I make require and support student engagement?	Students need to do the work to learn. Most students gain from scaffolds for engagement (e.g., sentence starters, graphic organizers).	▶ Make your engagement scaffolds English learner friendly. ▶ Build in checkpoints. ▶ Expect roadblocks and slowdowns.
Eliciting Understandings: **Finding the Zone**	What am I expecting to learn about the student in relation to their work/performance from this process? Is there enough time to learn that?	An effective formative feedback process makes participants aware of understandings/misunderstandings and strengths/weaknesses.	▶ Check for understanding of feedback continuously. ▶ Use multiple modalities and configurations to support your elicitation goals.
Extending the Work/Performance: **Stretching to the Next Level**	How will I know my feedback had an effect on the work/performance? Where is the next level and which steps can help students get there?	Feedback needs to catalyze student action, preferably in a positive direction that results in improved work/performance. Visible scaffolds and well-defined levels help students see growth trajectories.	▶ Have students share what feedback worked and how. ▶ Learn from what they report and plan to incorporate in lessons learned for next project/task.

A helpful way to consider what you're planning in terms of formative feedback with your students is to ask yourself the following questions:

- How do I *engage* students with cues, signals, **scaffolds**, and routines that keep them connected to my feedback?

- As students are engaged in the task/project, how do I locate their current levels of learning while working to *elicit* and extend these **first draft** performances in progress?

> How will what I am planning for students—written comments, verbal exchanges, body-kinesthetic gestures—help each student *extend* their work/performance and gain the confidence to keep trying to improve?

We can offer suggestions for how you might answer these questions. But you know your students and your context best and in ways we never could. You are the one who decides what's best for your feedback practice as a teaching professional. With that in mind, let's now examine what the research tells us when it comes to teacher-driven formative feedback.

What the Research Tells Us
Why Teacher-Driven Feedback Matters

The research tells us that how we, as teachers, see our role in the feedback relationship with our students matters (Harris et al., 2008). Our thinking about feedback influences our classroom practices (Hoy & Davis, 2006; Pajares, 1992). So, it's worth examining how each of us conceptualizes teacher-driven feedback:

> What do we see as its key purposes?

> What do we see as its benefits?

> How do we envision our role in it?

When we think of teacher-driven feedback, it's common to imagine the teacher running the process and doing the heavy lifting, so to speak. At first glance, this makes sense. After all, a teacher—typically—has much more familiarity with the qualities and characteristics of exemplary work or an ideal performance than students have. Further, unless it's the very first time you're helping students with a particular concept or project, you will have many more ideas about the next steps a student could take compared to the students themselves.

As a teacher of both subject content and skills—whether it's a unit on badminton, organic chemistry, transformative geometry, or conjugations in a world language—you have helped students improve in a specific area before. You know the response patterns and aims of the final work. Most students, if not all, are learning something new and they need their teacher's direct feedback to make progress.

Students Must Do the Work to Learn

But if we think of teacher-driven feedback in only this way, we will miss out on honing three essential skills for teacher-driven formative feedback:

1. Encouraging students to do the work (i.e., the heavy lifting)

2. Keeping students engaged with the work (i.e., doing the heavy lifting)

3. Helping students attend to what makes the most sense for them at a given moment in time (i.e., lifting *this* or *that* in this part of the cycle)

Students need to do the work to learn (Bransford et al., 2000). Therefore, we should envision our role in the feedback relationship in such a way that we are helping students as coaches and guides to get better at learning what to attend to over time with their own work. As teachers, it is always our goal to work ourselves out of a job, so to speak. Experts refer to this process as *gradual release* (Tharp & Gallimore, 1991).

So while we are calling this type of directionality *teacher-driven* (as compared to *peer-to-peer-driven* and *self-driven*) feedback, we suggest that you think of yourself as the driving instructor in the implied metaphor, not the actual driver. Your students need to be signaling left or right, pressing the accelerator, and turning the wheel. You're there to coach students in ways that help them become increasingly less dependent on your expertise (Gallimore & Tharp, 1990).

What's the Most Important Question to Ask?

Our role as teachers committed to feedback is to become skilled at asking, answering, and acting upon this question: Given this particular student, at this particular time, at this particular turn in the project or task, what formative feedback moves shall I make to promote the next steps in their learning?

The research suggests that students are best served when teachers answer this question with the students' phase of learning in mind (Hattie & Clarke, 2019). Are students in a phase of surface learning, deep learning, or transfer of learning? To what extent are they acquiring or consolidating their learning?

Is the student acquiring surface learning? If so, giving students feedback that gets them to summarize and relate the learning to **prior knowledge** is optimal. Is the student consolidating surface learning? If so, providing feedback that helps them practice with awareness is called for. Such feedback should catalyze students to practice deliberately with a specific focus for their practice in mind. Is the student acquiring a deeper understanding? If so, teacher feedback ought to help these students plan, evaluate, and monitor their own learning strategies. Is the student working on consolidating their deep understanding? If so, feedback that spurs and guides them on how to self-evaluate is the optimal choice.

Research also recommends that a teacher's formative feedback

- celebrate students' accomplishments related to the work,

- direct attention constructively to aspects most in need of revision or improvement (Graham, 2018),

- refer to changes in performance from previous efforts (Hattie & Clarke, 2019),
- be specific (Underwood & Tregidgo, 2006; Whitaker, 2011), and
- encourage student autonomy, agency, and responsibility (Hattie & Clarke, 2019).

There is mixed evidence on whether it is sound practice to include a grade with formative feedback (Black et al., 2003; Guskey, 2019; Kingston & Nash, 2011; Page, 1958). Several experts have argued that grades muddle the feedback signal, leading students to focus on the wrong indicators of success, which should be aimed at progress and next steps. Regardless of research, we know that feedback from teachers in classrooms aimed at **deeper learning** needs to send one clear, consistent message: We are not crossing the finish line (yet). Feedback for use during the instructional cycle on rich tasks reminds everyone that we are making pit stops, charging up, checking the distance traveled, and moving together toward the critical turning points as we approach the final destination. Grades and points won't tell us what to do next to move ahead. Besides, we know that combining grades with feedback is risky and often leads to students not paying attention to the feedback aimed at improvement.

How Students Hear and Respond to Feedback Matters Most

Finally, no matter which formative feedback **move** we make ("What's a next step you could take?" or "Tell me what's not yet finished about your project right now" or "I got a little confused by this part here; please clarify") what matters most is how students respond to our feedback moves. Therefore, we need methods that work for discovering these responses to our best efforts.

However, teachers need not wait to discover how their formative feedback is landing with students. They can take steps to frame their feedback for students. A body of research by David Scott Yeager and colleagues (2013) suggests teachers can preemptively and positively influence a student's response to—and uptake of—formative feedback. Yeager and colleagues found that when teachers explicitly stated, "I'm giving you this feedback because I have very high expectations and I know that you can reach them," as they gave students critical feedback, this made a significant difference in both how many students revised their work and how substantial their revisions were.

Significantly, the differences in revision were most notable among students found to harbor mistrust of their teachers and schooling, as determined by their responses to survey questions in the study. The researchers noted that minority students tended to mistrust white teachers giving them critical feedback and to attribute such criticisms to a perceived bias against them. But by explicitly and credibly working to "disabuse students of the belief that they are being seen as limited or as not belonging" and providing these students "with the resources, such as substantive feedback, to reach the **standards** demanded of them," teachers can lift a "barrier of mistrust" common "across the racial divide" (Yeager et al., 2013, p. 3). Not surprisingly, we also know that when students have opportunities to discuss, clarify, and communicate about their teachers' feedback, they are more likely to trust it, to understand it, and, therefore, to use it (Boon, 2016; Rotsaert et al., 2018).

Try It Tomorrow

How Is the Student Responding to Your Feedback?

	Look	What is the student's body language?
		Is the student leaning forward or backward?
		Frowning?
		Looking flushed in their face?
		Tensing up?
		Where is the student looking during the conversation?
	Listen	Is the student holding their breath?
		Sighing?
		Starting to say something?
		Possibly distracted by background noise?
		Fidgeting audibly?
	Ask/Say	"How are you feeling?"
		"What are you thinking?"
		"Your response matters. I am listening."
		"Ask me something. I am here to answer."
		"Is that a possible next step?"

Source: Icons by https://www.istockphoto.com/portfolio/-VICTOR-

Teacher Reflection

"But You Just Resolved My Comment Without Addressing It!"

I teach high school. When my students and I first started using Google Docs together and a student resolved a comment without addressing its specifics, I was like, "Wait, I wrote a comment!"

I actually felt frustrated.

Then I had to think about it. Did I expect *every single one* of my comments to get addressed? Did I not believe my students had agency? Did I trust that they could and would choose wisely from the array of comments I had made?

When I worked with students face-to-face, wasn't I okay with students leaving at least some of what I offered on the table, so to speak? Now that the feedback left on the table was more visible—and I got an email notifying me of it!—why did I suddenly feel differently?

It didn't add up.

When feedback dialogues are face-to-face, I am constantly reminded of what a negotiation right-sizing feedback is and how much give-and-take is involved. When face-to-face, I can more easily keep in mind that I am as much about preserving their sense of ownership over their work as I am about the best possible product being produced as a result of our (naturally hit-and-miss) dialogue. Somehow, though, sitting and typing at a laptop can get me feeling like an editor who subscribes to "my way or the highway." When typing, I can temporarily forget that I am a *teacher* communicating with young people who need to exercise agency as much as they need food, water, air, and love.

The medium through which the feedback dialogue occurs really does matter. If I wouldn't take offense at a student ignoring one of my suggestions during a face-to-face conversation (and I wouldn't), why would it matter so much to me online?

So I came around on that one. "It's okay to not take up some feedback," I tell students, "as long as you take up some other feedback." Without lowering expectations or defending the importance of my own time and energy, I now take steps to preserve students' agency—no matter the medium—and to remember that every learner *needs* to make choices and own their *own work process*.

Focus on Practice

Ask yourself: In your subject area and with the students in your classes, what motivates students to engage, persist, take risks, and ultimately succeed?

High school English teacher Kim Vinh learned that tying her feedback to a **rubric** wasn't what got her students to meet and exceed standards. Her approach emphasizes *why* we revise as much as *how* to do it. In the story that follows, note how Ms. Vinh's perspective on the role of formative feedback in motivating her students centers on

- *modeling* with many **exemplars**,
- *revising* as a professional practice,
- *eliciting* genuine interest in students and their drafts/current work,
- *encouraging* students' beliefs about themselves as creative thinkers, and
- *reminding* everyone of the real-life skills that are evolving in the process (by exploring the following questions: Why are we doing this? Why does it matter? How is it important?).

Teacher Reflection
The Importance of Feedback Not So Tightly Tied to the Rubric

Back in my early days of teaching, the only type of feedback I really planned for was tightly tied to the rubric. Informal conversations with students—supporting their ideas and supporting their revisions—were not included or highlighted in my lesson planning the way they are now. Instead, my focus was on the rubric, which I had spent hours crafting.

The rubric was a 20-box matrix: complex, jam-packed, and in 8-point font because I was trying to fit it all on one page. Analytic rubrics were popular then, and we all had to create and use one. I was backward planning because in our district, the emphasis was on knowing where you want your students to go. Students also had to know where they were going and how their final drafts would be assessed. So, I put lots of energy into the rubric and into getting students to engage the rubric. But the truth remained: No matter what we did, the rubric was not user friendly.

Add to this the fact that for my content area (English), students have preconceived notions of themselves as writers. They come into class thinking, "I'm a good writer" or "I'm not a good writer." So many students approached the performance tasks stuck in ideas like, "I'm good at English; I'm going to do this" or "I'm not good at English; I'm not going to do this." All of that needed to be broken apart, supported in multiple ways, and become something useful beyond English class. I asked myself: Why am I doing this? I want students to know that everything is a process. It's how life is. It's one of my core values as a teacher.

What I discovered—over time—was that the idea of the rubric and the "approaching, meeting, exceeding" standard was never what got students to produce a piece of writing that met the standards. Rather, what did get students to improve their writing was reading, responding to, and analyzing a variety of examples together; supporting students in revising their draft work—really revising, not just putting a comma here or adding a period there; and showing genuine interest in the beginnings of their ideas and encouraging them to expand on those beginnings, saying to them, "What a cool idea, let's play with that and see where it goes."

So I ended up articulating in much longer form every year how writing is a *process* of thinking. It's never about checking the boxes or turning the first draft in as if it were done.

I want students to know that the struggle with the thinking and creative process is often more important than the final, packaged product. The best writers—Morrison, Vonnegut, Lee—all struggled with crafting multiple drafts without a rubric!

Feedback on writing is more than a cat-and-mouse game. It can't be another way of going through the motions on the way to a grade. I want my students to experience what deep interest in their thinking feels like. Not only interest from me—although that's a start—but interest from their classmates as well. That's the power of feedback. It's one way I demonstrate professional care for them as human beings. It's all tied to formative feedback and the myriad ways I support their developing ideas.

The Role of PCK on Improving Teacher-Driven Feedback Practices

When talking about thoughtful teacher practices and exploring how they interact with student learning and performance, it's helpful to know and use the concept of *pedagogical content knowledge* (PCK), coined by Lee Shulman in the 1980s. When we're focusing on teacher-driven formative feedback practices, PCK can catalyze important insights. We invite you to ask yourself these questions as we proceed: Is knowing what PCK is and thinking about PCK in relation to teacher-driven formative feedback helpful? Is it useful? Does it enable a kind of nuance and thoughtfulness about your teaching practice that you, your students, and your colleagues find valuable?

But, first, what is PCK?

> ### Definition: Pedagogical Content Knowledge (PCK)
>
> *Pedagogical content knowledge* refers to a specialized knowledge that teachers have, knowledge that is beyond subject matter expertise alone. PCK is the information experienced teachers have about
>
> - **difficulties students typically encounter** as they try to learn about a topic,
> - **pathways students typically take** to understand that topic, and
> - **strategies that typically work** to help students overcome difficulties they face on their route to understanding that topic.
>
> PCK is an essential part of what teachers need to learn to be effective (Shulman, 1986, 1987).
>
> PCK is discipline specific. That is, PCK reflects the detailed information expert teachers possess about what aspects of the discipline are especially hard or easy for new students to master and what this means for instruction.

What Does PCK Have to Do With Teacher-Driven Feedback?

You aren't *just* a teacher. You are a teacher of a subject with disciplinary knowledge and skills. Whether you teach biology, choral music, economics, computer science, world history, composition and literature, mathematics, ceramic arts, world languages, or physical education, PCK will play a role in your assessment practices. The difficulties, pathways, and strategies for student success in each subject will differ. But feedback will be a constant.

Your PCK in your subject discipline will guide the formative feedback practices that work best for your students. For example, the formative feedback practices a mathematics teacher uses again and again to help their students enact the mathematical practice, such as attending to precision, will likely look very different from the ones a PE teacher might use to coach students' movements to be more precise. Even though the concept of *precision* appears, on the face of it, to be similar in both disciplines, the enactments of feedback moves will draw from your unique experiences on the field, in the lab, or in the classroom.

Your PCK includes knowledge about how students gain proficiency and sophistication with content and skills valued by your subject over time. This kind of expertise helps you predict where and how students will struggle. PCK has a lot to do with how you enact the three *E*s from Table 2.1.

You might **prime** students to engage with your formative feedback quite differently depending on not only the subject area but also the unit(s) and lessons unfolding over a semester. Your subject area will at least partially determine what you anticipate students will have a hard time hearing from you or answering during a feedback exchange. You will engage students differently while your formative feedback process is striving to elicit both understandings and misunderstandings as the project or task places demands on students' **zones of proximal development (ZPDs)**. After all, students' common **misconceptions, p-prims**, and so forth are particular to your subject area. Teacher-driven feedback must surface and address these challenges if students are to reach the next level. Finally, expectations for your feedback extending the current performance need to be informed by reasonable expectations concerning student proficiency in your subject area. Setting clear, visible, and proximal goals as you provide feedback is possible with **graphic organizers**, scaffolds, and tools such as **progress guides**, which are discussed in later chapters.

Teacher-Driven Feedback Practices in Multiple Modes

An Important Aspect of the Context of Formative Feedback: Synchronous or Asynchronous

As a teacher, you know well how much context matters. One aspect of context that can really make a difference is whether the feedback dialogue you are having—or attempting to have—with a student is in real time; is it synchronous or asynchronous?

When a formative feedback dialogue is said to be *asynchronous*, that means there are time delays built into the process. Often, these delays are largely or entirely out of your control. In other words, you don't initiate the time delays between turns in the feedback dialogue, as you may do when you initiate an intentional and strategic delay or **pause** when you are working in real time (i.e., synchronously) with students. You do this when you say, "Take a few minutes to see if you can come up with a way that works, then come back and show me."

Definition: Synchronous versus Asynchronous Feedback

Synchronous Feedback

In synchronous formative feedback situations, both teacher and student are present at the same time, considering the work they're discussing together. With distance learning, this is typically via Zoom, Meet, or any other web conferencing platform, or it may be via chat in those platforms or via a shared document.

(Continued)

(*Continued*)

> *Asynchronous Feedback*
>
> With asynchronous formative feedback, the two parties in the feedback exchange do not communicate in real time. Rather, each considers the work on their own. A teacher will insert comments and questions on a document; leave written, video, or audio comments about the work through a learning management system; or give feedback on the draft via email.

To become more intentional with your teacher-driven formative feedback practices, it's useful to reflect on the affordances and constraints (you might think of them as advantages and disadvantages) of synchronous and asynchronous formative feedback contexts. Let's consider synchronous feedback first.

Synchronous Feedback: Affordances and Constraints

AFFORDANCES (+)	CONSTRAINTS (−)
Immediate: Potential for dialogue is great because both parties are present.	It is easier to miscommunicate because interactions may put someone on the spot.
The student can ask for clarification immediately, which means time can be spent co-constructing meaning.	Turns of talk or text are quicker and may leave little time to digest.
Checking for understanding happens in a quicker (almost immediate) cycle, which means opportunity isn't lost forging ahead with feedback a student doesn't understand.	Students likely feel compelled to manage their emotions in front of the teacher and spend cognitive resources doing that, leaving fewer resources for processing what they're hearing/seeing/reading.
The teacher usually can tell if the student doesn't understand the suggestion/next step and invite more dialogue.	Silences and pauses (much needed for reflective thinking) can be challenging and uncomfortable for both parties.
The teacher may be able to see how feedback is going (e.g., body language and/or verbal cues).	
It is easy to ask, "What are you feeling or thinking when I say this/ask that?"	
Discovering how to work within the student's zone of proximal development (ZPD) is quicker.	

Tips for Synchronous Feedback

- Refer to a rubric or progress guide to help keep synchronous feedback grounded/anchored in visible criteria.
- Follow the 80/20 rule: Aim for the students to do 80% of the talking (How else can you learn what they are thinking?) and the teacher to do 20% of the guiding.

- Provide **think time** and use **wait time** (pausing moves) in the conversation at key points.

- Avoid using the word *but*. Students latch on to what comes after the *but* and effectively disregard what you said before it.

- Remind students that improving a draft takes time and effort and that your feedback is meant to support them.

- Prioritize next steps: Convey your top two positives and your top two next steps in a feedback exchange.

- Do what you can to preserve and encourage student agency; find out what they think is positive about their draft and where they want to take it next.

- Expect students to record their next steps at the end of a feedback session/exchange.

- Use a graphic organizer (such as a progress guide) to focus on opportunity for growth with revision.

Now let's consider the affordances and constraints of asynchronous formative feedback contexts, perhaps the most common context for teacher-driven formative feedback practices. How can we as teachers maximize the opportunities provided by an asynchronous context? Consider, for example, that when the student isn't right there in dialogue with you synchronously, you aren't able to interrupt their thinking. Note that we are not saying that a student's thinking—or your own—should never be interrupted. Intervention is key to formative feedback; it needs to be done with care, respect, and good timing.

Asynchronous Feedback: Affordances and Constraints

AFFORDANCES (+)	CONSTRAINTS (−)
Slower: This gives an opportunity to revise one's statements/questions/priorities before sending feedback.	The teacher can't immediately see/hear/read how feedback is being experienced by students.
Think time is built in. The need for processing without interruption is preserved.	The teacher doesn't know how feedback is landing until a reply comes back (if a reply comes back at all).
This is good for hearing a set of next steps: It is easier to take and you can return again at a later time to address feedback.	It may feel like the teacher is speaking (whether writing or audiorecording) to a void.
The student can postpone receiving feedback until they are ready to take it in.	Momentum in the virtual conversation can be difficult to achieve (having to pick up where one left off).
Running record: The comments, suggestions, and changes can be tracked and referred to later.	Following up and encouraging replies to your queries/comments can feel intrusive/harassing to students.

Tips for Asynchronous Feedback

- Use your communication wisely: Prioritize next steps, trim verbiage, and check for tone of written or audio comments.

- Invite students to ask for clarification of comments/suggestions/next steps using the reply to comments feature.

- Be authentic: Sound like yourself and try to personalize openings with first name (e.g., "Hi, Danny . . .").

- Close with an invitation to keep the dialogue going and offer a deadline for checking on changes with a reminder about final due date.

- Use a consistent set of **prompts**: "Does this help?" "Please let me know if there's something I've said or written that you don't understand." "Which of these 'next steps' do you think you can/will work on first?"

Take a Moment to Reflect

As you reread these two T-charts, consider what you might add to either column. Do you agree with how we've categorized what we've listed? Decide which of these tips you plan to use as soon as you can.

I'm a naturally empathetic person. That's what most people who know me would say. Yet when I'm looking at a student's draft work and trying to decide what to respond to and how to word my response, it's easy for me to enter a disconnected zone where my tone shifts. I can get sharp and clinical with 40 lab reports to review. Especially if the student isn't right there in front of me—which is so often the case in these days of remote instruction.

I have to remember this isn't Twitter or a science blog. It's my classroom and my students—all 160 of them! So, I've learned before I hit the send button to check my tone. It's what I have to do to make sure I'm staying positive and encouraging enough with my students, who I hope, after all, are socially and emotionally invested in the group lab work.

I've never once regretted the extra few moments I've spent revising my words to make their tone kinder, gentler, and more encouraging. I HAVE regretted times I've skipped that step!

Giving feedback to students asynchronously is intellectually demanding, but it's not *only* an academic enterprise. It's an exercise in expressing care for students' personal lives, too.

—Cassie, high school biology teacher

Scaffolds and Guided Practice for Individual Teachers

The Role of the Three Es in Putting Feedback Into Focus

When potentially adjusting our teaching practices, we all need support on how to get started. This section is intended to aid you in deciding what to focus on. This section (in each chapter, not only this chapter) also provides guidance—and sometimes concrete scaffolds—for how to approach the focus we offer.

We take it that you've already bought into the idea that as a teacher, reflection is valuable. We also recognize that as a teacher, knowing *what* to reflect on—what we like to think of as *fruitful reflection*—can be a bit tricky. Here we offer a quick check (the three *E*s) that you can use to assist your growth over time and to positively influence your students' learning and achievement:

Did the feedback—or formative feedback process—work to

1. engage,
2. elicit, and
3. extend students' *current levels* of understanding with the project, task, or long-term assignment?

As teacher educators and professional development consultants who've long worked with a diverse range of teachers, we've seen how much it helps to have a small set of questions you can ask again and again over time to gauge your progress with **assessment for learning** practices. Your interpretation of each of the three *E*s will grow more nuanced over time. For now, we recommend you start with three focus questions. You can ask yourself (or together with your co-teacher or instructional coach) the following at the end of the week:

Engage	Did the feedback engage students? Will it re-engage them to continue working on their first drafts?
Elicit	Did the feedback elicit both understandings and misunderstandings to improve at a given level of performance so far? Can it help to close gaps and address common misconceptions, p-prims, and procedural errors?
Extend	Did the feedback extend the current draft/performance by pointing in the direction of next levels along well-defined trajectories of mastery? Is it feeding forward toward more exemplary work?

One teacher we know, Ms. Gonzalez, reflected on how she sets students up to engage (or re-engage) with her formative feedback. See how Ms. Gonzalez primed her students through her email message to them in "Try it Tomorrow: Priming 'Hot off the Press' Feedback Cues and Reminders."

Try It Tomorrow

Priming "Hot Off the Press" Feedback Cues and Reminders

Priming refers to actions that teachers, and occasionally students, take to prepare the groundwork for learning (Duckor & Holmberg, 2017). Priming helps learners ready themselves for what's about to occur and get more out of the experience. A teacher's priming moves help establish and maintain norms and expectations.

During distance learning, high school teacher Ms. Gonzalez sent three periods of her Latin American politics and literature classes the following email. Notice how Ms. Gonzalez primes her students to engage with formative feedback routines. Ms. Gonzalez made her comments/gave her feedback via Flip. That's how students shared their practice speeches.

> Dear students,
>
> I finished making comments on all the practice speeches in first and second period. Sixth period: Rest assured, I am finishing as we speak.
>
> Here's the thing: I am doing this to help you improve. Please do not just turn in the same speech for your final with the same issues I mentioned in my comments on the practice. I really want you to do well, so I am giving you feedback to help you. If I mention, for example, that you should try to raise your camera, then try to do that by putting some books or a box underneath your computer. If I mention that your speech is too short, you will need to add more to make it longer.
>
> Overall, I am very pleased with what I am seeing. You have worked hard and it shows!
>
> Now, back to watching your videos,
>
> Ms. Gonzalez

Try It Tomorrow

Voice Typing

History and PE teacher Eric says voice typing on his smartphone has changed his approach to feedback for the better.

"I can give feedback on the go from my phone while I'm out on a walk or at the gym. Not having to stand there and type comments on a shared document, slide deck, or spreadsheet while in our faculty offices—because that's what I used to do—really works for me.

> I've noticed my voice-typed comments do tend to be a little longer than if I were typing them out, but an upside to that is they sound more like me. They just wind up friendlier, somehow, when I don't have to type them.
>
> Typing for too long—whether on my laptop or phone—exacerbates the pain from playing sports in college. With voice typing, I can engage in the feedback process without paying the price for it in my body physically. It's been a noticeable improvement to my teaching and my quality of life."

Setting Goals and Monitoring Progress With Teacher-Driven Feedback: Questions for Lesson Study and Professional Learning Communities

What Does It Take for Students to Want Feedback?

In your **professional learning community** (**PLC**), read the following conversation between two middle school teachers. Note what the teachers seem to believe about feedback. Also note what you think the faculty at this school might believe about assignments for students. Then discuss the questions that follow.

Teacher 1: Darned seventh graders. I'm so frustrated! You know that persuasive essay we do every year? The school mascot one, where they take a side? (*Continues, imitating a baritone-voiced announcer*) "The Spartan *is* . . . or *is not* . . . an appropriate mascot." Well, as they were working on their first drafts in class on Wednesday, I spent the *entire* block making comments on their Google Docs. And they were being *so* good. The room had that quiet work-hum. I got to every single draft. I made all kinds of comments about their introductions, their evidence, their use of "In conclusion." I pointed out where they should add examples to back up their opinions—the whole bit. I even wrote "More like this!" in places they were on the right track in the Chromebook app. I was on feedback fire!

It felt great. It was cracking me up, too, because the room was so quiet I could hear kids gasp when my icon popped up on their screen. Little surprised gasps around the room.

But now I feel like I wasted my time. They had two nights to revise. I just read their final drafts. And guess what?

Teacher 2: They ignored your feedback?

Teacher 1: Exactly. And the few who did any work did the minimum. (*Sighs, loudly*) It's like they didn't even *want* my feedback.

Discuss as a group:

1. Is unwanted feedback a problem? What does it take for students to want feedback and use it?

2. How do teachers get students to want feedback? Is there another way to think about this?

3. What, in your opinion, should Teacher 2 suggest to Teacher 1 to do or try next?

After reading the conversation and answering the questions, try to identify what some other modes and methods are for engaging students with the feedback process at your school. Note examples of what's working based on different faculty and staff experiences. Ask "Are we getting in our own way with too many assignments? Is there enough time set aside for authentic feedback cycles? Is there too much emphasis on **grading** and not enough on revising?"

Recap/Review

- How teachers envision their role in the feedback relationship with students influences their daily practices.

- Get feedback from students on how formative feedback *content and processes* worked for them as part of checking in and make adjustments based on what you've learned.

- What teachers believe about feedback matters as much as what they do to facilitate the flow of information about next steps.

- Your pedagogical content knowledge (PCK) will inform how you approach which feedback matters most, when, and for whom.

- What you learn as a teacher from your formative feedback processes/interactions with students matters a great deal. Have a system—even an informal one—for capturing insights and noting patterns to inform your instructional decision making.

- You can tailor your supports, scaffolds, and protocols for feedback-rich exchanges using the three *E*s (eliciting, engaging, and extending) with the current level of student performance.

- Be aware of the affordances and constraints of synchronous and asynchronous formative feedback processes so you can leverage them and adjust according to your own strengths and weaknesses to better support your students.

Ticket Out the Door

1. How have you primed students for engaging (the first of the three Es) in formative feedback processes in the past? That is, what have you said or done to establish expectations/norms and ready students for the experience of giving and taking up feedback?

2. Think of an upcoming performance task, project, or assignment for which you will be giving students formative feedback. What **formative assessment** techniques or moves will you try out with your students? Describe a move. Why that one? Explain.

3. Of all the content in the chapter, what was newest to you? What, if anything, did you find interesting about a particular concept and/or practice? What connections did it help you make?

4. Tell us about something else you think should have been included in this chapter on teacher-driven formative feedback. Use a bullet point list.

CHAPTER 3

Peer-to-Peer-Driven Feedback

> Peer assessment needs training and practice, arguably on neutral products or performances before full implementation, which should feature monitoring and moderation.
>
> —Topping (2010, p. 72)

No matter how carefully you orchestrate the pairings or groupings, how thoughtfully you **scaffold** the interactions, or how strategically you intervene during the activities, with peer **feedback**, someone is always going to struggle. It is the nature of learning to struggle for understanding. Peers can help one another, and they can also hinder each other.

Asymmetry in peer-based feedback exchanges happens. We all have different talents and dispositions. Our diversity can be a source of unity in the classroom. But we have to learn to collaborate. Activating students is a powerful way to teach the meaning of collaboration as we are working on a complex task, project, or performance. The question is, can we learn to work together and share ideas, comments, and questions—that is, to give feedback to one another as students?

Peer-to-peer feedback is messy, which can be unsettling at first. Many of us have worked for years to dismantle classroom assessment practices and routines that discourage students from exploring, changing, and growing as they learn to make mistakes. Mistakes are messy and necessary for children and teens to experience new ways of engaging one another.

We have worked toward more robust approaches to classroom assessment (Holmberg & Duckor, 2018) and documented examples of school improvement that involve students as assessors of each other's work (Duckor & Perlstein, 2014). But to strive for better **assessment for learning** approaches in today's classrooms, our students must join us. They must feel the power of their ideas to shape learning outcomes. They must feel empowered to collaborate and share ways to improve each other's (draft) work. If we are to move beyond an "us and them" sensibility in traditional assessment, everyone needs to invest in the act of listening to and hearing from others about work-in-progress.

We should expect that our students may not be prepared (yet) to support one another on a complex performance task or project. Despite everyone's best intentions, students also realize that group work can feel messy or awkward, or even pointless at times. In this chapter, we begin with the understanding that peer-based feedback can be challenging for students and teachers. For **formative feedback** to look and feel formative, we note that trust, respect, and positivity among peers is key. We must **prime** everyone for success with this type of feedback.

Peer-to-peer-driven feedback isn't as straightforward as it seems to adult researchers. Many of us live with middle and high school students. We know teenagers and young adults vary in their dispositions, personalities, and habits of communication. Since feedback at its core is about communication, we need to be curious about how it works with students who have their own ways of being in the world.

One child may regularly and consistently be a feedback giver. The feedback giver is communicative, confident, and wants to help at every turn. They make us wonder if one day they will be a coach, a counselor, or a teacher. Another child from the same family may be a feedback avoider; this one believes that the feedback others tend to offer isn't helpful. The feedback avoider is not as communicative, may feel less confident, and although they want to help and listen to others, it doesn't seem to work out.

As guardians/parents we wonder, why is it so easy for Sarah to jump into a group and offer feedback but so difficult for Ian? Or why does Jo seem so ready to share on the field or in the pool but so hesitant in the lab or science fair?

If peer feedback and communication dynamics in face-to-face settings prior to the pandemic were difficult to manage, they have only become more complex as students face a new normal of online, blended, and in-class instruction. Context—not only subject matter or unit goals—can open and shut down peer-to-peer interactions. Identity plays a role as do self-conception and perceptions about group status.

This chapter explores what we're calling *peer-to-peer-driven formative feedback* in all its complexity; "P2P" feedback, as we call it, sits between the teacher-driven and self-driven feedback chapters as one of three ways to see agency in feedback interactions. The following four guiding questions anchor our explorations on the power of peer-to-peer feedback exchanges.

Guiding Questions

1. Why plan, enact, and reflect on peer-to-peer-driven formative feedback? For whose good is this type of feedback intended? What educational goals and purposes does it serve?

2. What are the conditions necessary to support students in gaining habits with and skills in peer-to-peer-driven formative feedback?

3. How do we support peer-to-peer feedback activities in ways that get *everyone* better at giving and receiving feedback?

4. How can I help students get better at generating and following through on peer-to-peer formative feedback exchanges that move current performances forward *and* concretely show how to achieve the next levels with a task, project, or long-term assignment?

The modifier *peer-to-peer-driven* comes from the organizing principle we're using to categorize the different lenses through which we look at formative feedback. The three main feedback focal points in this book are **directionality**, **configuration**, and **modality**.

Figure 3.1 depicts three main focal points and their lenses. This chapter is about the focal point directionality and the second of the three lenses associated with directionality. We will interchangeably refer to this lens as *peer-to-peer directionality* or a *peer-to-peer-driven formative feedback approach*.

Figure 3.1 Formative Feedback Framework

Contexts for Learning		
Face-to-Face	Blended	Distance Learning
Focal Point		
Directionality	Configuration	Modality
Lenses		
Teacher-driven	Whole class	Written
Peer-to-peer-driven	Small groups (2–4)	Spoken
Self-driven	Individual (1:1)	Nonverbal
Tasks, Projects, Activities	Learning Goals, Standards, Skills	
	Rubrics, Progress Guides, "Next Steps" Organizers	

What we're calling *peer-to-peer-driven feedback* is typically delivered along with teacher-driven and self-driven formative feedback protocols and practices. By calling attention to this peer-to-peer lens, we are not isolating it from other practices in the directionality domain. Rather we are directing attention to how students may activate one another as **formative assessors** differently from their own perspective. The framework depicted in Figure 3.1 allows all stakeholders to see the possibilities of practice within and across various domains.

Defining What Peer-to-Peer-Driven Formative Feedback Is and Isn't

To begin, let's define what we mean by peer-to-peer-driven feedback. *Peer-to-peer-driven formative feedback* refers to qualitative comments and questions provided by learners of approximately equal status about a work product or performance in process. Peers can be classmates, other students of similar age and experience, or students of different grade levels working on a shared project. Peer-to-peer feedback can occur in any configuration: pairs, triads, small groups, and so on.

The key to peer-to-peer-driven feedback is agency: Who is offering feedback to whom? The feedback offered by students to one another can be reciprocal or unilateral and can be given anonymously or identified, publicly or privately. Empowering and activating students to help each other with a suggested next step or invitation to support revision or encouragement with a do-over are the hallmarks of peer-to-peer-driven feedback from the research on what works. Case studies and common sense tell us that communities of learners in which peer-to-peer exchanges elevate the collective work lead to better outcomes for all.

The table below outlines what peer-to-peer-driven formative feedback is and how it differs from other kinds of feedback.

PEER-TO-PEER-DRIVEN FORMATIVE FEEDBACK	
What It Is	**What It Isn't**
• uses qualitative comments (e.g., sticky notes, comments features, chat)	• a set of scores or points added on to the evaluation process
• asks questions about the current work	• a letter grade assigned to the current work by one student to another
• offers positive, specific statements about performance/work product with concrete suggestions for improvement	• offered from the point of view of a curricular expert
• reciprocal or one-way/unidirectional	• often highly accurate without the need for teacher review or expertise
• of variable quality: recipients of this feedback often have reservations about its accuracy; clarifications may be required	• necessarily transferable from one context to another
• can spur discussions, clarifications, and behaviors that seek confirmation or disconfirmation of success criteria	• statements of praise by a peer
	• a popularity contest or opportunity for showing who is best
• a learnable skill and practice	• a guarantee that students will learn from suggestions, comments, and/or advice from each other
• best when accompanied by a graphic organizer, evaluation guide, or next steps protocol	• a skill set that doesn't require modeling and practice
• an opportunity to grow the depth and quality of relationship between students	• time for students to operate without goals or expectations

> Before COVID, I always prompted my eighth graders to shake hands at the end of a Gallery Walk session. I wanted them to convey respect for the feedback process and one another. Now, we do a hands-up "shout out" with the words "Appreciate you."
>
> —Leon, middle school English language arts teacher

As you well know, planning for instruction makes a difference in the quality of experience that you and your students have. Surprises and unexpected teachable moments are welcome. But it helps to have a unit and/or **lesson plan** that systematically invites different aspects of feedback processes and protocols for students.

As you plan activities, scaffolds, and **prompts** in relation to peer-to-peer feedback, we offer some important aspects for consideration. Table 3.1 presents multiple aspects and explains why they matter for successful peer-to-peer feedback experiences. Use the tips and questions from the table to guide your decision-making process at the lesson and unit level. Don't forget to keep asking "Why does it matter?" for each choice you decide upon. Effective peer-to-peer feedback exchanges are contingent upon varying contexts, the curriculum, and as always, the kids. But you can anticipate and ready yourself for contingencies with forethought and reflection.

Table 3.1 Planning for Peer-to-Peer Feedback: What to Consider and Why It Matters

ASPECT	ASK YOURSELF	WHY IT MATTERS	TIPS AND TO-DO'S
Your Primary Purpose/Goal Behind Peer Feedback	Why am I having my students engage in giving each other feedback?	So I can evaluate the success of the peer-to-peer feedback activity in light of my goal.	• Be transparent with students about why they're engaging in this process. • Have students reflect in a way that supports this goal/purpose.
Student Understanding of What Makes a Quality Work Product or Performance	How familiar with what makes an exemplary performance are my students? Do they know the success criteria? Have I modeled the process (e.g., shared a moderation video, peer-to-peer exchange clip)?	Increased familiarity → increased chances of helpful feedback. When students see themselves in the process, they can visualize successful exchanges with peers.	• Check students' understanding of the success criteria using an exemplar. • If students don't know the criteria, it's too soon for them to be engaging in peer-to-peer feedback.

ASPECT	ASK YOURSELF	WHY IT MATTERS	TIPS AND TO-DO'S
Timing in Relation to Self-Assessment and Teacher Assessment	Have they self-assessed their performance/draft work product yet?	Having students assess their own work/performance before engaging in peer feedback encourages receptiveness to peer feedback. Engaging in self-assessment often increases familiarity with success criteria, which leads to better peer feedback.	▶ Think of self-assessment as preparation for peer feedback activities. ▶ Remind students of the three directionalities of feedback for the project, task, or long-term assignment: self, peer-to-peer, teacher. ▶ Talk about how all feedback directionalities are necessary and how their order of use and intermingling can be helpful. Discuss: Why does the order of self → peer to peer → teacher comments/suggestions make sense? ▶ Use similar tools (e.g., progress guides).
Timing in Relation to Final Deadline	What opportunities do students have to incorporate peer feedback into their work/performance? Do class time and deadlines support and respect peer feedback?	It takes time to enact peer feedback suggestions. Since the act of revising (redoing) is a part of learning to learn, students need time and support to incorporate the feedback they have received.	▶ Remind everyone: It's not merely about learning to meet deadlines in the real world. ▶ Collaboration requires processing time for everyone. ▶ Dedicate class time to addressing feedback received from peers (rather than treating it as homework).
Interactivity	How much do I want there to be back-and-forth between peers? How can I encourage recipients of peer feedback to take an active role?	Feedback that is not understood can't be used. Clarification requires interaction.	▶ Support and monitor peer-to-peer interactions and, when necessary, coach students to get back on topic or to switch speaking/listening roles. ▶ Invite reflection. Ask students, "What will make the process more interactive and shared right now?"

(Continued)

(Continued)

ASPECT	ASK YOURSELF	WHY IT MATTERS	TIPS AND TO-DO'S
Configuration, Privacy, and Proximity	What setup aligns with my goal and students' needs? Who will need a sense of privacy or more safe space? Who will need a coach/advocate to bring their voice to the fore?	Students with more expertise at the targeted skill/performance will tend to give better peer feedback. Peer dynamics influence the process, as will your presence. The more bystanders are listening in, the higher the stakes for the feedback giver and recipient.	▸ Assign pairs/groups thoughtfully and be prepared to swap them out. ▸ Students gain from repeating a feedback procedure. Say it out loud and often: "How are we doing?" ▸ Real or virtual gallery walks are powerful opportunities for students to practice giving targeted, nonjudgmental, focused feedback. ▸ Back channel, if necessary, with vulnerable students to ensure they are doing well with feedback in their group.
Familiarity With Peer Feedback Process	How familiar are my students with peer feedback in general? How familiar are they with this particular peer feedback process?	Their familiarity with peer feedback influences how you ▸ prepare students beforehand, ▸ support them during, and ▸ lead them through reflection afterward.	▸ Prime students for awkward moments: "Remember, we are all learning to learn from one another in this world." ▸ Coach students (before, during, and after) about the value of gaining a new perspective: "That's what formative feedback is—it helps you get better *together*."
Scaffolds and Accountability	Do the scaffolds I'm planning reflect my goals for this unit? How will I know students have engaged in the process? What tools do I have to keep everyone explicit about success with learning criteria?	Scaffolds convey, "This process is worth working at and can be learned. There are clear steps to success. Each level of progress counts." To ensure equitable learning opportunities and experiences for students, you need to know how students are engaging with learning criteria and incorporating other people's feedback.	▸ Invite students to help improve the scaffolds and tools to guide the peer feedback. ▸ Ask, "Is everyone clear on [this level of performance descriptor]? How can we improve it or make it clearer? How can we make it more useful for you as you help your classmates?" ▸ Strategically walk around and listen in for where students are stuck, seem to have difficulty using the scaffolds, or may need more assistance/modeling.

Note that *timing* is addressed twice in Table 3.1: first in relation to **self-assessment**, next in relation to the final deadline. Each merits separate consideration. Yet it makes sense to first consider whether students have self-assessed their work *before* they are expected to offer their peers formative feedback. Typically, students give better feedback to their peers when they have first self-assessed their own work and generated next steps for themselves.

A final takeaway from Table 3.1: Any scaffolds for supporting peer-to-peer feedback processes that you develop and revise should align with your students' learning context. You are in the best position to know the most about this context. The school's mission, the curricular demands, and the students' cognitive, social, and cultural **assets** will guide how you approach peer-driven feedback in your classroom. Strive to be thoughtful and artful in how you support peer-to-peer feedback. As the table suggests, invite students to help improve your scaffolds. After all, they are the ones who can help you improve the user experience.

What the Research Tells Us
Peer-to-Peer Feedback Supports 21st Century Skills and Deeper Learning

When students engage in peer-feedback processes, they are enacting the four Cs of 21st century skills: *critical thinking, communication, collaboration,* and *creativity* (National Research Council, 2012; Pellegrino, 2017). No matter the specific tool or scaffold they use to guide the process, students must think critically about the work or performance on which they are offering feedback.

As students learn to describe the strengths and improvement opportunities of a draft or a performance, they develop their critical thinking and communication skills. We know that **peer assessment** causes a very substantial increase in the quantity and immediacy of feedback to the learner. As Topping (2010) notes:

> As the learning relationship develops, both helper and helped should become more consciously aware of what is happening in their learning interaction, and more able to monitor and regulate the effectiveness of their own learning strategies in different contexts. . . . Development into fully conscious explicit and strategic metacognition (level 7) not only promotes more effective onward learning, it should make helper and helped more confident that they can achieve even more, and that their success is the result of their own efforts. In other words, they attribute success to themselves, not to external factors, and their self-esteem is heightened. (p. 65)

In gallery walks at an art **exhibition**, in pairs while lifting weights, or in groups during a science lab, students can learn to conduct themselves as caring and competent peer evaluators. When working on science exhibitions or troubleshooting a robotics project, we see how students engage one another with verbal and nonverbal feedback. During loosely and more formally structured peer feedback sessions, we can observe students of various backgrounds supporting one another in a spirit of collaboration in which they exercise their voices and creativity.

We don't want our students rigidly following a peer-to-peer feedback protocol in lockstep fashion. Rather, we encourage them to look for signs of their peers' needs for affective support, explanation, and clarification. They can then adjust accordingly. It's the back-and-forth nature of peer-to-peer feedback processes—students' questioning, clarifying, and reflecting on the feedback from their peers and comparing and contrasting it with their understanding of the learning task—that leads to **deeper learning** (Filius et al., 2018; Gold & Lanzoni, 1993; Li et al., 2010).

Essential Peer-to-Peer Feedback Practices Supported by Research

Encourage/Require Justification

- It's imperative to coach students to justify the feedback they give to their peers, since research demonstrates that students who receive justified feedback improve their work the most (Gielen et al., 2010).

Use Written Prompts

- Giving students sentence starters, scaffolds, and other written prompts to use while generating feedback has been found to make a significant difference in terms of increasing suggestions for improvement and feedback focused on learning processes needed to understand the task at hand (Gan & Hattie, 2014).

Discuss the Feedback

- Student discussion of the feedback they have received, as well as supported time to act on it, is critical (Boon, 2016; Rotsaert et al., 2018).

For English Learners: Support Strategically

- In supporting English learners, it is important for teachers to not only focus the peer feedback work on course content but also to partner students strategically and with consideration for students' growing awareness of their social status in peer groups (August, 2018).

Focus on Practice: Using a Scoring Guide to Facilitate Peer-to-Peer-Driven Feedback

Giving students a concrete **graphic organizer** helps orient their feedback in a targeted direction, and when students compare several samples of work to a **scoring guide**, they gain familiarity with the success criteria (Wilson & Sloane, 2000). These guides help students explore together in groups to address questions such as: (1) What elements are required in a piece of quality work for this assignment? (2) How do drafts of work on this task vary from more accomplished to still developing? (3) What is the actual difference between scores (levels of performance) on a classroom peer assessment guide?

Students need this understanding of exemplary (and developing) performance so they can give specific, well-informed, and ultimately helpful feedback to a peer who may be struggling. Since it is difficult for children and teens to make meaning of scores or grades or any markings without first comprehending what the levels of performance mean, we suggest introducing many **first draft** examples across a range of performances. The goal of a peer-to-peer-driven feedback session is to model what's next and which actual steps can be taken by one's peer. Scoring guides, **progress guides**, and similar tools are key to keeping everyone focused.

To come up with useful feedback for their peers, students first need to determine the following:

- What is the work sample (i.e., current draft or activity) doing well?
- Where could it be improved specifically?
- How can I/we suggest a next step by [student's name] that can be reached with our/my assistance?

> ## Author Insight
> Lev Vygotsky
>
> **Zone of Proximal Development**
>
> the distance between the actual developmental level as determined by independent problem solving and the level of potential development as determined through problem-solving under adult guidance, or in collaboration with more capable peers.

Source: Vygotsky (1978), p. 86.

Scoring Guides as a Powerful Tool to Guide Feedback Among Students

What is a scoring guide? How does it differ from an **answer key** or **rubric**?

Answer keys are everywhere. They often help grade efficiently. In some cases, students are asked to use these keys for test correction exercises. But using an answer key is different from providing peer feedback protocols to deepen feedback practices.

Rubrics are also ubiquitous in many classrooms. Rubrics help us to set **learning targets** and **standards**, identify benchmarks along a skills trajectory, and grade more fairly. But rubrics can be unwieldy and, in too many cases, hindered by dysfunctional detail (Popham, 1997).

A scoring guide is a user-friendly alternative to a rubric and an improvement on traditional answer keys. Scoring guides contain less verbiage and dysfunctional detail that might overwhelm students (remember our discussion of right-sized feedback and rubrics in Chapter 1).

Scoring guides offer students ways to unpack qualitatively distinct levels of response—without the added pressure of **grading** and distracting labels.

Scoring guides prioritize skills, often one strand at a time. Over the course of a **unit of instruction**, students and teachers may use multiple scoring guides to check progress toward the final performance, which will eventually be graded with an analytic rubric. For an example of a scoring guide from a research project conducted by University of California, Berkeley in a yearlong middle school science curriculum called "Issues, Evidence, and You" (IEY), see Figure 3.2.

Figure 3.2 Applying Relevant Content Scoring Guide

Score	Applying Relevant Content: Response uses relevant scientific information in new situations, such as solving problems or resolving issues.
4	Accomplishes Level 3 *and* extends beyond in some significant way.
3	Accurately and completely uses scientific information to solve the problem or resolve the issue.
2	Shows an attempt to use scientific information *but* the explanation is incomplete; may have minor errors.
1	Uses scientific information incorrectly and/or provides incorrect scientific information *or* provides correct scientific information but does not use it.
0	Is missing, illegible, irrelevant, or off topic.
X	Student had no opportunity to respond.

Setting Students Up for Success With Peer Feedback: A Middle School Science Case Study Example

Let's look at what Ms. Denton, a middle school science teacher, does with her students before expecting them to give peer-to-peer feedback on their own. After briefly reviewing the characteristics of helpful formative feedback with her students, Ms. Denton prioritizes setting up an interactive task activity that students will evaluate together. The activity's purpose is to get students familiar with the elements and qualities of exemplary work (**exemplars**)—the success criteria of using relevant scientific information in new situations—and it relies on students using a scoring guide to justify their claims. Note that scoring guides are not new to Ms. Denton's students. They have been introduced to scoring guides in previous units.

In this unit, Ms. Denton's seventh-grade science students are learning to apply what they know about acids and bases to solve a problem in the IEY curricular unit:

> A student conducts an investigation to see which is more concentrated, a sample of acid or a sample of base. He finds that it takes four drops of acid to neutralize one drop of base. Which is more concentrated, the acid or the base? Explain your answer. You may wish to include a diagram.

Before expecting her students to give peer feedback on their answers, Ms. Denton prepares them with the following activity/protocol: She gives all her students three anonymous responses to the problem above. The anonymous responses are from seventh graders Ms. Denton has taught in the past. Each response can be improved, though in different ways.

Ms. Denton's directions on the projector to her current students are as follows:

1. Read each of the three anonymous responses: Draft A, Draft B, and Draft C. (2–6 minutes)

2. Then score using the Applying Relevant Content Scoring Guide. (1–4 minutes)

3. In your group of three, compare the scores you gave to each draft. (2–3 minutes)

4. Discuss any disagreements you may have about scores and come to consensus about one score for each draft. (10–12 minutes)

5. Next, as a group, give one piece of feedback to the student who wrote that response. (3–6 minutes)

6. Write a justification for the feedback in the "Justification" column. (3–6 minutes)

    NOTE: Write it as if you were writing it to the student, but do *not* give the student the correct answer or missing information. We are practicing how to give feedback. We are not about doing the work *for* the other person.

To support the **English learners** in her class and to help all her students develop their **academic language** skills, Ms. Denton reminds her students to open a window/tab on their school-provided computer, which displays these phrases/**sentence starters**:

> I'm not sure what _____ means.
> We can't come to consensus until I understand the reasons why. Can you explain it another way?
> So you're saying that . . . [restate in your own words what your classmate said] _____.

Peer-to-Peer Feedback in Small Groups: Diving Deeper Into the SEPUP Example

Peer-to-peer feedback can be part of any embedded assessment framework (Wilson & Sloane, 2000) that focuses on activating students to support one another. In collaboration with curriculum developers at the Lawrence Hall of Science at the University of California, Berkeley; assessment developers from University of California, Berkeley's graduate school of education; and teachers and students in a school district in Kentucky, an assessment process called **moderation** demonstrates the use of scoring guides to explore levels of progress. The collaboration, known as SEPUP or the Science Education for Public Understanding Project (Roberts & Sipusic, 1999), used visible tools and protocols for guiding peer interactions focused on analyses of students' work. The team designed and piloted a yearlong middle school science curriculum (IEY) that innovated a comprehensive, integrated system for assessing, interpreting, and monitoring student performance.

The episode in *All Things in Moderation* shows how Ms. Denton and her students took up the challenge of learning to provide specific, timely, and useful feedback to one another. Ms. Denton models the process of offering feedback (in this case, a justification and explanation of what needs to be improved) in a whole-class configuration before moving the students into smaller groups. In a peer-to-peer exchange, we see several students interacting with the work samples.

WATCH THIS

All Things in Moderation

Please use the QR code above and watch the video before proceeding.

Jeff:	I gave it a 1.
Teacher:	Why?
Jeff:	Because for one, it (*reading from scoring guide*) "inaccurately identifies and/or describes scientific information." First of all, the numbers aren't exactly what the question asks. It says 4 times as many, except it doesn't explain, describe the scientific information. It just says 40 drops and 10 drops, it doesn't say what of. It doesn't say, it doesn't give the answer to the question, "Which is more concentrated?"
Russell:	Yeah, but it says it "incorrectly identifies" (*reading from Level 1 of scoring guide*).
Jeff:	Yeah, it incorrectly identified it, well, because it didn't give either one. So you could say that 10 drops could be either an acid or base, and 40 drops could be acid or base.
Pam:	But it identified scientific information . . . well, it didn't, like, put it in words, but it showed the point of what it was trying to get across by the 40, 10, and the 4 times as many.
Jeff:	Except what point is that? Because you don't know what it even has to do with. You don't know what substance it is. I mean, it could be water or orange juice for all you know.
Teacher:	If you read the answer by itself, Pam, would you, without having any knowledge of the question, would that be enough information to tell about the concentration of acid and the base?
Pam:	No. I guess not.
Jeff:	It also doesn't answer the one question. It says, "Which is more concentrated, the acid or the base?" That's the final question and it doesn't answer that.
Pam:	Okay. I see what you mean.
Jeff:	You see how I got the 1?
Pam:	Yeah, I see. (*to the other two students in the group*) Do you two understand how we got the 1?

Other two students nod their heads.

Teacher:	Well, Russell, you sound like you're just caving in. Do you fully agree? Do you understand what Jeff's explanation was? Tell us why you . . .
Russell:	I still think it's a 2.
Teacher:	Well tell us why. Give us—
Russell:	Look. It tells what the question is. It answered the question. It just doesn't explain it much.
Jeff:	But the question is—
Pam:	Yeah, it does answer the question.
Jeff:	But the question is, "Which is more concentrated, the acid or the base?" And if you just looked at this *(referring to student sample answer B)* you, well, even if you knew what the question was, you couldn't tell which is acid and which was base.
Russell:	It could have been anything.
Jeff:	Yeah. So *(looks at Russell)* it doesn't answer the question.
Russell:	I can go with 1.

Notice how the students (as peers working to arrive at a consensus) in the video read from the Figure 3.2 scoring guide as they discuss areas for improvement and how they work together to arrive at agreement on the level of the current draft. This process of moderation is a powerful tool for activating students to think critically about the current level of a given task performance. Moreover, the moderation process in peer-driven exchanges demonstrates (through a form of learning by doing) that judgments about grades and/or scores require evidence. The students in this example are learning about science (bases and acids) and how to use evidence in verbal discussions to justify their reasoning.

Scaffolds and Guided Practice for Individual Teachers

Know Your Primary Goal

To get started with peer feedback—or to improve what you've done so far—it's smart to clarify your primary goal. Researchers have identified five primary goals for having students engage in peer-to-peer assessment and feedback (Gielen et al., 2011). Many of these lessons hold for working with middle and high school students, in our experience.

As you read the following list, consider how frequently each goal is used for your students. Also note any goals you have that don't appear on this list. What are they? Why are they important to you?

Goals for Peer-to-Peer Feedback Exchanges and Why You Might Have These Goals

GOAL	WHY YOU MIGHT HAVE THIS GOAL
Motivation/Social Control	
To get students to spend time on a task	▸ Knowing a peer is going to look at their work or performance can be an external motivator for students to work harder and perform better
Replace, Augment, or Triangulate Your Feedback	
To increase the amount of feedback students receive	▸ You can't possibly give feedback on every piece of work or performance students do
	▸ You want to compare what feedback your students give to your own, more expert feedback
Learning More About the Performance Expectations (Project or Task Specific)	
For students to discover how others are interpreting and responding to a complex project or parts of a task	▸ You want students to revise how they are approaching a task; responding to peers' work gives them ideas on how to approach first drafts
To familiarize students with success criteria	▸ When students are expected to explicitly look for success criteria and judge these criteria at play in their peer's work, they often become better at reaching the next level
Learn How to Give and Take Feedback in Collaborative Settings (College, Work, and Life Skills)	
To foreground lifelong learning processes	▸ Learning how to give and receive feedback is a powerful tool in one's lifelong learning toolkit
Active Participation in Verbal, Written, and Other Feedback Modes	
Action promotes learning how to learn from others	▸ You want to empower students to make judgments that count
Peer-based exchanges develop student autonomy and the ability to co-regulate learning	▸ Students' active participation increases student awareness of many inputs/factors that support academic success

Align Student Reflection on Peer Feedback Activities With Your Primary Goal

To reinforce the learning students gain from the peer-to-peer feedback activity, encourage them to reflect on what worked and what needs improvement with the peer-based feedback sessions. But be particular with your reflection prompt. Make sure it aligns with your primary goals and the success criteria embedded in the performance task, project, or long-term assignment.

For example, if your primary goal for feedback on a collaborative project is for students to make progress as a team and commit to a set of concrete next steps, the reflection (an **exit ticket** or quick write) prompt might be something like the following:

Name:
Date:
Period:

1. Describe a next step that would be valuable for you (or your team) to take in your project.

2. To take this next step, what do you (or your team) need to do?

3. Before you (or your team) turn in the next draft, how can you all agree you've taken those next steps? (Mark as many boxes as apply.)

    ☐ We have a checklist.

    ☐ Everyone signed off as ready to go.

    ☐ Our progress guide (attached) shows the next steps.

But if your primary goal is for students to learn how to give formative feedback in collaborative settings (as they learn college, work, and life skills), the reflection prompt might look more like this:

Name: _____
Date: _____
Period: _____

1. How did you know that your feedback is being understood today? You might use one of these sentence frames:

> At first I didn't know how _____ was responding to my feedback. But when _____
> I noticed that they were taking next steps.
>
> I had to clarify my feedback to _____ because
> _____.
>
> I knew that _____ was understanding my feedback because
> _____.

Try It Tomorrow

Share and Celebrate Peers' Work-in-Progress With Flip

Have your students give positive feedback on each other's in-progress work using Flip. For example, students could all post short videos of themselves calling attention to an aspect of the in-progress work they're proud of (e.g., showing a portion of an artwork, reading aloud one paragraph of an essay). Their peers view these and compose video responses, providing one piece of specific, positive feedback. You can require everyone to comment on two or three classmates' works-in-progress. Students gain practice giving positive feedback, learn what their classmates are up to, and often experience more buy-in for the project.

> Peer-to-peer feedback activities aren't just about keeping your class busy while you help individual students. Kids really do wind up helping each other in ways I couldn't dream up. It's important to give them that opportunity during class. I learn so much about what's working and where they are stuck as I move from table to table.
>
> —Raquel, social science teacher and drama coach

Setting Goals and Monitoring Progress With Peer-to-Peer-Driven Feedback: Questions for Lesson Study and Professional Learning Communities

Sharing, Considering, and Adapting Scaffolds

In your **professional learning community** (**PLC**), consider the different scaffolds you're using to support peer-to-peer feedback.

1. Have volunteers who have brought a scaffold introduce it by sharing

    - its primary purpose,
    - how students use it,
    - what, if anything, they'd like to change about it, and
    - its best feature.

2. Give plenty of time for group questions and answers (Q&A) regarding each scaffold.

3. Reflect as a group: How do the scaffolds relate to the goals of peer-to-peer feedback outlined in "Goals for Peer-to-Peer Feedback Exchanges and Why You Might Have These Goals"? How accessible to English learners are these tools and scaffolds? As a group, what do the scaffolds prioritize?

4. Discuss what kinds of peer-to-peer feedback scaffolds for English learners, students with special needs, and other designated students you would like to see shared in a future PLC meeting.

5. Before closing, have each member share aloud what they learned and/or are excited about trying with their students.

Recap/Review

- When students discuss the feedback they have received from peers and have time to act on it, they are more likely to take up that feedback.
- Coaching students to justify the feedback they give to their peers is one of the most powerful peer-to-peer feedback practices teachers can enact.
- Providing students with scaffolds (e.g., sentence starters, progress guides, graphic organizers) is essential if we want all students to get better peer-to-peer feedback.
- When students are expected to refer to a scoring or progress guide *during* peer-to-peer feedback activities, they become more familiar with the success criteria of the task.
- Teachers ought to be transparent with students about why they are engaging in peer-to-peer feedback activities.
- It's sound practice to align student reflection prompts on the peer-to-peer feedback activity they've just engaged in with the primary purpose of the activity.
- Invite students to critique the peer-to-peer feedback scaffolds they use. Students can help you make them better. Revising feedback protocols and reflecting on their usefulness matters for users.

Ticket Out the Door

1. It's your turn. Based on your experience, what, in your opinion, did we miss when promoting the use of peer-to-peer feedback exchanges to advance learning? Say more.

2. Tell us about something else you think should have been included in this chapter on peer-driven formative feedback. Make a checklist that everyone should consider.

3. Name as many different reasons as you can think of why *trust*, *respect*, and *care* are important for the peer-to-peer formative feedback process.

4. A student who has never engaged in peer-to-peer feedback joins your class. Will you do anything different before your next peer feedback activity? (Hint: See the glossary entry on *priming*.)

CHAPTER 4

Self-Driven Feedback

Why do we ask students to self-assess? I have long held that self-assessment is feedback . . . and that the purpose of feedback is to inform adjustments to processes and products that deepen learning; hence the purpose of self-assessment is to generate feedback that promotes learning and improvement in performance. This learning-oriented purpose of self-assessment implies that it should be formative: If there is no opportunity for adjustment and correction, self-assessment is almost pointless.

—Andrade (2018, p. 337)

Students aren't known for having consistently accurate **self-assessments** of their work (Brown & Harris, 2013). There are many reasons why. But without an accurate assessment of your own performance, how can you generate helpful **feedback** for yourself? Is it possible to improve one's use of self-assessment in the classroom? Yes. But students will need support from teachers and peers to self-assess more effectively.

We can make self-assessment part of the lives of our students who are learning how to learn. In fact, part of the self-regulation process is having access to new habits of thinking. "What is next for me to do now?" is an essential question for all learners.

For many of us, an important question that also emerges is this: What kinds of self-driven feedback matter?

If the self-driven feedback students give themselves is along the lines of "Keep at it," "I can do it," "Take a breath before trying again," "I need to think about where I got confused last time," or "Try not to freak out," they are likely to benefit. Self-assessment techniques of this sort help regulate their stress and anxiety with complex tasks and long-term projects.

Significantly, this sort of self-driven feedback is not content-, domain-, or even necessarily task-specific. We can categorize these self-driven **moves** for students in different ways: self-regulatory ("I need to take a breath"), mindset-oriented ("I can do it if I try again"), meta-cognitive ("Where I get confused is"), and strategic ("I think it's time to try a new tactic"). Each represents a repertoire of self-driven feedback moves/skills that can be acquired by our students with practice.

Yet we know that learners also benefit from subject- and discipline-specific **formative feedback** moves. These sorts of moves are often challenging for our students to generate on their own. For example, it takes deep content knowledge and experience in assessing a particular type of performance, not to mention a degree of accuracy, to be able to say to oneself, "I should shift my weight at this point as I drive toward the hoop, not sooner," or to ask oneself, "What are some different methods I could use to draw the viewer's eye more toward the figure in the foreground of my collage?" or "I'll go back and check our sources of evidence sheet to better distinguish between primary and secondary sources."

As educators preparing students for the world of work and college, we want our students to be in the habit of giving themselves these general and subject-specific types of feedback. But we also want and need our students to cultivate skills with self-assessment that address learning goals, cross-cutting concepts, and higher-order thinking skills related to the academic/subject discipline. Studying mathematics, science, language arts, world languages, music, art, physical education, history, civics, economics, and ethnic studies requires feedback from experts. Self-assessment only works in the company of those experts—in this case, teachers and peers working as knowledgeable guides on the side.

Students who are learning to self-assess will need **prompts**, cues, tools, and routines that allow them to engage feedback for themselves and with others. Since we want our students to generate—and act upon—content-, domain-, and task-specific feedback for themselves, we must create soft landings and accessible on-ramps during self-assessment practices and procedures.

It's time to ask, "What are the conditions necessary to support our students in gaining skill in several kinds of self-driven formative feedback?"

This chapter explores what we're calling *self-driven formative feedback* and its connections to the previous two **directionality** chapters. The following four guiding questions anchor our explorations. Taken as a whole, each chapter on directionalities describes the challenges and opportunities with separating and connecting different angles of feedback-rich information exchange in the classroom. This particular lens points to the need for weaving well-defined, consistent, and reflective student-based feedback practices into your lessons and **units of instruction**.

> ## Guiding Questions
>
> 1. Why plan, enact, and reflect on self-driven formative feedback? Who is self-driven formative feedback good for? Self-driven formative feedback is used for which educational goals or purposes?
> 2. What are the conditions necessary to support students in gaining habits and skills in self-driven formative feedback routines?
> 3. How do we support self-driven feedback activities in ways that get *everyone* better at giving and receiving feedback on their first drafts and next steps?
> 4. How can I help students get better at generating and following through on self-assessment protocols and practices that move current performances forward *and* concretely show how to achieve the next level with a task, project, or long-term assignment?

We'll answer these questions together. For now, let's define what we mean by *self-driven feedback*.

The modifier *self-driven* comes from the organizing principle we're using to categorize the different lenses through which we look at formative feedback. Figure 4.1 depicts three main focal points and their lenses. This chapter is about the focal point—*directionality*—and the third of the three lenses associated with directionality. We will refer to this lens as the *self-driven formative feedback approach*.

From the perspective of directionality, self-driven feedback is grouped with teacher-driven and peer-to-peer-driven formative feedback. Examining formative feedback this way helps keep our focus on what is unique about a student (typically a student who is not an expert in the subject area) who is generating feedback for themselves.

Figure 4.1 Formative Feedback Framework

Contexts for Learning		
Face-to-Face	Blended	Distance Learning
Focal Point		
Directionality	Configuration	Modality
Lenses		
Teacher-driven	Whole class	Written
Peer-to-peer-driven	Small groups (2–4)	Spoken
Self-driven	Individual (1:1)	Nonverbal
Learning Goals, Standards, Skills		
Tasks, Projects, Activities	Rubrics, Progress Guides, "Next Steps" Organizers	

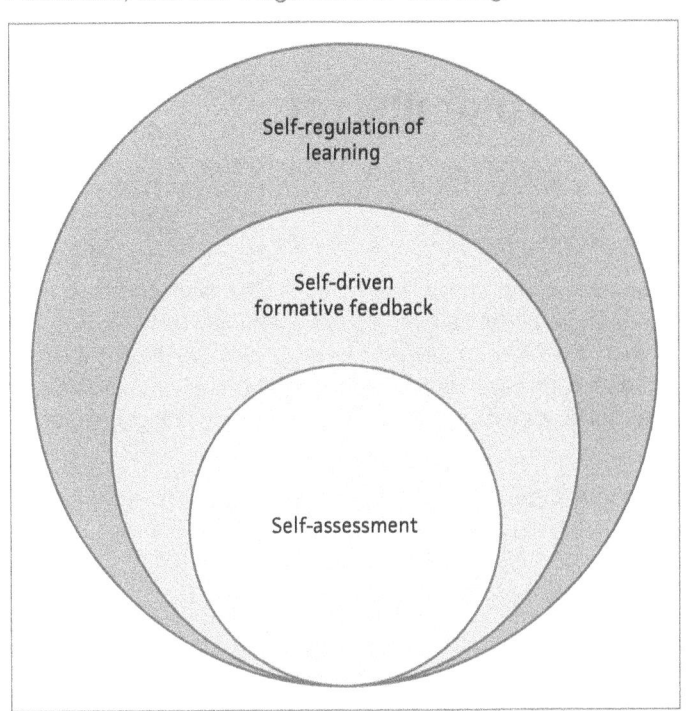

Figure 4.2 On the Relationship of Self-Assessment, Self-Driven Feedback, and Self-Regulation of Learning

Defining Self-Driven Formative Feedback

Self-assessment and self-regulation of learning are related but not synonymous concepts (see Figure 4.2). According to experts, "self-regulation and self-assessment are complementary processes that can lead to marked improvements in academic achievement and autonomy" (Andrade, 2010, p. 91).

Self-assessment is a process of **formative assessment** during which students reflect on the quality of their work, judge the degree to which it reflects explicitly stated goals or criteria, and revise their work (Andrade, 2010; Andrade & Boulay, 2003). Panadero, Jonsson, and Strijbos (2016) note that self-assessment may "involve a wide range of activities, from asking students to **grade** their own work without further reflection (i.e., self-grading), at one end of the spectrum, to having them make comprehensive analyses of their own performance on complex tasks at the other end of the spectrum" (p. 314).

Self-regulated learning is a process whereby learners set goals for their learning and then attempt to monitor, regulate, and control their cognition, motivation, and behavior to reach their goals (Andrade, 2010; Pintrich, 2000). Brandmo et al. (2020, p. 322) note that self-regulated learning "can be described as the process where the learner activates and sustains their cognition, motivation, behaviors, and feelings toward the attainment of a learning goal."

> ## Author Insight
> ### Brandmo, Panadero, and Hopfenbeck
>
> **Self-Regulation and Co-regulation**
>
> Self-regulated learning is about students approaching academic tasks in a planned way, while adapting their learning activities/performance to the context and text in order to achieve progress toward the learning goal. . . . [It] can be described as the process where the learner activates and sustains their cognition, motivation, behaviors, and feelings toward the attainment of a learning goal.
>
> Co-regulation is described as a process in which the social environment supports the emergence of regulation.

Source: Brandmo, Panadero, & Hopfenbeck (2020), p. 322.

In recent assessment literature, the recognition that self-regulation of learning involves a reciprocal process of co-regulation is gaining attention from scholars. Andrade et al. (2021) note that "because self-regulatory processes often occur under the joint influence of students and other sources of regulation in the learning environment such as teachers, peers, interventions, curriculum materials, and assessment instruments, classroom assessment is a matter of mutual co-regulation" (p. 2).

Self-driven formative feedback refers to what students think and say—and sometimes write or gesture—to themselves in order to further their learning and improve their performance. In school-based learning contexts, self-driven feedback is catalyzed, facilitated, and monitored by teachers. Teachers and peers can coach students who are learning to give themselves feedback. In other words, we learn from others how to coach ourselves better.

Think of students coaching themselves out loud as they play complex video games at home or when they decide to take a back seat in a game and watch a more expert player while they take mental notes on their own moves, make comparisons, think about the differences, and attend to what's possible for them. It's not merely about regulating oneself with a prompt or quick check such as "How am I doing?" on this assignment. Rather, effective self-driven feedback is like the **habit of mind** (perspective). It includes the voice in one's head that says, "Okay. Relax. Step back and watch what I am doing or thinking from this perspective." The skills and habits associated with self-directed feedback are fundamentally about learning how to feel and see that progress is possible at this moment in the project or task.

Students may not be accustomed to or motivated by particular school subject disciplines or units of instruction in the same way they are with video games, outdoor play, and other forms of nonacademic expression.

This is frustrating but true for parents, guardians, and teachers alike. We want to see students grow more independent, learn how to regulate their learning, and generate feedback for themselves within school contexts and classroom learning environments.

The good news is we have examples and evidence of student-driven feedback all around us. Yet our students will need to be coached—and set up for success with peers and teachers—in places where self-assessment is a core value at our own schools. We will have to show them as teachers and guides on the side how we, too, commit ourselves to getting better at our craft by self-assessing, daily. We've got to walk the walk, not just talk the talk of self-assessment.

Self-Assessment Is Necessary, But Not Sufficient, for Generating Feedback for Oneself

To generate self-driven feedback, students must self-assess. They do this by comparing their performance or work to an **exemplar**, another available performance, or their memory/record of their own past performance.

Hovering between self-assessment and self-regulation, self-driven feedback is hard to make visible to observers (Figure 4.2). Students may think, say, or feel things we can't observe as they work on a draft or project activity. We will discuss concrete ways to advance the goals of self-assessment with visible procedures and tools in the classroom. The **scoring guide** that we introduced in the last chapter invites students and others to reflect upon a range of possible actions, but we also hold space for informal conversations among peers and teachers that reveal how students are learning to self-assess. In this and the next few chapters, we will explore how a **progress guide** can take self-assessment to deeper levels of engagement but only with conversation and multiple **feedback loops**.

We often see teachers attempting to gather evidence of students' self-regulation. New technologies and software applications promise more self-regulation on the fly. But the call for thumbs up/thumbs down or quick poll techniques on Zoom are not enough. Too often we see teachers asking students, "Are you okay? Everything good? Are you ready to move on?" These questions may or may not engage the students in self-reflection moves that lead them to concrete, specific, or targeted next steps.

Knowing the difference between where you want to go with your work and where you are with your work is not the same as knowing what actions to take to narrow the gap! Helping students understand their own **zones of proximal development** (**ZPDs**) with a task or performance requires tools and **scaffolds** that are shared. We can say that developing the general skills at self-assessing one's own work is necessary but not sufficient for being able to generate quality, actionable, next-steps–oriented formative feedback for oneself on a particular project at a particular moment in the feedback cycle.

It is our job to communicate that self-assessment is an opportunity to adjust, to revise, and to improve—in this current learning cycle!—in order to motivate next steps and go beyond simple encouragement or self-affirmation of oneself. To do this well, we must make time and create space for modeling and practicing self-assessment together, in groups, and by ourselves.

SELF-DRIVEN FORMATIVE FEEDBACK

What It Is	What It Isn't
• often akin to self-talk or the voice one hears saying "I can do this"	• wholly synonymous with self-assessment (self-assessing is a prerequisite for generating sensible next steps one could take)
• frequently oriented to self-regulation	
• can be metacognitive	
• benefits from having concrete and visible scaffolds, such as a progress guide for student self-assessment	• only an evaluation, although evaluating one's performance is part of the process of being able to come up with feedback for oneself
• dependent on one's familiarity with the domain at hand when it comes to being able to generate *specific* feedback for oneself	• a letter grade, score, or points one gives to oneself
	• self-affirmation (e.g., praise or boasting)
• a skill that gets better over time with peer and teacher supports	• polling and thumbs up/thumbs down signals
	• a nod to the rhetorical question, "Are you good?"
• something people, as human beings, naturally do but need coaching to advance their learning	• always productive
	• often well-aligned with subject-specific learning goals
• a learnable skill and practice	

> My kids love to monitor their social media. They are always looking at ways to be seen and influence others. I've been working on harnessing that energy and showing them new, productive ways to self-evaluate with fitness, finance, and other apps. If they are going to self-monitor, why not put it to use at school for important educational goals?
>
> —Nina, history/economics teacher and softball coach

Having students self-assess and generate formative feedback for themselves is one of the most important learning activities we as teachers can support. After all, we are responsible for teaching students to learn how to learn as much as we are for ensuring they master specific knowledge and skills in particular subject areas (although this is undoubtedly important!). Doing this well takes planning.

As you plan your lessons and unit, we invite you to consider

- how to *prepare* students for self-driven formative feedback routines and protocols you assign, set up, and/or assist with;
- how to call attention to the *process of learning*, not only the delivered work product;
- how a potential routine/protocol/scaffold helps *all* students understand the *relevant success criteria* for the task, project, or assignment; and
- how **academic language** and **register** will play a part in cycles of feedback.

In each case, effective feedback requires us to carefully attend to the language load and academic language demands involved in the routines/protocols/scaffolds we are embedding in the lesson and units in our subject discipline. Students engaged in deeper feedback routines should be practicing and making sense of subject-specific language, not merely new vocabulary. Deep feedback practices offer students many opportunities to speak the language of science, sports, mathematics, music, economics, civics, art, history, and so on. We learn by speaking, not only by doing, as the familiar adage goes.

Table 4.1 presents helpful questions to ask yourself when considering these aspects, why they matter, and offers "Tips and To-Do's" you might try with your students.

Table 4.1 Planning for Self-Driven Feedback: What to Consider and Why It Matters

ASPECT	ASK YOURSELF	WHY IT MATTERS	TIPS AND TO-DO'S
Priming Students Appropriately	What can I do to help set students up for making the most of this self-driven formative feedback experience I want them to engage in?	What teachers do matters for student learning, but what students do themselves matters even more.	Reassure students, "You're new at this. You're learning it! You're not supposed to know it and be able to do it skillfully *yet*—that's what we're working on." Remind them how they got good at something they love and how they choose to do it in their free time now (e.g., video games, singing, playing an instrument, rock climbing). Help them make connections between places they self-assess in the real world and what they're working on for your class.

(Continued)

(*Continued*)

ASPECT	ASK YOURSELF	WHY IT MATTERS	TIPS AND TO-DO'S
Calling Attention to the Process, Not Only the Product	How much and how often do I foreground that we are focused on learning how to learn (i.e., teaching for transfer) and not only on learning the knowledge and skills of this unit?	As much as we love and want all our students to do well in our subject area, it is our responsibility to help them better learn how to learn. We are helping prepare them for life beyond our subject area.	Ask students to monitor their effort and attention as they are working in class, not retrospectively (i.e., interrupt them strategically). Have them journal, log, and talk with a partner about process goals (e.g., moving from first drafts to the next steps). Provide sentence starters for students to use to monitor progress before the final deadline.
Helping Students Understand Success Criteria	If students *aren't* familiar with the success criteria, what will they get out of this self-driven feedback process/procedure/routine I am planning? If students *are already familiar* with the success criteria, what will they get out of this self-driven feedback process/procedure/routine I am planning?	Self-assessment and self-driven formative feedback protocols/routines can be a way students become more familiar with specific success criteria. When students understand success criteria, their self-assessment tends to become more accurate. Using increasingly accurate assessments (whether they come from the teacher, a peer, themselves, or someone else) is an essential part of students being able to generate sensible feedback for themselves.	Exemplars, exemplars, exemplars! Structure formal and informal ways for students to interact with these worked examples from previous semesters. Create activities for students to get to know success criteria that are social and interactive. Invite students who generate effective self-driven formative feedback to share gems with the class. Support a culture of "I find this works for me" or "I also got stuck here and then I did this."
Paring Language Down	Where can I trim the language load down for students in this self-driven feedback process?	Because what you're asking students to do is already cognitively demanding, it helps to address relevant academic language and to eliminate extraneous information not germane to the task or project.	Provide sentence starters. Focus students' attention on the top task priorities only. Offer a concrete tool such as a progress guide to help students engage in self-assessment and offer assistance on its specific uses.

A key idea to take away from Table 4.1 is related to the second aspect listed in the left-most column, "Calling attention to process, not only the product." We hope you'll agree that an effective use of a teacher's efforts during class time is to thoughtfully and strategically intervene with students *as they are working* on a task or project. At key junctures, on occasion, we need to call our students' attention to monitoring their effort and attention. Remind them with cues and prompts: "Hey, everybody, time for a project check-in. Write down two things you need to do next and one thing you feel stuck on at the moment."

This suggestion is supported by empirical research (Panadero et al., 2012). Such thoughtful, brief, in-class interruptions may help students take heed of their own cognitive and social-emotional (sometimes called *noncognitive*) processes. Likely, such gentle but strategic interruptions will support students in learning to better self-regulate, particularly when it comes to engaging in new and complex academic performance tasks. No one is born knowing how to write a lab report or build a software code or hurl a discus. We all need help learning how to assess how we are doing at key junctures with these complex tasks.

We know that interventions to support students' self-regulation of learning can have a positive effect on students' achievement (Dignath et al., 2008; Jansen et al., 2019). As teachers, we can play a unique role in helping our students become agents who drive their feedback. Eventually, self-driven formative feedback will become second nature as our students learn to do it for themselves.

What the Research Tells Us

Formative feedback to oneself—self-driven feedback—requires lots of self-assessment opportunities that promote students' knowledge and skill development (Andrade, 2018; Tan & Wong, 2018; Wong, 2017). Much of the research on self-assessment focuses on the accuracy or consistency of students' self-assessments. Perhaps unsurprisingly, students' self-assessments tend to be inconsistent with judgments by external—and more expert—evaluators (Admiraal et al., 2015; Baxter & Norman, 2011; De Graz et al., 2012). Age and maturity are factors in keeping students' judgments on target. We also know that high school and college students who are more academically inclined are more accurate in their self-assessments (Alaoutinen, 2012; Hacker et al., 2000; Lew et al., 2010).

Recent self-assessment research has turned toward students' perceptions of the processes behind self-assessment routines (van Helvoort, 2012; Wong et al., 2019). Teenagers moving toward adulthood enjoy being involved in formative aspects of self-assessment. They perceive the feedback gathered from self-assessment activities as useful to the extent that this feedback reduces anxiety and helps to set expectations. Younger students tend to have unsophisticated understandings of the purposes of self-assessment (Bourke, 2016; Brown & Harris, 2013). This doesn't mean they shouldn't be expected to generate and be supported in generating formative feedback for themselves, however. It merely reminds us to take a developmental perspective on who is ready to self-assess more readily than another.

Recent meta-analytic research tells us that interventions focused on supporting student-initiated formative assessment practices, which include students generating formative feedback for themselves, make a greater difference to student learning than interventions designed to promote teachers' formative assessment practices (Lee et al., 2020). A key takeaway is this: While of course what *teachers do* matters for student learning, what *students do* with peer and teacher feedback matters even more. Supporting students to generate their own formative feedback regarding their draft work products and performances aligns with this finding. But let's not forget: Teachers are always the guides on the side even in exemplary feedback-rich classrooms where students appear to be driving their own feedback processes.

Essential Self-Driven Feedback Practices Supported by Research

Keep It Formative, *Truly*

- Always have students self-assess and generate feedback for themselves formatively, when they still have plenty of opportunity to improve their work.

Familiarity With Success Criteria Matters

- Avoid having students attempt to generate content-, domain-, and task-specific self-driven feedback too early, before they are familiar with the success criteria.

Scaffold Students Through the Process

- Take care to support novices (who may not have much prior knowledge about and expertise in the task at hand) through the processes of self-assessment and generating formative feedback for themselves. Use tools, organizers, and sentence starters to model the way.

Give Yourself and Others Permission to Model

- It's okay to be the guide on the side. The cognitive processing skills required for self-assessment are not innate; they are learned in the company of others. Show videos, movie clips, and social media examples of people engaged in self-driven feedback.

> My music coach was fond of telling their students—and they said it often—"Work smarter, not harder." Self-driven feedback routines are about helping our students do just that: Commit to smart, micro-adjustments you can make now. Chunk it if you have to.
>
> —Stefan, high school music teacher

Research also supports these approaches to guiding and aiding novices who are learning to self-assess their work-in-progress.

Teachers Can Set Everyone Up for Success in These Four Ways:

Chunk It

- Structure complex tasks into shorter cycles of goals, performance, and self-reflection (Panadero, Brown, et al., 2016).

Provide Focus

- Focus students' attention on evaluating one component of a work product's quality at a time (e.g., examine only the structure of an essay's argument rather than considering several components at once; Andrade et al., 2008).

Attend to Process

- Bring attention to process, not only the product. Ask students to monitor their effort and attention *as* they are engaged in working, not after the fact (Lui & Andrade, 2022; Panadero et al., 2012).

Use Tools and Scaffolds

- Teach students explicitly about self-assessment and guide their practice with tools and scaffolds such as progress guides, rubrics, checklists, scripts, and prompts (Andrade & Valtcheva, 2009; Nielsen, 2014; Panadero, Johnsson, et al., 2016).

Focus on Practice Reimagined: Looking Backward and Looking Forward at the Case of Central Park East Secondary School

Self-regulation comes in many forms—some of it spoken, some of it written, some of it nonverbal, which we address in the **modalities** chapters (Chapters 8, 9, and 10). For now, let's remember, when students tell themselves, "I need to slow down," or "I need to just relax, and try to explain myself," or even when they decide to move themselves to a quieter location to focus better, they are exercising a skill/disposition toward self-driven formative feedback.

Encouraging and scaffolding self-regulation reaps multiple rewards. Students who have been coached into practicing self-regulation over many years, particularly in middle and high school, are poised to gain more from self-directed feedback processes and their own attempts to generate content-specific feedback for themselves and others.

In this "Focus on Practice Reimagined" section, we hear from educators who help coach students for practicing self-regulation at a nationally recognized secondary school in the U.S. Our reconstruction is based in part on what we know about self-regulation from research literature today and in part on what we know from teaching at the school when these powerful examples were on display at a high school in District 4 in New York City (Bensman, 2000; Darling-Hammond et al., 1995; Meier, 1995).

Situated in Harlem and serving the area's youth, Central Park East Secondary School (CPESS) offered a progressive, **constructivist learning approach** to economically and politically marginalized students. The school's learning goals reached beyond conventional questions of subject content mastery, as measured by standardized Regents exams at the time, and included goals such as readiness to graduate from high school; attend a four-year college; find a productive, meaningful career; and engage in civic life. Duckor and Perlstein (2014) write:

> CPESS served as the flagship of American secondary school reform. School founder Deborah Meier's *The Power of Their Ideas* and Frederick Wiseman's documentary *High School II*, along with the reports of countless visitors, touted CPESS's achievements, and educators and reformers across the nation sought to replicate the school. (p. 3)
>
> With a "waiver" from New York's Regent's diploma requirements, CPESS and a growing number of small public schools were able to pursue educational reforms that emphasized personalization, critical thinking, real-world experience, and respect for the individual child. CPESS's influential backers included the Center for Collaborative Education and the Coalition of Essential Schools, and supporters ranged from newspaper tycoon and Reagan administration insider Walter Annenberg to the stalwart liberal senator from Massachusetts, Ted Kennedy. (p. 3)

In the decade-and-one-half following CPESS's 1985 founding, a teacher-designed and teacher-implemented assessment system played a central role in the school's efforts to re-center assessment and accountability. Learning by doing became synonymous with assessing by doing.

What was less known to outside policymakers and observers was the central role of the habits of heart in the learning environment at places such as CPESS, Fannie Lou Hamer Freedom High School, and the Coalition of Essential Schools (Meier, 1995; Meier & Schwartz, 1995; Palladino & Shepard, 2022; Sizer, 1996). Care, compassion, and respect for the learner's ability to learn at CPESS (what we now see as essential to self- and co-regulation) stood at the fore of teacher, peer, and student exchanges in these middle and high schools. Self-assessment, something we would never have called it at CPESS, was nonetheless a key feature of the school's equity-focused assessment practice.

Having read about CPESS through the eyes of others (Darling-Hammond et al., 1995), we notice that researchers correctly focused on portfolios and **rubrics** and the role of graduation committees in assessing the accomplishments of CPESS graduates. These thick descriptions of the work from these well-researched accounts, documentaries, and stories are invaluable to remembering what made schools such as CPESS special in an era of assessment innovation and locally controlled, school-based accountability prior to No Child Left Behind and the Every Student Succeeds Act.

In this chapter, we will more closely examine the turns of talk and self-driven feedback exchanges that show schools and classrooms where students are in the habit of saying aloud, "I just need to relax and try to explain myself," or the all-too-familiar "I understand it but I can't explain it." Each statement is self-assessment in action. To better understand what students are conveying in these moments, we will take the time to unpack student talk with these vignettes.

Reimagining Conversations in an Urban School Community With a Well-Grounded System of Support

We would like to begin with conversations that faculty had about a student named Betty (all names in this example are pseudonyms). Let's consider how these educators collaborated to recognize the individuality and value of each of their students, all of whom had a unique story, personal history, and set of positive **assets** as human beings.

Among those educators was Manny, a resource room teacher who was charged with student **individualized education plans** (**IEPs**) and 504 plan documentation and who also served as an academic advisor and informal tutor/coach at CPESS. There was also a ninth/tenth-grade math/science teacher named Debbie, who had worked at the school since its inception and shared many perspectives on her students. Debbie had an **advisory** at CPESS and served as an assistant coach for girls' basketball. In this reconstructed vignette, Manny and Debbie tell us about how they support Betty, a sophomore at CPESS.

Betty learned when she came to high school that she would get stressed easily by deadlines, particularly for big projects and assignments. The nearer the deadline, the more stress Betty would feel. While Betty saw shutting down as normal, to the outside world, her shutting down looked like defiance and having an attitude. Betty's teachers had talked with one another about this. Everyone acknowledged that Betty needed space sometimes. One strategy they agreed to use was giving her space to work through something by herself in the classroom alone or with a peer.

Manny, the resource room teacher charged with supporting Betty and several of her classmates, explained it like this:

MANNY: Betty is a real firecracker and always has been. Ever since she came to us, she's made a real big impression. She gets frustrated easily. And shows it! We also know she wants to achieve and be successful. We see her drive. She puts it all out there. Just like she does on the basketball court. What appears as attitude and disrespect, though, when she feels frustrated, threatened, or even just confused by her own feelings, is actually more complicated.

We all know she needs support. Sometimes, the best way to provide that support is to teach her how to support herself. So all the teachers in her cohort agreed that there are a few basics to help her get back on track: Give her time and space to cool off, let her work with a buddy, and trust that she won't give up.

We also have been working with Betty on relaxing and taking a breath when she feels angry at her situation. Sometimes Betty uses other cues. For example, we've coached her to say to herself, "This is doable. Just not all at once. One thing at a time."

Our community understands that many kids are like Betty. They go through cycles and waves of emotion when they're engaged in hard work in the classroom. Encouraging self-driven feedback—having them pay attention to what they're telling themselves in the moment—helps. We want to give all our students the tools, cues, and scaffolds they need to cool off and work out what they need to—on their own terms.

But we're always there to help. Betty needs her study buddy. She needs her check-ins with her teachers. And she needs her own progress guide connected to the project rubric so that she knows she's on track.

Teaching Betty how to support herself requires that we all learn when what we have to say is useful and when we have to sometimes allow her to work through her own process. The word *process* is key because it reminds us that whatever roadblocks or stumbling blocks are in front of the learning situation, Betty will move through them.

Sometimes it only takes a gentle nudge from her classmates, like when Danni, her study buddy, tells her, "Don't throw that away. You can use this," or when Debbie, Betty's teacher, tells her, "I see the words there, but I need you to give me some evidence. Back it up," using a firm but respectful tone of voice.

Now, we'd like to revisit a reconstructed feedback-driven conversation that exemplifies the power of self-driven feedback in the company of others. We have changed the names and created composite conversations in order to better unpack the approach to formative feedback in the school. You can watch the following video for more context.

In the following reconstruction, we imagine how Debbie, Betty's science teacher, relates her experiences with Betty and how different **configurations** of feedback help her to succeed with her least-favorite subjects: math and science. No configuration stands alone. Peer-to-peer feedback is critical, notes Debbie, as it provides a safe space for Betty to self-assess as part of what experts call *co-regulation*. Regardless of the terminology, teachers like Debbie recognize that we're all here to support and give space to students like Betty in our community.

WATCH THIS

Graduation by Portfolio

Please use the QR code above and watch the video starting at 9:12. You can stop the video after 14:32.

DEBBIE: Betty gets frustrated, like a lot of kids, especially when they're pushed to explain how they know something. At CPESS, we value evidence not just in science class, but in all our classes. We're always asking, "How do we know? What's the evidence?" Kids know they have to back up a claim.

Like this morning, when Betty showed me what she had written up so far for her sound **exhibition**. I told her, "You've got to write it so that it makes sense to you." She wanted to be done with the assignment, but it wasn't there yet. I know she's capable of more. I told her, "You've got the words in there, but it doesn't look to me like you've really internalized it, that you fully understand."

Betty pushed back at me, completely frustrated, "I understand it! But I can't explain it!"

So I gave her some space. But I wasn't that far away. Betty worked with Danni, her study buddy. I overheard Danni telling her, "Don't throw that away because you can use that. Just word it differently. And put in the equations and explain it."

I love it when students tell each other what we'd tell them. It's great when it comes from a classmate.

Betty really is putting into practice her self-regulation tactics. We have evidence! This morning I heard Betty say out loud to herself—and to Danni, sitting next to her—"Wait, wait. I want to explain the formula first. I just have to relax and try to explain myself. Wait." Betty was literally naming her next step and calming herself down.

I was so proud of her.

As we reimagine the possibilities and practices aimed at supporting students' ways of self-regulating, particularly when we assume all students can and will take up the task of self-assessment, let's slow down and rethink our assumptions. Here is a quick set of questions anyone committed to self-assessment for diverse groups of students might ask:

- How well do we know students like Betty? What is her story and history as a learner at our school?

- How will our contexts for learning embrace Betty's culture, gender identity, race/ethnicity, sexual orientation, age, and personality?

- What do we need to know and ask as we check in with Betty so that she feels more—not less—empowered to engage in self-reflection? What do we need to know and ask as she learns to assess her draft work and next steps?

Now, more than ever, educators need to rethink how new developments (beyond buzzwords and slogans) might have augmented the work at schools such as CPESS. But we also must consider whether these new terms and concepts are in fact an advance of the wisdom of practice (Shulman 1986, 1987) from schools like CPESS.

Having taught at the school in the 1990s, we know that students at CPESS used an overarching rubric based on the habits of mind for every major course assignment in every subject. Whether these artifacts and tools led to better forms of co-regulation we do not know. Looking back, we do wonder if some students might have benefited from a work-in-progress guide tied to these rubrics to help them track and write down next steps. Could progress guides have made a difference—in terms of self-regulation and co-regulation—for those students who struggled more than Betty with the complex, challenging task demands over the unit?

In this new scenario, we imagine students other than Betty and Danni working together and by themselves with opportunities to self-assess their **first drafts**. We ask, in focusing on different parts of the rubric for the sound exhibition (aided by a progress guide to unpack a key aspect of the performance), could students have started circling places where they felt stuck, giving the teacher more information about emerging patterns and trends? We saw in the *Graduation by Portfolio* video how Betty thought her draft was okay and how she got frustrated when others pointed out it needed more work.

We ask with the benefit of hindsight: What if Betty had the opportunity to make some notes on her draft and did some self-assessment with a progress guide *before* these encounters with peers and the teacher? Would that process have prepared her for what others observed and had to say? Or perhaps she was fine with the process and didn't need that extra scaffolding and support.

For many students, there is not enough time during class to carry out the work on the next steps we imagine as teachers. Students can use a scaffold such as a progress guide to remind them where their work currently is (at which approximate level) and what are options/steps to close the gap to improve the first draft performance. Importantly, these tools and scaffolds allow paraprofessionals and resource room support providers to serve as guides on the side who are in alignment with clear **learning criteria** and subject-mastery goals. Everyone needs guidance on where the student is and what may be next to advance.

Scaffolds and Guided Practice for Students and Teachers

A Scaffold That Supports Student Self-Assessment and Self-Driven Formative Feedback: The Role of Progress Guides in Supporting Self-Regulation

In this section, we introduce you to the concept of a progress guide and offer guidance on using them with your students to support self-driven formative feedback processes in your classes. First, we define what a progress guide is. Then, we illustrate with an example of a progress guide from a middle school social science class. Finally, we offer suggestions and guidance on using progress guides (in paper and digital form) to support self-driven formative feedback practices with your students.

> Progress guides are great at orienting the whole class. Everyone has a place. Sometimes you find yourself adding more levels to include abilities and assets and next steps you didn't imagine. Students help you to rethink what progress means and revise your own thinking!
>
> —Jorge, sixth/seventh-grade math teacher

What Is a Progress Guide?

A *progress guide* is a tool (typically a graphic organizer or handout) that assists in orienting students toward next steps and focuses them on formative feedback (Duckor & Holmberg, 2017). A progress guide helps students (and teachers, who create key features of any progress guide) to identify and work within a student's ZPD with a task. A progress guide describes a continuum of possible current performance levels with a task.

A progress guide is a supplement to a rubric. Typically, a progress guide focuses on only one strand of an analytical rubric (e.g., weighing evidence). In this way, a progress guide *does not* aim to be comprehensive in terms of describing *all* possible progress related to an important performance task; rather, a progress guide is much more strategically prioritized, streamlined, and student friendly.

A progress guide *does* aim to be comprehensive in the sense that it accommodates and aims to be helpful to *all* students, no matter where their current performance is on the evolving continuum. This includes students at the topmost and bottommost levels/ramps on a progress guide.

A progress guide helps students answer the following questions:

- Where is my current work/performance on a continuum?

- What are concrete, specific next steps I can take to move my current work into the next level of performance?

- What formative feedback will help me achieve this next level of performance?

Teachers can develop and support students in using more than one progress guide during a unit. For example, students may use one progress guide on weighing evidence and another progress guide for writing conventions.

A key feature of progress guides is that they *do not* include numbers, points, or scores.

A Progress Guide From a Middle School Classroom: Tools for Guiding the Process of Self-Driven Feedback

We illustrate the concept of a progress guide for helping students self-assess and generate next steps with an example from a sixth-grade social science class. Students in this class were engaged in a unit on the Dust Bowl and its causes. They were in the process of revising and expanding their first draft responses to the prompt, "After reading, viewing, and discussing articles and the video about the Dust Bowl, would you agree or disagree with this statement: *The Dust Bowl was a man-made problem with man-made solutions?*"

Since students' skills at weighing evidence were the top priority at the time, you'll see that the progress guide focuses on that element. By using this progress guide, students are invited to identify the level (using "I can" statements) that best describes their present draft and then are prompted to write down ("one or two") specific next steps needed to advance their work to the next level.

The power of the progress guide resides in its simple yet direct message to all learners: "To improve my draft, I will . . ."

There are many formal and informal ways to set up self-driven feedback loops in our classrooms. Sometimes we want to encourage **sentence starters** and **priming agreements** about how to handle stressors, anxiety, and uncertainty with the task or project. Other times, we want to put attention on the formative evaluation tools and protocols we use to advance our subject content–based understandings individually and in groups.

Progress guides allow many students to do both formally and informally. The message of the progress guide is this: You are working to improve your draft as you self-assess, and together we can figure out how to get to the next level with concrete actions.

Depending on the subject content in the unit, the aims of the project or performance task, and the cross-cutting skills, we must decide how much scaffolding and support will be needed to engage students in the self-driven assessment process.

But we must remind ourselves and our students—again and again—even as they engage in self-driven feedback practices and routines: We are not alone; you are not alone. Rather, we self-assess to get started. Then we peer assess in pairs and small groups to get more help figuring out where we are currently. And last but not least, we can at any time during the lesson call upon the knowledge of others (teachers, advisors, paraprofessionals, after-school program staff, and/or district support staff) as we work together to decide how to get to the next draft or redo/replay the task, assignment, or project.

Figure 4.3 Progress Guide for Students to Self-Assess and Generate Next Steps for Causes of the Dust Bowl: Understanding and Weighing Evidence

CAUSES OF THE DUST BOWL: UNDERSTANDING AND WEIGHING EVIDENCE	
My Current Draft Demonstrates (Circle One)	My Next Steps Are
I can weigh evidence.	To improve my draft, I will . . . 1. 2.
I can add some evidence.	To improve my draft, I will . . . 1. 2.
I can take a position.	To improve my draft, I will . . . 1. 2.
I can restate the prompt.	To improve my draft, I will . . . 1. 2.
I'm not yet ready.	I need to meet with . . . to get started.

Available for download at **resources.corwin.com/ContinuousImprovement**

Suggestions on Using Progress Guides to Support Self-Driven Formative Feedback

Suggestion #1:

Before using a progress guide to assist your students in generating self-driven formative feedback, we recommend first familiarizing yourself and your department or team with its key features by studying Figure 4.4.

Figure 4.4: Key Features of a Progress Guide for Students to Self-Assess and Generate Next Steps

---

Key Features

- ❏ Is written in student-friendly language
- ❏ Has an appropriate number of levels (accommodates all levels of performance a teacher reasonably expects to see in their class)
- ❏ Is oriented vertically
- ❏ Uses age-appropriate graphic cues for identifying levels ("Circle the image that best describes . . .")
- ❏ No points or scores!
- ❏ Uses a first-person point of view: "I . . ."; "My draft . . ."
- ❏ Uses sentence starters appropriate to language learners
- ❏ Has age-appropriate amounts of space for students to fill in responses

---

Suggestion #2:

- ▶ Provide plenty of time and support the first time you expect students to use a progress guide. Make it an in-class activity. Prepare students with an I Do, We Do, You Do routine, as you might with other lessons.

- ▶ Orient students to how and why a progress guide is laid out the way it is (up/down, left/right).

- ▶ Talk about why they are first self-assessing (identifying the level that best describes their present work) and then have them generate formative feedback for themselves (writing down one or two specific next steps they think could advance their work to the next level).

- ▶ Be sure to circulate to not only help your students but also to learn from them. What they may be struggling with might surprise you!

Suggestion #3:
During the inaugural use of a progress guide with your students, make notes of how you may need to revise it.

- ▶ Would adding another level or two help?

- Was there some language that tripped up students?
- How could you revise it based on your students' feedback?
- What revisions to the right-hand column (the "Next Steps" column) would be helpful?

> ### Try It Tomorrow
>
> Making Student Self-Assessment Progress Guides Student Friendly
>
> Suggested Next Steps in the Form of Check Boxes
>
> Sometimes it helps to make a progress guide for student self-assessment "student friendly." This can be done by offering easy-to-select "next steps." A sixth-grade math teacher we worked with, Mr. Cheng, decided his students could benefit from suggested next steps in the form of check boxes.
>
> | Next Steps |
> | --- |
> | **To go even deeper, I will...**
 ☐ Create a graph and label the X and Y axis correctly
 ☐ Show my answer on the graph using ordered pairs |
> | **To improve my work, I will...**
 ☐ Use sentence frames to explain my answer using words |
> | **To improve my work, I will...**
 ☑ Review my notes
 ☑ Review LCD and equivalent ratios |
> | **To improve my work, I will...**
 ☐ Review my notes
 ☐ Review LCD and Equivalent ratios
 ☐ Use sentence frames to explain my answer using words |
> | **To improve my work, I will...**
 ☐ Make time to meet with the teacher |
> | **I need to...**
 ☐ Ask a classmate or teacher what I missed |

Try It Tomorrow

Voxer or Other Audio Messaging Applications

Voxer is a walkie-talkie messaging app for smartphones that features live voice, text, and photo sharing. There are other apps such as Hey Tell, Zello, Zulip, Telegram X, and LINE. Some are proprietary and have a cost, others are offered for free. Your school district likely has a policy on app use and may offer other tech solutions for communicating information. We don't endorse these products—we only point to how they can, when used appropriately, change how feedback is produced and exchanged in the 21st century classroom.

You can use this voice recording tool to let students self-assess their ideas and assignments and float possible next steps. Consider sending recordings to parents so they can hear how their students are doing and perhaps even give their student feedback. For students who would prefer to speak their thoughts rather than write them out, Voxer or other similar apps can be used in place of completing written scaffolds to support self-driven feedback.

Show them. Model it. *I Do, We Do, You Do* is the self-assessment motto in my classroom now. Give them a chance to practice this new skill and watch them take to the progress guide like naturals. I did and it changed our school's idea of assessment.

—Alex, seventh/eighth-grade science teacher and department lead

Try It Tomorrow

Google Docs on a Project

Self-assessment using a progress guide with Google Docs is easy. While you've got a progress guide projected where all can see it, help your students make connections to it and the task at hand. Show them where to add comments and next steps, and how to circle the current level with a cursor. You can comment on their self-assessments and annotate later. It's a running record that everyone (including parents/guardians, paraprofessionals, and instructional support staff) has access to down the road.

Setting Goals and Monitoring Progress With Self-Driven Feedback: Questions for Lesson Study and Professional Learning Communities

In your **professional learning community (PLC)**, consider the different scaffolds/tools you're using to support self-driven feedback.

1. Have volunteers who have brought a scaffold/tool that supports students' self-assessment with a performance task introduce it by sharing

   - its primary purpose,
   - how students use it,
   - what, if anything, they'd like to change about it, and
   - its best feature.

2. Give plenty of time for group questions and answers (Q&As) regarding each scaffold/tool.

3. Reflect as a group on how the scaffolds/tools are aligned with the goals of self-driven feedback?

   a. How accessible are these scaffolds/tools to **English learners**?

   b. Are there any modifications for students with special needs?

4. What do the scaffolds/tools for self-driven feedback practices seem to prioritize? Is there a pattern?

5. Discuss what kinds of scaffolds/tools you would like to see shared in a future PLC meeting.

6. Before closing, have each member share aloud what they learned and/or are excited about trying with/adapting for their students.

In the "Focus on Practice Reimagined" section, you read how Manny (a special educator) and Debbie (a math/science educator) had a conversation about Betty, a **focus student**. The inspiration for this vignette/reconstructed conversation was based on an actual documentary, *Graduation by Portfolio*, which shows Betty engaged in self-driven feedback practices in the ninth/tenth-grade science classroom while working with her peers and teacher throughout the 90-minute block. (Betty's school uses **block scheduling**.)

Let's return to today's special educators and lead teachers who, like Manny and Debbie, are fortunate to work with colleagues well-versed in the theme of deep equity and **continuous improvement** plans (California Collaborative for Educational Excellence [CCEE], 2019; Coburn, 2003; Fullan & Quinn, 2015) at their school site. They've decided to use a **fishbowl** technique to dive deeper into equity: At the next staff meeting, a few instructional leads work to help others figure out how to connect with a focus student, who has an IEP. In the fishbowl, a person talks about working with "Yesmina" (the real student's name is not always used, depending on a school's context and policy). The instructional lead talks about how the focus student typically gives and takes up feedback as a learner. The fishbowl session always offers an academic background, a developmental context, and a review of the assets/strengths the focus student brings before moving toward any challenges and/or concerns. Usually, one or two other teachers who have had success with the focus student add to what has been working well with offering feedback and what mistakes they've learned to avoid. The goal is to deepen the relationship with the **focal student** (and others like her) in part by bringing out the best in her work. Feedback is a window into ways of building more concrete, strategic support for student success at the school.

Here are some guiding questions to support collaborative work unpacking feedback practices that empower focal students to move forward with challenging academic projects, performance tasks, and long-term assignments (both within and across departments).

> **WATCH THIS**
>
> **Graduation by Portfolio**
>
> Please use the QR code above and watch the video starting at 9:12. You can stop the video after 14:32.
>
> Please also see the Appendix at the end of this chapter.

For a Department- or Subject-Specific PLC

1. As a group, after watching the *Graduation by Portfolio* video, come up with two or three observations about Betty's composure during the formative feedback exchange.

2. Discuss: How does she seem to internalize others' feedback? When does she offer self-regulation techniques as part of that process? What are others doing to encourage her to reflect on the draft or task?

3. How would you characterize students like Betty in your classrooms as they try to take up formative feedback? Make a

list of what is working and what isn't. Compare how it may differ from Betty's experience in this formative feedback exchange.

4. What role, if any, does directionality (teacher, peer, and self) seem to have with what's working for Betty? Brainstorm how to build on wins. In other words, what might be some additional, alternative ways of fostering agency for students like Betty who are learning to self-assess and feel safe enough to do so in the company of others?

5. Commit to change: As a result of your PLC's discussion so far, consider and then share out to the group how you will be striving to change what you do regarding self-assessment routines and formative feedback practices. Consider what's next with department-level projects or standard performance tasks embedded across each classroom. Be specific.

6. *Bonus/Extension Activity:* Create a few progress guides aligned with a shared rubric to help orient your students and faculty/staff toward this practice.

For PLCs Across Many Departments and Subject Disciplines

1. Explain why self-driven feedback matters. For whom does it matter? (If you are focused on **opportunity gaps** for special education or youth experiencing homelessness or youth in foster care at your school, try to imagine why feedback matters from each perspective.)

2. Share out what you think is the most important advice about self-driven formative feedback across classrooms, labs, the theater, playing fields, and any other relevant learning settings. Why must soccer players, musicians, historians, scientists, and others know how to self-assess? In which contexts or parts of their careers should they self-assess?

3. Brainstorm what you want all new teachers in the building to know about the power of self-driven feedback from the perspective of equity. Try to take the viewpoint/perspective of a classroom teacher, a coach, a paraprofessional, or a counselor, for example.

4. Compare: To what extent did teachers of different subject areas or staff perspectives or even learning settings (field, classroom, lab, studio, theater) at the school influence how we see the possibility of feedback directionalities?

5. Make a list of five core feedback practices that exemplify the value of self-assessment for everyone at the school. Imagine it will be a poster placed everywhere students, staff, and teachers interact on your campus. When students come into the learning spaces you offer, have them stop, read, and tell you why a particular practice/value matters for them today or this week.

6. Commit to change: As a result of your PLC's discussion so far, consider and then share out to the group how you will be striving to change what you do regarding formative feedback that elevates self-regulation and self-assessment practice. Be specific.

7. *Bonus/Extension Activity*: Create a few progress guides for assessing progress with self-assessment aligned with good feedback techniques, cues, and moves to help orient your community toward this practice. Ensure that students self-assess at the beginning and end of a signature project or performance task in a few classrooms. Talk about what you all found.

Recap/Review

- Giving oneself formative feedback requires self-assessment. Most human beings want to avoid judging themselves, their work, and their performances in ways that will bruise their ego or lead to hurt feelings.

- Work to normalize what students may consider a negative self-assessment and focus on the power of positive, constructive next steps. Reassure students, "You're new at this, you're learning it. There's time to improve it. You're not supposed to be at mastery level—yet."

- Being able to give oneself helpful content-, domain-, and task-specific formative feedback takes expertise and experience. Scaffolds are needed. So are routines for feedback from peers and teachers in the classroom, lab, theater, or field.

- Zones of proximal development matter for self-assessment. This means knowing where one currently is in the flow of work. Finding the right next step will vary by student. A graphic organizer helps one focus on where one is (at this moment).

- When students are coached to self-regulate, their attempts to generate content-specific self-driven feedback tend to improve.

- Make sure your self-driven feedback routines support student autonomy and encourage independence over time. Over time and with practice, students become better self-assessors.

- Considering what's working with students' self-driven feedback routines (before you or peers offer feedback) can help everyone feel empowered to lean into the project, performance task, or long-term assignment.

Ticket Out the Door

1. Look over the progress guide (Figure 4.3). How might this example support your students at self-assessing and coming up with next steps? Do you think it's likely to work in your class? Who specifically might a progress guide help in your current unit? Think of a focal student and explain why a progress guide may help them.

2. Write down your favorite phrases/cues/signals that you use to remind your students of the value of self-assessing. ("Let's be kind and keep it real—everyone needs a moment to consider 'How am I doing?'") Throw your favorites into a chat or on the board. What do you think will happen?

3. Give a current example from your own life or a project that requires you to self-assess. Tell your students about it and how you are learning to provide feedback to yourself so you don't give up. ("I try to be kind with myself when I hit the gym and keep it real. I tell myself with each station rotation, 'Relax. I've got room to improve.'")

4. True or false: Students can give themselves useful formative feedback even when they don't understand the success/**learning criteria** well. Explain your reasoning to a colleague or friend at your school. Why does understanding success criteria make a difference in how students approach self-assessment in your classroom?

Did You Know? Discourse Analysis Helps Us Look at Feedback Practices

Researchers have long been interested in making turns of talk visible to teachers as they try to study what works. Rather than focus on metrics alone, it can be useful to examine which feedback moves elicit which kinds of responses to actual content in the classroom learning environment. Companies are attempting to provide solutions focusing, for example, on the amount of time spent on feedback or the ratio of teacher-to-student talk. Key to formative feedback practice will be the quality of teacher, peer, and self-assessment talk as it relates to actual subject matter and learning progressions in a domain. (See the Appendix at the end of this chapter for a real-world example.)

Appendix: Unpacking Formative Feedback Moves: A Dialogic Approach to Analyzing Turns of Talk Related to Informal, Short-Turn Cycles of Self-Assessment

We're recreating for you here a scene that occurred at CPESS in the 1990s because it captures a **dialogic** approach to formative feedback. To watch the scene described here, go to minutes 9:12–14:32 of the documentary, *Graduation by Portfolio* (Gold & Lanzoni, 1993).

Let's set the scene. Students in a ninth/tenth-grade integrated science and math class are engaged in uncovering how musical instruments and the properties of sound can be described by equations. This is an active, noisy, non-tracked classroom that respects different ways of uncovering the material of the unit, the main task of which is known as the "sound exhibition." Students are drawing sine waves on the chalkboard, manipulating stringed instruments, working in pairs at computers, and striving to write out and explain their thinking. From the variety of different activities students are engaged in concurrently, it's evident that in this classroom, students are free to pick the primary modality in which they carry out the task they're facing: to identify, describe, and explain (using equations) the phenomena at play in the instrument they have chosen.

In the dialogue we unpack here, we see multiple formative feedback moves in play as two students, Betty and Danni, interact with each other and with their teacher, Debbie. We see Debbie engaged in high-leverage instructional practices:

- seeking evidence of student understanding (by listening in and asking questions)
- holding fast to high expectations
- being flexible
- not being deterred by Betty's pushback and expressions of attitude
- offering a next step, without spelling out the exact, specific content of the next step (that would be doing the work for the student)

We'll unpack the short-turn feedback loops Debbie, Betty, and Danni engage in. First, let's see the moves Debbie makes during whole-class configuration to set the stage for the short-turn formative feedback exchanges she knows will come during class.

While Debbie has everyone's attention, she reminds them of the elements involved in their task: to use equations to explain the phenomena of sound for their chosen instrument for the sound exhibition. These elements include finding frequency, using the symbol *tau* to represent tension, and representing mass per unit length correctly using *m* as they write about their instrument. Betty, we'll soon see, is working with a thumb piano.

Note that Debbie's whole-class interactions set the scene for her to press all her students to elaborate, to expand upon, and to support their reasoning with oral and written explanations. "You owe me the how and why of the pitch changes," she tells them all. "Remember to use these equations," she says, underscoring what she's written on the board. These are **standards**-based learning goals, rooted in the habits of mind framework we discussed in Chapter 1.

Debbie: Okay, but I want to know frequency; how do I find frequency? (*DEBBIE stands at the chalkboard, pointing to an equation that includes* tau *and* m.) All right, any guesses for what this might represent? What might this stand for? (*She is pointing to* tau *in the equation.*)

A student calls out: Tension.

Debbie: Tension, good. The tau is the tension. (*DEBBIE writes on the board, tagging this response, and then pauses.*) What do you think *m* is?

Another student calls out: **Mass.**

DEBBIE is still priming at the board and probing for how *and* why *in this assignment (the sound exhibition).*

Debbie: Yes, but it's not just mass, it's mass per unit length. So as *m* gets bigger, as you use a thicker, heavier string, the wave speed goes down. I want you to work on your sound exhibition, due today. You owe me the *how* and *why* of the pitch changes. Remember to use these equations.

(*The camera settles down on an extended exchange between BETTY and DANNI.*)

Betty (*to her partner, Danni*)**:** I understand, but I can't word it, like. I'm gonna try . . . (*looks down at her notebook and draft paper*). The longer the bar is, the lower the pitch. (*She starts to write.*)

CHAPTER 4. Self-Driven Feedback

Clearly, written explanations are valued in this class, as they are in all the classes at CPESS. We see how Betty feels comfortable verbalizing her present state of struggle ("but I can't word it") and witness her self-regulation ("I'm gonna try . . ."). We don't know exactly what Debbie has done to help make her classroom a place where such spoken feedback to oneself occurs; we highlight that we see Betty's "I'm gonna try" as evidence that sticking with learning is normalized in her classroom.

In this next section, note how Debbie takes time to listen in on how Betty's study buddy, Danni, is trying to help. Note also how Debbie presses Betty to elaborate, to expand upon, and to support her reasoning.

Betty (*reading her work to Debbie, hoping it's right*): The instrument is called a thumb piano. A thumb piano is made up of bars with different lengths. The reason why it has different lengths is so you can create a different pitch. (*BETTY looks up at Debbie.*)

Debbie: Okay.

Betty (*turns to Danni, her study buddy, smiling big*): Uh-hunh. (*meaning, "Yeah, see how I'm on track?!"*) (*BETTY looks down and continues to read from her draft*). The bars are tied on a wooden board, which has a hole in the middle so when you pluck the bars, it hits the wooden board, causing it to vibrate.

Betty (*looks up at Debbie*): Okay. I don't understand, like, where it vibrates, but I know that it makes a sound.

Danni (*jumps in*): It vibrates like this. (*DANNI moves both her hands up and down, opposite of each other, pantomiming vibration.*) And then the hole in there makes like a sound box so it can . . . (*DANNI holds her left hand like she is holding an imaginary softball, presumably representing a sound box, for BETTY.*)

Betty (*talking softly to herself while writing in her notebook*): . . . makes a sound . . .

Danni: Because if you have that thing there, and you hit it, it would vibrate, but you wouldn't hear nothing. (*BETTY picks her head up to look at DANNI at this last part.*)

Betty (*looking at Danni*): The holes . . . ?

Danni: Because it vibrates, the little wood thing vibrates. (*DANNI is looking at BETTY, moving a hand up and down and continues to provide feedback on the explanation.*)

(Continued)

(Continued)

Debbie: Yeah, when the little wood thing vibrates (*holding up her right index finger and moving it up and down rapidly pantomiming vibration*) what does that make vibrate?

Betty: The inside, the . . . (*DEBBIE moves her right hand around in a circle, looking at BETTY, giving body-kinesthetic clues and visual feedback.*)

Debbie: What inside?

Danni: No, it makes the top, the thing that's holding it, vibrate, which makes the whole thing vibrate.

Debbie: Which makes the body vibrate, which makes what vibrate?

Betty: The air.

Danni: (*at the same time as DEBBIE*) air inside the box . . .

Debbie: The air inside the box, yeah. That hole . . .

Betty: You want me to write all that in this paper?!

Debbie: Sure! Yeah, well, part of that you can include in the part . . .

Betty: It vibrates, and then, which makes the sound. The longer the vibrating part, the lower the pitch.

Debbie: Okay, but now I want you to include some of these equations. Now prove it. This is good for general description. This is excellent, okay? (*BETTY smiles.*) Now I want more detail. Give me some evidence, you know. You're just making this statement that, "The longer the vibrating part, the lower the pitch." Now back it up with something. Give me some evidence.

(*DEBBIE leaves the pair. BETTY and DANNI continue working together.*)

When Betty says, "You want me to write all that in this paper?!" she's asking it of Debbie but she's also verbalizing her frustration to herself aloud. It's partly a matter of Betty's new understanding of the success criteria; it's also a form of venting, which is normal and expected for complex work. Debbie is not deterred by the outward expression of emotion; she invites it, as does the whole school. In fact, Debbie is the embodiment of steady encouragement; her calm response to Betty's frustration is a social-emotional scaffold. Supporting students to get better at self-driven formative feedback takes this kind of steadiness and perseverance.

CHAPTER 4. Self-Driven Feedback

The scene then cuts to a student plucking strings on a harp-like instrument. Neither writing nor verbalizing, this student is working through the tension exhibition as a musician might, plucking and poking. It is clear there is space in the classroom to apply a multitude of intelligences to the problem presented by the sound exhibition before having to write or speak about one's writing.

The camera cuts back to Betty and Danni. They are still persisting despite the frustrations and setbacks. After all, this is conceptually difficult material. It is a **higher-order question** with a performance task that draws on many skills.

Betty (*trying to stay positive and using her metacognitive skills*): Wait, wait. I want to explain the formula first. I just have to relax and try to explain myself. Wait. (*to DANNI*) I didn't write that in no way here. All I wrote was that the longer the vibrating part . . .

Danni (*looking at Betty*): Then do it over.

Betty: *the lower the freq—*(*BETTY picks up her paper, starts to fold it in half, and is about to throw it away, but DANNI intervenes. Peer-to-peer feedback provides encouragement and reminders that this is a draft, a work-in-progress, something to reword and revise.*)

Danni: Don't throw that away because you can use that. But just word it differently. And put in the equations and explain it.

Betty: All right. So the shorter the vibration, the lower the pitch. That's what you say right?

Danni: You know, like, yeah, the shorter—No, the shorter the length of your thing, is going to be higher the pitch. Because that's going to be the higher frequency.

Betty: So I did that! (*BETTY picks up her paper and begins reading from her paper with attitude.*) "The longer the vibrating part, the lower the pitch."

Danni (*patiently, to Betty*): Right.

In this last set of turns of talk between Betty and Danni you just read, we see again Betty verbally reminding herself of her goal—to explain the formula first—and speaking out loud about her efforts to self-regulate: "I just have to relax and try to explain myself."

We also see Betty self-assess when she says to Danni (and herself), "I didn't write that in no way here." Self-driven formative feedback encompasses such self-assessments of one's work.

> *The scene cuts back to DANNI and BETTY working together. BETTY is now writing on her draft. She lifts her head and tries to verbalize what she has just written. DANNI jumps in to help.*
>
> **Danni:** Okay, the higher the frequency . . . (*scaffolding with a sentence starter*) the higher the frequency . . . the higher the pitch. (*BETTY is nodding, writing what DANNI says.*)
>
> **Betty:** The higher the pitch.
>
> **Danni:** Exactly. And explain you get a high pitch when you have a little . . .
>
> **Betty** (*volunteers*): Lambda?
>
> **Danni** (*guiding but not telling her what to write*): You have a little length. The length of your thing is going to determine your pitch, right?
>
> **Betty:** Yeah, I just said that. The higher the frequency, the higher the pitch. (*BETTY looks frustrated. Drops her writing hand down quickly onto her notebook.*)

Students' self-assessments of their work are often helped by their interacting with peers about their work. As Betty is working to understand how frequency and pitch are related, she compares what she hears her classmate Danni saying to her with what she's already written. It's in this comparison, self-assessment, and declaration ("Yeah, I just said that") that meaning making is occurring. Danni doesn't seem convinced that Betty has done yet what is required of the task, and Betty herself seems to be expressing frustration (she drops her hand down quickly) that she, too, knows she's not yet confident in what she's writing and what it means.

We also get the sense that Betty has been down this road before, that she knows that by sticking with the process of writing, talking with a classmate, checking in with her teacher, and revising, she will come to an understanding that makes sense to her, her peers, and her teacher.

In this next set of turns of talk, notice how Betty feels it is safe to say to Debbie, "I understand, but I can't explain it." Haven't we all been right where Betty is in that moment?

The camera cuts away again to other students working independently. The classroom appears chaotic; students are seated and unseated. They are making noise, playing with instruments, and talking around the computers.

DEBBIE approaches BETTY and DANNI again. In this scene, DEBBIE is standing next to BETTY, using proximity to soften the feedback. Her hands are gesturing as if to invite BETTY closer. Nonverbal communication is a big part of effective formative feedback that invites uptake from students.

Debbie:	Well, you've got to write it so that it makes sense to you.
Betty:	But it don't! (*Looks up at the DEBBIE.*) Did it make sense?
Debbie:	(*flips BETTY's paper over.*) You've got the words in there. What does not, what doesn't look clear to me, it doesn't look to me like you've really internalized it, that you fully understand.
Betty (*retorts*):	I understand it, but I can't explain it.

Betty, like most of our students, needs time to revise. She needs us as teachers to exercise patience as we are inviting her efforts at self-driven feedback moves. We must allow her to persevere—on her own terms—with respect.

Time passes as the video cuts back to BETTY. By the end of the period, BETTY is shown standing next to DEBBIE, reading from her paper aloud. We only hear a segment of the conversation.

Betty:	The equation length equals n divided by two, which shows that when the length gets smaller, the lambda gets smaller also.
Debbie:	Good.

(Continued)

(*Continued*)

> **Betty** (*continuing to read*): When converting the length to lambda, you can find the frequency by v equals f times lambda. This will show that as the wavelength gets smaller, meaning the length as well, the frequency will get higher, causing the pitch to get higher.
>
> **Debbie:** That is so clear.
>
> *BETTY grins and throws her hands up in celebration, joy on her face.*

Betty crosses the finish line (a first, second, and almost final draft of the sound exhibition) with the help of many, including her table partner and friend, Danni.

CONFIGURATION

CHAPTER 5

Feedback With the Whole Class

> When a teacher provides feedback to students based on the evidence analyzed, the purpose is not to "fix" or "correct" a problem but rather as we engage students' thinking and provide sufficient guidance, without offering a total solution, for the students to take the next steps in learning on their own.
>
> —Heritage & Wylie (2020, pp. 36–37)

There are always students who say they are not ready to receive **feedback** on their work, particularly in front of others. And we remind them: You may not feel ready—yet. But how we talk to our students—with which kind of intention—matters. Our voice and choice of words also matter. Students are attuned to the feedback we offer, particularly in the company of others. Believe it or not, a lot is at stake when we address young people.

It's natural for students to worry about whole-class feedback. In larger classroom **configurations**, feedback can feel like being put on the spot or being lost in a crowd. It's not that students don't want to do what we suggest in front of everyone. It's that the way we communicate counts as much as the communication itself.

Collaboration, teamwork, sharing suggestions with a group of people—these are 21st century skills in action. As a confident expert working with a team, it's your job to remind everyone, "We are working together on a complex but manageable task." It's important your students understand there are no *gotcha*'s or "Why didn't you do that?" questions in your classroom. People in collaborative learning environments aren't being judged; they are being offered new ideas and directions to move the work forward.

Being mindful and patient with the process of **formative feedback** in whole-class configurations (large working groups) is essential because there are always those who need more time and more reassurance to take the next steps together. We have to constantly remind our students to keep their eyes on the prize. We are their guides on the side—together.

Teachers who value formative feedback will put a working definition of formative feedback on the dry-erase board, an electronic page, or a laminated poster for all to see. They know we all need guideposts and road maps. Before the journey begins, have a few students read the following aloud with you, slowly, one sentence at a time:

> Formative feedback is the exchange of information aimed at improving everyone's work on this task/project. Formative feedback is a process that occurs *during* our work as we assess how far we've come and what is next. This feedback occurs during the learning cycle and provides you (the learner) with just-in-time information regarding what's next. Your current work is a draft that requires **continuous improvement** *before* you turn it in for **grading**. Formative feedback can and will come from teachers, peers, and students in our community. Expect the feedback to include written, oral, and/or body-kinesthetic communication. Get ready for formative feedback happening over the next several weeks in different configurations, including whole class, small groups, or one-on-one. You will succeed and grow. Feedback is the way we work together as a class. And don't forget: Use your **progress guides** so you can see what's ahead!

Here is a **move** to consider: Before a whole-class feedback session, ask the whole class: "What's the first thing that comes to mind when you hear or see the word *feedback*?" **Tag** all the responses, and **probe** on a few. Then put "Why feedback?" on the board and tag and **scribe** responses so everyone is **primed** for what is to come. Now the whole class is ready for what is next.

Using a Progress Guide to Support Differentiating Formative Feedback for Equity and Inclusion Before Speaking to the Whole Class

We may not have visible protocols and procedures in place to support, guide, and orient our students to what matters most with respect to feedback sessions for whole-class configurations. But if we are going to offer feedback to the whole class, it's imperative we provide everyone with the tools needed to succeed. This chapter offers a tool called a *progress guide for teacher use* that can help you direct feedback more effectively to who needs it, when they need it. A progress guide for teacher use helps you analyze student work (a set of **first draft** responses, whether in the classroom, on the field, or in the auditorium). These guides help you decide what feedback you need to give to which students in your class.

Moreover, a well-crafted progress guide helps you see patterns in a student's provisional response and group students' draft work by levels. With this more strategic view of response levels, you can also make decisions about next steps during the lesson or for the next day's instruction. The progress levels for grouping responses address where the student's work is at a particular moment in the task cycle. The corresponding "Next Steps/Request" column allows you to offer a customized and systematic set of feedback moves for that particular response level.

Similar to the example from the Dust Bowl unit in Chapter 4, this "Using Evidence" progress guide (Figure 5.1) allows the teacher to see trends by percentages, examine a range of performance by levels, and plan the differentiated feedback students will receive over the cycle of a task. As teachers gain more pedagogical content knowledge (PCK) with the kinds of task responses they expect on the task project or assignment, the "TBD" strategies are filled in and implemented across the unit. Each time the task is offered, modifications and improvements can be made to the progress guide to improve its usefulness.

Figure 5.1 Progress Guide for Teacher Use: Using Evidence to Examine Causes of the Dust Bowl

PERCENTAGE OF CLASS	RESPONSES	NEXT STEPS/REQUEST
Exemplary 5%	▶ Weighs evidence	1. TBD 2. TBD
Advanced 20%	▶ Adds some evidence	1. TBD 2. TBD
Developing 45%	▶ Can take a position	1. TBD 2. TBD
Emerging 15%	▶ Can restate the prompt	1. TBD 2. TBD
Beginning 10%	▶ Not yet ready	1. TBD 2. TBD
Needs another (supported) opportunity to respond 5%	▶ "Not sure," "I don't know," or no response	1. Review the task handout. 2. Identify where to start.
Needs first opportunity to respond 0%	▶ Absent	1. Talk with student about what was missed and next steps. 2. Consider pairing with an on-task student.

online resources Available for download at **resources.corwin.com/ContinuousImprovement**

Teachers, instructional coaches, and administrative leaders talk about equity all the time. We know of few more effective ways to make classrooms more equitable than by increasing the quality and quantity of

differentiated formative feedback. A progress guide will help you differentiate formative feedback to meet *all* your students' learning needs: students who sailed through responding to the task in exemplary fashion, students who struggled with the task in myriad ways, students who may not have struggled but who also need to improve their performance, students who may have scarcely responded to the task, and students who were absent or had trouble starting.

We have learned from personal experience that a progress guide for teacher use supports good teaching practices as much as it does good learning assessment. It allows everyone to share in the work of what is next by setting clear goals. Each goal is well-defined, is accompanied by next steps, and most importantly, can be shared among all sorts of stakeholders in the learning system/environment (e.g., paraeducators, tutors, family/care providers).

Making Whole-Class Feedback Work Best by Knowing What Your Students Know and Can Do at This Moment in the Cycle

Simply put, whole-class configurations of formative feedback are information exchanges that everyone needs to know before breaking into other configurations.

If you're speaking to everyone in your class, your formative feedback needs to apply to every student. Feedback in this configuration often includes teachers sharing anonymous student work/draft examples, soliciting students' thinking about next steps, and modeling how we approach others' work with care and a tone of respect.

If your feedback practices and protocols in this setting fail to reach everyone, it's not an effective use of your time or theirs. Standing at the front of the class and running through a checklist or showing "do this, do that" steps is common but not always helpful.

Instead, whole-class formative feedback should be thought of as an invitation to dialogue with the whole class. It helps when there is a shared **graphic organizer** such as a progress guide to support the different entry points and therefore next steps with the work. At minimum, a teacher needs to check that everyone understands the feedback protocol and that they have an opportunity to ask clarifying questions. This is one of the most common pitfalls of whole-class configurations of formative feedback: presuming that students know what you're talking about and rushing ahead as if they all did.

This chapter launches our exploration of whole-class configurations of formative feedback. Whole-class feedback practices are interconnected with small-group and individual configurations in any feedback-rich learning environment. Finding the balance between each is part of the art of teaching and assessing well.

The following guiding questions anchor our exploration of the power of this approach and the means by which it supports other configurations, which we discuss in Chapter 6 (small groups) and Chapter 7 (individuals). Taken as a whole, each chapter on feedback configurations points to the challenges and opportunities that arise from separating and connecting feedback methods according to the audience, while pointing to the need for well-defined and consistent whole-group feedback practices across a unit of study and within your **lesson plans**.

> ## Guiding Questions
>
> 1. Why plan, enact, and reflect on whole-class configurations of formative feedback? For whose good is this particular type of feedback most helpful? For which educational goals or purposes is this feedback most useful?
>
> 2. What are the conditions necessary to support students in gaining habits and skills related to whole-class configurations of feedback?
>
> 3. Can progress guides or other formative evaluation tools help students get the differentiated formative feedback they need while helping you monitor and respond to trends?
>
> 4. How can I set my students up for success with tools and procedures that tell me where we are in the feedback cycle and which next steps everyone needs to revisit as we move ahead in the project, performance task, or long-term assignment?

Throughout this book, we've been using focal points to unpack and explore formative feedback practices. These are ***directionality***, ***configuration***, and ***modality***.

Configuration refers to the primary arrangements of people in which the formative feedback occurs or is situated. The organizing principle we're using recognizes three configurations for formative feedback dialogues: whole class, small groups, and individual. Figure 5.2 depicts the first of the three lenses for configurations: whole-class formative feedback.

We will anchor our exploration of whole-class formative feedback to a progress guide, one version for teacher use and the other for student use. We do so because such tools are integral to making classrooms more equitable learning spaces and because the research shows that it's important to align feedback with **learning targets** and success criteria.

Now let's define what we mean by formative feedback in whole-class configuration. Then we'll take a look at some of the potential challenges and opportunities as we go deeper.

Figure 5.2 Formative Feedback Framework

Contexts for Learning		
Face-to-Face	Blended	Distance Learning
Focal Point		
Directionality	Configuration	Modality
Lenses		
Teacher-driven	Whole class	Written
Peer-to-peer-driven	Small groups (2–4)	Spoken
Self-driven	Individual (1:1)	Nonverbal
Tasks, Projects, Activities	Learning Goals, Standards, Skills Rubrics, Progress Guides, "Next Steps" Organizers	

Defining Whole-Class Formative Feedback

Configuration refers to the number of students involved in a formative feedback interaction. If the entire classroom's participation (e.g., a **moderation** technique using **exemplars** of student work) is expected during a lesson, then that's *whole-class configuration*.

FORMATIVE FEEDBACK IN WHOLE-CLASS CONFIGURATION

What It Is	What It Isn't
▸ formative feedback with the expectation that every student in the class will be engaged in the process	▸ going over test scores with a class after a test
▸ scaffolded in a visible learning process/segment with tools, roles, and objectives defined	▸ "Keep in mind for next time" advice to all students
▸ the teacher communicating patterns they have noticed about current drafts of (anonymous) student work and making observations about next steps for everyone	▸ a way to avoid giving individualized feedback because "I told you all yesterday at beginning of class what everyone has to do"
▸ the teacher facilitating a whole-class discussion about a common piece of feedback many individual students (or groups of students) have received	▸ only showing an example of an *A* paper or "Excellent" performance to whole class
▸ most often synchronous, but can be asynchronous if delivered to all	▸ giving advice to everyone: "You should all pay attention to how Beth does it"
▸ builds toward another configuration (small group or one-on-one) to ensure different ways to engage students	▸ "Pay attention—you have to turn this in by Friday"
▸ primes students for next steps and asks them for thoughts, concerns, and questions during the feedback session	▸ "Look at the rubric handout"
	▸ "Everyone ask Selene, she's doing it right"

Feedback is about dialogue. Sometimes you feel heard, other times you don't. It is no different for your students. In your approach to formative feedback in the classroom, on the field, in the theater, in the lab, you should consider the following questions:

- Did that work today?
- Who seemed engaged by the feedback example?
- Who still struggled to follow along with the progress guide and how we talked about using it?

We invite you to think about the opportunities and challenges that come with planning, enacting, and reflecting upon feedback practices in whole-class configurations. What will it take to meet those challenges? What will it take to create opportunities that work for your kids?

> If it's worth telling everyone, it's worth checking that everyone understands. Feedback depends on others taking up what we are saying and asking questions. I always say to the kids "Listen up, then listen in." They need space to ask me, "Can you show us that again?"
>
> —Daniel, physical education and algebra teacher

Table 5.1 presents four aspects to consider when planning for formative feedback in whole-class configurations. Use it as a planning guide to determine how different aspects of whole-class feedback will influence your choice of practices and protocols.

One of the most important ideas to take away from Table 5.1 is the need to prioritize the context of the whole-class formative feedback interaction as you are lesson planning. It is essential you consider these two questions about context:

- What percentage of the class does this formative feedback apply to?
- Will students be able to use the formative feedback immediately (or be supported to use it)?

Table 5.1 Planning for Whole-Class Formative Feedback Interactions: What to Consider and Why It Matters

ASPECT	ASK YOURSELF	WHY IT MATTERS	TIPS AND TO-DO'S
Context	What percentage of the class does my formative feedback apply to? Will students be able to/be supported to use the formative feedback immediately?	Students have little incentive to engage if the formative feedback doesn't apply to them. When formative feedback sits in "cold storage," it fades. Examples should represent the range or levels of different performances in the class so everyone sees what's next for them.	• Use a progress guide for teacher use. Use your analysis of student work/performance by level (the leftmost column of the progress guide) to help you determine the content of the whole-class formative feedback interaction you're planning. • Leverage the students who "got it" to help the students who haven't yet demonstrated they've gotten it. • Plan your whole-class formative feedback interactions for the beginning of class and provide time and support for students to implement the feedback during class.
Engaging	How will the whole-class formative feedback process be an active one for students? What am I expecting students to say, write, and do?	Even taking small actions tends to build motivation, which leads to taking more action, which feeds motivation further. Multiple modalities of engagement are better than a single modality.	• Expect and support students to speak about, write about, and take physical actions (as appropriate) related to the formative feedback. • Celebrate even small steps/actions taken because they help build momentum. • Challenge, support, and encourage students to get past the six-minute mark (if students can get into a task/next step for six minutes, they can usually continue in it for two, three, and four times longer).

(Continued)

(*Continued*)

ASPECT	ASK YOURSELF	WHY IT MATTERS	TIPS AND TO-DO'S
Eliciting	What do I expect to elicit from students during this whole-class formative feedback interaction? How will I get students to do this? How will knowing what I hope and expect to elicit help me? How will it help students?	A formative feedback interaction without eliciting an interpretable response from students isn't an interaction; it's dictation. The quality of your decision making depends on what you elicit from students. What you elicit should help students as well, not only you.	▸ Have a system for keeping track of what you elicited from students during the formative feedback interaction. ▸ Verbalizing encourages retention; summarizing your key takeaways back to students is an informal way for you to keep track and review with students at the same time. ▸ Coach students to use the information you have elicited from them to inform their next steps (e.g., when you've elicited from students where they need to focus their attention/effort next, remind them of one or two specific strategies they could try).
Extending	What's going to make it likely that students will take up this formative feedback? How will I know the formative feedback worked?	If formative feedback is offered but no one takes it up, it's not really formative feedback.	▸ Give students class time to implement the whole-class formative feedback immediately. ▸ Let students know you will have them reflect on what it was like to take up the formative feedback. ▸ Celebrate incremental successes along the way.

A progress guide for teacher use (e.g., Figure 5.1) can help you answer the first question by identifying how many students' responses/performances are roughly at each level of performance. This rough estimate of the various levels (of students' current work) informs you of what formative feedback is likely to be most helpful to offer during the whole-class configuration. It guides your choice of examples and brings your potential feedback, including possible next steps, closer to students' **zones of proximal development** (**ZPDs**) with the skills represented in the performance task.

There are many ways to use teacher and student versions of the progress guide. This chapter offers several. However you choose to use it, we hope that you'll also ground what you do in practices informed by research. With that in mind, let's now look at what the educational research can tell us about formative feedback in whole-class configurations.

What the Research Tells Us

Educational researchers exploring formative feedback processes have yet to fully focus on the whole-class variable as compared to small-group or individual interactions. They have either ignored these distinctions or treated them as roughly equal with respect to their influence on student achievement. There are, however, some essential whole-class formative feedback practices **extant** in the literature.

Black et al. (2003) note that questioning and feedback are distinct but interrelated goals of **formative assessment**. Researchers have long held that sharing criteria for success is an essential component of helping orient learners, and such efforts play a crucial role in **self-assessment** and **peer-assessment** protocols inside the classroom. From the teachers' perspective, much of the emphasis in the literature (e.g., Butler, 1987) has been on the type of feedback students get in terms of comments and "marking" (grades). In one study, Black et al. (2003) note,

> Peer- and self-assessment helped the project teachers to make the criteria for evaluating any learning achievements transparent to students, so enabling them to develop a clear overview both of the aims of their work and of what it means to complete it successfully. *Such criteria were sometimes abstract and so concrete examples were used in modelling exercises to develop understanding.* Suitable models were often drawn from other students' work, either from previous years or from the class itself, although these pieces were sometimes modified by the teachers to emphasize particular aspects or the lack of evidence for a specific criterion. (p. 52, italics added for emphasis)

We've known for decades that teachers must introduce, model, and explain features of both the task and the criteria for success. Less emphasis has been placed on how different configurations of feedback over a set of lessons (whole-class, small-group, and individual exchanges) can advance student success with those criteria. **Formative assessors** deploy a range of strategies and tactics to check in with students on their progress. Sometimes there is a need for whole-class feedback before breaking into other configurations to support students more directly, and often one must come back to summarize takeaways and next steps for all.

Essential Whole Class Feedback Practices Supported by Research

Make the Time to Take Up Feedback

- Brookhart (2007) says to plan lessons that include time for taking up feedback during the learning segment.

Align Feedback to Where Students Are in the Learning Cycle

- Formative feedback should be appropriately related to where the students are in the instructional cycle (Hattie & Timperley, 2007).

Teach How to Use the Feedback (i.e., Model Taking Up Specific Feedback, Engage in Role Play, and Use Other Pedagogical Methods to Demonstrate How to Take a Next Step)

- Whole-class configuration can be wisely used to model for students how to take up and use the feedback they've all been given (Brookhart, 2017).

Prepare for Whole-Class Feedback by Using a Scaffold

- Progress guides, scoring guides, and other visible tools allow students to work with teachers on next steps. Researchers (Roberts, Wilson, & Draney, 1997; Wilson & Sloane, 2000) have shown that scoring guides, for example, can be used in whole-class and small-group configurations effectively. These tools allow for focusing on students' zones of proximal development (Shepard, 2000, 2005) while modeling the socio-cultural work of learning to revise one's first draft responses in the learning community.

Unpack Academic Language Together

- Walqui and Heritage (2018) note that structured conversations with clear, visible scaffolds for student talk make a difference for English learners.

Grades and Comments Aren't the Point—Modeling How to Take Next Steps Is

- Effective feedback, must give students a sense of where they are and what they need to do to improve (Duckor & Holmberg, 2017).

More recent meta-analytic research into the effectiveness of feedback done by Wisniewski et al. (2020) explored six moderators of feedback in order to draw some conclusions about the power of feedback. Of the six moderators identified by the experts, three are of particular interest to formative assessors working with feedback:

- *Type of feedback*: reinforcement/punishment, corrective, or high information

- *Feedback channel*: spoken, written, or video/audio/computer-assisted

- *Feedback direction*: by teachers to students, by students to teachers, or by students to students

It is important to note that configurations (whole-class, small-group, or individual feedback exchanges) were not analyzed as moderators in this report. In other words, regardless of the feedback direction, the meta-analysis did not specifically distinguish if, for example, teacher-to-student feedback during whole-class configuration, during small-group work, or during a one-on-one interaction contributes to effect sizes. Nonetheless, we know based on our experiences as teachers and the research in the field that configurations not only matter but they also organically occur as part of classroom assessment practice.

The Case for Differentiating Feedback: Aligning Purposes, Tasks, and Tools

Over the next chapters, we will use progress guide exemplars to show the power of feedback that is grounded in a rich learning task on a unit-level topic that advances the goals of **assessment for learning**. The **prompt**/task is also aligned with clear **standards**-based learning objectives and goals (Nitko & Brookhart, 2019). Each task, project, and assignment—if it is to be formative for the student and teacher—must establish **learning criteria** that help to measure where we are going in the curriculum and larger subject discipline.

In Chapter 1, we highlighted the role that purpose-driven feedback plays in ensuring students receive the feedback they need. We noted that *purpose-driven feedback* is anchored in well-defined competencies, skills, and dispositions; that is, in learning goals for an academic subject. Formative feedback moves learning forward when we clearly and consistently define a set of learning goals (LGs) within and across units of study.

In this example from a unit on climate change in a middle school science class (Figure 5.3), the teacher has carefully articulated and planned a task that will reveal where her students are with the standard and learning targets. Rather than wait for the summative end-of-unit test to **pose** this question, Ms. Davies places this task/prompt in the second week of her course. Ms. Davies gives her students two days to work on the task because, at the end of the first day, after introducing the task/prompt, she collects the first draft to gauge progress. The progress guide for teacher use (Figure 5.4) shows us how Ms. Davies will make sense of and see patterns in the student responses across a range of current performances (or first drafts).

There are a few things to notice about this feedback **scaffold** before moving forward. First, the students and teacher use similar versions of the progress guide to ground their discussion of current work. This allows everyone to see where their draft is along a continuum of task performances and to collaborate on the next steps leading to their finished work. In the student's version, certain columns are slightly modified to encourage more student ownership over the self-assessment process (see Chapter 7). For the teacher, it is important to assess first drafts (or first tries) before handing them back to the students. Observation of these proverbial drafts is key. With this provisional "snapshot" of information, patterns begin to emerge on how the class is going at a particular moment in the project/task cycle. This adds important data to the teacher's approach to feedback and instruction in subsequent lessons.

Figure 5.3 Unit: Climate Change

Lesson Objective

- **Teacher View:** Students will be able to identify the human causes of climate change and their direct impact on ecosystems.

- **Student View:** I will be able to identify human causes of climate change and how they impact ecosystems.

Prompt: Based on what we have talked about today, name at least three causes of climate change and their direct impact on ecosystems.

Prime: "Think back to what we have talked about today. We have had excellent discussion around this topic. We live in a world that is changing with our behavior. What does that change look like?"

Habit(s) of Mind: Relevance and Connections

Depth of Knowledge Level: 2

Learning Target: Students will connect ecosystem changes with behaviors that have contributed to climate change.

California State Standard (Partially addressed):

HS-LS2-6: Evaluate claims, evidence and reasoning that complex interactions in ecosystems maintain relatively consistent numbers and types of organisms in stable conditions, but changing conditions may result in a new ecosystem.

Modality Adjustments

Face-to-Face: Students will write their responses on slips of paper.

Distance/Online Learning: Students will record their responses on a Google form.

In the following example of a progress guide for teacher use in a whole-class feedback protocol, Ms. Davies has collected all available responses to the task/prompt on a Tuesday. She has reviewed the progress of the class with a quick-sort **binning** procedure. That is, she **bins** the drafts into piles on her desk and then uses hash marks in the leftmost column on the progress guide (Figure 5.4) to see the distribution of responses. Within a matter of minutes, Ms. Davies is able to determine which responses roughly fall into which categories by level (converting hashmarks to percentages). A back-of-the-envelope calculation reveals a distribution of students within and across the progress guide.

CHAPTER 5. Feedback With the Whole Class   131

Figure 5.4 Progress Guide for Teacher Use for Binning Student Responses: Causes of Climate Change and Their Effects on Ecosystems Tasks

APPROXIMATE LEVEL	PROMPT RESPONSE	NEXT STEPS
Exemplary 5%	▸ Identifies multiple human causes of climate change ▸ Connects each cause with a specific impact on an ecosystem	▸ Explore further: What are potential solutions to climate change? How can humans change their behavior? How can we reverse the impacts on the environment?
Advanced 20%	▸ Identifies human causes of climate change ▸ Makes weak connections with their impacts on ecosystems	▸ Explore connections between climate change and its impacts ▸ List impacts that identified causes have on existing ecosystems ▸ In what other ways can you connect changes in ecosystems to human behavior? Are there behavior changes that could improve the environment?
Developing 40%	▸ Identifies either human causes of climate change *or* impacts to ecosystems ▸ Makes no connections between the two	▸ Review notes/discussion, list climate change causes or their impacts (depending on which is missing) ▸ Connect identified causes to identified ecosystem impacts ▸ If causes are named, ask "What are the results of these?" *or* if impacts are named, ask "What may have brought upon these changes to the ecosystem?"
Emerging 20%	▸ Names one cause of climate change ▸ May also show major misconception or common p-prim	▸ Refer to notes/discussion: Name additional causes of climate change ▸ Connect those causes to changes in ecosystems ▸ What changes to the environment are due to this cause? Are there other human behaviors that are changing the environment?
Beginning 10%	▸ Attempts by restating prompt or assignment description	▸ Refer to notes/discussion on climate change and its causes ▸ "If you are still confused, ask a classmate for help on where to start." ▸ "If you need additional help, meet with me one-on-one."

(Continued)

(*Continued*)

APPROXIMATE LEVEL	PROMPT RESPONSE	NEXT STEPS
No response yet (present) 0%	▸ "Not sure," "I don't know," or no response	▸ Refer to notes/discussion on climate change and its causes ▸ "If you are still confused, ask a classmate for help on where to start." ▸ "If you need additional help, meet with me one-on-one."
No response yet (absent) 5%	▸ Absent	▸ "I need to talk with you about what was missed and how to get started." ▸ "Let's start by working with another student."

These quick analyses of student work play a key role in setting expectations on what is achievable for the class by the end of the week. More importantly, it gives Ms. Davies a clearer view of the middle range (for example, 40% of the work is "Developing") and the extremes (who is only beginning to engage the task and who can produce an "Exemplary" response).

For each response level, Ms. Davies had determined which kinds and types of next steps she could offer across each configuration by **binning for feedback**. These targeted, actionable next steps informed her choice of teaching and learning activities for subsequent classes as well.

But a major finding was that Ms. Davies needed to carve out time for the whole class to engage together the next day. She would use a sample student response (i.e., Theo's first draft) from the "Emerging" level on the shared progress guide to help focus everyone on self-driven and peer feedback protocols. While the sample was taken from last year, it represented a safe method for modeling how to help Theo so that he could move—with specific, targeted next steps—from an "Emerging" understanding to an "Advanced" one.

As Ms. Davies prepared the next lesson, she noted places where the current batch of written responses offered opportunities to address **academic language** demands and review the **register** of language expected in scientific discourse with a graphic organizer/**sentence starter**. But Ms. Davies reminded herself that teaching students how to use the student progress guide for self-assessment (Figure 4.3, featured in Chapter 4) was as important as the content because, at this stage, it would guide them with self-assessment and peer table work later in the week.

> ## Author Insight
> Darling-Hammond, Ancess, & Falk
>
> **Authentic Assessment in Action**
>
> The process of evaluating, revising, and re-evaluating makes the assessment process fundamentally a learning process, one that promotes both self-evaluative capabilities and habits of work (the internalization of standards) for students as well as for staff.

Source: Darling-Hammond, Ancess, & Falk (1995), p. 54.

Focus on Reflective Practice

Experienced teachers use whole-class formative feedback judiciously and strategically. They tend to incorporate feedback at key junctures in the lesson: sometimes at the launch/opening with an **entrance ticket**, other times at the closing/takeaway portion of the lesson. When supporting a task or project element, formative assessors will implement a feedback configuration such as whole class → small group → whole class in a lesson.

With such a pattern, class begins in whole-class configuration, with the teacher leading students through orienting/opening interactions. This is followed by small-group and/or individual student work time during which the teacher circulates, helping and observing. This portion of class is typically the bulk of the class period. As the teacher interacts with students, the teacher notes any emerging patterns.

Patterns will inform any whole-class feedback the teacher decides to offer before the closing of the class. Before having students engage in an individual closing/**exit ticket** task, the teacher provides the whole class with targeted takeaways (i.e., formative feedback). The whole-class communication is brief but freshly obtained, relevant, and immediately useful to the learner.

These sorts of just-in-time feed forward moves are hard-won evidence of learning (Hattie & Timperley, 2007). They can only be gained through real-time qualitative observations by teachers. In multiple configurations, they can be gathered during a lesson. The goal in this example is for students to use this whole-class feedback right away in the closing/exit ticket task to augment and improve understanding.

We observed Augustin follow this structure with his sixth-grade science students during a unit on traits and reproduction at a local K–8 school. With this illustration, we highlight that Augustin made a choice that helped keep his whole-class feedback within students' ZPDs and

> **WATCH THIS**
>
> *Introducing Self-Assessment Using a Progress Guide*
>
> Please use the QR code above and watch the video before proceeding.

tightly focused on the learning target, which was that students will be able to explain with evidence why traits vary, even between parents and offspring and among siblings. Augustin did this by inviting his students to self-assess the first drafts of their written explanations to a series of prompts about whether or not specific traits are heritable among family members. The progress guide Augustin created offers his middle schoolers a student-friendly self-assessment based in well-defined learning criteria and the goals of the standards-based assignment.

Augustin Orients Students to the Self-Assessment Task With Feedback on Where We Are Going as a Class

Once every student has their own copy of a self-assessment progress guide, Augustin begins by instructing students to reread what they wrote the day before. "After rereading carefully what you wrote yesterday, circle the category that you think you're in. So, even if you were absent yesterday, there's a category for that." Augustin offers guidance for students who might not know where to begin: "If you're looking at your answers from yesterday, and you're not really too sure, this would be the category that you would choose." Augustin points to the category "Absent/No Response," which states, "I'm not sure or don't know."

Once all of his students have an entry point, Augustin spends time at the lesson opening orienting students to a key aspect of the progress guide. He carefully draws attention to the "Next Steps" column as the objective of the day's lesson. "Remember everyone, as we answer the questions, we are looking for evidence to support our explanation. For many of you, finding and adding that evidence is today's goal."

Augustin then calls the whole class's attention to places on the progress guide in the boxes of the "Next Steps" column where it uses a sentence starter ("To improve my work, I will . . .").

"Here's where you will put your next steps," Augustin says. "Why do we need next steps?" Hands go up. He circles *next steps* and **pauses**. Augustin probes on more than half a dozen initial responses.

A student calls out, "To get better."

Augustin probes, "What does it mean, *to get better*?"

A different student calls out louder, "To improve!"

Augustin probes again, "What does that mean in science, *to improve*?"

Another student offers, "To have bigger vocabulary and know what you're talking about?"

"We call that academic vocabulary . . ." [He points to the task objective "Using Evidence"] "Can anyone say more?"

Another student volunteers in a quiet voice, "To give evidence."

Still, Augustin probes. "What's *evidence*?" The class discusses evidence for a few more minutes in a quick one-minute pair share. Responses vary along the lines of something to prove your point, something to show what you've done, facts to support your claim, support for your main statement, and information from a source. With this level of reassurance that his students know they need to incorporate evidence into their explanations, Augustin pivots his class to engaging in the self-assessment activity using the progress guide and working individually and in pairs as he circulates the classroom.

Augustin Gathers Observations in Other Configurations to Adjust the Direction and Pace of Feedback

During this middle portion of class time, Augustin checks in with over a third of his students. As he circulates, he adjusts his interaction style (using proximity, hand gestures, and other nonverbal feedback moves discussed in Chapter 10) to meet students' needs. With some students, Augustin is very direct: "Did your use of the simulation support the answer you had earlier?" With others, Augustin is more roundabout: "You don't know which one to choose? How about we don't even look at this right now. You just tell me how you're feeling about this task instead. We'll start there."

As he meets with students, Augustin notes how over half his class categorized their work in the second-highest category, "I can identify the correct answer with evidence," and that seven students had explanations for their answers but the answers were scientifically incorrect (e.g., parents and children sometimes having the same hair color and eye color meaning that traits cannot vary or that living near a body of water will cause the trait of being a strong swimmer). Augustin also notes on his own clipboard with his progress guide which students are seemingly self-aware regarding their beginning use of academic language, "I can list words that have to do with the topic."

Augustin Regroups and Shares Observed Trends and Offers Feedback on Next Steps With the Whole Class

Toward the end of the period, Augustin calls everyone back to whole-class configuration and offers feedback on what he sees as trends/next steps for the whole class. Like a scientist, he models how observations require notetaking; he shows the students by waving the clipboard before he returns to the progress guide shown on the projector. "Today as I was going around, I was really looking for evidence. I liked what I saw at this stage. I asked myself as I met with you, 'What evidence were you using in your explanations?' And I noticed some of you talked about this as the 'examples' in your answers. That's one way to think of it.

"I also noticed today that many of you were using the word *trait* correctly. That's terrific. I'd like to see just as many of you use the word *heredity* in your explanations, too. So, I want to challenge you on that."

Now comes the whole-class feedback garnered from Augustin's careful observations of the drafts of students' work: "Remember I promised at the beginning of class to offer you all some feedback on how to improve? Well, here's something I think we can all work on based on what I've seen so far."

Augustin puts the feedback (from his notes) under the document camera. He reads his written "whole-class next steps" comment: "Before expanding your written answers—which everyone is going to do, by the way—talk it out with a partner. Remember, the highest level on the progress guide is, 'I can explain to the class.' So, an important next step for everyone is explaining it to a partner. Science is about communicating your ideas and results. Also, if you can explain to a partner first, there's a pretty good chance you can explain it in writing."

Augustin poses one last question for the class: "Before we close today, I want to know if your level on the progress guide changed." Some hands go up. Others look around at each other, not sure. "Okay, so for many of you, it did! And for the rest of you, I know that it can."

As he closes the lesson, Augustin invites everyone to do some more writing. He puts the task/prompt on the projector: Explain why you agree or disagree with this statement: *Each person in a family has the same traits. There are no differences in traits between parents and offspring or among siblings.*

"So right now, go back to your response to Question 4 and try to revise your answer. I want you to rewrite it. Add a sentence or two. This is going to be your exit ticket for today."

Scaffolds and Guided Practice for Individual Teachers: Five-Step Scaffold for Designing Progress Guides

So, we've talked about other people's progress guides. Let's put the focus back on your practice and what's next to get started with differentiated formative feedback for all. These steps for designing a progress guide are preliminary ones. Our goal is to provide a rough sketch to get you started.

Five-Step Scaffold for Success

1. Identify an assessment task, project, and/or long-term assignment from a unit.
   - List the skills needed to complete the task.
   - List the learning target(s) aligned with these skills.
   - Crosswalk these skills with standards and taxonomies for alignment with larger educational goals in the subject.

2. Anticipate student responses to the task, project, and/or long-term assignment.
   - List particular procedures and/or operations that must be completed to successfully complete the task.
   - List typical places where students get stuck with the task.
   - List typical major **misconceptions** and/or procedural errors related to the task.

3. Organize anticipated student responses by levels.
   - Identify a range of possible responses into groupings.
   - Delineate a trajectory of these groupings (starting with *absent, no response, off topic, restates, major procedural error or misapplication of formula*, etc.).
   - Carefully consider how partially correct responses in the middle levels can be differentiated.

4. Determine next steps for each level of response with feedback cues/prompts.
   - Differentiate feedback by successive levels.
     - Offer general and specific instructional activities.
       - Model problem solving with actual or anonymous response leading to self-assessment.
       - Group by adjacent levels to offer feedback leading to peer assessment.
     - Offer general and specific assessment moves.
       - Reteach an aspect of a task/skill while checking for understanding (posing questions).
       - Review a task/response by moving to different tables and asking questions (with specific probes and requests for **elaboration**) by level.

5. Design progress guides for teacher use and student use for self- and/or peer assessment.
   - Review teacher-friendly exemplars.

- Note essential characteristics: Percentage of responses at a given level in left column, "Student can . . ." in middle column, and "Feedback Strategies" in right column
  - Review student-friendly exemplars.
    - Note essential characteristics: Non-graded symbols at a given level in the left column, "I can currently . . ." in middle column, and a sentence starter "My next steps are . . ." in the right column

These steps are not always linear, and sometimes you will want to iterate and start building your progress guide where it feels right. The goal is to sketch out a trajectory of levels of progress or waypoints that you feel best map out where drafts of student work are likely to appear in the feedback cycle. We use the words *likely*, *roughly*, and so forth to convey that our estimates of progress are provisional. Unlike grades, we aren't marking students up or down on a scale that becomes an academic record. The progress guides for teacher and student use are intended to help re-form and refocus attention and energy on what's next for students during the learning cycle. To be formative, these guides must ensure students can move their work ahead to the next level. The design and intended uses of progress guides are formative. They are guides to support progress—not tools for recording summative results.

Try It Tomorrow

Getting Started With Binning for Feedback

Look at responses to an exit ticket aligned with the unit goals in your course. Bin all student responses into four or five categories using the scaffold language provided in Ms. Davies's example ("Using Evidence to Examine Causes of the Dust Bowl").

- Ask yourself how the responses are distributed (i.e., what percentage for each level?).
- Pick one level to focus on preparing feedback strategies for and identify three next steps for students in this range.
- Consider using a whole-class to small-group to whole-class cycle to support student uptake of the feedback.

CHAPTER 5. Feedback With the Whole Class

I just started my first semester of student teaching at the university. My university supervisor and assessment professor has been inviting us to get more information out of looking at student work than just assigning points. I was grading a CFU (check for understanding) that the geometry students took on trigonometry ratios for my placement. As I looked over the responses, before meeting with my mentor teacher, I noticed four specific bins that the student work was falling into so I went ahead and made a progress guide as practice for myself. I showed my mentor teacher the progress guide and she loved it! We are using it as we hand back the CFUs. Since the students have two more chances to tackle the CFU task, I made sure to include next steps that will set the students up for success.

—Stacey, pre-service teacher candidate

Misa's Reflection on Whole-Class Feedback

Tips From My Department Chair, Joan, on Opening the Class

"Give 'em Some Good News and Something to Grow On"

First off, I learned early in my career that any feedback I give to the whole class needs to be brief. Otherwise, students tune out. (I teach freshmen.) Personally, I have about a three-minute limit. If the feedback I'm giving the whole class needs more than three minutes, then it's not really feedback; it's a lesson.

Second, what I tell my class needs to apply to everyone—or at least *almost* everyone. What's the point of talking to all of them if only a third of them need to hear it? I'd be better off talking directly with just that group of students and letting the rest work on something else. (I get that this takes planning and trust.)

Finally, it never hurts to start off with positive feedback. It sets a good tone. I think of what I do at the beginning of class as my back-of-the-envelope, "Good News and One to Grow On" routine. It's *back-of-the-envelope* in my mind because I was coached to do so by my department chair, Joan. Joan told me:

(Continued)

> *You make a few notes on the back of an envelope as you're reading. It doesn't have to be fancy. The point is that it's not. It's real. And you bring this envelope to class, and before they get their drafts back, you hold it up for them. Explain to them what you did. If your envelope's got tea rings on it, all the better. Show those off. Paint a picture. Make it personal. Share how you were reading their drafts. Maybe one of your cats was on your lap as you were reading. Draw them in. Then give them the good news and let it sink in. Celebrate some.*
>
> *Then, you must give them something to grow on, especially at the beginning of the year.*
>
> *My advice: Do this at the beginning of class and get them diving back into their draft with a partner within five minutes.*

Setting Goals and Monitoring Progress With Whole-Class Feedback: Questions for Lesson Study and Professional Learning Communities

In this chapter's "Focus on Reflective Practice," you read Augustin's story about whole-class formative feedback. Augustin was fortunate to have been mentored by a department chair who gave Augustin specific advice about feedback practices that, like Joan's, have worked well over the years. Department chairs and instructional coaches can help with supporting teachers' work in best feedback practices.

Augustin is fortunate. His high school's **professional learning community (PLC)** team is working on the theme of Dive into Deeper Learning as part of its schoolwide improvement plan. The reading resource list includes the work of Quinn et al. (2019), Shepard et al. (2017), and others. The goal this year is how to connect feedback for all by diving into a variety of current classroom assessment practices. Here are some guiding questions to support the work of various teams.

For a Department- or Subject-Specific PLC

1. As a group, come up with the top three pieces of advice about whole-class formative feedback you'd give new teachers in your subject area.

2. Discuss whether any of the advice applies particularly to your school or to the students in your school. If so, in what way? What's unique about your context/situation that makes you say this?

3. How would you characterize students' uptake of formative feedback in your subject area? Make a list of what is working and what isn't.

4. What role, if any, does configuration (whole class, small group, individual) have to do with what's working? Brainstorm how to build on wins for each configuration.

5. Commit to change: As a result of your PLC's discussion so far, consider and then share out to the group how you will strive to change what you do regarding whole-class formative feedback. Be specific. If you're not planning any changes, share what's vexing you or what you're mulling over, since one of your colleagues could suggest something you haven't thought of yet.

For PLCs Across Many Departments and Subject Disciplines

1. Explain why feedback matters. For whom does it matter? (If you are focused on **opportunity gaps** for students with special education needs or youth experiencing homelessness or youth in foster care at your school, try to imagine why feedback matters from each perspective.)

2. Share what you think is the most important advice about whole-class formative feedback across classrooms, labs, the theater, playing fields, and any other relevant learning settings. Try to connect the proverbial feedback dots across these settings from the students' point of view. Are there gaps in practices? Are there places to link up and leverage what is working from one setting to another?

3. Brainstorm what you want new teachers to know about the power of feedback from your perspective (e.g., as a classroom teacher, as a coach, as a paraprofessional, or as a counselor). Each perspective matters to create continuity and care for students.

4. Compare: To what extent do teachers of different subject areas, staff perspectives, or learning settings influence how we see feedback in large groups?

5. Make a list of five core feedback practices/values. Imagine it will be made into a poster and displayed in every place students

interact with teachers, staff, and principals. When students come into these learning spaces, invite them to pause and tell you why a particular practice/value matters for them.

6. Commit to change: As a result of your PLC's discussion so far, consider and then share out to the group how you will strive to change what you do regarding whole-class formative feedback practices and moves. Be specific. If you're not planning any changes, share what's vexing you or what you're mulling over regarding feedback. Ask a colleague whose teaching you respect. Perhaps one of your colleagues could suggest trying something with feedback you haven't thought of yet.

Recap/Review

- Collaboration, teamwork, sharing suggestions with a group of people—these are 21st century skills in action. Each assumes we can give and take feedback from one another.
- While teachers are guides on the side of any project or task, we set the stage for learning to listen. Activating students for one another requires teachers to walk the walk. We must model how to use feedback with the whole class first.
- Teaching how to use feedback (not merely offering it) is essential in any configuration. Whole-class configurations allow us to role-play how to approach feedback. Using authentic exemplars, we can engage everyone in worked examples and collectively strategize what's next for this first draft.
- Visible scaffolds, similar to the progress guide, can help us leverage the opportunities for differentiated formative feedback. Using examples of student work at a particular level of performance to model what's next allows us to share feedback more effectively and efficiently in whole-class configuration.
- Progress guides help teachers plan how to differentiate formative feedback to support students at all levels of performance across the classroom. These shared tools and scaffolds also help students when they move into other configurations, such as one-on-one and peer groups. Competence with feedback is tied to what students focus on and how they take up next steps to advance the work.
- Content of feedback should be aligned with learning goals (LGs) and criteria for success yet also be appropriately related to where the students are (i.e., which proverbial or actual draft) in the instructional cycle. ZPD applies to feedback choices.
- Supporting students in understanding and using formative feedback often requires using and teaching academic language. Unpacking academic language embedded in progress guides (aligned with a standards-based rubric) can be an informative, helpful, and wise use of time spent in whole-class configuration.

Ticket Out the Door

1. This chapter has looked at formative feedback practices through the lens of whole-class configuration. What are you still wondering about with respect to the best use of time in this configuration?

2. It's your turn. Based on your experience, what, in your opinion, did we miss when discussing the opportunities and challenges of practicing feedback strategies and moves in whole-class configurations?

3. What's one idea from this chapter you want to try? In what context might you try it? Why that one in particular?

4. Create a tool for differentiating feedback. Look over Figure 5.1 and identify a task aligned with a learning goal in your curriculum that requires students in each subject to demonstrate their understanding of evidence. Then build a progress guide for teacher use by employing the five-step scaffold presented in this chapter to aid you in differentiating your feedback for the next unit in your course.

CHAPTER 6

Feedback With Small Groups

> Students are essential players in the feedback process. In addition to being recipients of feedback, the students have a role as partners in each of the forms of the feedback activities (i.e., clarifying learning goals or success criteria, comparing current performance with success criteria, and using the information to formulate an action plan) and as feedback providers and developers of actions to be followed.
>
> —Ruiz-Primo & Li (2013, p. 221)

As teachers committed to **formative assessment** as a learning practice, we take steps to ensure active listening—whether as a whole class, small group, or one-on-one—is occurring during a **feedback** exchange. We remind our students of the power of feedback to help them make progress with a **big idea**, a new skill, or a complicated task or project.

We try to help students understand why and how what we expect them to learn, to do, and to revise *matters*. At our best, we convince our students daily that how, why, and what we are studying is relevant to their lives (one of the essential **habits of mind** we discussed in Chapter 1). If they care about what they're attempting to do individually and collectively, our students are more likely to listen to our and others' feedback with a growth mindset.

We know from well-documented research and from our own teaching experience in high school that students tend to listen to **formative feedback** when they

- trust the process,
- see that feedback is timely,
- have an opportunity—preferably multiple opportunities—to respond and to revise or practice, and
- have past experience that what's suggested can make a positive difference in their personal learning outcomes.

So we agree—listening and learning to listen matters. The extent to which students are actively listening during formative feedback interactions in any **configuration** is very important. And, yes, we can work to increase the chances that our students *are* listening to suggestions and considering next steps by mixing configurations of feedback.

Yet the *configuration* in which the formative feedback interaction occurs—the size of the audience, if you will—is also important to both students' and teachers' success.

We see challenges and opportunities with each configuration we've identified in this book. Attending to the challenges and opportunities of any configuration *before* diving into classroom learning opportunities and assessment procedures can help set everyone up for more productive, feedback-rich conversations. In the case of peer-to-peer and small-group feedback configurations, students will need guidance and practice with how to help one another.

Adults often forget: Peer dynamics easily and often become a major influence in students' learning experiences. So as teachers, we want to take actions that help the dynamics between students become as equitable and productive as possible while in a small-group configuration.

Small groups are likely to be filled with students wondering, "How do I appear to Clarissa right now?" or observing "I don't get why Antonio is always cracking jokes when we work together," or noticing "That's not how Bryan acts when Ms. Benson *isn't* standing right here." It's not that students aren't thinking similar things during the whole-class configuration. It's that as teachers orchestrate feedback exchanges in different groupings, the dynamics and tone and energy can and will shift. Our point is simple: The dynamics between *each* student come to the fore in small-group configurations, and we must anticipate challenges and be flexible as guides on the side.

If we want to consider how we activate students as learning resources for one another (Wiliam, 2018), then attention on feedback exchanges by configuration is paramount. To ensure a small group's productive functioning when we are *not* there, we can help establish norms, make visible **moves** to aid co-regulation, and set up clear, well-defined routines that promote participants feeling safe and help them keep their work on track.

A few thoughts as you read along and explore this configuration with us more deeply: First, formative feedback needs to be a two-, three-, or four-way street when peers are interacting with one another at a table, during a lab, or on the field. Monitoring, intervening, and supporting young people as they learn to offer feedback to one another takes time, intention, and skill.

Next, we as teachers need to be able to hear what students are saying to us—and to each other—when they're operating in small-group configurations. By listening in and asking questions, we can coach these teams toward reflection and self-regulation (Andrade & Heritage, 2017). Sometimes we will ask our students to substantively reflect together on their responses to an **exit ticket**; other times we can do a quick whole-class check-in to reset norms within and between groups. If repair or reflection is necessary, we will know and speak with each group. But only by listening carefully and monitoring group dynamics consistently can we take positive action to steer everyone back to feedback interactions that work for each person in small groups.

Configurations of feedback significantly influence how a teacher learns from students. Clearly, whole-class, small-group, and one-on-one feedback dynamics differ. During a lesson, we can ask ourselves, what are we hearing in this particular configuration? Is this configuration working to advance feedback for all, for some, or for a few? Might another configuration work better? Whose voices are most audible in the group? Whose voices does the group—whether it's a group of four students or the whole class—need to hear from? As we are listening to our students interact in small-group configurations, what are we learning about how students are coaching one another? Where can we as guides on the side and role models committed to collaboration make a positive difference in their group functioning?

This chapter explores what we're calling *small-group configurations* of formative feedback; it is situated between the whole-class and individual feedback chapters as a link between the two approaches. The following four guiding questions anchor our explorations on the power of small-group and peer-to-peer feedback. Taken as a whole, each chapter on feedback configurations points to the challenges and opportunities with separating and connecting different aspects of information exchange on projects, long-term assignments, and performance tasks.

Guiding Questions

1. Why plan, enact, and reflect on small-group configurations of formative feedback? For whose good is this configuration beneficial? What educational goals and purposes can this configuration serve?

2. How do I know what my students are getting out of the feedback loops and exchanges with me as the more knowledgeable expert in configurations?

3. When I observe that communication strategies in small groups aren't working as well as I intend them to, what can I do to facilitate, repair, and restart a more dialogic exchange?

4. How can I help different groups become more independent and more confident to take up feedback from each other and move to concrete next steps?

Guided by these questions, we'll explore formative feedback with small groups of students. Let's be sure we're clear about what we mean by *small group* and how it differs from whole-class and individual configurations. Let's also begin by reminding ourselves how these configurations of feedback fit within an array of practices.

The formative feedback framework represented in Figure 6.1 directs our attention to *configuration* and refers to the primary arrangements of people in which the formative feedback occurs or is situated. Each of these focal points sharpens our understanding of the dimensions of feedback practice while helping us to better examine where we can combine them for better effect.

Figure 6.1 Formative Feedback Framework

Contexts for Learning		
Face-to-Face	Blended	Distance Learning
Focal Point		
Directionality	Configuration	**Modality**
Lenses		
Teacher-driven	Whole class	Written
Peer-to-peer-driven	Small groups (2–4)	Spoken
Self-driven	Individual (1:1)	Nonverbal
Tasks, Projects, Activities	Learning Goals, Standards, Skills Rubrics, Progress Guides, "Next Steps" Organizers	

Defining Small-Group Configuration

Configuration refers to the number of students expected to be involved in the formative feedback interaction. Typically, three or four students (sometimes more) comprise a small group. The members will have a common aim when working together on a performance task or project.

Students may have chosen their group or team or they may have been assigned to it. Each group engaged in a feedback exchange must share expectations, be supported in the process, and most importantly, have a visible **scaffold** to guide them. Setting reachable goals within the feedback cycle matters, as does monitoring the progress of each group as it works collaboratively to achieve next steps.

FORMATIVE FEEDBACK IN A SMALL-GROUP CONFIGURATION	
What It Is	**What It Isn't**
• typically three to four students	• two students (two students is a dyad)
• a group that meets together to collaborate	• an unwieldy number of students—whatever this number is for your students
• a group that meets together once or multiple times	• a guarantee that students will interact more
• a group that meets synchronously or asynchronously or a combination of both	• a chance to have the natural class leader dominate the group
• a group with a common aim and shared task	• a guarantee of independent work by each group member
• an opportunity for increasing student participation	• a guarantee that students will work together productively
• a good opportunity for teachers to listen and observe students in action	• easy-to-manage flows of information, particularly in distance learning contexts
• a challenging situation for students who prefer to remain independent from classmates	• a feedback solution for not having enough time to meet with individual students
• a way to model collaboration skills and constructive feedback habits and routines	

> Dropping in on a small group of students working together in a Zoom breakout room is altogether different from what I used to do in-person with groups at tables. I really did do a lot of "stealth listening" and casual monitoring in the physical classroom space. Nothing about monitoring group work during online instruction feels casual to me.
>
> —Christina, middle school science teacher

Table 6.1 presents five aspects to consider when planning for formative feedback interactions with small groups of students. The table invites you to examine

- how "worthy" of small-group formative feedback the task you are expecting students to do together is; that is, the task's "feedback worthiness,"
- what formative feedback you expect to *give* each group,
- what formative feedback you expect to *receive* from students,

- how you can encourage equitable participation, and
- the supports (such as scaffolds, agreements, protocols, and routines) that you do (or don't yet!) have in place for the phases of *pre-*, *during*, and *post-group work* activities.

We offer questions to "Ask Yourself" about each of these five things to consider and also invite you to attend to "Why It Matters" to give thought to each *before* you begin group work with your students. Table 6.1 presents "Tips and To-Do's" that can help you focus on what's most important for you to do with all the complexity and buzzing action that are the hallmarks of small groups of students working together on a rich, authentic, complex task or project (as we discussed in Chapter 1).

Table 6.1 Planning for Formative Feedback Interactions With Small Groups of Students: What to Consider and Why It Matters

WHAT TO CONSIDER	ASK YOURSELF	WHY IT MATTERS	TIPS AND TO-DO'S
Feedback Worthiness	Is what the students are engaged in worthy of cycles of formative feedback?	Quality of formative feedback is related to richness of task. All else being equal, the more complex the performance or project, the more cycles and configurations of feedback are needed.	• If it's not worthy of feedback, ask yourself, "Why am I expecting students to do this at all?" • Involve students in deciding *what kind* of feedback they'd like and, to the extent you can, *how* they'd like it.
Giving Formative Feedback to Students	What is my top priority? How much am I focusing on content for the group? How much am I focusing on process/participation for the group?	Group participation rates and patterns affect how much and how well content/skills are learned.	• Focus. Stick to your top priority. Use a graphic organizer (e.g., progress guide, scoring guide, or graphic organizer of your own creation) to anchor student talk. • Take stock of students' participation rates to balance and rebalance voices. • Use bouncing moves to ensure better sampling of student work in progress.

(Continued)

(Continued)

WHAT TO CONSIDER	ASK YOURSELF	WHY IT MATTERS	TIPS AND TO-DO'S
Receiving Formative Feedback From Students	What do I most want to know from students in small groups? How can I discover what I'm most interested in learning from each group of students before I give feedback? How can I keep track of what I discover?	Your instructional decision making depends on eliciting useful information from students.	• Try saying out loud to the group, "I just learned . . ." or "It looks like a pattern across groups is emerging . . ." • These feedback/feedforward moves give students the opportunity to correct your inferences. • Keep a running record by tagging learnings to help you and students record and reflect on what's been discovered.
Equitable Participation	How am I supporting more equitable functioning in each small group? Can I anticipate bottlenecks or places where my students tend to get stuck communicating?	Rate of interaction in a group is a strong predictor of learning gains (Cohen et al., 1989). A teacher's interactions with a small group can make a big difference in students' overall participation in other configurations.	• If you haven't already, make group work norms explicit. Create a "Let's Try Now" poster or digital slide. • Ensure there are many ways for students to be successful with different modalities (spoken, written, nonverbal) of communication. • Intervene when necessary to support group members who may not be fully contributing and/or participating (yet).
Supports Before, During, and After Formative Feedback	How am I preparing students for the small-group formative feedback process *before* I engage them with the lesson? What protocols/agreements do we have in place *while* the formative feedback cycle is ongoing? What's our routine for debriefing *after* a session? How did the formative feedback process go? What can we do as a small group to improve for next time?	Scaffolds, agreements, and explicit routines make a difference. Helping students to be intentional, metacognitive, and reflective is a critical part of teaching for transfer and supporting students to learn how to learn.	• Keep your routines as simple as you can. • Ask aloud, "Can we all follow the 'feedback trail' without using a special handout?" If not, then make an agreement with students about how to keep track of trends and takeaways during group work. • Demonstrate that feedback is a two-way street. Let your students see and experience how their reflections/suggestions make a difference in future formative feedback sessions. In other words, take up some of what they suggest!

A key idea behind Table 6.1 is that a teacher interacting with a small group of students and engaging them in a formative feedback dialogue requires us all to make choices. Frequently, these choices emerge in response to observations we make on the fly while circulating around the room or dropping into a group conversation at some point in the task, assignment, or project cycle. We note that it is necessary, at times, to intervene in group work and offer feedback on both the process and the product as part of the learning cycle. This may sound like:

"I've noticed Valerie hasn't spoken yet. Can we hear from her?" (teacher feedback to students on process)

"What has been working well for your group so far in terms of supporting equity of participation? Remember, we want to share our voices before revising." (teacher inviting feedback from students on process)

"I see an error in the units where you've chosen to express a quantity. Can someone suggest a correction? Or suggest a place to double-check each other's work?" (teacher feedback to students on content)

"Tell me why you've labeled this *anomalies*. Let's hear from each of you about this decision. If you want to amend or elaborate why in your draft, now is a good time." (teacher inviting feedback from students on content)

As teachers committed to formative feedback, we don't necessarily need to strive for the impossible ideal of a perfect balance between giving and receiving formative feedback. Similarly, we may not always be able to strike the optimal balance between content-focused and process-focused formative feedback *all* the time.

Yet, with preparation, planning, and reflection aided by Table 6.1, we can gain awareness about our feedback practices so that we may be more intentional in our actions/interactions with our students in their groups going forward.

What the Research Tells Us
Peer Dynamics in Small-Group Configuration Affect Students' Learning

There's no getting around it—an instructional dilemma inherent in group work is that some students come to certain tasks with perceived higher status than others. These students typically talk more and, as a result, learn more (Cohen & Lotan, 1997). This has significant implications for teacher practice in diverse classroom and school settings: To ensure equity with formative feedback interactions in small-group configurations, we must monitor and sometimes intervene.

Researchers have found that "even during cooperative learning designed to promote equity, *unless the teacher intervenes to equalize rates of participation,* the rich get richer, and the gap in academic achievement widens" (Cohen et al., 1999, p. 84, emphasis added). Cohen et al. (1999) recommend two general strategies teachers can use to treat status problems with group work in the classroom: (1) broaden students' ideas about what it means to be competent, contributing, and smart; (2) praise the work of all students, particularly those who are at the margins and/or may feel marginalized in the group.

Providing Structure and Calling Attention to Higher-Order Thinking Skills During Small-Group Work Makes a Difference

It's no surprise: When teachers expect students to work together in groups, whether the task is as simple as answering a set of questions on a worksheet or as complex as preparing an interactive presentation to the class, providing structure for students supports more effective and productive interaction (Chan, 2020; Gillies, 2008; Gillies & Ashman, 1998; Kablan, 2014).

We know that what teachers say to students during group work makes a difference. We don't have to engage in overelaborate preparations for peer-to-peer feedback protocols or design the perfect **lesson plan** to support small-group configurations. Sometimes, less really can be more when setting our students up for successful interactions. Lin and colleagues (2015) found that during small-group collaborative discussions, a teacher calling specific attention to the students' uses of cognitive or interpersonal strategies helped everyone feel more competent with higher-order thinking (i.e., engaging in analogical, causal, logical, and hypothetical reasoning) in the group.

The Role of Co-regulation of Learning in Small-Group and Peer-to-Peer Configurations for Exercising Habits of Mind

Heritage (2016) notes that **assessment for learning** (AfL) conceptualizes assessment as integral to teaching and learning. Interaction is considered a primary source of evidence in AfL. *Co-regulation* refers to the joint influence of student self-regulation (and regulation from other sources, including teachers and peers) on student learning. Andrade and Heritage (2017) note that purposeful modeling can be a powerful pedagogical response to evidence of learning. Students can ask each other, "How do you know? How can we prove this? What is our evidence to support our claims?" Feedback, centered on how we all use evidence as a core habit of mind, feeds many proverbial birds with one seed.

We know that teachers who create, facilitate, and sustain a culture of questioning in the whole class and in small-group configurations of learning offer their students opportunities to respond to ideas, question assumptions, and practice the values of democratic education (Dewey, 1916; Meier, 1995; Newmann, 1996). These peer-to-peer experiences in small-group configurations position students for seeing formative feedback as part of assessment for learning and what true participation in decision making means in a democratic society. To improve their learning to meet the multiple purposes of education we discussed in Chapter 1, students must activate one another in a community of learners (Brown & Campione, 1998; Darling-Hammond, 1997) to build shared understandings.

Using the Teacher and Student Self-Assessment Progress Guides to Enhance Formative Feedback-Focused Interactions in Small-Group Configuration

In Chapters 4 and 5, we introduced you to the ideas of a **progress guide** for student use and a progress guide for teacher use. Designed for multiple uses, these progress guides are intended to scaffold, support, and guide feedback-rich conversations about concrete, actionable next steps for improving students' work. Now we will apply what we learned about the role of progress guides to the small-group configuration.

Student Self-Assessment Progress Guides Ready Students to Be Better Peer Feedback Participants

A student **self-assessment** progress guide is tailored specifically to help students self-assess their work/performance and generate next steps that will help them take their work/performance to the next level. For the key features of self-assessment progress guide intended for student use, see Figure 4.4 in Chapter 4.

We recall that as students complete a self-assessment progress guide, they

- begin to understand the criteria for success better,
- dialogue with peers,
- become more invested in the work of next steps revision,
- surface questions they have about the work in its current draft form, and
- grapple with **academic language** embedded in the task.

Taken altogether, students' engagement with a progress guide prepares them to be better peer feedback givers and receivers—whether for a single partner, a small group of students, or the whole class. Before one can offer feedback to others, it helps to try to see in one's own draft, movements, or actions what might be next, with assistance. We have found that having students use the self-assessment progress guide regarding their own **first drafts** on a performance task makes a difference in how they approach others. Again, it's not that a student *can't* give helpful formative feedback to a peer *before* completing a self-assessment progress guide, it's that it's more likely they will give more targeted, goal-specific peer feedback once they have completed their own self-assessment with the same progress guide.

Progress Guides Prepare Teachers to Make Better and More Equitable Instructional Decisions

We pointed out in Chapter 5 that a progress guide helps teachers

- see emerging patterns, including bottlenecks and where students seem stuck,
- analyze how many students' current performances/responses to the task are at each level described on the progress guide (and where additional levels may need to be added to the progress guide),
- plan what feedback and next steps could help students' performance/responses to the task get to the next level, and
- differentiate feedback within and across **zones of proximal development (ZPDs)** in a heterogeneous classroom setting.

The sorts of analyses of student work we do as teachers, paraprofessionals, and instructional coaches help us to be strategic, targeted, and intentional in how we use class time in whole-class, small-group, and one-on-one configurations. When it comes to planning support for formative feedback in small-group configuration, typically there are two ways to leverage the results of our analyses of students' current drafts based on a progress guide for teacher use:

1. *Group creation*, which means the thoughtful, intentional creation of the small groups. (Who is going to work with whom? Will groups be heterogeneously grouped? Will groups be more homogeneously grouped? What is the common element amongst members? Can we rotate participants in groups so, for example, those who are more accomplished in particular skills can help those who are still developing those skills?)

2. *Group interaction focus*, which offers several possibilities: (a) What will the teacher ask the students to focus on as they work as a group independently (i.e., without the teacher present)? (b) What will the teacher focus on (often content-oriented or process-oriented) while interacting with each group to gather information, see patterns, and offer class-level feedback?

How Ms. Davies Leveraged Her Completed Progress Guide for Teacher Use to Support Formative Feedback-Focused Interactions in Small-Group Configuration

Let's revisit Ms. Davies, to whom you were introduced in Chapter 5, and see how her completion of the progress guide for teacher use informed her formative feedback practices with small groups. Review her completed progress guide for teacher use (Figure 6.2) in which she sorted a set of students' written responses to the **prompt**, "Based on what we have talked about today, name at least three causes of climate change and their direct impact on ecosystems." Note what Ms. Davies plans to say to students or have students do differs depending on the results in how she has **binned** their written responses.

Figure 6.2 Schematic Representation of the Percentages of Students by Performance Level on Ms. Davies's Progress Guide for Teacher Use for a Class of 30 Students

APPROXIMATE LEVEL	RESPONSE TO PROMPT	NEXT STEPS
Exemplary 5%	• Identifies multiple human causes of climate change • Connects each cause with a specific impact on an ecosystem	• Explore further: What are potential solutions to climate change? How can humans change their behavior? How can we reverse the impacts on the environment?
Advanced 20% (Angela's work as a possible exemplar for whole-class feedback) 6 students (out of a class of 30)	• Identifies human causes of climate change • Makes weak connections with their impacts on ecosystems	• Explore connections between climate change and its impacts. • List impacts that identified causes have on existing ecosystems. • "In what other ways can you connect changes in ecosystems to human behavior? Are there behavior changes that could improve the environment?"

(Continued)

(Continued)

APPROXIMATE LEVEL	RESPONSE TO PROMPT	NEXT STEPS
Developing 40% (Theo's work as exemplar for whole-class feedback) 12 students (out of a class of 30)	• Identifies either human causes of climate change *or* impacts to ecosystems • Makes no connections between the two	• Review notes/discussion; list climate change causes or their impacts (depending on which is missing). • Connect identified causes to identified ecosystem impacts. • If causes are named, then ask, "What are the results of these?" *or* if impacts are named, ask, "What may have brought upon these changes to the ecosystem?"
Emerging 20% (Luis's work as a possible exemplar for whole-class feedback) 6 students (out of a class of 30)	• Names one cause of climate change	• Refer to notes/discussion; name additional causes of climate change. Discuss *climate* and *change*. • Connect those causes to changes in ecosystems. • "What changes to the environment are due to this cause? Are there other human behaviors that are changing the environment?"
Beginning 10%	• Attempts by restating prompt or assignment description • May also show major misconception or common p-prim	• Refer to notes/discussion on climate change and its causes. Discuss *causes*. • "If you are still confused, ask a classmate for help on where to start." • "If you need additional help, meet with me one-on-one."
No response yet 0%	• "Not sure," "I don't know," or off-topic response • Present in class	• Refer to notes/discussion on climate change and its causes. • "If you are still confused, ask a classmate for help on where to start." • "If you need additional help, meet with me one-on-one."
No response yet 5%	• Absent	• "I need to talk with you about what was missed and how to get started."

Group Creation

Looking at the range of current work in her class of 30 students, Ms. Davies decides to group students heterogeneously. Ms. Davies chooses to create seven groups of four students and one group of two students. Ms. Davies spreads the seven students whose work currently is binned as "Advanced" (six students) and the topmost level on the progress guide, "Exemplary" (one student), among the groups so that there is one of these students per group of four. Sixty percent of Ms. Davies's students in this class period currently have work at the "Emerging" (six students) and "Developing" (twelve students) levels. Ms. Davies spreads these 18 students around to the six groups that have a student whose work was binned as "Advanced." Ms. Davies puts the three students whose work was binned as "Beginning" with the one student whose work was binned as "Exemplary." Finally, the two students who don't have a response yet—because they both were absent—form a group with Ms. Davies. She can talk to them together about the task, get them started with a first draft, and then integrate each into the other groups when the next rotation occurs.

Group Interaction Focus

Once the groups are formed, Ms. Davies thinks about how she'll encourage the groups to work independently while she's helping a different group. She decides to focus on two things: the concept of *connections* and the academic language of *direct impact*. Her decision is informed by the fact that 75% of her class has not yet demonstrated that they know/understand the connections between human causes of climate change and their direct impacts on ecosystems.

Ms. Davies comes up with a **graphic organizer** that illustrates that each cause needs to be associated with a particular ecosystem and that each ecosystem must have a specific way in which it is directly impacted. Ms. Davies presents the graphic organizer to her students with an example already completed. She plans to leverage that example as she goes from group to group.

Before group work begins, Ms. Davies reminds everyone of two of their norms: "You have the duty to assist anyone in your group who asks for help," and "You have the right to ask anyone in your group for help." She lets them know, "As I come around to each group, I'll be looking to hear about how you explained *direct impact* to one another. I'm interested in learning better ways to teach it to other class periods."

By explicitly letting students know of her authentic interest and purpose in dialogue, the feedback cycle feels a bit more genuine to students. Ms. Davies really is keen to learn from her students during small-group configurations. While Ms. Davies certainly is, as experts put it, "a more knowledgeable other" to her students, she knows how to model an ethos of collaboration. By walking the walk, not just talking the talk, Ms. Davies's students watch how her own energetic participation with group-level conversations energizes the class. Students appreciate when teachers are learning with them and taking the time to move around, ask questions, and offer next steps. These configurations of feedback feel more like a journey of mutual discovery than a to-do list before the bell rings.

Focus on Practice

Teachers give formative feedback to small groups of students often. Whether we teach in a fully online, a hybrid, or a completely in-person instructional context, engaging small groups of students as they grapple with subject-specific content, work on complex projects, and prepare authentic performances to practice habits of mind in the company of peers is core to our work as teachers.

On the field, you'll see our physical education teachers working with teams. In the music room, you will see students working in trios, quartets, and other performance configurations. Similarly, in the art and science room, you'll see teachers moving across the classroom to check on different teams across tables and lab stations. English/language arts and history teachers use stations and table work, too. All teachers at one point or another work with these teaching, learning, and feedback-rich configurations.

When we interact with a small group in any subject or setting, let's keep in mind our two goals:

1. To offer the kinds of support students aren't yet generating for themselves

2. To guide or spur them toward more productive group work when we're not interacting directly with them (i.e., support their independent functioning)

These two goals are not mutually exclusive. What you do for one goal tends to feed the other. Facilitation of small-group interactions requires us to guide and, at times, step aside.

It may help if we **pose** these learning goals as questions for our own professional growth and practice. Let's ask ourselves the following questions as we circulate the physical or virtual learning space:

- What am I adding that only I, as a more expert other, can add to this interaction?

- How am I helping, with my feedback, to support the group in becoming more independent?

Generally, the first question is about content knowledge and subject matter–specific skills that you have but students don't yet have. Teachers are the mentors and content experts in their classrooms. But that expertise must be "right sized" to the group dynamic and interaction. Part of the art of teaching is knowing how and when to offer your expertise in a feedback exchange.

The second question is about group processes. You are the guide on the side, and you have facilitation skills that are necessary to keep everyone on track and practicing good feedback habits. Often, you will need to check in with everyone by using the following verbal prompts:

- "Okay, how are we going?"
- "In what ways—and hopefully multiple ways—are we conveying respect to one another?"
- "Remember, start with a positive: 'One thing I like is . . .'"

Supporting classroom norms for group work in a feedback-rich learning environment requires teachers' skills with and a disposition toward "activating students as learning resources for one another" (Wiliam, 2018, p. 23). Now it is time to contextualize these aspirations with what the work looks like for teachers and students working in different feedback configurations.

The Case of Mr. Aaron: One Teacher's Take on Using Time With a Group to Probe and to Support Students to More Effectively Interact With One Another

Mr. Aaron, an experienced teacher, teaches at a Northern California Transitional Kindergarten (TK)–Grade 8 school with a racially and linguistically diverse student body in which over a third of students are officially designated as **English learners** and nearly all students qualify for free or reduced lunch. The following dialogue was captured in his seventh-grade mathematics classroom. As you read, note what Mr. Aaron does to invite students to speak to him and to one another. What do you think of his approach in this segment (i.e., turns of talk)?

Context: Four students are seated together: two girls and two boys (JUNE, LYDIA, ARTURO, and RAMON). LYDIA and JUNE sit side by side. ARTURO and RAMON sit across from one another. MR. AARON has pulled up a chair and sits between ARTURO and RAMON. It is his second visit to this group during the lesson. LYDIA is an English learner and has strong math skills.

Mr. Aaron: All right! June's got the tool down.

June: What?

(Continued)

(*Continued*)

Mr. Aaron (*to Lydia*): Lydia, you are doing it. All right. (*to Ramon*) You're starting to make the tool. Okay, what about you, Arturo?

Ramon: I've been telling them . . . ah . . . I'm choosing. You want me to do two, not three.

Arturo doesn't answer Mr. Aaron's question.

Mr. Aaron (*to June*): So, June, do you understand what Lydia is doing?

Lydia (*to June*): Do you?

June: A little bit.

Mr. Aaron (*to June*): Okay, why don't you ask her? Why don't you ask her what she [Lydia] is doing?

June (*in an altered, extra-deep voice that conveys she is asking this to comply with Mr. Aaron's expectation*): What are you doing, Lydia?

Mr. Aaron (*to Lydia*): Explain it, Lydia.

Lydia (*plaintively*): I don't know how to explain.

Mr. Aaron: Well, I can help you. So, go ahead.

Lydia: Uh . . .

Mr. Aaron: So explain what the numbers are that you put on there first.

Lydia: Oh, these numbers!

June: Oh!

Mr. Aaron: Okay? Explain why you put those on there first.

Lydia and June interact, but their exact words are inaudible. Mr. Aaron turns his attention to Arturo.

Mr. Aaron: Okay, so, Arturo, why don't you make the graph there?

Ramon (*to Arturo*): It's right here.

Arturo (to *Mr. Aaron*): This one?

Mr. Aaron: No. Remember we did this one yesterday. Oh, were you here?

Arturo:	I wasn't here.
Mr. Aaron:	Oh, okay. Just make a graph like this, but don't put any numbers in yet. Ramon can explain to you how you decide what numbers to put in. Okay? So just make a quick graph.
Ramon (*to Mr. Aaron, before he helps Arturo*):	So the numbers, the negative numbers go on the *x*-axis and the positive numbers go on the *y*-axis?

Mr. Aaron and Ramon go back and forth until Ramon starts helping Arturo.

Mr. Aaron (*to June*):	So you're understanding now, June?
June:	Yeah.
Ramon (*to Mr. Aaron*):	There is -1, -2, 1, 0, and 2.
Mr. Aaron (*to Lydia*):	Lydia.
Lydia:	Yeah?
Mr. Aaron (*to Lydia*):	What is he [Ramon] doing wrong?

Lydia stands up and leans over to look at Ramon'S work.

Lydia:	Oh! You have to put like the same number this side, this side.
Ramon:	Oh, like . . . ?
Mr. Aaron (*to Lydia*):	Yeah, because why?
Ramon (*to Lydia*):	What do you mean?
Lydia (*to Ramon*):	Like, um . . . like the same number . . .
Mr. Aaron (*to Lydia*):	Point to the graph. (*Lydia points to the graph.*) There you go.
Lydia:	Like the same number, on this side. Bigger . . .
Ramon:	Oh! So they have to be in *order*!
Lydia:	Yeah. I think.
Mr. Aaron:	You got it, you got it.

(Continued)

(Continued)

> *Mr. Aaron gets up from his chair, still listening in the interaction.*
>
> **Ramon:** In order, from smaller to bigger.
>
> **Lydia:** Yeah, *(pointing at the numbers in turn)* -2, -1, 0, 1, and 2.

Discuss:

1. What does Mr. Aaron do well in this segment?
2. How does Mr. Aaron activate Lydia to support others?
3. Without knowing the full context of the situation, what do you wish Mr. Aaron had done differently with this feedback cycle? Why?
4. Do you consider what Mr. Aaron does—or attempts to do—formative feedback? How is it formative? For whom might it be formative?
5. What teachers receive from students—what teachers learn about students—during formative feedback interactions is important. What do you think Mr. Aaron might have learned from interacting with this small group (e.g., about uses of academic language)?

Scaffolds and Guided Practice for Individual Teachers

Supporting Formative Feedback in Every Phase of a Small-Group Project

You don't have to be a **project-based learning** advocate to understand the value of having scaffolds, agreements, protocols, and routines to support your formative assessment-based interactions with students. Most teachers engage in classroom assessment practices based on complex tasks, projects, or assignments that involve longer cycles of feedback than the time it takes to say, "Great job," "See if you can do better," or "Now that's an *A*."

We note that these three phases of rich formative feedback practice are part and parcel of any small-group work project. The three phases occur

- *before* the feedback is offered (*pre-formative feedback*),
- *during* the formative feedback cycle (*feedback enactment*), and
- *after* the project is complete or the performance given (*post-formative feedback* or *reflection*).

Sara, a high school history and civics teacher, discovered this in a new way during the pandemic when all the instruction at her school moved fully remote—and stayed that way for months until the end of the school year. Sara's story about supporting her world history sophomores through a small-group project—a team-teaching group presentation—illustrates and contextualizes some of the procedures, practices, and routines we're recommending. In preparing this case study, after conducting several Zoom-based interviews, we decided to have Sara tell this story in a reconstruction of our dialogue in a first-person narrative voice.

Sara's Story: Learning to Learn about Group Feedback During the Pandemic

As I tell you my experience during the pandemic, I invite you to listen for what you can use. We might not teach the same subject, but it's likely you can borrow the essential components of my story: what I put in place during distance learning to help my students before our small-group formative feedback interactions, during the formative feedback process, and after. My students have given me the feedback that this was one of the most valuable, and enjoyable, learning experiences they had all year.

It's worth noting that the three phases of formative feedback highlighted here—*before*, *during*, and *after* the main formative feedback cycle—align with a cycle familiar to nearly any teacher, especially teachers who have mentored teacher candidates (or *student teachers*, as many people call them). And that's the cycle of plan, enact, and reflect. Some folks like to put an *assess* in there, too. I don't usually, since I'm assessing all the time.

The Small-Group Task/Assignment: Team Teaching in a Group Presentation

Students in my world history class are expected to team teach in a group presentation format each semester. They do this in groups of three, or sometimes four, depending on how the sign-ups work out for topics. Though we are in fully remote instruction, this is still the case. They teach by Zoom, just as I do. The expectation is that within 20 minutes, the group will

- teach three core aspects of the topic (these core aspects may differ depending on the topic),
- engage their classmates through oral and written (e.g., chat) participation, and
- seek evidence of their classmates' understanding (e.g., with an exit ticket) and share the results with me.

Support for Formative Feedback Cycles/Phase

Phase 1. Pre-formative Feedback Preparation: Setting Project/Performance Task Goals and Procedural Expectations

To kick off the small-group presentations project, I meet with the team first. A meeting with only the team-teaching group members present is a must. I think of it as frontloading. It's essential to set their expectations for how the feedback and revision process is going to go. During pre-pandemic days, I would have met with the group—in-person, of course—during class time. I do the same now by either creating a breakout room for me and the team, or, if I'm able to, by dismissing the rest of the class early and keeping the small group with me on Zoom.

The agenda of this meeting is to answer these questions from the students' perspective:

- What are the expectations of the project/assignment?
- Where/how do we find the information we'll need?
- How will we communicate with each other?
- What will the feedback–revision loops be like?
- What's our group's preferred method of communication? When will we communicate next?

In distance learning, it's imperative that we're all on the same shared documents at the same time. I used to rely on paper handouts and watching the students take notes as I set expectations. With shared documents, I can better see what students are writing as they write it without being obvious and obtrusive.

Figure 6.3 shows the important components of pre-formative feedback support for this project. Notice I'm clear about what I'm aiming to give them in this phase and what I'm seeking to learn from them (the "Process Expectations and Norms" and "Watching/Listening for" rows). Our school uses Google Docs as part of its learning platforms but any electronic system for sharing documents, videos, and so on works. In my experience, it's not about who owns it but how we (students and teachers together) use it. It is critical that this electronic document is shared and that each group member uses the comment feature and/or adds to the document as we meet. Otherwise, feedback won't be collaborative or lead to many revisions.

Figure 6.3 Key Components of Pre-formative Feedback Support to Small-Group Members

Scaffold/Handout	*Performance task description* that succinctly describes the assignment (teaching presentation), objectives, context, materials, accommodations, and success criteria.
	Actual *slide deck* the team will use for their team teaching. This template-type slide deck communicates the basic elements I expect of their team teaching (e.g., their topic's three core aspects) and is the foundation of their teaching/presentation performance.
	The project *progress guide* the team will use to assess the first draft (slide deck) before our meeting to discuss next steps before the final performance.
Agreements "on the Wall"	"If I'm not sure about a comment, I'll ask."
	"There are no right or wrong questions—just ask."
	"Feedback is not a 'click and done'—it's a give and take."
	"When in doubt, ask about . . ."
Protocol	1. When the first draft of your slide deck is ready for feedback, have the group decide it's time to communicate with me.
	2. Send me an email with the link to your draft slides and CC all group members.
	3. As you read/listen to my comments, ask clarifying questions on the comment threads and wait for my reply (48 hours).
	4. Don't resolve any comments/suggestions until the group has read them all and agrees on a revision strategy or solution.
My Process Expectations and Norms	▶ A concrete example of how they'll communicate to me when they are ready for feedback (i.e., send me an email with the link to the slide deck and CC all group members).
	▶ "I will use 'Reply All' to let you know my formative feedback is there."
	▶ "When you read my comments/suggestions/questions, contact me if you don't understand what I mean. Otherwise, take up my feedback by incorporating it or replying to the comment (i.e., making it a dialogue rather than a monologue)."
	▶ "Don't click 'resolve' (since if you do that, the comments aren't visible)."
	▶ "Leave all the feedback loops up for us to revisit later."
I Am Watching/Listening for	▶ Have they worked with one another before?
	▶ How familiar with using the comments or other editing features are they? Will I need to do a quick demo?
	▶ Have they read the topic material already? Are they using the scaffolds? Which skills are on display?
	▶ What do they think is a reasonable length of time between my formative feedback and their next iteration? Should I extend the cycle? Which adjustments will help them now?

Phase 2. Observing, Reading, and Listening to Exchanges as the Formative Feedback Process Unfolds

Of course, this phase doesn't go perfectly, even when I feel I've done a good job setting expectations and reaching agreements with a small group. They're still sophomores, after all, and I'm still human. For example, they don't always email me that they're ready for feedback by the time we agreed (life happens). And I don't always get my formative feedback back to them as quickly as I'd like (again, life happens). But, just as often, a group will email me sooner rather than later. That's when the communication cycle I enjoy the most begins!

Figure 6.4 communicates what I consider to be the most essential components of this phase—the formative feedback enactment phase. Notice that I pay attention to who in the group gets comments from me—everyone does—and roughly what percentage of comments I am expecting replies to in this phase. In other words, how many of my comments and which kinds of comments/queries are initiating online exchanges (i.e., opening a **feedback loop**) on the task?

Figure 6.4 Key Components During Enactment of Formative Feedback

Principles I Follow	Don't do the work for my students.
	Give them the space to self-evaluate after the performance.
	Make it a learning experience.
Personal Protocol	In my "Reply All" email to the group members telling them my formative feedback is ready, I say something encouraging and inspirational related to how they are gaining subject matter expertise.
My Formative Feedback Analysis	▸ Have I given enough positive, actionable comments?
	▸ Has each group member received at least one "next step" comment (to obtain a more equitable distribution)?
	▸ Of all the comments I made, what percentage do I expect them to reply to?
	▸ What are the patterns, if any, of response/nonresponse across each group?
	▸ Do I need to reteach a concept or skill based on the formative feedback I am getting from this process?
My Process Expectations and Norms	▸ Positive comments, specific next steps I expect them to take with regard to content knowledge (e.g., elaboration, follow-ups, additions)
	▸ Questions about the collaboration process that I expect them to answer with regard to participation, division of labor, specific roles during their group teaching presentations

I Am Watching/ Listening for	▶ Are the students having issues communicating with one another? Has someone emerged as the dominant leader? Are others handing off responsibility without knowing it? Is the work shifting toward one person? How do I intervene to rebalance the division of labor?
	▶ Which comments do the students seem confused by? Are students in certain groups confused? Is this related to my style or tone rather than their content knowledge or skill set? Can I mix up the modalities more to invite more group participation?
	▶ Which scaffolds are they using and which ones do not seem to be useful?
	▶ Should we huddle before I react or respond to the slowdown in this feedback exchange?

Phase 3. Post-formative Feedback Reflection: Noticing What Works and What Still Needs to Be Worked on to Advance the Work

I always aim to get the students talking right away after their performances. During our debriefs, usually, they each have quite a bit to say. I learn very quickly what I won't have to focus on with my comments—or, conversely, what I will have to focus on—when it's my turn to speak. If I speak too much first, I miss the opportunity to discover this.

Notice that part of the private team debrief (Figure 6.5) is dedicated to my getting the students to talk about their experiences with the formative feedback process itself. It's valuable for them to hear each other's perspectives, particularly as we do **peer assessment** later on.

I also learn in this feedback process where people are getting stuck or where they have needed a nudge. And the focus on the "Process Expectations and Norms" with "Agreements 'on the Wall'" helps my students see themselves as people who can revise. Revision has gotten a dirty name. Even adults think of it as "what I did in English class." Not true. All of us are revising constantly. Success in the world of work and college assumes one knows how to revise, to rethink, to redo.

Students (and many adults in our building, in my opinion) have come to hold a **misconception** about revision and its crucial role in the learning process. They think of it as a time-consuming luxury or oddity that some teachers push. Yet folks in the professional world revise with input from others all the time. When I worked for a sports apparel company part-time last summer, our teams were constantly rethinking and revising our thinking about scripts, layouts, and approaches to what works.

I developed this key components list (Figure 6.5) as a personal reminder. If this is something I want my students to have experience with—revising in response to well-informed comments and doing so as part of a team—it's important that we talk explicitly about it. That's largely what this post-formative feedback phase is about: putting language to their experience, reflecting with others, and using 21st century skills, as my principal puts it.

Figure 6.5 Key Components of Post-Formative Feedback Reflection

Principles I Follow	Warm feedback is the place to start.
	Classmates (the audience) are invited to offer warm feedback immediately after each team teaching presentation.
	Any cooler feedback that's needed can come from me in private with only team members present and after I've gauged their readiness to engage.
Whole-Class Public Protocol	1. Prime the class ahead of time: Note something specific and positive about the team teaching presentation to share with everyone after.
	2. Immediately after, everyone writes in the chat at least one specific positive comment (and waits to press send until I give the signal, so that the chat populates nearly all at once).
	3. While classmates are writing, team members can be thinking of advice/suggestions they'll give to the next team to teach.
	4. After the class's positive feedback appears in the chat, the team members who just taught read it aloud.
	5. The team gives advice/suggestions to the team that will teach next (so there is a cumulative add-on effect to the feedback).
Team Group Private Debrief Protocol	▸ Meet with small group members to debrief.
	▸ Get them talking first with my opening questions (e.g., how do you think it went? Knowing what you know now, what might you have done differently? What, if anything, surprised you?).
	▸ Talk about the formative feedback process itself: What do you have to say about it? What's not working? How can we do better?
	▸ Always close the debrief on a positive note.
Process Expectations and Norms	▸ Remind the group of all the specific positives they received (point out any patterns to them) on their presentation.
	▸ Acknowledge and celebrate any risks they may have taken (regardless of outcome).
	▸ Focus on one major takeaway (a feel-good one or one that may be tougher to hear, if I judge it's needed).
Watching/ Listening for	▸ Their analysis—are they reflecting on things I would have brought to their attention?
	▸ Their experience of the formative feedback process: Is this new to them? Were there any rough patches? Did intentional successes occur? Did happy accidents happen?

It's Your Turn

You've just read about what Sara does with her sophomores in world history to support them through three distinct phases of a group-based learning project. These projects are multifaceted, and they require lots of collaborative skills in addition to subject knowledge. With the shifts in instructional settings brought on by the global pandemic, Sara reminds us that formative feedback must go on. The next generation of students will rely on so-called distributed and blended learning in ways we cannot yet quite fully imagine.

Now think of an upcoming group project your students will do. For each phase of the project, use the structure of Figure 6.6 to list the scaffolds, agreements, and protocols you intend to use with your students. By doing this before you introduce the project to your students, you'll have a better sense of how to use your time (e.g., what handouts/documents might you need to create or what resources might you need to curate for your students?) and how balanced and visible your supports may or may not be through each phase of the upcoming project feedback cycle.

Figure 6.6 Graphic Organizer for Analyzing the Support You Will Offer Your Students Through Three Phases of a Group-Based Project Feedback Cycles

Phase 1. Before formative feedback cycle has begun (feedback preparation)

Scaffolds/Handouts/Resources:

Agreements:

Protocol(s):

Phase 2. During the formative feedback cycle with students (feedback enactment)

Scaffolds/Handouts/Resources:

Agreements:

Protocol(s):

Phase 3. After the project is complete (post-feedback reflection)

Scaffolds/Handouts/Resources:

Agreements:

Protocol(s):

Getting Started: Revisiting Your Small-Group Norms

Norm-setting—and maintaining group work norms—is critical for feedback-rich exchanges in small-group configurations. Even if we teach at a school where students engage in group work in every class, we cannot take for granted in our own class that each group is prepared to function as well as it needs to for effective feedback routines. Our responsibility to support equitable learning environments requires us to focus on small-group interactions and dynamics.

Too often, our students miss the mark with feedback-rich exchanges. They get stuck, they slow down, they spin in circles. Giving and taking feedback from peers brings pressure. It can feel painful and embarrassing. Many adults also struggle with feedback-rich exchanges. No wonder why we as humans tend to avoid it.

There is nothing inevitable about this. We all need to rethink how we think about feedback norms and practices in small groups. One step in the right direction is to slow down and draw attention to what matters most to us. Let's start providing visible, tangible scaffolds and supports such as task checklists, progress guides, and "right-sized" **rubrics** to put the focus back on the work from first drafts to last draft. We must remember that people, especially young adults, need constant positive cues and reminders. They also need to know we are assessing the work, not the person, with a growth mindset. Progress—not final judgment—is what it is all about with assessment for learning.

To make progress, group norms need to be explicit, monitored, and revisited.

Group Work Norms That Support More Productive Independent Functioning

How We Learn Together

- ☐ No one is done until everyone is done.
- ☐ You have the right to ask anyone in your group for help.
- ☐ You have the duty to assist anyone in your group who asks for help.
- ☐ Helping means explaining our thinking, not giving answers or doing work for others.
- ☐ Provide justification when you make a statement or claim.
- ☐ Rely on each other first. Ask the teacher only if it's a team question.
- ☐ Work together. Don't divide up the work so no one knows what the others are doing.
- ☐ None of us alone is as smart as all of us together.
- ☐ We communicate when things aren't working or we feel left out.

Maintaining group work norms is everyone's responsibility, not only yours as a teacher. Have students reflect on group functioning regularly. This can be done in several ways. One of the simplest and quickest is a "whip around" by a group where each group says aloud the best part of their group's functioning that day. (Each group will need to decide ahead of time what this is and who will share it.)

It helps if you invite students to pay attention to a particular norm that is a focus for the day before small-group work begins that day.

While whole-class discussions and "whip arounds" about the functioning of group norms can be an important source of information for the teacher and a healthy experience for a learning community—since students get to hear one another's perspectives—having students write their reflections down and share anonymously can lead to a different kind of information exchange. Teachers learn from these informal sources of information: When they know what's working for their students, they can make adjustments to improve group performance.

During online learning, many teachers drop a link to a Google form in the chat to do this. The example in Figure 6.7 presents a paper exit ticket for students to better focus the group's feedback to the teacher. The idea is to gather a sample of responses (feedback for adults) to better understand what is and is not working for students in different teams.

Figure 6.7   Exit Ticket to Support Reflection on Group Norms

---

Name:

Date:

Period:

Today as you worked with your group, our focus was on our group work norm, "Rely on each other first. Ask the teacher only if it's a team question."

1. How did you rely on each other today? Be specific.

2. If your team asked me a question today, remind me what the question was. Then tell me what you tried in order to answer your question before you asked me your question. Be specific.

3. Looking back, what might you have also tried to do or say to each other before asking me?

Try It Tomorrow

Trello and Other Project-Based Collaboration Tools

Trello is a visual collaboration platform designed for project management. There are many other apps in this space, including JIRA, Pivotal Tracker, Clubhouse, and Basecamp. Some apps are proprietary and have a cost, others are offered for free. Your school district likely has a policy on app use and may offer other tech solutions for communicating information. We don't endorse these products—we only point to how they can, when used appropriately, change how feedback is produced and exchanged in the 21st century classroom.

Trello is one example of how to teach students to organize, collaborate, and communicate on projects and assignments. Users create boards, lists, and cards. Each *board* is a single web page. *Cards* make up each list and can be dragged and dropped onto other lists or reordered within lists. There is no limit to the number of team members that can be shared on a board. Students can move their card from one list to another as they accomplish that stage. Links, attachments, and comments can be part of each card.

One way that teachers can use Trello is to keep tabs on students as they complete several stages of a project, even if it's not a team project. For example, each stage of the project (e.g., understand the success criteria, brainstorm, research, first draft, get feedback from an outsider), can be a list on the Trello board.

I never cease to be amazed by how different some students' small-group work personas are compared to their whole-class selves. Imagine if my only impressions of a student were based solely on my interacting with them one-on-one or during whole-class situations.

—Kyle, high school art teacher

Setting Goals and Monitoring Progress with Small-Group Feedback: Questions for Lesson Study and Professional Learning Communities

Sharing Stories of Success: When Small Groups of Students Have Demonstrated Independence

Learning from each other doesn't always require us to focus on instructional challenges and problems. We can learn from and learn to celebrate one another's successes with things we haven't yet tried. In your **professional learning community** (**PLC**), what are some of the successes with small groups you've had over the years? It's important to reflect together on how students in small groups at your school learn and have learned to become more independent, more competent, and more accomplished by helping one another grow as a team.

- Think of a specific action/intervention you tried to get a small group to become more independent that worked! Then take turns communicating to each other:
    - What was the action/intervention?
    - How do you know it worked? Say more.
    - What do you think made the difference?
    - Did the students offer each other feedback? Which kinds?

- Have someone in your group **scribe** and **tag** responses on visible media so everyone can look for emerging patterns and make connections (a critical habit of mind).

- As a group, consider whether there any patterns emerging from your discussion on these actions/interventions. What seems to be working across all your lived experiences?

- From the lens of feedback, what meaning can we make of these small-group success stories? Try to distill in a few statements what works when kids give and take feedback. Agree to post them for students to see in a few of your classrooms this year.

Recap/Review

- Peer dynamics can play an influential role in students' experiences of small-group work. Our formative feedback interactions with students should thoughtfully serve to prevent, address, and reflect on issues related to group members' sense of well-being and depth of participation.
- Since students' rates of interaction in a small group are a strong predictor of learning gains, some of a teacher's formative feedback interactions with groups needs to focus on equalizing rates of participation, particularly in terms of how we assign (and sometimes reassign) roles to advance the work.
- Students and teachers both benefit from explicit protocols, agreements, and routines designed to assist small groups at each phase of formative feedback interactions (planning for pre-, during, and post-feedback cycles helps integrate the power of feedback across the project or task).
- Having students self-assess with a progress guide or other success criteria organizer can aid in the quality and quantity of feedback in small-group configurations.
- Completing a progress guide for teacher use can help teachers to create small groups that are strategically formed and purposefully aligned with class goals and to make good choices about potential foci (e.g., skills development) for small-group interactions.
- Students and teachers can benefit from having a content and/or process focus for formative feedback interactions in small-group configuration.
- Regarding the formative feedback you give to a group, it can be helpful to think in terms of which of your comments or questions are more *content-focused* and which are more *process-focused*. The point is to be intentional with both and aware of your ratio of one to the other.
- To improve your formative feedback interactions with small groups (and to foster more productive and independent group work), establish, maintain, and regularly reflect on the functioning of small-group work by addressing norms.

Ticket Out the Door

1. What's one idea and/or tool from this chapter you want to try? In what context might you try it?
2. Name a current strength you have when it comes to formative feedback interactions with students in small groups. How did this particular strength come to be the one you named?
3. A new teacher, not familiar with your school culture, joins your department and seeks your advice regarding small-group work. What would you tell them?

Self-Assessment

Take a moment to reflect on your past experiences giving (and receiving) formative feedback to (and from) students in small-group configurations. Were you face-to-face with the groups? Did you meet in a Zoom breakout room? Did you communicate on a shared slide deck?

Now, try to respond to the following self-check questions. There are no right or wrong answers. This is an opportunity to check for your own understanding and reflect on your own experiences:

1. When I think of my formative feedback interactions with students in small-group configurations, the benefit(s) that come to mind are: (Please list as many benefits as you can.)

2. My biggest concern with formative feedback interactions with small groups of students is: (Please share.)

3. The best advice I've ever received about interacting with small groups of students is: (Please be as specific as you can.)

4. One way I address the challenge of listening in when it comes to small-group formative feedback is: (Please give an example.)

CHAPTER 7

Feedback With Individuals

> Few physical, intellectual or social skills can be acquired satisfactorily simply by being told about them. Most require practice in a supportive environment which incorporates feedback loops. This usually includes a teacher who knows which skills are to be learned, and who can recognize and describe a fine performance, demonstrate a fine performance, and indicate how a poor performance can be improved.
>
> —Sadler (1989, p. 120)

We all learn from each other, typically one person at a time. If asked to think in general about **formative feedback**, as teachers, we often think of what we do in our classrooms. When working with students, we offer **feedback** to individuals one at a time. We know that each of our students is unique, and they need us to meet them where they are in the trajectory of learning on a project or task everyone is working to complete. It makes sense that to progress, to move forward on a current draft or part of the assignment, everyone needs or will need individualized attention and support.

Personal experience and research on formative feedback tell us that working closely with individual students requires a focus on engaging, eliciting, and extending each student's sense of what is next. We often have a destination or goal in mind, but that picture of progress needs clear and consistent communication routines in addition to visible **scaffolds** and protocols to mark progress for each person in the classroom. Let's explore what engaging, eliciting, and extending our feedback **moves** and strategies look like when we focus on feedback for individual students.

Engaging

Teachers often picture how to approach their individual students to offer feedback. We like to think before we speak. Even before we engage our students' myriad needs, orientations, and dispositions in our classrooms, we find ourselves rehearsing how to size up that first turn of talk with a student. As we recall previous feedback sessions with individual students, we remember there are many approaches to starting the cycle. We make small talk with some students, checking in before we come to the point of the actual feedback exchange. With other students, we dive right in to the exchange because we sense they prefer a no-nonsense approach to feedback. These students are ready to make next steps on the project draft; we sense they need to get it done. Still others may need us to circle back or slow down and take a deep breath before they can hear our feedback or offer theirs. These students may need to review the **progress guide** again, talk with a classmate, and come back to engage in the next steps tomorrow or the next day after our one-on-one talk.

Eliciting

We know that teachers also tend to think of ways of eliciting information from a particular student during a formative feedback cycle or loop. Elicitation is an invitation to think through what we are doing and why. As **formative assessors**, we seek a dialogue with students together and separately. The goal is to engage students and elicit responses by communicating about what can be done to move the work (a project, performance task, or longer assignment) forward. Whether that one-on-one dialogue occurs asynchronously via typed comments in a shared document or whether it happens synchronously in-person or via Zoom does not matter. Our goal is the same: We want to elicit productive responses to feedback so that progress can be made by our students and we can learn better how to assist as guides on the side.

Across the literature on **formative assessment**, there are many well-documented elicitation strategies that are intended to generate productive feedback-rich conversations. Our work has focused on how elicitation and **elaboration** improve when teachers and students employ combinations of **posing, pausing,** and **probing** moves (see Figure 7.1) to advance **feedback loops**. To deepen and sustain the cycles of dialogue/feedback on a performance task or project, one can probe by asking, "Can you say more? Try to describe it. What comes to mind when . . . ?" As we note in Figure 7.1, probing is the art of asking follow-up questions that utilize information from actual student **first draft** responses. When combined with posing and pausing routines, probing moves support our assessment of our students' understanding while also revealing gaps and bottlenecks they may be encountering along the way.

Students who are working one-on-one with teachers to meaningfully take up feedback in a **dialogic** way must also feel free to probe on that feedback. For feedback loops to work authentically and effectively, there must be a give and take (Carless, 2019). Students can and should ask the teacher, "Can you say more? I am still unclear." "What can I do, specifically, to make this revision?" or "Why does it matter to add this or reconsider that?" To achieve authentic communication, that is, dialogue about feedback and next steps, both parties must be able and willing to probe on those concrete, specific next steps to reach shared understanding and agreement.

CONFIGURATION

Figure 7.1 Formative Assessment (FA) Moves

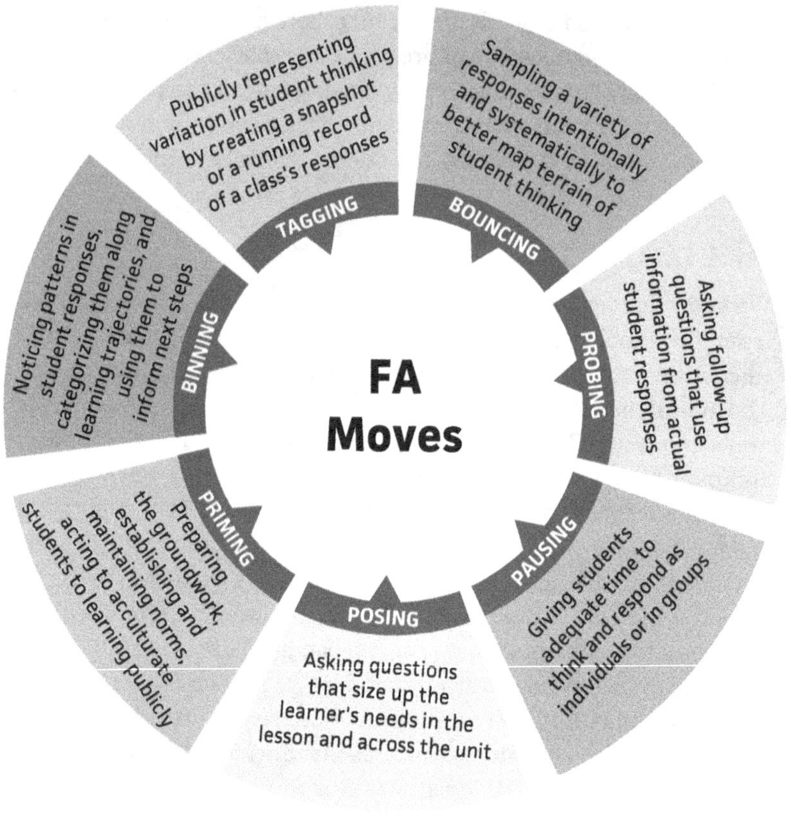

FA Moves wheel with eight segments:

- **TAGGING**: Publicly representing variation in student thinking by creating a snapshot or a running record of a class's responses
- **BOUNCING**: Sampling a variety of responses intentionally and systematically to better map terrain of student thinking
- **PROBING**: Asking follow-up questions that use information from actual student responses
- **PAUSING**: Giving students adequate time to think and respond as individuals or in groups
- **POSING**: Asking questions that size up the learner's needs in the lesson and across the unit
- **PRIMING**: Preparing the groundwork, establishing and maintaining norms, acting to acculturate students to learning publicly
- **BINNING**: Noticing patterns in student responses, categorizing them along learning trajectories, and using them to inform next steps

Source: Adapted from Duckor & Holmberg (2021a).

Available for download at **resources.corwin.com/ContinuousImprovement**

In one-on-one settings, we sometimes rely on directive invitations to elicit information. These exchanges look and sound like this: "Tell me what you were striving for here," or "Show me the part you think is strongest right now." As formative assessors in the classroom, on the field, or in the lab, we demonstrate our commitment to growth and progress by inviting inquiry and problem solving. Thus we tend to ask the same clarifying questions repeatedly to elicit information from students about their first draft responses to performance tasks. Visibly making these probing moves in different **configurations** allows everyone to ask questions such as: "What's another way you could approach this?" or "What is the best part so far?" or "Where are you stuck?"

Extending

Teachers can think they are too busy to re-engage with every child who fails to act upon suggestions and advice. We can put forward one-on-one meeting routines (such as conferencing, huddling, etc.) and look for results. We naturally get frustrated when our feedback is ignored or not incorporated in the next drafts. Add this to the fact that teachers face competing demands (curriculum pacing, testing, the bell schedule, etc.) and it seems there isn't always time for extending one-on-one feedback loops and experimenting with different configurations to make feedback more formative.

Nonetheless, all is not lost. Everything takes practice, including making feedback work. We can start thinking about *how* we know whether our students use feedback loops and dialogues. We can ask ourselves, did our attempts at communicating with a student help them extend their performance? How do we know? What is evidence that some things (sticky notes, comments/reply feature, nonverbal cues, etc.) are working for some and not others (yet)?

For example, before bringing to a close a feedback loop with an individual student, do we typically invite the student to express commitment to revision and improvement? ("Let's hear what you're ready to work on. Why that first?") Answers can often be surprising. Do we ask the student to summarize or prioritize next steps? ("So what are the first two things you're going to do? Why those two?") If so, at what level of specificity and with what visual and body-kinesthetic supports to bring it home in multiple **modalities**?

Each of these extending-type questions leads to an internal dialogue that supports reflection for teachers and students who are collaborating on a project or performance task. It is through teachers' own reflection on engaging, eliciting, and extending student engagement with rich tasks, projects, and longer-term assignments in one-on-one dialogue that feedback practices flourish and take root.

Dialogue May Lead to Misunderstandings

An important point to make at the outset of this chapter is that when thinking about our formative feedback practices with individual students, we often do so with the assumption that verbal communication is the most effective means to share information. This is often not the case with our students. Young people naturally get stuck, forget what is being asked, and have difficulty monitoring their next steps, which is a **metacognitive skill** in itself.

Instead of assuming real-time dialogue is always the answer, it may be wiser for teachers and other adults to remember that young people think differently and therefore process information in different ways. In addition to developmental differences, generational gaps can lead to misunderstandings between teachers and students. The communication processes and feedback expectations among Millennials and Gen Z students differ from those of Gen X and Baby Boomers.

Given this, and to ensure equity and authenticity, it is important to build a customized toolkit of communication facilitation and repair strategies to use during formative feedback cycles. Meeting students where they are and supporting them requires that we have a variety of tools, strategies, and protocols in our formative feedback toolkit. Partly, this means realizing that dialogue is difficult at times because there are different expectations (cultural, developmental, generational) at play in the work.

This chapter explores what we're calling *individual configurations* of formative feedback and is connected to the previous two *configurations* chapters. The following four guiding questions anchor our explorations.

Guiding Questions

1. Why plan, enact, and reflect on individual and one-on-one configurations of formative feedback? For whose good are these configurations? What educational goals and purposes can individual/one-on-one configurations serve?

2. How do I know what my students are getting out of the feedback loops and exchanges in one-on-one configurations?

3. When I observe communication strategies aren't working as well as I intended, what can I do to facilitate, repair, and restart a more dialogic exchange?

4. How can I help my students in all their diversity become more independent, more confident to take up feedback, and more likely to move to the next level?

Guided by these questions, we'll explore the practice of formative feedback with individual students. We'll start by focusing on what we mean by individual formative feedback and what its hallmarks are. But first, we need a reminder of where we are with the formative feedback framework that anchors our work.

Figure 7.2 depicts three main feedback focal points and their associated lenses. This chapter is about configuration and the third of the three lenses for it: individual or one-on-one formative feedback. Remember: *Configuration* refers to the primary arrangement and number of people in which the formative feedback occurs or is situated.

We're using configuration as a lens to explore how formative feedback practices can work better for both our students and ourselves. But we should always keep in mind that **directionality** and modality matter, too. How such facets influence one another within and across each lens matters for advancing the depth and breadth of feedback practices. For now, let's look at how individual one-on-one interactions can set students up for success in your classroom and beyond.

Figure 7.2 Formative Feedback Framework

Contexts for Learning		
Face-to-Face	Blended	Distance Learning
Focal Point		
Directionality	**Configuration**	**Modality**
Lenses		
Teacher-driven	Whole class	Written
Peer-to-peer-driven	Small groups (2–4)	Spoken
Self-driven	Individual (1:1)	Nonverbal
Tasks, Projects, Activities	Learning Goals, Standards, Skills Rubrics, Progress Guides, "Next Steps" Organizers	

Defining Individual/One-on-One Formative Feedback

When we say *individual formative feedback*, we are referring to scenarios in which a teacher or a student attempts to support a **formative feedback loop** on a particular task, project, or assignment. It involves a one-on-one situation, whether the feedback dialogue is initiated by a student or the teacher. The feedback loop may occur through a single modality (i.e., spoken, written, or nonverbal) or a combination of modalities (such as when an in-person conversation is supported by notes or comments written by one or both parties).

Though peer-to-peer formative feedback is frequently conducted in pairs, which suggests a one-on-one configuration, this chapter will focus primarily on a one-on-one configuration in which one member of the pair is a teacher and one is a student. Please refer to Chapter 3 for additional guidance on supporting peer-to-peer feedback, whether it is in a one-on-one configuration, a small-group configuration, or a whole-class configuration.

Formative Feedback Is an Individual Experience

All formative feedback is individual at some level. For example, if a teacher engages a small group of students and has a feedback dialogue with that group, each student is making meaning of the experience for themselves. We tend to process what is most important to ourselves as individuals first. Similarly, when a teacher offers feedback to the whole class simultaneously or engages the whole class in a feedback dialogue, individual students still cognitively process and act upon that feedback experience as individuals even when in a group. We may inhabit a community of learners, as experts note, but we are nonetheless individuals in a group or classroom and school-based setting.

Individual Formative Feedback and Differentiation

The hallmark of individual formative feedback is that it is tailored to and adjusted for individual students. In other words, individual formative feedback is, by definition, **differentiated formative feedback** customized to a student's **zone of proximal development (ZPD)** with a task, **prompt**, or **stimulus**. Additionally, individual students bring personal **assets**, experiences, and **prior knowledge** to feedback exchanges. Linguistic, ethnic, economic, and cultural experiences inevitably shape our one-on-one dialogues about student work and next steps. To differentiate feedback one on one, we need to see the whole person in the exchange.

The following table summarizes one-on-one formative feedback and distinguishes it from other assessment practices.

FORMATIVE FEEDBACK IN AN INDIVIDUAL CONFIGURATION

What It Is	What It Isn't
▶ Differentiated in content and tone/style to better meet each student's learning needs and personal dispositions	▶ A one-size-fits-all approach (although teachers can begin developing their skills with "base recipes" from which they improvise)
▶ Dialogic	▶ Writing the same comment again and again on students' papers
▶ A process where misunderstandings in communication are the norm, not the exception; therefore, specific moves intended to check for understanding and enhance understanding are necessary	▶ Something only English language arts teachers do
▶ Considered the crux of meaningful teaching and deeper learning by many at-promise students	▶ A monologue delivered by a teacher who is rushed and batch processing "do this, do that" instructions for all
▶ Significantly influenced by subject content, task difficulty, and the nature of the project cycle	▶ A guarantee that students will learn a skill because "I explained how—now you carry it out"
▶ Requires attention to dialogue dynamics and turn-taking	▶ As efficient as assigning points and grading
▶ Builds metacognitive skills	▶ Grades on a performance with generic advice such as, "Try to use the rubric next time."
▶ Equity-driven responsive teaching that conveys "I value your learning enough to take time to talk with you about it."	▶ Offered without exemplars and protocols

> It really helps with individual formative feedback when you know your students well. You know what examples will resonate with kids and which metaphors will stick. I use real-world examples to bring home why feedback matters.
>
> —Alice, sixth/seventh-grade teacher

Planning for Four Key Aspects of Feedback-Based Dialogue With Individual Students

Table 7.1 presents four aspects to consider when planning for individual formative feedback dialogues. The table explains why these aspects matter and provides tips and questions to guide your decision-making processes as you plan, so you and your students can better optimize the time you each spend in dialogue. As you begin launching turns of talk and working toward a productive feedback loop or cycle, use the table to check and correct course, if necessary.

Table 7.1 Planning for Individual Formative Feedback: What to Consider and Why It Matters

ASPECT	ASK YOURSELF	WHY IT MATTERS	TIPS AND TO-DO'S
Making the Process Visible to Both You and the Student	If key components of the formative feedback loop are not visible to me or to the student, how can either of us really know what's occurring in our communication?	Visible scaffolds make a difference in teacher practice and student learning. Both teacher and student can reflect on spoken-only feedback and structures to guarantee (for example) the aim of consistently identifying strengths and next steps during a feedback loop, but when a structure to support this aim is present (e.g., a progress guide for student self-assessment) students and teacher can both benefit more.	• Use progress guides for teachers and for students (self-assessment) to plan for and to carry out individual formative feedback dialogues. • Come up with your own ways to visually represent to students where you are in a formative feedback loop/dialogue (e.g., opening the loop, reflecting on the effectiveness of the recommended next step, closing the loop).

(Continued)

(Continued)

ASPECT	ASK YOURSELF	WHY IT MATTERS	TIPS AND TO-DO'S
The Student's Perspective/ Perception of the Feedback Loop/ Dialogue	How do I know how this student is perceiving and understanding this feedback content and situation/ process?	The same move you make (whether it's asking a question, giving a suggestion, or simply telling the student what to do next) may be understood, interpreted, and felt by different students in surprisingly different ways. What may work or feel good to one student may not work for (or may even feel terrible to) another.	▸ Offer students choice in how they would like their feedback dialogue with you before it starts (e.g., would they like to speak first?). ▸ Work to discover how it went for them. Try a closing check-in move such as asking, "What was the toughest part of that conversation/ dialogue for you?" ▸ Pay attention to body language—your own and the student's—but don't draw conclusions based only on body language. ▸ Ask, "What parts of the formative feedback process/conversation were working for you?" Encourage specificity so you can make repairs if necessary.
Communication Repair Strategies (Because Misunderstandings Happen)	What's most important in this moment: cognitive-focused repair efforts on my part or affective-focused repair work?	Deciding which takes priority can help you do a better job in your repair efforts.	▸ If body language, energy, and communication tell you that student affect is taking precedence, address it gently and in an age-appropriate manner. ▸ When the repair is cognitive-focused, try an alternative explanation, analogy, or other solution. ▸ Signal that a fix is needed, but also try giving yourself the opportunity to come back later with an alternative explanation, analogy, and so forth. You don't have to repair every misunderstanding on the fly.

ASPECT	ASK YOURSELF	WHY IT MATTERS	TIPS AND TO-DO'S
Range of Implementation Strategies With a Similar Aim in Mind	How else could I achieve the same goal (e.g., the goal of engaging this student in the formative feedback dialogue)?	Serving students equitably requires having a variety of means to achieve similarly oriented ends.	▶ Seek students' input on how else the goal could be achieved. ▶ Let feedback techniques from outside your discipline or profession inspire you. ▶ Consider how you are intentionally supporting pausing with different students.

When it comes to planning high-quality formative feedback loops with individual students, it helps if you ask yourself the following questions first:

- How do I make the process visible to both myself and the student?
- What are the likely student perceptions of the experience?
- What communication repair strategies might I use if things need a reboot?
- How can I ensure that a range of reengagement techniques/strategies are available to both of us during the information exchange?

These aspects are covered in the "Ask Yourself" column of the table: They remind us that good feedback practice doesn't just happen, it is brought to life with reflective practice (Burns, 2010; Duckor et al., 2017, 2018).

We also invite you to ask why having a range of techniques available matters (see the "Why It Matters" column). Assessing for learning and deep equity requires we have a range of feedback moves, even for the same aim (e.g., the aim of inspiring more substantive revision with a work-in-progress). Kids are not one-size-fits-all problems waiting for magic solutions. If there is one enduring truth about formative feedback, it is that the same feedback offered in similar circumstances can work for some students and not others, depending on many factors.

To be the best we can be with all our students, we need flexible and adaptable tools and strategies in our feedback toolkit. These tools and strategies can help us anticipate and guide the dynamics of intersecting influences on feedback exchanges with real individuals. Table 7.1 also presents relevant "Tips and To-Do's" to help us all achieve what matters—student engagement with the work to take it to the next level.

Both the "What the Research Tells Us" and "Focus on Practice" sections that follow offer research-backed suggestions for how to make what you do with individual students more visible, more effective, and (we hope) more engaging for all.

What the Research Tells Us

Tailor the Message and Timing of Feedback to the Work at Hand

If there's one thing the research tells us, it's that there isn't one kind or type of formative feedback that suits every occasion (Nottingham & Nottingham, 2017). Context, curriculum, and kids matter, and each will influence what works when it comes to one-on-one feedback.

However, most experts agree that you ought to avoid mixing praise with substantive feedback about the task, project, or assignment. Praise acts as a diluter and fails to stimulate cognitive engagement with the task demand (Hattie & Zierer, 2018; Skipper & Douglas, 2012). It is better to focus on observational statements to bring the **learning criteria** and curricular goals into sharper focus:

- "One thing I see that is working well with this current draft is . . ."
- "I really like your use of [this success criteria] because it shows how . . ."
- "The work in its current form is not yet at [this **standard**]. Here is a way we can get to the next level . . ."

These sorts of messages offer the student opportunities to reorient their first drafts to the current level of performance and envision possible next steps.

In addition to the message, the timing of feedback matters (Brookhart, 2017; Shute, 2008; Wiggins, 2012). According to some researchers, immediate feedback tends to work well for low-achieving students (Gaynor, 1981; Mason & Bruning, 2001; Roper, 1977). But this may not be the case for everyone in every subject all the time.

There is a place for timing when it comes to feedback: The time to offer or withhold feedback is based on individual students' needs. Some scholars call for delaying, "judiciously withholding," and reducing feedback to boost students' long-term retention and to lead to more sustained learning (Soderstrom & Bjork, 2015). Such holding back tends to be effective when students have already moved through the surface learning phase (when they are first gaining needed information). As Hattie and Clarke (2019) point out, feedback can be timed with deeper phases of learning, such as when students are manipulating, relating, and applying information to a problem or task.

Feedback Should Be Intentional, Strategic, and Personalized

We know that teachers need to be intentional and strategic about the timing, mode, and content of the formative feedback they provide in a learning segment or **unit of instruction**. We also know that aligning feedback with where a student is in their various learning trajectories in the project or task makes a difference. When in doubt about what formative feedback to provide, ensuring there is specific, tangible, and actionable feedback about next steps is good practice (Hattie & Zierer, 2018). Generic, haphazard feedback tends to miss the mark.

Cowie (2005a) found that individual configurations of feedback work for students. In one study,

> [Student] consensus was that teacher feedback provided during these relatively private interactions was particularly useful because students themselves were more explicit about what they did not understand. Teachers had a better appreciation of their 'level' of understanding and were able to 'target' their problem areas. The students were unanimous in their desire for more opportunities for one-to-one interaction with teachers. (pp. 203–204)

Moreover, students' consensus was that

> teacher feedback, provided during relatively private one-to-one or one-to-group interactions, was particularly useful. The reason given was that pupils themselves were more explicit about what they did not understand and so the teacher had a better appreciation of their 'level of understanding' and could 'target problem areas.'" (Cowie, 2005b, p. 142)

Not surprisingly, it turns out that the perceived efficacy of our feedback matters more than our need to communicate specific informational content (as we talk!) to students in these exchanges. Moreover, what students share about what, where, and how they may not understand often matters greatly to the quality of the feedback interaction.

Confusion Around Feedback Happens and Is Normal

A few studies point to how common it is for students to find teachers' feedback confusing. It turns out many students are unable to interpret teachers' feedback correctly (Goldstein, 2006; Higgins et al., 2002). Some students may understand the feedback but are unsure about how to use it. Too often, confusion arises because communication is not aided by clear, well-designed scaffolds or procedures that keep our students on track. New learning platforms and high-tech media can allow for in-document commentary to track feedback exchanges but low-tech solutions such as printed progress guides with written notes can also aid in monitoring and supporting uptake of next steps.

Frequent Check-Ins Are Necessary

For all these reasons, it's critical that teachers always check to see how students are interpreting the feedback they have received. These can be thought of as check-in or "How's my feedback going?" moves. Teachers can ask their students the following:

- What sense are you making from what I've said? Am I being clear?
- How do you see yourself making use of this particular part of feedback?
- What can we talk more about right now that might help you with your next steps?

Each of these moves requires a degree of metacognitive skill (for teachers and students). We must take steps with feedback to support learners who are learning how to learn. Check in and ask, "How is it going with what I said on the progress guide? Does my feedback—the comments on the electronic document—make sense? Can I say it again right now or show you what's next in a different way?"

Wise Feedback Promotes Trust and a Tone of Respect

Research shows that when teachers are of a different race/ethnic/linguistic background from their students, there are specific moves teachers can make to support students' uptake and use of formative feedback. Yeager and colleagues (2013) have coined this "wise feedback," which emphasizes both high standards and the belief that the student can meet those standards. In a double-blind randomized field experiment, teachers who explicitly stated "I'm giving you these comments because I have very high expectations and I know that you can reach them," made a significant difference in both how many students revised their work and how substantial those revisions were.

How a Feedback Dialogue/Loop Opens and Ends Matters

Where we start and stop a feedback cycle matters. Researchers have identified a so-called ***peak-end effect***, which describes how people's retrospective evaluation of an event tends to be based on how the experience felt during the most intense moment and the last moment of any feedback session (Kahneman et al., 1993). It often helps to have a feedback protocol in place that ensures the last moment of a formative feedback dialogue is a positive one (Hoogerheide et al., 2018).

Consider summarizing the highlights of the session together and add, "One thing I liked about today's feedback session was . . ."

Try It Tomorrow

Make Your "Positive" Really Stand Out

Lots of learning management systems, such as Canvas, offer an option for recording audio or video feedback and attaching it to a document, post, or message.

Use this feature to make a specific, positive comment that will direct attention to success. "One thing I like about this current draft is how you were able to . . ." is the kind of feedback sentence starter that focuses on the work. It can be used when offering feedback on art projects, musical performances, math exhibitions, science investigations, language arts essays, historical research papers, autoethnographic stories, world language assignments, sports games, and so forth.

The point is to offer the warm tone of your voice alongside the positive content-focused feedback tied to learning goals.

Positive feedback on work-in-progress is not praise; it is acknowledgment of learning that is unfolding toward a visible learning goal.

Feedback Builds a Schoolwide Culture of Deep Equity

All these findings are consistent with research on high-performing schools that serve historically underserved students, in particular, our students of color (Darling-Hammond, 1996, 1997, 2006). In schools that promote trust and a tone of respect, Theodore Sizer of the Coalition of Essential Schools notes that it is reasonable for students to ask themselves, "How am I doing?" Unless a student knows how they are doing, they are unable to adjust the regimen of their learning (Darling-Hammond et al., 1995). In the Foreword (Darling-Hammond et al., 1995), Sizer also adds,

> "Assessment" thus has many functions. It is only as good as its instruments, and it is defensible only to the extent that it actively forwards and enhances a child's learning.
>
> Good schools not only frequently tell their students "how they are doing" but get youngsters into the habit of asking the question for themselves. The expectation is that illuminating feedback—indeed aggressively searching it out—is a universal characteristic of an educated person.

> ## Author Insight
> ### Brown and Campione
>
> The core participant structures of our classrooms are essentially dialogic. Sometimes these activities are face-to-face in small or large group interactions; sometimes they are mediated via print or electronic mail; and at still other times, they go underground and become part of the thought processes of members of the community. . . . Dialogues provide the format for novices to adopt the discourse structure, goals, values, and belief systems of scientific practice. Over time, the community of learners adopts a common voice and common knowledge base, a shared system of meaning, beliefs, and activity that is as often implicit as it is explicit.

Source: Brown and Campione (1996), p. 319.

Focus on Practice: Using the Progress Guide for Teacher and Student Self-Assessment to Support Individual Students

In the following vignette, we illustrate one way a progress guide can serve dual purposes—for a teacher's use and for a student's use for **self-assessment** (one of the directionality lenses we introduced in Chapter 4). The progress guide can be used by both teachers and students as they prepare for and carry out formative feedback dialogues in one-on-one/individual configurations. As you read, keep in mind the importance of progress guides for teacher use to aid in decision making for formative feedback delivery; these tools help inform and bring coherence to the individual, small-group, and whole-class configuration decisions you will make in your class.

Revisiting the Scenario in Ms. Davies's Middle School Science Class

Recall Ms. Davies's feedback practice that we first introduced in Chapter 5. Ms. Davies's students are studying the human causes of climate change. Partway through the unit, the students drafted a written response to a task/prompt that has them (1) identify human causes of climate change and (2) connect each human cause with its direct impact on the affected ecosystem.

Recall that after Ms. Davies collected all her students' written responses and analyzed them, she discovered that 40% of her class wrote responses categorized as "Developing" on her progress guide (Figure 7.3). Her next **lesson plan** was built around these findings. She decided to move forward with two configurations of feedback.

First, Ms. Davies planned time for a whole-class feedback session revisiting the prompt on the projector/smartboard. She unpacked the embedded **academic language** in the ecosystems task/prompt and then analyzed in front of the class the strengths of a typical "Developing" response, contrasting it with "Advanced" and "Emerging" ones. She had students share observations with each other and then **scribed** the potential next steps for each example.

Next, Ms. Davies set the class to work revising their written responses with a self-assessment protocol using the student version of the progress guide (Figure 7.4). Their task was to work in teams to help each other with identifying and writing down one or two next steps. During this part of the lesson, Ms. Davies was able to focus on students at the top and bottom of the progress guide distribution as she moved around the classroom to check in one on one.

Figure 7.3 is a schematic representation of the percentage of students by performance level according to Ms. Davies's progress guide. Only the qualitative descriptions for work at the "Developing" and "Emerging" levels are present because that is where we will focus our attention. Teachers who engage in formative assessment must be careful to send the right message: We don't **bin** students and assign them grades; we identify current levels of performance in student work and focus on these as first drafts. All work is subject to improvement and revision. Grades are a summative affair, used at the end of the unit when final work is due.

Figure 7.3 Schematic Representation of the Percentages of Students by Performance Level on Ms. Davies's Progress Guide for Teacher Use

APPROXIMATE LEVEL	PROMPT RESPONSE	NEXT STEPS
Exemplary 5%	▶ Description here	▶ Possible next steps here
Advanced 20% [Angela's work as possible exemplar for whole-class feedback] 6 students (out of a class of 30)	▶ Description here	▶ Possible next steps here

(Continued)

(Continued)

APPROXIMATE LEVEL	PROMPT RESPONSE	NEXT STEPS
Developing 40% [Theo's work as exemplar for whole-class feedback] 12 students (out of a class of 30)	• Identifies either human causes of climate change *or* impacts to ecosystems. • Makes no connections between the two.	• Review notes/discussion and list climate change causes or their impacts (depending on which is missing). • Connect identified causes to identified ecosystem impacts. • If causes are named, ask "What are the results of these?" or if impacts are named, ask "What may have brought about these changes to the ecosystem?"
Emerging 20% [Luis's work as possible exemplar for whole-class feedback] 6 students (out of a class of 30)	• Names one cause of climate change.	• Refer to notes/discussion and name additional causes of climate change. • Connect those causes to changes in ecosystems. • "What changes to the environment are due to this cause? Are there other human behaviors that are changing the environment?"
Beginning 10%	• Description here	• Possible next steps here
No response yet (Present) 0%	• Description here	• Possible next steps here
No response yet (Absent) 5%	• Description here	• Possible next steps here

Leveraging the Breakdown of Current Student Performance by Percentage

The range of current work is significant. Five percent of the class completed "Exemplary" responses at the highest level of Ms. Davies's progress guide. These students may need feedback that focuses on extension activities or they may be invited to support their struggling peers. Another 5% of the responses are categorized under "no response yet." These students will need immediate feedback to get them started when they return to class. Similarly, 10% are "Beginning," which may mean they copied the prompt and wrote one or two ideas. It may also mean their responses were off-topic or vague.

Ms. Davies's analysis of student work the day before revealed that most of her students' work rests in the middle of the progress guide. Twelve out of the 30 student responses (40%) are at the "Developing" level and another 12 of the 30 student responses (40%) are represented by the "Emerging" and "Advanced" levels.

So, by looking at the breakdown of student performance on this task so far, Ms. Davies saw that it would be wise to engage the whole class in examining "Theo's" first draft, an anonymized student response from last year with no personal identifiers. Working together in a whole-class configuration, Ms. Davies then modeled and engaged everyone in how to help Theo's work move toward the next level. They asked questions together as a class:

- What steps can Theo take next?
- What would carrying out those next steps look like?
- Specifically, how can Theo revise his written work so that it will be *binned*, or categorized, at the "Advanced" level?

Ms. Davies's pedagogical and instructional choices would have been different had she discovered that 40% of her class's responses were at the "Exemplary" and "Advanced" levels instead.

Students Introduced to Student Self-Assessment Progress Guide Before One-on-One/Individual Conversations

Another way Ms. Davies used class time in whole-class configuration was to introduce students to the student self-assessment progress guide depicted in Figure 7.4. This student self-assessment progress guide is structurally like the one in Chapter 4 (Figure 4.3) about weighing evidence, but it is specific to the prompt on human causes of climate change. As we noted, all student self-assessment progress guides share key features:

- Written in student-friendly language
- Appropriate number of levels/**bins** (accommodates all levels of performance a teacher reasonably expects to see in her class)
- Oriented vertically
- Age-appropriate use of graphics to direct attention
- Names the strand or skill being worked on
- No points or scores!
- First-person point of view: "I" "My draft"
- **Sentence starters** as appropriate
- Age-appropriate amount of space for students to fill in or comment

Figure 7.4 Student Self-Assessment Progress Guide: Human Causes of Climate Change and Their Direct Impact on Ecosystems

Directions: Circle a level that best describes your work at this moment. Then write two next steps you can take to bring your work to the next level.

IN MY RESPONSE TO THE TASK OR PROMPT	NEXT STEPS
▸ I can name multiple human causes of climate change. ▸ I can make direct connections between those causes and changes to specific ecosystems.	To go even deeper, I will . . . 1. 2.
▸ I can identify human causes of climate change. ▸ I know that climate change impacts ecosystems but am unclear on exactly how.	To move ahead, I will . . . 1. 2.
▸ I know that humans cause climate change and that ecosystems are changing. ▸ I don't see the immediate connection between the two.	To move ahead, I will . . . 1. 2.
▸ I think humans cause climate change but I don't know many causes.	To move ahead, I will . . . 1. 2.
▸ I don't know whether or not humans cause climate change.	To move ahead, I will . . . 1. 2.
▸ I'm not sure, I don't know, or I didn't write a response.	To move ahead, I will . . . 1. 2.
▸ I was absent.	To get started, I need to talk with you and one or two classmates about what is next.

Unit and lesson planning matters for the formative assessor. One must plan lessons with time for instruction and assessment. Protecting the work of formative feedback requires planning so that students get the message: It's time to see where we are, what is next, and how we can help one another to go to the next level.

Ms. Davies's students know they are expected to revise their written work. (Just as they do in physical education, art, music, and world language classes that emphasize practice!) Ms. Davies's students also know they are supposed to decide where their own work currently is and to commit in writing to two next steps they will take to improve. Sometimes Ms. Davies collects these student self-assessment progress guides for one-on-one meetings; other times, she asks questions, listens carefully to their answers, and puts a stamp on them to keep in students' folders. The students know without a doubt that these guides are a part of each unit—they count as much as quizzes, tests, and homework for learning to learn.

Finding a Place to Start One-on-One Feedback Sessions During a Lesson

Now that the preparation (reviewing class response patterns, introducing to the whole class how to use a progress guide, and offering Theo's work as an example of the process for finding next steps) has occurred, it is time to pivot to individuals. By analyzing the initial results from the progress guide (Figure 7.3), Ms. Davies is now ready to be strategic about which one-on-one conversations to prioritize during class time and which to pursue over the week in a variety of media.

Ms. Davies has a good rapport with Luis. This rapport was strengthened by her positive relationship with him outside the classroom. Ms. Davies coached Luis on the cross-country team and Luis was an enthusiastic and talented runner. Ms. Davies figured that by talking with Luis first, she may garner insights with similar students whose work is emerging on this project.

Before sitting down with him, Ms. Davies reminded herself why she had binned Luis's written response as "Emerging." Luis's response had named only one cause of climate change: "burning coal," which was accurate.

Ms. Davies, however, expected her students to name multiple human causes of climate change (the prompt required three, among them deforestation, transportation, the manufacture of goods and consumerism, farming, overfishing, etc.). The learning activities that Luis and the rest of the class had experienced leading up to this task/prompt had everyone delving into the "Top 10" human causes of climate change.

The prompt also sought the direct impact on an ecosystem of every cause of climate change named (e.g., Earth's atmosphere, the oceans). Notably, Luis's response made no mention of an ecosystem impacted by burning coal (neither did the three other students whose work was binned in the same category).

Because all of Ms. Davies's students had started a student self-assessment progress guide before she began her one-on-one conversations, Luis was already **primed** to think about possible next steps for improving his work (the right-hand column of Figure 7.4 asks students to write two next steps for their draft). The ability to self-assess is an important skill for students to have generally (Andrade, 2000, 2010; Boekaerts, 1999; Panadero et al., 2017). But, as Ms. Davies has discovered over the years when looking at drafts of students' work, self-assessment is critical for productive, focused feedback exchanges as they enter a one-on-one interaction with a teacher. Progress guides provide coherence across each configuration of feedback exchange and allow everyone to keep the focus on visible learning goals and criteria for success on the task/project.

The student self-assessment progress guide, in particular, prepares the teacher for one-on-one conversations by providing a sense of the student's accuracy with respect to self-assessment (see Figure 7.4, where the first step for a student using a progress guide is, "Circle a level that best describes your work at this moment."). This is critical to determine how to best work within a student's ZPD.

As she sat down next to Luis, Ms. Davies immediately saw that he had assessed his own work at the same level she had. To her, this meant the one-on-one with Luis was going to take a familiar tack; they would immediately focus on next steps to reach more advanced performance levels on the project. When students haven't assessed their own work accurately, Ms. Davies begins another way. The progress guide gives Ms. Davies and her students a chance to find a foothold and calibrate the distance between their respective judgments about what next steps are toward success before completing the work and receiving a final grade.

Ms. Davies relies on the following rule of thumb/**mental model** (Figure 7.5) for all one-on-one formative feedback conversations with her students. She refrains from discussing grades and points. The aim of all these conversations is formative, with a focus on qualitative feedback. While she and the student are reviewing the first draft work and the self-assessment progress guide, Ms. Davies stresses the dialogic quality of the feedback. It is a two-way street. She is a guide at the students' side, working to keep everyone moving forward with care and respect.

Figure 7.5 The Mental Model/Rule of Thumb Ms. Davies Uses During Conversations With Students to Increase Engagement With Feedback

Review	Have we talked about some positives of your work so far?
Ask	Have I answered your question(s) about the current work *and* do we agree on possible next steps?
To-Do	How do I know you understand how to carry out the next step(s) or what to do next and when to see me or others if you feel stuck?

This mental model helps Ms. Davies live out her values for engaging with all students: keeping positive, fostering agency and autonomy, and coaching the hard feedback with care (most often the formulation of harder-to-reach next steps) while checking for the student's understanding of the conversation.

Ms. Davies reminds herself of her rule of thumb by thinking *review*, *ask*, and *to-do* before and during her one-on-one conferences. But she also expresses these thoughts to the student, ensuring she has talked about the positive aspects of the student work and answered all of their questions, especially concerning next steps.

After seeing that Luis had an accurate assessment of his written response, Ms. Davies began by asking Luis what he thought was good about his work so far. Luis replied, "I named the cause of climate change that Manolo and I read about" (during independent work time).

"Yes, Luis," Ms. Davies replied. "That's terrific. Because burning coal, specifically, wasn't one of the causes of climate that we talked about as a class when I was putting up all those slides. Good for you and Manolo for coming up with that one." At this point, Ms. Davies was impressed that in his answer, Luis had prioritized the originality of his response. This was something Ms. Davies hadn't considered about Luis's answer beforehand. Then she did some checking for understanding by probing: "We talked about burning other fossil fuels. Do you remember which ones?"

"Oil?" Luis answered.

"Yes, that's right. And gas. Oil and gas, along with coal, as you wrote in your answer, are *fossil fuels*. You wrote, 'burning coal,' which is one specific kind of fossil fuel."

Luis smiled.

Now Ms. Davies turned to the second part of her one-on-one conference **schema**: eliciting a student's question to create autonomy and ownership over next steps. "What's something you have a question about, Luis?"

Luis thought for a moment, then put his finger on the following prompt: *Based on what we have talked about today, name at least three causes of climate change and their direct impact on ecosystems*. He said, "I know what *ecosystem* is. But I don't know what this is." Luis's finger was pointing to the words *direct impact*.

"*Direct impact*?" Ms. Davies asked.

"In football?" Luis responded. "Like a concussion?"

Ms. Davies smiled, "Yes, in a way." She then pointed to the sentence starters on the back of the progress guide. "Let's also look at some sentences that use this term from the reading."

Other Pedagogical Choices Ms. Davies Could Have Made

Ms. Davies chose to talk one-on-one with Luis first. She could have spoken with one of the three students whose work she binned as "Beginning" first. She could have also focused on having one-on-ones with as many of the 12 students whose work she binned as "Developing" as possible, with the goals of discovering why their work was binned together at that level and the extent to which she found herself giving different kinds of formative feedback.

No matter her pedagogical choices, though, Ms. Davies always strives to align them with one of her core values: Supporting students in revising their work-in-progress. A visible, sustained commitment to the art of revising is the deepest sign of respect for a person's intellectual and personal growth in Ms. Davies's teaching practice. Science, like all subjects at her school, requires a disposition toward improvement. All good things take time, and there is always time for feedback to improve our knowledge and build our skills.

Focus on Practice: Ms. Singh and Sam in a Feedback Episode During Biology Class

Analyzing how other teachers have conducted one-on-one formative feedback conversations with their students is a great way to add new tools to our own formative feedback toolkit. Let's try another example.

In the following pages, we will read 10 actual turns of talk between a beginning teacher and a ninth grader. The class is biology, and all the students in it are preparing individual presentations that they will give to their classmates in a few days. Each student is responsible for teaching their classmates about a particular animal species and its habitat. Because the class has been learning about various marine ecosystems, students are also expected to know and communicate their animal's habits and how their animal functions in the specific marine ecosystem in which it lives. The unit goal is to have students create a PowerPoint presentation. But there are many components in the feedback cycle before this long-cycle destination is reached by Ms. Singh's class.

In this particular lesson highlighting Sam's work, 10 turns of talk were exchanged in less than a minute. As you read the dialogue, consider what needs to be in place for it to occur, then describe what you see going on in each turn. Please note, this dialogue is not meant to represent the most skillful, intentional, or strategic dialogue possible. What we're suggesting is that by analyzing such conversations between teachers and students, you can become more attentive to the dynamics, tone, and pace of feedback.

You won't always have a transcribed guide at hand for you to analyze feedback moves. It's more likely that you'll be talking one-on-one with a student in real time and will be improvising to some extent. But breaking down short-cycle feedback loops and exchanges can reveal much for those working to become formative assessors (see Chapter 1).

TURN	SPEAKER	TRANSCRIPT	NOTES WHAT IS GOING ON IN THIS TURN?
1	Ms. Singh	Okay, Sam, let's take a look at what you've got so far. So, Sam, first off, you're doing your species on the marine iguana. Right?	
2	Sam	Yep.	
3	Ms. Singh	That's a great choice! That's a good one because it's a unique species—the only marine lizard in the world. Very cool. So what are some things you're starting off with?	

TURN	SPEAKER	TRANSCRIPT	NOTES WHAT IS GOING ON IN THIS TURN?
4	Sam	The physical appearance of the marine iguana.	
5	Ms. Singh	That makes sense. Your classmates will want to know the colors they come in, their size. Those are all straightforward things you can pretty easily find, right?	
6	Sam	Yeah.	
7	Ms. Singh	What about anything you're having difficulty finding? Maybe we can go through that.	
8	Sam	Um, actually, everything is like here on this National Geographic website. I just found this and it's like super useful.	
9	Ms. Singh	Good.	
10	Sam	But um . . . the habits. I don't know what that is.	

Pivot Points and Just-in-Time Assists

That last comment is a **pivotal point** in the conversation. Before reading further, answer this question: Why do you think this particular point in the conversation is important?

_____

_____

_____

_____

During turn 10, Ms. Singh discovers that Sam is still unclear about at least one of the success criteria for the assignment: that students know and be able to communicate to their classmates what their animal's habits are. How can Sam convey the marine iguana's habits to his classmates if Sam is unsure what an animal's habits are? Complicating matters, the website Sam has found does not have a paragraph or section that uses the word *habits* explicitly. Sam will need to dig around and make connections between what he is reading and his understanding of the concept.

Given this, which of the seven move(s) do you think Ms. Singh should make next? (See Figure 7.1.) Name as many possibilities and combinations as you can before reading ahead.

Possible Moves Ms. Singh Could Make at This Point

_____

_____

_____

_____

How the Feedback-Focused Conversation Actually Continues

As you read the conversation as it unfolds, take special note of Ms. Singh's response to Sam's question about habits. How does Ms. Singh handle this? Would you have chosen differently—for example, to offer more probing feedback or pivot to review and direct instruction? If so, why and how?

Also consider Ms. Singh's strategy for helping Sam identify a second habit without telling him exactly what it is. As before, jot down what you think is going on in each turn of conversation in the right-hand column.

TURN	SPEAKER	TRANSCRIPT	NOTES WHAT IS GOING ON IN THIS TURN?
1	Sam	But, um . . . the habits. I don't know what that is.	
2	Ms. Singh	Okay, yeah. We can go through that together. So, habits . . . would be . . . it's kind of just another word for their behavior. So part of what that can be is . . . what they eat. So are they an herbivore or a carnivore?	
3	Sam	Herbivore.	
4	Ms. Singh	So there we go. That's the first thing we can put down there. [5-second pause] _(Sam types on his laptop.)_ Yeah, and so . . . yeah, that's what they eat, so part of that is, so they're an herbivore. They eat plants. What kind of plants do they eat?	
5	Sam	They eat algae.	

CHAPTER 7. Feedback With Individuals

TURN	SPEAKER	TRANSCRIPT	NOTES WHAT IS GOING ON IN THIS TURN?
6	Ms. Singh	Okay, algae, so how do they . . . so something else like that would be . . . how do they get to it? Because it's algae growing on rocks, right?	
7	Sam	Yeah.	
8	Ms. Singh	That's where there's a lot of surf action.	
9	Sam	Yeah . . . well, (*Sam makes a strong medial brow pinch, looks confused and surprised*) what do you mean *surf*? Like people?!	
10	Ms. Singh	Well, *surf* would refer to the waves.	
11	Sam	Oh.	
12	Ms. Singh	Lots of wave action. Lots of hard waves. [2-second pause] So they need to be able to have a way to get around those rocks without getting hit by the waves so harshly. So there is a behavior that they're able to do with that. That's something we can make a note about to look for.	

Now try using the lens of the three *E*s to analyze the individual formative feedback conversation between Ms. Singh and Sam. Try to find evidence of Ms. Singh's actions to engage, elicit, and extend in her conversation turns with Sam. What are some alternative ways Ms. Singh could have accomplished the same goal? List those in the right-hand column.

THE THREE *E*S	DIALOGIC EVIDENCE IN THE TURNS OF TALK	ALTERNATIVES MS. SINGH COULD HAVE USED
Engaging		
Eliciting		
Extending		

> ### Teacher Reflection
> #### Individual Feedback Takes Time and Is About Relationships
>
> No doubt about it, individual formative feedback dialogues take time. Lots of time and skill. Maybe even lots of patience.
>
> Especially at the beginning, when you're finding your way with each individual student, learning new names, noticing their unique personalities and styles of engaging with a challenge. And so much of getting this process right has to do with tone and setting. My same students on the field act differently in the classroom.
>
> I have noticed that at the beginning of the year, when the feedback process is new to my students, that I have to patiently lay out what we are doing, why we are doing it, and allow space for everyone to say aloud, "I don't really like this . . . it's not something my other teachers expect us to do."
>
> I've learned to slow down, back up, and give space to those who feel unsure or unsettled about sharing feedback in our geometry class. I tell them a story about when feedback on the field felt more like a dress-down or pile-on from my college football coach. They laugh—it's relatable, they say. Then we agree—these dialogues are for real and we will keep positive and keep it real this semester.
>
> —Tony, high school math teacher and football coach

Scaffolds and Guided Practice for Individual Teachers

Self-Assess

In the "Tips and To-Do's" column of Table 7.1, we invited you to consider how you support pausing moves with different students. **Think time** matters in all formative feedback cycles and exchanges (Tobin, 1980, 1986, 1987) and one-on-ones are cognitively demanding for everyone. There is often an unspoken pressure to keep things moving quickly so that you can help another student soon.

For that reason, we want you to use the tool below featuring the **SOLO taxonomy** to self-assess and see where you are in terms of supporting students to pause during one-on-one formative feedback conversations. Put a check mark by the level that best describes the current state of your instructional practices as a teacher responsible for supporting students (and yourself) in engaging in deeper, quality conversations during a formative feedback dialogue.

SOLO LEVEL	DESCRIPTION	PUT A ✓
Extended Abstract	My students and I have systematic, visible routines, scaffolds, and protocols for differentiating the ways we support each other in pausing during one-on-one formative feedback dialogues.	
Relational	I give students different ways to express a need to think about something more (e.g., by telling them, "It's okay to say, 'I need to think about that next step some more—it's the kind of learner I am.'"). I offer different culturally responsive ways to support pauses for students and pauses for myself. We talk about the fact that sometimes a pause in a feedback exchange can feel awkward or uncomfortable because of language demands.	
Multi-structural	I make a habit of pointing out to the student I'm conversing/dialoguing with that we both need pauses to gather our thoughts. I also remind the student that not having an answer/response immediately is okay.	
Unistructural	I allow think time for the student I'm having a formative feedback conversation/dialogue with.	
Pre-structural	Why would I need to always support pausing (think time) during a formative feedback dialogue? There is too much material to cover in too little time.	

Reflect

Now take at least 10–15 seconds to reflect on how you assessed your feedback practice in one-on-one configurations with your students. What do you need to improve? In the following space, write one next step you could try this week to support pausing during a pivotal turn of talk in a one-on-one feedback session.

_____

_____

_____

_____

If you're already at the topmost level, what could you do to differentiate options to support pausing even further? What other ways could you make these options more visible to both you and your students?

Try It Tomorrow

Prime for Applying the "Tincture of Time"

Applying the "tincture of time" means intentionally and strategically giving students a break from interacting with you about the work at hand. Sometimes you might be overt and explicit about this—for example, when you say, "Let's have you think about this for a bit. I'll check back in with you after I've talked with Anita."

Other times, you might simply do it without letting students know you're intentionally slowing the dialogue down. This is more easily accomplished when the feedback is digital (versus in-person)—you just don't reply quickly on the shared document or to the message.

Tell your students, either at the outset or during dialogue, something along the lines of

> I'm probably going to call for us to slow the conversation down a bit at some point. What we're engaged in isn't easy. We both need time for processing and reflection. When I do this, it's a positive sign that we're really getting to the hard stuff. If it were easy, we wouldn't need to slow down.

You can prime a student individually or you can prime your entire class with a quick explanation about why slowing things down at different times in a project helps improve outcomes and smooths expectations about work flow.

> Working with students one-on-one is what it's all about as far as I am concerned. These conversations are really the best part of the job. Students' *aha*'s and my own during these dialogues keep me energized more than any other part of the school day. That's why I prioritize meeting with several students each period. The kids need my feedback and they appreciate the care for their work.
>
> —Priya, social science/history teacher with college prep advisory

Setting Goals and Monitoring Progress With Individual Formative Feedback: Questions for Lesson Study and Professional Learning Communities

Principal Garcia has led his school for over a decade. He previously worked with a nationally recognized high school redesign team that produced some outstanding results in several urban school districts. Mr. Garcia now leads faculty, staff, and parents in a rural community that has embarked on **continuous improvement** reforms (Fullan et al., 2018; Fullan & Rincón-Gallardo, 2017; Furger et al., 2019).

At the cornerstone of the **professional learning community** (**PLC**) focus at Carquinez High School is a commitment to seeing students as change agents whose school projects inform the community. Part of this vision includes finding new ways of working with student work (projects, performances, and real-world assignments) so students can express what they know and can do in preparation for college and 21st century work. "Less tests, quizzes, and homework sheets—more real-world projects, rich tasks, and long-term projects" is the motto at Carquinez High. But to implement this ambitious deep equity–focused vision, Principal Garcia has had to study the success (and failings) of previous assessment and instructional reforms. **Project-based learning** is only a part of what the students need at Carquinez High.

Without a sustained commitment to formative feedback—hour by hour, day by day, week by week—Principal Garcia knows that the students will rightly struggle with how to grow, to progress, and to improve their work. That is why this year's PLCs will focus on feedback for all. Interdisciplinary teams, in collaboration with paraprofessionals, instructional coaches, and counselors, are working together to answer the **essential questions** this year: Do you give and take feedback? Where? When? How? With whom? Why?

In faculty and staff meetings, people in the school community are invited to freely admit that sometimes the formative feedback that works well for one student doesn't work so well for another. Principal Garcia and teachers know that even when you offer feedback on students' work, not everyone takes it up. Too often, as teachers say, it goes in one ear and out the other. Over the course of the monthly meetings, a set of warm-ups invite everyone to reflect deeper on these and other feelings about feedback.

Principal Garcia writes on the dry-erase board, "Differentiated feedback strategies matter in one-on-one settings." He hands out a sheet for those who prefer to write and a link to a shared electronic document for those who prefer to type their responses. This is the start of several conversations at the school to unpack beliefs, attitudes, and dispositions toward feedback across all subject areas and grade levels. Nothing changes, he knows, unless our **habits of mind** and heart do first.

Let's imagine we are working across the district collaboratively at our own school with Principal Garcia and his team. We can put the same prompt up—"Differentiated feedback strategies matter in one-on-one settings"—and ask everyone to take a few minutes to discuss and write their responses to the following:

- Do you agree with this statement/observation?
- If so, why?
- If you do not agree, why not?
- What do your experiences with differentiation imply when it comes to formative feedback? What does this mean for your students? What does this mean for you? What does this mean for our school community?

At the next PLC meeting, we can ask everyone to reflect through a self-assessment.

Self-Assessment/Quick Check

1. What I like best about engaging students individually in formative feedback dialogues, loops, and conversations is . . .

_____

_____

_____

_____

_____

2. Rank the following in order of most difficult to least difficult for you in a one-on-one feedback session. Then add other skills/moves that come to mind but aren't on this list.

Rank From Easiest to Hardest (1 = Easiest, 4 = Hardest)	Skill/Move
	Involving students in the prioritization of next steps
	Closing the formative feedback loop on a positive note
	Staying positive during the one-on-one session
	Communicating the hard feedback
	Checking for student understanding of feedback takeaways from the session

Not on the List Above But Also Important	Level of Difficulty (Circle)		
	Easy	Moderate	Difficult
	Easy	Moderate	Difficult
	Easy	Moderate	Difficult

3. I have a diverse range of moves (e.g., priming, posing, pausing, probing, **tagging**) to engage students with widely differing learning needs and personalities in formative feedback conversations. (Please share how.)

4. One way I address the challenge of time when it comes to individual formative feedback is . . . (Please give an example.)

As you work together, what are the common themes emerging about feedback in your meeting. Share and discuss the results of the self-assessment together. Have someone scribe and take notes. Start looking for patterns and gaps in experience across different classrooms and different learning contexts such as the lab, theater, gymnasium, or field.

These prompts can aid in the discussion:

- **In response to Question 1:** What did everyone like best about one-on-one feedback with their students? Explain why.

- **In response to Question 2:** What skills/moves were ranked easiest? Which ones were ranked hardest? Do you think other skills/moves should be on the list of important practices that were not? List them. Explain why you picked these skills/moves.

- **In response to Question 3:** What are some of the skills/moves you use to engage students with different learning needs to take up feedback? Try to see if there is any overlap (**English learners**, students with special needs, etc.) between different types/groupings of students. Discuss.

- **In response to Question 4:** Talk about the challenges of time in the context of individualized feedback. Share ideas and strategies for creating efficiencies and wins. Acknowledge anxieties and concerns. Agree to try out a colleague's suggestion.

Before closing, formulate a plan together (maybe in a department or with a study buddy) to generate some new strategies to achieve a feedback-focused skill/move that you agree is important for you and your students. Together, try to commit to in your classroom

1. a feedback goal, such as individual one-on-one meetings with at least 20% of my "Developing" students each week;

2. a specific next step, such as introducing and collecting results from a self-assessment–focused progress guide before the individual meetings with students;

3. a date/time in the unit or lesson plan for when you will take these next steps with visible tools; and

4. a check-in for assessing the strategies that put formative feedback at the center of your unit and lesson planning this year.

Recap/Review

- Equity demands that we approach feedback strategies and tactics with care. How students perceive and respond to formative feedback—what they do or don't do in response to it—is the most important aspect of good formative feedback practice.
- Teachers and students both benefit when the process of formative feedback is made visible with shared tools, graphic organizers, and norms.
- Progress guides for teacher use for whole-class assessment and for student use for self-assessment make individual/one-on-one formative feedback dialogues richer, more tangible, and more focused on learning goals and criteria for success.
- Knowing that misunderstandings happen in all feedback exchanges can help us to be better guides on the side.
- Wise feedback and a tone of respect have important roles to play in every exchange of information and classroom assessment practice aimed at growth.
- Helping students identify the positives in their current performance and concrete next steps can help foster student agency.
- Encouraging metacognition during individual formative feedback dialogues is one of the most effective practices for helping students learn how to learn.

Ticket Out the Door

1. Name something that occurred recently during a one-on-one formative feedback conversation you had with a student that helped you do better with the rest of the class (or in other class periods).
2. How do you address the challenge of time when it comes to individual/one-on-one configurations of formative feedback?
3. List at least three ways you stay positive with students when it comes to individual formative feedback sessions.

Looking Back on the Configurations Chapters: Reflection

As you continue to learn about and reflect on different configurations of formative feedback, we'd like you to self-assess. Take a moment to consider what you've experienced and what you value about various configurations of feedback (whole class, small group, and individual/

one-on-one). Then, with respect to your current students, determine where you are in your thinking about these different configurations.

1. List: The most important aspects to consider when planning to give whole-class formative feedback are . . .

2. Complete this sentence starter: It is a good idea to use anonymous examples of student work when showing how to use feedback because . . .

3. Complete the following sentence starters: My go-to method of checking for student understanding depends on the configuration.

    a. For whole class, I tend to . . .
    b. For small groups, I tend to . . .
    c. For individuals/one-on-one, I tend to . . .

4. Complete this sentence starter: The hardest thing about differentiating formative feedback is . . .

MODALITY

CHAPTER 8

Written Feedback

> The [written] feedback message does not sit by itself on an assignment but is inextricably linked to the work of the student that engendered the message, the goal of the [feedback writer] who constructed the message, as well as how that message is received by the student on the return of the assignment.
>
> —Murray, Gasson, and Smith (2018, p. 95)

As teachers, we may want to write and teach **formative feedback** that is clear and certain. Yet, when it comes to classroom assessment practices and procedures that involve people learning to provide, engage, and take up **feedback**, nothing is simple. Our ideas and our writing may be clear to us, but our students may rightly struggle to interpret them.

Meaning and intent are often fuzzy, especially when there aren't well-defined pathways or clear rules for engagement. Texts (written comments we make to students) don't always speak for themselves. We have to offer ways to make sense and meaning of what is written while also offering procedures for taking students' work to the next level.

Too often, we forget that students have been acculturated to "do" school (Lortie, 1975). This can mean they don't see the value in rethinking, revisiting, or revising their work. Those who do see the value may be motivated by incentives such as points or extra credit. Those who don't—the majority in many cases—simply want to move on. As teachers who know the power of formative feedback on learning outcomes, we need to address these dynamics and dispositions.

When our students get their performance tasks, projects, and assignments back for review, they may gasp, sink their heads down, or feel like giving up. You may hear replies like "What? I followed the instructions. Now I have to rewrite?" or "I did the same thing as Rebeca and I have to revise. That's not fair!" or overhear a student say to a classmate, "What does Ms. Pierson want me to do with all these comments on the Doc? I'll just hit resolve. I really don't understand why she writes so many comments anyway."

Such student reactions are the consequences of treating classroom assessments (tests, quizzes, homework) as one-offs. Most students have been led to believe, based on deep experiences with the schooling system, that schoolwork is a one-and-done process. Many have gotten the proverbial memo that there really aren't second chances or opportunities to improve one's work by using others' feedback.

The next few chapters on **modalities** will help us to differentiate written, spoken, and nonverbal modes of communication of feedback. In this chapter, we begin with the challenge and opportunity for taking action to ensure that any written feedback we write to students is as clear as we can make it. We will also put emphasis on the importance of laying out clear, accessible pathways and routines that engage students in **feedback loops** as they recognize what we have written and try incorporating our feedback.

Always Support Written Comments With Other Feedback Modalities

Formative feedback in the written modality must not stand alone. It has too many inherent weaknesses (including fuzzy interpretations and indeterminate meanings) to stand by itself. When rushed or overwhelmed, we may want to say, "Just read it," but that won't work for most of our students.

An overreliance on written feedback in distributed learning platforms in secondary school settings is especially problematic, partly because teenagers and young adults already feel pressed for time (and motivation!) on many fronts. They may not process our commands, particularly if they feel overwhelmed by the volume of other web-based apps competing for their attention.

Written feedback via any digital media should be used judiciously and in balance with lots of opportunities for verbal dialogue. Why? People need multiple modalities to agree upon next steps or to clarify meanings. Most will also benefit from the accompaniment of concrete **exemplars** and **scaffolds** that are **criterion-referenced** (such as **progress guides**) to better situate the feedback along a well-developed, visible learning trajectory.

Dutch researchers have corroborated what many teachers have experienced themselves: Secondary students engage in more reflective thinking after receiving written feedback when that feedback is also accompanied by an actual conversation—a "feedback dialogue"—with the teacher (Van der Schaaf et al., 2011). These researchers found that "the number of [audio recorded] segments containing [teacher and student] interaction was positively correlated with students' use of thinking activities" (p. 227).

Less Is More

We should be incredibly intentional about how we approach, engage, and support students through formative feedback in the written modality. Whether the written feedback is teacher-driven or peer-driven, the rule of thumb should be "less is more." With acknowledgment to Walter Tevis, author of *The Queen's Gambit* (1983), you can think of written feedback as a potent spice: A pinch wakes you up. Too much dulls your senses.

There really is no need to increase the **cognitive load** of our students with lots of extraneous bells and whistles such as color codes, special symbols, and emojis when offering written feedback. A smiley face or exclamation point may feel friendly or useful next to a written comment on a cloud-based document, but it's unlikely to invite our students' focus on the success criteria or learning trajectory for the task.

We often sugarcoat written feedback with well-intentioned encouragements or even emojis, usually to soften the blow or ease the pain of a challenging or critical comment. Wiggins (2012) and others have pointed out that effective feedback relies less on praise and more on focused support with tangible, specific, concrete next steps.

Written feedback practices are interconnected with verbal and nonverbal modalities in any feedback-rich learning environment. It is critical to consider the intersections of each modality and how they can be leveraged to reinforce the impact on students' work and growth.

The following guiding questions anchor our exploration of the power of written modalities of feedback to launch into and support other modalities, which we discuss in Chapters 9 and 10. Taken as a whole, each chapter on the modalities of feedback points to the challenges and opportunities with separating and connecting different aspects of information exchange for projects, performance tasks, and long-cycle assignments while emphasizing the need for well-defined, consistent, and reflective lesson and unit plans that incorporate written modalities of feedback practice.

Guiding Questions

1. Why plan, enact, and reflect on written modalities of formative feedback? For whose good is this modality potentially most helpful? For which kinds of educational goals and purposes is this modality?

2. How can we meet the challenges that come with formative feedback in the written modality? What opportunities arise from its use?

3. In what ways can written formative feedback be more like a back-and-forth conversation between giver and recipient(s), where all participants exert influence?

4. What are ways that written formative feedback can be scaffolded and connected to other modalities (spoken and nonverbal) to strengthen feedback loops?

Throughout this book, we've been using focal points to unpack and explore formative feedback practices. These are ***directionality***, ***configuration***, and ***modality***.

Figure 8.1 depicts three main feedback focal points and their associated lenses. *Modality* refers to the primary mode of communication/expression through which the formative feedback unfolds. The organizing principle we're using in this book recognizes three *modalities* for formative feedback dialogues: written, spoken, and nonverbal. This chapter is about modality and the first of the three lenses for it: written formative feedback.

Many, if not most, feedback loops that lead to changes in student work performance are made up of multilayered conversations and feature multiple modalities that appear in various combinations throughout the entire run of a feedback loop. Some of these layers emphasize simultaneous use, while others focus on the sequential use of each modality. If the participants in the **formative feedback loop** are mostly writing, then the feedback modality is considered written. It will appear to the reader (our students!) as a text to be deciphered.

Simultaneous use of different modalities occurs all the time. One example is when a choir teacher asks a practicing soloist to "draw out your breath here, across these measures," and the student marks/draws the suggestion on their sheet music in order to remember it. This is feedback in spoken and written modalities. Another example is when a physical education teacher says to a student while pressing on their tennis racquet, "Push your racquet into my hand to feel where you want your power to come from." This is feedback in spoken and nonverbal (i.e., physical) modalities simultaneously.

Sequential use of different modalities is also common, particularly when the work, project, or learning occurs over several lessons or weeks. For example, it is common for a formative feedback loop to begin in person (synchronously, in real time) and in a spoken modality, only for it to be continued via the comments feature on a shared digital platform (asynchronously and in a written modality). Such written feedback can then be revisited and elaborated upon in a verbal and nonverbal mode of conversation, whether in person or online in the next phases of the feedback loop.

Let's look at some of the strengths and challenges of using the written modality to advance new habits of **assessment for learning** practice. Remember, we are all struggling for deeper connections between good instruction and good assessment, and formative feedback practices build the bridge between them.

A quick glance at the Formative Feedback Framework (Figure 8.1) will heighten our awareness of the challenges with building bridges between effective instruction and assessment while promoting opportunities to reframe and focus on the combinations that can advance student learning.

Figure 8.1   Formative Feedback Framework

Contexts for Learning		
Face-to-Face	Blended	Distance Learning
Focal Point		
Directionality	**Configuration**	**Modality**
Lenses		
Teacher-driven	Whole class	Written
Peer-to-peer-driven	Small groups (2–4)	Spoken
Self-driven	Individual (1:1)	Nonverbal
Tasks, Projects, Activities	Learning Goals, Standards, Skills	
	Rubrics, Progress Guides, "Next Steps" Organizers	

Defining Feedback in the Written Modality

Whether provided by a teacher or peer or offered as a note to oneself, "written feedback is a genre all its own" (Brookhart, 2017, p. 36). Word choice, tone, and style matter in written modalities, as they do in verbal and nonverbal modalities. One must gauge who the audience is and what they are prepared to incorporate in the learning cycle.

One of the affordances of working in the spoken modality is that all participants can walk back their words, utterances, and even gestures or body language. Because the turns of talk occur on the fly, each party can add, retract, or rephrase what they say. Adjustments to tone, style, and demeanor can be made, in most cases.

But written feedback is different. It involves a time-lag between turn-taking in the feedback process. When we write comments, questions, symbols, and even emojis, they become what experts call "**extant**" texts. When we meet to discuss what we wrote, we are often talking backward, focusing on the past. Since our goal is to move students forward, we must take care to keep things fresh and orient ourselves toward larger learning goals.

For the most part, written feedback dialogues are conducted *asynchronously*. An exception to this is when the formative feedback interaction/dialogue occurs as an online chat during Zoom or as messages online during class. Nonetheless, *asynchronous feedback loops/exchanges* typically occur among students and teachers as they work on shared documents, slide decks, and spreadsheets together. Feedback among participants on the same shared document at the same time is a powerful way to experience collaborative thinking and teamwork. But it requires being able to give and take feedback over time.

FORMATIVE FEEDBACK IN THE WRITTEN MODALITY	
What it is	**What it isn't**
▸ interpersonal	▸ a grade, even if accompanied by a comment: "now see if you can improve your work/performance before the final deadline."
▸ custom-tailored with careful regard for students' skills, dispositions, and needs	
▸ qualitative comments on digital or hard copies of work-in-progress	▸ a numeric score or symbols (on a part of or all of a work-in-progress)
▸ questions or probes on digital or hard copies of work-in-progress	▸ a spoken conversation about a performance of work-in-progress with a checklist
▸ most often asynchronous (delayed time between exchanges/turns of talk) but can be synchronous if participants are in an online chat or are texting one another	▸ anonymous, unless explicitly part of a protocol (e.g., comments on a gallery walk)
	▸ generic cut-and-paste comments without regard for particular students' skills, dispositions, assets, and needs
▸ can be a dialogue as part of a review session of how to approach incorporation of feedback	▸ generated by an automated scoring program
▸ may include posted links to video tutorials, exemplars, definitions, and other resources to complement the written comments, suggestions, questions, and so on	

Written Feedback Is Frequently Asynchronous

Compared to talking in real time—or compared to typewritten conversations held via online chat or text—the back-and-forth "turns of talk," as researchers call them, are slowed down during written feedback processes. The time elapsing between message and reply can vary widely.

While it may be a delay of mere minutes, turn-taking delays can also occur across hours, days, and even weeks. This pace brings with it potential strengths and challenges, which we've outlined in the following table.

ASYNCHRONOUS FORMATIVE FEEDBACK DIALOGUES VIA WRITTEN MODALITY IN DIGITAL MEDIUM

Strengths	Challenges
Participants can postpone reflecting on feedback until they are ready	No access to nonverbal communication to supplement reactions to written comments/questions
Participants can look up vocabulary or definitions contained in the feedback in private	Participants must rely on written text to do all the communicating
May lower affective filter and reduce cognitive load by increasing processing time	Delays in the comment–reply–comment cycle may cause participants to lose momentum when drafting/revising
Participants can consider their words and revise before submitting initial feedback and responses to feedback	More challenging for the feedback provider to check for understanding
Greater opportunities for clarification using "reply" features (if students are primed in advance)	Clarification process typically takes longer than spoken-only modality
Builds confidence for real-world independent learning that approximates college and career skills	Use of emojis/emoticons may distract from the criterion-based focus of feedback
	May lead to premature use of the "resolve" function to reduce anxiety or stress

Self-Assessment for Modalities Chapters Ahead

As you begin to engage with these next few chapters on the modalities of formative feedback, we'd like you to reflect and self-assess. Take a moment to consider what you've experienced and what you value about written, verbal, and nonverbal feedback. Try to consider not only what you value but also what your students have appreciated and gained from formative feedback exchanges conducted asynchronously and in real time.

1. Describe a time when a particular modality really worked for a student you had experienced as hard to reach. Which combinations of modalities made a difference for your student? Please explain why.

2. My favorite way of having students digest my written feedback is . . . (Please share.)

3. Complete the following **sentence starters**: My go-to method for checking student understanding of my feedback depends largely on the modality.

    a. For written feedback, I tend to . . .

    b. For verbal feedback, I tend to . . .

    c. For nonverbal feedback, I tend to . . .

4. Complete the following sentence starter: The hardest thing about getting students to engage with written formative feedback is . . .

5. Making connections exercise: Draw a line from the "Primary Goals for a Feedback Cycle" in the first column to the "Best Modality" for achieving those goals in the second column. (Note: You may have more than one line for each.)

PRIMARY GOALS FOR A FEEDBACK CYCLE	BEST MODALITY
To be able to check for students' understanding	Typed
To foster students working at their own pace	Handwritten
To build relationship by communicating warmth, respect, and encouragement	Spoken
To power through the process as efficiently as possible	Nonverbal
To foster dialogue about the revision process	None of the above

> During the pandemic, now that we switched to blended and distance learning, I've given more written feedback than I ever have before. This has had its ups and downs. Sensitive topics make me ensure we are talking about my feedback in their journals—not just assuming my students understand why I am writing, "Please elaborate" or "Say more" so often.
>
> —Roberta, high school English language arts and ethnic studies teacher

Engaging in written formative feedback is a demanding task for yourself as a teacher and for your students. Be sure to plan support *before*, *during*, and *after* writing formative feedback.

Table 8.1 is organized by directionality of feedback: teacher-driven, peer-to-peer-driven, and self-driven. It offers suggestions for

- readying students to understand and engage with written formative feedback *before* a single word is written,
- supporting yourself and your students to ensure the best quality feedback *during* the process of writing, and
- encouraging you and your students to reflect on the process itself *after* writing.

We invite you to use it as a planning guide in choosing and prioritizing the practices, protocols, and scaffolds to use with your students.

Table 8.1 Planning for Before, During, and After Written Formative Feedback: Suggestions to Increase Effectiveness For Teacher-, Peer-, and Self-Directed Contexts

DIRECTIONALITY AND CONTEXT	BEFORE	DURING	AFTER
	What preparation is needed to ensure students will understand the upcoming written feedback?	What support/intervention during the feedback-generation process is needed to ensure it engages, elicits, and extends?	What actions after the formative feedback will assist students in using the feedback and reflecting on the feedback process?
TEACHER	colspan across: Teacher-driven formative feedback in the written modality should, above all, be focused, not overwhelming for students, and supported by classroom activities. If you're going to write feedback, it's imperative to use class time to have students read or reread it and for you to discover what meaning they make—or don't make—of your feedback.		
Asynchronous	Before writing feedback, explain to students what the focus will be. If you can, remind them of this focus before they read your written feedback. Both actions will give them context and help them understand your written feedback.	Take advantage of the opportunity to reread your feedback before delivering it. Check for *quality* (How well does what I've written communicate next steps and beyond? See the "What the Research Tells Us" section later in this chapter.), *invitation to engagement* (Where/how have I invited students to continue dialogue with me?), and *tone/balance* of valence (Is there enough positive feedback? Is my tone warm, respectful, and encouraging?).	Have students reflect on the easiest and hardest feedback to take up. This can be done after synchronous written feedback dialogues, too.

CHAPTER 8. Written Feedback

DIRECTIONALITY AND CONTEXT		BEFORE	DURING	AFTER
TEACHER	Synchronous	Teach and practice phrases to use/type during synchronous, written formative feedback dialogue (e.g., "I have a question about that," "Before we move ahead, please . . . ," or "Can we return to something you wrote earlier?").	Check for understanding in real time and use this opportunity to clarify while ideas are fresh in participants' minds.	Find out from the students' perspective what was valuable about the synchronous written feedback.
	Either Asynchronous or Synchronous	Prioritize the focus of written feedback by using/creating progress guides that are connected to the rubric(s) for the task/project. Anticipate academic language (AL) you might use in your comments; teach/review that AL. Leverage use of student work in your efforts to help students understand success criteria and quality. Teach what *using formative feedback to improve work* means. Have students write questions that you will respond to in your feedback.	Consider using a mental model/rule of thumb to guide yourself as you write formative feedback. +, ?, To-Do Rule of Thumb + = Am I giving positive feedback? ? = Am I answering students' question(s)? To-do = Are possible next steps clear?	Create a class T-chart that captures what feedback was used and what feedback wasn't (this can be done anonymously). Facilitate an activity that requires the processing of your written feedback and ask, "Is there something that still needs clarification?" Invite spoken feedback on your written feedback. This can be done in whole-class configurations. Have students tell you (or one another) what they learned from the feedback content/process. See "Try it Tomorrow: Invite Feedback on Your Written Feedback" (p. 245).

Peer-to-peer formative feedback in the written modality can help students use academic language in context, gain insight into their own current work/performance, and build classroom community. Even though students may have engaged in peer-to-peer feedback processes in other classes and contexts, discussing how your class will engage in peer-to-peer feedback—and why—is essential. The aim is for students to feel seen and respected by one another as well as help one another.

(Continued)

(Continued)

DIRECTIONALITY AND CONTEXT		BEFORE	DURING	AFTER
PEER	Asynchronous	Brainstorm the advantages of peer-to-peer feedback in the written modality with your class. Coach students ahead of time to take advantage of the opportunity to reread their typed feedback before they post it. Strive to achieve clarity with your class regarding the purposes of this particular episode of peer-to-peer feedback.	Remind students to interrupt their own formative feedback process and do a self-check on one aspect of the feedback content or process (e.g. "Am I offering a possible next step?" "How specific is what I'm writing?" or "Have I pointed out what is uniquely positive about the work?")	Make time in class for peer-to-peer clarification of written feedback. If some students do not require/desire clarification, invite them to begin revising immediately.
	Synchronous	Prepare students to take advantage of the opportunities for real-time clarification that synchronous feedback dialogues afford. Teach and practice possible phrases to use during the synchronous written formative feedback dialogue with students.	Interrupt their working once to ask a targeted question on content or the process. Ensure that the target focus is not a surprise to students.	Ask students, "Did being interrupted help you execute the target focus? How so?"
	Either Asynchronous or Synchronous	Give students a progress guide for peer-to-peer feedback and teach them how to use it. Give students a menu of examples, questions, and next steps they could offer classmates. Prep students for the target focus of the process.	As students are working, observe them to the extent you can. Make yourself available, if feasible, to help them through the process.	Facilitate a whole-class activity (or set of activities) to learn from the peer-to-peer written feedback process. Try to do it within a reasonable length of time, while feelings and/or thoughts are still fresh. See "Try it Tomorrow: Invite Feedback on Your Written Feedback" (p. 245).

CHAPTER 8. Written Feedback

DIRECTIONALITY AND CONTEXT	BEFORE	DURING	AFTER
SELF	*The concept of having an asynchronous written feedback dialogue with oneself can occur in this sense: One can intend to write some hard feedback to oneself, knowing that it will be put aside for a time (perhaps to gain critical distance or perhaps to let the sting of the feedback subside) before coming back to it later to respond. The key is to leverage the time between the initial writing and the response to gain new perspectives and new skills that could inform your response to your initial feedback to yourself.*		
Asynchronous	Prime students: Aim to give yourself the most incisive feedback you can. Remind students: "You can give yourself feedback though you don't *yet* know how to implement it or follow through."	Tell students they can use their time between the initial written feedback and their response to • give themselves a break from the work/performance, • actively seek out new perspectives on the question/issue/suggestion, or • investigate what it will take to gain the new skill(s) they might need to follow through on your feedback. Help students with the three preceding bullet points.	Celebrate that your students were able to mentor themselves toward a significant revision/improvement in performance.
Synchronous	Students: Be clear with yourself about the main purpose of your written feedback. If you're not aware of your purpose, explore that. The idea is to increase your capacity to work metacognitively.	Strive for honesty and authenticity. Be curious and kind to yourself.	Remind students to take a moment to reread the feedback to themselves and recognize/affirm its level of expertise or silliness.

(Continued)

(Continued)

DIRECTIONALITY AND CONTEXT	BEFORE	DURING	AFTER
SELF — Either Asynchronous or Synchronous	Make sure students have samples of student work (anonymous and/or identified) at various levels of performance to learn from.	Help students use the scaffold you provide. We recommend a progress guide tailored to their needs (augmented with sentence starters/frames, a menu of possible next steps, etc.).	Spur reflection on content or process through a modality other than writing ("What did you learn from giving feedback to yourself?") See "Try it Tomorrow: Invite Feedback on Your Written Feedback" (p. 245).

A central premise of this chapter is that formative feedback via any written modality does not stand alone. It is always embedded in other parts of the feedback process/cycle, including the directionality and configurations of your feedback-rich practices.

Whether it is feedback driven by the teacher, feedback between peers, or feedback by a student to themselves, we will need tangible, visible supports, scaffolds, and processes to guide the interpretation and use of written clarifying comments and suggestions for next steps.

I've been a teacher for over 20 years.

I'm kind of embarrassed to admit this, but I remember vividly the day my son asked me, "Mom, what's *frag*? It says here *frag* on my justice essay." My son was in middle school then and his English language arts teacher had put comments on his paper, among them *frag* in the margins.

That day was the first time I stopped to ask myself, "What am *I* writing in the margins of papers that my own students don't understand?"

I really had no idea that my comments were based on how I was taught freshman English in college. Now I know better than to take cryptic shortcuts my students shouldn't be expected to comprehend or respond to.

—Nanette, middle school humanities teacher

What the Research Tells Us

Students Frequently Don't Understand Written Feedback

For feedback to be effective, students need to understand it. Yet students often do not understand written feedback or interpret it accurately (Glover & Brown, 2006; Higgins et al., 2001, 2002; Hyatt, 2005). Researchers have documented what beginning teachers often learn the hard way: Providing written feedback does not automatically lead to student understanding nor does it guarantee students can use the feedback in subsequent drafts or performance attempts (Havnes et al., 2012).

There is also a common **misconception** that designated **English learners** (**ELs**) struggle more than non-designated students to understand written feedback, but it turns out written feedback can be equally baffling to ELs and non-ELs alike.

Writing direct comments, using simple vocabulary, and using expressions students are familiar with tend to help them improve their work (Bruno & Santos, 2010). But teachers should ask, how simple does the vocabulary in their written feedback have to be? And more importantly, when do **academic language** (**AL**) demands go beyond simple vocabulary review (a common misconception of *only* what AL development is or entails)? Teachers know that reading comprehension must be contextualized and that motivation to understand a particular text varies from student to student. It is no different for our written commentaries and suggested next steps on **first draft** work.

Students' frustration and disappointment with written feedback is well-documented in the research literature (Ferguson, 2011; Glover & Brown, 2006; Hounsell et al., 2008; Hyland, 2013; Price et al., 2010; Weaver, 2006). Unless we have asked students to read or reread their written feedback during class time, we may not have directly observed their challenges with comprehending the written feedback we have offered. Students, of course, respond to frustration and disappointment in different ways. Some responses are productive—for example, when they seek clarification or ask for help; other responses are less so—for example, when students disengage completely (not temporarily) and give up on the task, project, or assignment.

Student Perceptions of Feedback Matter; Conveying Warmth, Respect, and Encouragement Without Lowering Expectations Matters

Students' perceptions of feedback are important (Agricola et al., 2020; Rowe, 2011; Yeager et al., 2013). Student perceptions of feedback are often misaligned with the intentions of the one sharing the feedback (Van der Schaaf et al., 2011). In this way, feedback exchanges are multidirectional. Each participant is struggling to convey meaning while also trying to maintain the intent of their work.

We know that conveying warmth, respect, and encouragement during feedback processes impacts whether students revise their work and how substantially they revise it (Darling-Hammond et al., 1995). Failing to communicate warmth, respect, and encouragement in a feedback loop can mean students feel biases are at play in the exchange. Conveying warmth, respect, and encouragement—the parallel to demonstrating "nonverbal immediacy behaviors" while in person (Martin & Mottet, 2011)—should be a top priority.

With Written Feedback, a Feed-Forward and Next-Steps Orientation Is Necessary

Studies of teachers' written feedback to students show that feed-forward feedback is rare (Hattie & Timperley, 2007; Murray et al., 2018). Such feedback communicates where students should go next. Written feedback that aims at next steps not only points out what is right or wrong, it conveys *why* actions are being taken to improve the task performance. Feed-forward feedback has the immediate goal of helping students understand the underlying reasons for the specific comment/question. It also aids students in making judgments about their own work (Sadler, 2010).

Essential Written Feedback Practices Supported by Research

Encourage Next Steps and Focused Action Going Forward

- Use common language (such as *next steps*) and invite students to prioritize their next steps numerically (1, 2, 3). Discuss how these next steps bring one closer to the demonstration of excellence with the performance task, project, or long-term assignment.

Align Comments, Questions, or Notations With Visible Scaffolds and Learning Goals

- Use a progress guide and/or modified rubric to orient your written feedback in learning goals and success criteria along a continuum of next steps leading to the next level. Offer a glossary of academic language terms (domain-specific and general) to help students define and make sense of what you mean with your written comments.

Invite Opportunities to Unpack Academic Language in the Feedback Process

- Signal registers and domain-specific language cues in your written comments. While striving to avoid jargon or dysfunctional detail, uncover and discuss academic language demands in the task, evaluation tools, and your own written comments. Written feedback is a powerful means of helping students acquire and gain facility with academic language demands when the written feedback process is dialogic and supported by other modalities.

Avoid Complexity, Confusion, and Extraneous Cognitive Overload

- Shy away from emojis, use of all capitals, and punctuation mark–only "comments" (e.g., "!!!" or "?"). Written feedback that is clear, concise, and learning path–driven opens the way to revision and next steps.

In the vignette that follows, we will see how high school science teacher Mr. Roy took the **rubric** provided to him by his department and broke it down into two progress guides aligned with the rubric. Mr. Roy developed a short glossary of terms as well as specific science phrases and conventions that the task evoked and the rubric and progress guides employed in this three-week project. Mr. Roy's students referenced this glossary as the feedback sessions went forward. The investment in these tools and organizers helped Mr. Roy use his time wisely because they gave his students multiple ways of making meaning beyond the all-too-familiar and well-intended "Read my comments."

Judiciously Using and Supporting Written Formative Feedback: The Case of Mr. Roy and Ms. Marsalis on the Green Island Design Project

Mr. Roy has taught science at a large, comprehensive high school in northern California for over a decade. Ms. Marsalis has been teaching for three years in the same science department with Mr. Roy. When Ms. Marsalis was hired, she was a big advocate for **project-based learning** (**PBL**). Both teachers found lots of common ground in their philosophy of equity and excellence in STEM (science, technology, engineering, and mathematics) education. Over the summer, they worked collaboratively on ways to provide better assessment strategies for struggling students. A big part of their commitment to school improvement was to encourage the use of sustained formative feedback strategies with their students at their Title I school. Their school is known for its strong science department, collegiality, and openness to innovation. It also serves a wide range of linguistically, culturally, and economically diverse students from urban communities in San Jose, most of whom qualify for free or reduced lunch.

Both Mr. Roy and Ms. Marsalis began their teaching careers as the **Next Generation Science Standards** (**NGSS**) were being adopted. When each joined the science department, they were encouraged to use a standard format for rubrics, one that vaguely described components of student performance at four levels: *exceeds standard, meets standard, emerging skills,* and *insufficient evidence*. They felt that students were not connecting with these assessment categories of evaluation used to represent achievement, so they came up with a few creative and manageable solutions for guiding written feedback, with an emphasis on progress markers and academic growth over time.

We interviewed Mr. Roy, Ms. Marsalis, and several other teachers at the school as part of a yearlong case study. Our goal was to learn from practitioners how they align **standards**-based educational purposes with authentic projects and tasks to assess for **deeper learning**. Key to our study was to better understand how traditional evaluation tools such as rubrics could be augmented with progress guides to deepen feedback practices for students and teachers.

We started the interviews with Mr. Roy and others with a focus question: *What makes formative feedback formative?* Mr. Roy jumped right in with a firm answer: "When my students seek out my written comments and ask me to talk about what's next, then I know it's formative for them. It's that simple."

What follows is a case study that highlights Mr. Roy's and Ms. Marsalis's experiences in bringing complex formative feedback practices into alignment with rigorous standards while foregrounding the use of an intentional process of revision. In their classrooms, students are invited into cycles of feedback that involve written commentary (complemented by spoken turns of talk) anchored in assessment tools such as rubrics, progress guides, and scaffolds that document next steps.

Mr. Roy's Case

Mr. Roy has been working on the design and delivery of the Green Island design project for a few years. He likes the idea that the project allows students to be creative, to use their imaginations, and to apply their knowledge of the unit in a personal way. The big question for the assignment is this: Can one provide for the well-being and livelihoods of 1,000 people living on an island while also leaving the smallest carbon footprint possible?

As part of this project, Mr. Roy's students are expected to design, evaluate, and test a solution to human impact on the environment. In addition to demonstrations of mastery of the core content, the students in Mr. Roy's class are expected to rate each other's work based on their proposed solution and the impact it could have on anthropogenic climate change.

Figure 8.2 is the scenario Mr. Roy presents to his students. This project is typically assigned after his students have learned about biogeochemical cycles on Earth as well as population dynamics/ecology in biomes.

The Green Island design project is aligned to two NGSS performance expectations: HS-LS2-6 and HS-LS2-7 from the Life Science Standards.

> **HS-LS2-6 Ecosystems: Interactions, Energy, and Dynamics**
> *Evaluate claims, evidence, and reasoning that the complex interactions in ecosystems maintain relatively consistent numbers and types of organisms in stable conditions, but changing conditions may result in a new ecosystem. (Clarification Statement: Examples of changes in ecosystem conditions could include modest biological or physical changes, such as moderate hunting or a seasonal flood; and extreme changes, such as volcanic eruption or sea level rise.)*

> **HS-LS2-7 Ecosystems: Interactions, Energy, and Dynamics**
> *Design, evaluate, and refine a solution for reducing the impacts of human activities on the environment and biodiversity. (Clarification Statement: Examples of human activities can include urbanization, building dams, and dissemination of invasive species.)*

Figure 8.2 Task/Prompt: Scenario for Designing Your Green Island

---

It is the year 2100 and a new island, one completely untouched by humans, has been discovered. There is now a competition to decide who will be allowed to colonize the island and establish a society there. An Intergovernmental Panel on Climate Change (IPCC) has decided that whoever takes over the island must create the smallest carbon footprint possible. You and your group members must come up with a plan for how you would set up a new society on the island. You will present to the committee your plans for the island's food/agriculture, transportation, and power sources. You must provide for 1,000 people on your island. Remember, the groups that create designs that leave the smallest carbon footprint will win the committee's votes. When you design your island, you should be creating an island that puts very little greenhouse gas into the atmosphere while still meeting the needs of your citizens.

Objectives: Students are to apply their knowledge of carbon footprint production, global climate change, and the link among CO_2, human economy/impact, and global warming to build and analyze a sustainable model of habitation for 1,000 citizens.

Project Task: Create a poster that illustrates (with a map and action plan) how one can build a sustainable model of habitation in a closed ecosystem.

Based on the alignment of the project task with the science standards, Mr. Roy notes that his students have the opportunity to demonstrate understanding of HS-LS2-7, that is, they can "design, evaluate, and refine a solution for reducing the impacts of human activities on the environment and biodiversity." By working on this project, they are also able to demonstrate understanding of HS-LS2-6 to show they can "evaluate claims, evidence, and reasoning that the complex interactions in ecosystems maintain relatively consistent numbers and types of organisms in stable conditions, but changing conditions may result in a new ecosystem." Mr. Roy always takes the time to remind students that their work is evidence (a key **habit of mind** from Chapter 1) of what they know and can do with science standards.

Mr. Roy inherited the two rubrics he uses with the Green Island project. See Figure 8.3 for the CO2 Footprint Action Plan rubric and Figure 8.4 for the Island Map rubric. As Mr. Roy explains, "These are the kinds of rubrics that we use throughout the year at my department. At the end of the project, I will fill in scores (0–4 scale) with my grades and, when necessary, justification for each individual part. Each column has associated expectations with it that we have gone over."

Figure 8.3 CO_2 Footprint Action Plan Rubric

	EXCEEDS STANDARD	MEETS STANDARD	EMERGING SKILLS	INSUFFICIENT EVIDENCE
Provides sufficient food, transportation, and energy for all 1,000 citizens				
Chosen options reflect purposeful CO_2 reduction strategies				
Calculation and presentation of CO_2 footprint data analysis is complete and formatted correctly				
CO_2 footprint is competitive and comparable with similar groups				

Teacher comments:

Figure 8.4 Island Map Rubric

	EXCEEDS STANDARD	MEETS STANDARD	EMERGING SKILLS	INSUFFICIENT EVIDENCE
Map is informative to the reader; nation, flag, or island name is easily seen				
Key or legend is present, colorful, informative, and easy to understand; symbols are properly calibrated/ calculated and consistent				

	EXCEEDS STANDARD	MEETS STANDARD	EMERGING SKILLS	INSUFFICIENT EVIDENCE
Essential island infrastructure is completely represented and in an easy-to-interpret method. Land area is proportionate and clearly outlined				
Organization of the island clearly shows purposeful planning and strategy				
Execution of the map presentation shows care, time, and effort in its creation				

Teacher comments:

Mr. Roy, in His Own Words

"When it comes to formative feedback for this project, I give a lot of it. I am a creature of habit. My primary means of seeing what my students are working on and how they are progressing is going around and checking in with each group in a rotation. Often, despite my best-laid **lesson plans**, I learn that my students may need more (or less) in-class work time.

"I also use the comments feature on Google Docs (which is what they share as a group to make their individual contributions). I try to add daily comments or critiques as they work on different drafts over the course of the project. This process also gives me insight into pacing of the project workflows. My science students, like all students, have different needs: Some need more guidance with my written feedback, others seem to take it up rather easily.

"This last year, I started using more **self-assessment** tools to complement the rubrics. It's additional data on the 'How is it going?' question. I noticed there are places where my students tend to get stuck or seem to need more targeted feedback and guidance. I put together these progress guides, which serve to focus everyone in the first and second weeks of the project."

From Rubric to Progress Guides: Designing My Own Tools That Promote the Use of My Written Comments

"Rubrics can really help us be clear with our students about what they're aiming for in a project, but I've found that, truthfully, photos and actual examples of previous Green Island design projects are much more effective than going over a rubric with students in terms of getting students to understand what a quality performance looks like. Yet students do need to be familiar with 'rubric speak,' I think.

"Part of gaining experience in a discipline is learning how the criteria on a rubric match—or don't match, as the case may be—with what we're seeing in a work sample, whether the work we're looking at is their own work-in-progress or an anonymous completed work sample from a previous year. Students need practice and support at comparing the language of the rubric with the actual work in front of them. But doing this with a densely worded, entire document filled with 20 boxes of details is overwhelming to most students. I've relied on full-blown department rubrics to keep standards, but I now create my own set of progress guides, which are much more streamlined and user friendly.

"Progress guides based on rubrics have a role to play in helping teachers be strategic in their written feedback to students. What I've done to help my students—and myself—to be focused in my written and spoken formative feedback with students is to take one strand (or component) of the Island Map rubric and turn it into two progress guides: one for me as the teacher and one for the students to self-assess their work-in-progress and/or give their peers formative feedback."

Thoughtfully Choosing a Skills Strand of a Rubric to Check on Actual Progress

"Of the five components on the Island Map rubric, over the years, I've learned to 'focus in' on how students are developing their island infrastructure. I use the self-assessment check as a proxy for gauging their understanding of ecosystem infrastructure. This helps me decide if I need to offer materials, reteach, or do a few one-on-one sessions. The "Understanding and Representing" strand also encompasses how my students have chosen to represent their decisions visually. We need our attention on those choices at this stage in the project's development, too.

"Past experience with students and the Green Island design project has taught me that students may make sound decisions regarding their infrastructure but run into significant trouble when it comes to representing it clearly and proportionately—or vice versa. I want to interact with them about this while they have plenty of time to change up what they're doing.

"Figure 8.5 presents my progress guide for formative feedback to students on island infrastructure. The first icon indicates the response so far is making excellent connections, the second icon indicates the response has a good focus, the third icon indicates the response is on target, the fourth icon indicates the response still lacks focus, and the last icon indicates the response is not yet on target. I use these symbols to communicate with my students who like visuals, but the written feedback is where the action is."

Figure 8.5 Progress Guide for Guiding Teacher Feedback

Bins	% of Class	Can Currently Do	Next Steps/Feedback
(palette icon)	5%	▸ Essential island infrastructure is completely represented in an easy-to-interpret method. Land area is proportionate and clearly outlined.	[note formative feedback and identify 1–2 next steps here]
(pencil cup icon)	10%	▸ Essential island infrastructure is partially represented *and* the method of interpretation is visible. ▸ Land area is almost proportionate and/or clearly outlined.	[note formative feedback and identify 1–2 next steps here]
(pencil and ruler icon)	60%	▸ Essential island infrastructure is not yet represented. ▸ The method of interpretation is not yet visible or clear. ▸ Land area is neither proportionate nor clearly outlined.	[note formative feedback and identify 1–2 next steps here]
(notepad icon)	15%	▸ Essential island infrastructure is not yet identified.	[note formative feedback and identify 1–2 next steps here]
(pencil icon)	10%	▸ No response or off-topic response.	[note formative feedback and identify 1–2 next steps here]

The symbols used in this table are intentionally vague. Rather than focus a student's attention on such language as *exceptional* or *needs improvement,* we want them to have a more accessible entry point to identify their level. Visual entry points can add to engagement and reduce stress concerning a value judgment about their performance.

Icon sources: iStock.com/bsd555, iStock.com/TuracNovruzova, iStock.com/-VICTOR-, iStock.com/nickylarson974, iStock.com/SergiiTiliegienov

"Here's how I use the progress guide for making decisions about feedback delivery. I observe students' first drafts and identify which of the statements in the "Can Currently Do" column best describe the draft overall. I use hash marks to tally the number of students for a particular level, then convert that to percentages. Then, in the right-hand column, I type out what next steps students (at each level) can do to revise their work. I consider grouping and pairing students to allow coaching and peer support for the speaking and writing demands of the task (e.g., revision process over the following days of instruction).

"Results from my quick review of drafts on Day 3 showed that over 60% of my students' current work was at the "Emerging" skill level. I expected this, to a degree, but for the project to move forward, we all had to get on the same page about this strand. Of all the **learning criteria**/skills on my rubric for this assignment, "Understanding and Representing Island Infrastructure" is one that we need to close the gap on before moving into more complex **depth of knowledge** aspects of the project.

"After my review of their work in Google Docs, I decided to give the students an opportunity on Day 5 to self-assess their drafts with a student-friendly progress guide focused on this success criterion. (See Figure 8.6.) My main modality for this phase of the feedback cycle is written comments, and we use the tracking feature to ensure we have a **running record** of the exchanges. I don't want to rewrite my feedback because someone accidentally erased or misplaced it!

"I invite the students to fill out the self-assessment guide and add one or two next steps. Sometimes I ask them to circle the icon first that best describes their current draft. Once they know the key for each icon (which we use a lot) it gives them a place to choose by circling a visual icon, which my students like. In my mind, this is like an **entrance** or **exit ticket**: It helps me see where they think they are. Sometimes their next steps are spot on; other times they are vague or formulaic. Either way, I get a picture of the places where my students are bunched up. It makes it easier to target my written comments on the Google Docs and be consistent.

"Then I add an actual comment on their next steps with a question: 'When will I see this?' 'Can I help you with this for the next draft?' 'If you feel stuck making this change, who can help?'

"By using the student's own progress guide and the comments feature, I can address a few additional skills with the Green Island design project. Students are learning to collaborate with me and each other using technology. Our feedback practices are typical of the real world. You need to be ready to take up feedback in different modes but also get very comfortable with written feedback, no matter how it comes to you."

Figure 8.6 Progress Guide for Guiding Student Feedback on Their Current Draft

LEARNING TARGET/SKILL: UNDERSTANDING AND REPRESENTING ISLAND INFRASTRUCTURE		
My Current Level of Progress Is	**My Current Draft Shows**	**My Next Steps/ Feedback**
(palette & brush icon)	▸ The essential island infrastructure on our map is completely represented in an easy-to-interpret method. Land area is proportionate and clearly outlined.	My next steps are 1. 2.
(pencil cup icon) ✓	▸ The essential island infrastructure on our map is partially represented *and* the method of interpretation is visible. ▸ Land area is almost proportionate and/or clearly outlined.	My next steps are 1. 2.
(crossed ruler & pencil icon)	▸ The essential island infrastructure on our map is not yet represented. ▸ The method of interpretation is not yet visible or clear. ▸ Land area is neither proportionate nor clearly outlined.	My next steps are 1. 2.
(notepad icon)	▸ The essential island infrastructure is not yet identified on our map.	My next steps are 1. 2.
(pencil icon)	▸ Does not have a response yet or is off topic at the moment.	My next steps are 1. 2.

Icon sources: iStock.com/bsd555, iStock.com/TuracNovruzova, iStock.com/-VICTOR-, iStock.com/nickylarson974, iStock.com/SergiiTiliegienov

Focus on Practice: Taking Up the Challenges and Opportunities With Written Formative Feedback

Ms. Marsalis teaches in the same science department with Mr. Roy, and she is still considered new. When Ms. Marsalis was hired, she was a big advocate for PBL. She still is. Ms. Marsalis's more seasoned colleagues are impressed with her energy, knowledge, passion, and advocacy for authentic assessment. At her previous school, she was a leader for a school-based PBL network. The students at that school presented their science portfolios in front of a panel of adults from various backgrounds, including parents, community members, and people working in STEM fields in the San Francisco Bay area.

In what follows, we will learn about the challenges Ms. Marsalis faced with formative feedback in the written modality, which she encountered during the pandemic as distance learning was mandated.

As you consider her situation, ask yourself what you think Ms. Marsalis has done well so far. What might she be able to do differently now that everyone is face-to-face again at her school? Most importantly, how can Ms. Marsalis's story help you reflect on your own instructional and assessment practices?

Ms. Marsalis, in Her Own Words

"I teach integrated science to ninth and tenth graders. As a lead-up to a big group project we call the Green Island design project—where groups of students are challenged to create a sustainable island that supports 1,000 citizens—I ask small groups of students to teach their classmates about different aspects of the carbon cycle. Everyone will need what they learn from the experience of teaching their classmates—as far as content and process—to engage successfully in the Green Island design project in the very next unit. This includes

- knowing specific subject content and academic language such as *carbon footprint, function, resource constraints*;
- being able to work with peers on a project;
- taking up my formative feedback as I support them for a successful presentation experience; and
- being able to execute what they've planned (with my support) with their classmates.

"Before distance learning, when it came to this part of the school year, I worked with the small groups in person to help them prepare for their team presentation experience. This year, I've had to depend on giving each group written feedback on a shared slide deck. It really doesn't matter which platform you use, as long as we can exchange feedback and keep a record.

"Students know when their group's presentation is, and I've been crystal clear with them: 'I need to see your slide deck before you all actually present so I can give you feedback. Send me an email letting me know when you're ready for my feedback.'

"Last week, two groups were to present on Monday: Hector's group and Priya's group. On Sunday, I received emails from both. Their first drafts were ready for my feedback. I was out and about, but on my phone, I was able to open their slides and add several comments to each presentation. Both groups had their feedback before 2:00 PM. I gave several positive comments to each group as well as four or five (what I thought were explicit) next steps. I wrote each group back letting them know my feedback was there for them. Then I got back to my Sunday.

"Monday arrived: team presentation time. As the class presentation began, I noticed Hector's group had resolved all my comments and incorporated almost all my formative feedback into their presentation. They had revised!

"Priya's group, on the other hand, had resolved all my comments but had not taken up any of my suggested next steps. They had revised their draft slides some but not in the ways I had expected them to.

"As the presentations wrapped up that day, I wondered, what went wrong? I had followed the same procedure with both groups. Why such different outcomes? Most importantly, what could I learn from this experience? How could I better support groups like Priya's in the future?"

Reflections on What Is Working and What Needs Improvement

1. In addition to the questions Ms. Marsalis asked herself above, try to speculate: Why do you think Hector's group and Priya's group responded so differently?

2. Make two lists, "Things Ms. Marsalis Can Change to Improve Student Uptake" and "Things Ms. Marsalis Can't Easily Change." What should Ms. Marsalis focus on first? Be as specific as you can. Imagine you are mentoring her. Give Ms. Marsalis some concrete feedback on her current feedback practices.

Things Ms. Marsalis Can Change to Improve Student Uptake	Things Ms. Marsalis Can't Easily Change

My advice to Ms. Marsalis is

Finally, read the following list of questions Ms. Marsalis generated for herself in her journal where she reflects on just-taught lessons. What question or questions would you add? Which would you prioritize?

Ms. Marsalis's Own Questions About Next Steps

- Was my mistake in letting the groups send me their first drafts at the last minute (the day before they were to present)?

- Should I have set a deadline for them to get their first draft to me?

- Should I have contacted both groups on Friday and asked about delivery dates? Should I have then reminded them that they will need time to act on my feedback and not left it to the weekend?

- To what extent were the different outcomes about the feedback itself and not about deadlines?

- Did I expect Priya's group to carry out next steps that were too difficult for them to carry out by themselves in only the written modality? If so, why hadn't I sensed this when I wrote the feedback?

- In what ways can I check—in multiple modalities if necessary—that a group is able to carry out the next steps I suggest?

- Is it reasonable that I expect all groups to take up every suggestion I make? If so, am I communicating this expectation to them clearly and effectively?

- Do I need some way to signal in my written feedback "This is a next step I expect you to take" versus "Here's some food for thought, act on it as you wish"?

- What kinds of scaffolding (e.g., progress guides) should I put in place to help groups like Priya's?

- How do we build more visible, consistent norms around written feedback practices and procedures? Do we need a short checklist to ensure we resolve next steps?

- How can I discover what frames/conditions/presumptions my students are working under with this type of project (whole-class presentations) and how much revision matters to their success?

- Once I learn these frames/conditions/presumptions, can I change up what I'm doing to better meet them where they are in a particular feedback cycle or exchange?

All of these questions are normal and lead all of us to wonder what answers would serve the students and Ms. Marsalis best. Like Ms. Marsalis, we might feel overwhelmed by the sheer number of issues and concerns the reflective assessment practitioner faces when engaging in formative feedback practices. Our advice typically is to prioritize and pick one or two immediately addressable practices. But we didn't offer directions or 1–2–3 steps in our case studies with Mr. Roy and Ms. Marsalis. Why? Because we trusted in their process as colleagues who talk, share, troubleshoot, and answer their own questions together.

We can offer tips and observations based on our experience in secondary schools, but we deeply respect all teachers' collaborative and creative energies. The goal of all reflective practice in the teaching profession is and should be growth—not summative judgment. We mean it when we say, "You decide." You are the professionals in your school, and you are positioned to make the best decisions on the way to **continuous improvement** in the classroom.

Try It Tomorrow

Reflection Prompts for Students After Self-Driven, Written Formative Feedback Exchanges

As you know, prompting students to reflect on an experience helps them learn from it. But that's not the only reason to have students reflect. You also want students to reflect—and communicate their reflections to you—so *you* can learn from them!

As you read your students' written responses, pay attention to patterns that arise. Let what your students say and write inform your feedback practices moving forward.

Although having students reflect in writing is typically sound practice, it's a good idea to mix things up. Have them reflect via another modality—namely by talking and listening to one another. You might have them turn and talk with a partner while reading written comments or queries aloud. You might also have them share immediately or record their reflections to those comments/queries on audio or video.

Prompts you might use to motivate student reflection include the following:

- What did you learn from the written feedback?
- How did it feel to see the strengths/positive parts of your performance acknowledged at this stage in the work?
- What assistance will you need to carry out using the written feedback and to revise before the final version is due?
- What written question or comment, if any, could you *not* answer for yourself? How can I help?
- Is there an aspect of your work/performance that you know needs improving but you're not sure how to improve it? In other words, did you have trouble generating a next step for yourself? Can we work on that together?

Teacher Reflection

AP Humanities Courses Need Writing Conferences

I learned about feedback modality making a difference by accident. As a first-year teacher at a high-performing public school, when I started teaching a semester-long AP [Advanced Placement] government class, I committed myself to having one-on-one writing conferences during class time for every major writing assignment.

Doing well on the AP exams and preparing for college requires many skills. Learning to write persuasively is a signature of my approach in AP courses. At my college, I was lucky because we all had to read Calkins, Elbow, and others to learn how to write, no matter what our major.

It's funny because students tell me I am known as "Mr. Revise and Resubmit." Apparently, I have a reputation for writing lots of comments on documents and, worse, expecting them to be resolved before anyone gets a grade in my classes.

The problem is, despite my best efforts with feedback during conferences, I was so *bad* at them. In the beginning, they were long—much too long. We're talking over 10 minutes per conference sometimes. I would read their work silently (rather than have the student read their work aloud) and sit there stumped, unsure what to say but forging ahead anyhow.

It was painful. Everything was new to me then: the assignments, the kids themselves, and the stunning variety of ways in which their writing could be quirky, simple, fascinating, technically incorrect, full of opinions, and often a combination of all those at once.

But I kept at the writing conferences. Problem is, I wasn't getting to all my students in time. So I didn't have a choice, really. To be fair to my students, I had to take their drafts—we're talking mostly handwritten drafts, with some printouts mixed in—home.

I soon learned what I'll never forget: The most important part of the experience of writing formative feedback to students is learning what to say to students. By having to write my comments to some of them on their drafts (the drafts of the students I hadn't been able to conference with during class time), I got much better at knowing how to point out positives, ask questions, and suggest next steps. There was something about having to write it down to communicate it to them that made the difference for me.

Evidence of my journey on this learning curve showed up quickly in subsequent writing conferences. It was like once I had written out a set of feedback on several papers for a particular writing assignment, I really began to hit my stride with the writing conferences. Each year it got easier to know what to say.

> Couple this experience with the fact that I didn't have in place *any* routines designed to help the students who had received written feedback from me process the feedback, respond to it, or ask me questions about it, and you can see why I decided early on in my career that if I expected students to revise their writing in ways guided by my feedback, then we had to have actual conversations about their drafts.
>
> Nowadays, actual conversations via typewritten (or voice-typed) language are possible. But that wasn't the case back then. I still much prefer in-person conversations about their work. I feel I get much better results with in-person conversations. Yet I also appreciate that so many other options are out there today—options that make written feedback merely a mode for having a real formative feedback *conversation*. Written feedback no longer means a one-way enterprise.

Scaffolds and Guided Practice for Individual Teachers

When writing formative feedback to your students, ask yourself the following:

- Is the written feedback for short turns or long turns of talk when it comes time to speak about my comments and suggestions?

- Is the written feedback going to use *synchronous*, *asynchronous*, or *both* modes for communicating my comments/suggestions/queries?

- Is my written feedback intended for **elaboration** to push to the next level or is it more like scaffolding/reinforcing the current level of understanding on our progress guide?

- What opportunities are built into the feedback cycle to ensure my students understand and can clarify the meaning of the written feedback *before* taking action?

Decision 1: Long Turns versus Short Turns of Feedback

Whether you give written feedback on students' work that occurs over a short or long time depends on the nature of the performance task. Big assignments like the Green Island design project tend to occur over the course of a unit. Subject matter content and student skills will also inform the duration of feedback and the kinds of cycles required to ensure revision.

For big projects and complex tasks, some decisions will need to be made and agreed upon in advance of the feedback exchanges. If you are planning to incorporate written comments, questions, and notes in these exchanges, consider the following:

- **For teachers:** In designing the unit, determine whether and how much students will be engaged in longer or shorter turns. How will you handle the first draft and subsequent drafts before the due date? Is revision expected based on the resolution of comments/questions/notes you provide? Will students have to show evidence of their use of these in the final product?

- **For students:** As you work on the project, what will you need to stay on track? When will you ask the teacher for help or clarification with comments/questions? Will you need a checklist, a progress guide, or a glossary? If you get stuck, who can you reach out to for help? Do you need a study buddy (for feedback)?

- **For paraprofessionals:** As you work with your students on the project, what will you need to help them stay on track? Can you ask the teacher for clarification with comments/questions before meeting with students? Will you need a copy of the task checklist and/or progress guide and rubric for the assignment? Will a glossary or some other tools help you to unpack written comments with your students? Do you need permissions to add comments/feedback in the learning management system or drive platform?

Decision 2: Synchronous versus Asynchronous Feedback

It helps to set and manage participants' expectations around written formative feedback (its uses and purpose). You also need to ask yourself, will the dialogue about the written feedback occur synchronously or asynchronously? For this decision, it helps to decide and act upon the following factors:

- **From a teacher's perspective:** Are you **priming** your students to reply to your comments and questions without resolving them in the document, particularly when the feedback is occurring in real time? If you know the written formative feedback dialogue is going to be asynchronous, have you tried coaching your students to leverage their ability to read all the comments without acting on them immediately? Sell your students on the value of thinking over feedback for a bit of time before immediately responding to it.

- **From a student's perspective:** During an asynchronous, typewritten feedback dialogue, it's okay to communicate your need for processing and **think time**. It's also okay to ask for examples. Additionally, part of being a student is learning to communicate in a professional **register**. Use this time to find the most professional words and tone you can access to respond—if you need to respond at all. Sometimes all that's needed is for you to "reply" by doing the work of taking up the feedback and revising. That is often the most professional response of all. Either way, a great rule of thumb with asynchronous feedback conversations is to do your part by attempting revision(s) before you continue the feedback dialogue.

- **From a paraprofessional's perspective:** Keep in mind that feedback can sting. Watch for signs that a student you are working with might be experiencing what some experts call "emotional flooding" in response to written feedback. When people are affected this way, they are ready to fight, flee, or freeze and are not in the best state to resolve conflict rationally. For many students, feedback feels like conflict and can produce cognitive dissonance. You can help students by practicing active listening and empathy and a degree of mindfulness. Say something like, "I can see why you'd feel like that . . ." or "I can understand the way you feel . . ." Model taking deep breaths. Let students know it's okay to take a break.

Decision 3: Scaffolding to Reinforce Current Level of Performance versus Seeking Elaboration Through Probing to Advance to Next Level

As you're writing, be aware of whether your feedback aims to reinforce the current level of performance or whether it seeks elaboration from the student in order to push a performance to the next level. The point isn't to always do one or the other or even to try to balance these two aims. The point is to know which type of written feedback you are giving so that you become more intentional and nuanced in your practices. For this decision, it helps to consider the following for each participant in advance of the exchanges that revolve around written feedback:

- **A teacher might consider:** If I'm reinforcing by asking for rewriting or redoing, why am I reinforcing this next step in particular? If I'm **probing** or seeking elaboration on the current performance, have I primed my students for feedback that can feel pushy, nosy, or harsh to them? How do they know I believe they can take their performance to the next level?

- **A student might consider:** Why would the teacher ask for more or push me to the next level if they truly believed I couldn't do it? How has my teacher worked with me before to improve? Why is the feedback focusing on this specific skill again? Is there a pattern? What can I learn from that?

- **A paraprofessional might consider:** How do I set the students at ease? Can I ask gently but explicitly, "Why do you think [your teacher] is focusing their feedback on this element or aspect of the work?" I might listen actively, then probe: "So, what can we learn from this specific comment or question? How can I help you move this forward to 'resolve it' today?"

Decision 4: Opportunities for Clarity/Clarification

All formative feedback dialogues, whether they feature writing or not, should invite opportunities for clarification. An advantage (and disadvantage) of written feedback is that the clarification process can be quite slow. For this fourth and final decision, it helps to consider the following in advance of the feedback exchanges:

- **Teachers might consider:** Am I being clear? Have I explicitly asked the students what questions they have about my written feedback? Can I choose a written feedback example (comment, suggestion, next step) that could work for several students with similar needs (not only one student)? What am I learning about my use of written feedback on this assignment? Where do students consistently need clarification of my comments? Are there patterns in my suggestions? Are the next steps meaningful for improving performances? If so, for whom?

- **Students might say (with a set of sentence frames or worksheet questions):** "Can I explain in my own words what the written feedback means to me? If any of these written feedback (comments, questions, suggestions for next steps) do not yet make sense to me, can the teacher clarify? Can I ask a peer? If I am feeling stuck, can I ask the teacher for clarification about the next steps? I am going to type out what I think your written feedback means in terms of one or two next steps and ask you/my peer if that seems right."

- **Paraprofessionals might say:** "I am your guide on the side, too. I can coach you. We can tackle this together." By being an authentic sounding board for the students they work with, paraprofessionals can ask students directly, "Tell me in your own words what the teacher is asking you to do here." Focus on unpacking written feedback, then follow up with, "How does this extra work feel? Can you do it? How can we get started with the suggested next steps on this assignment?"

Try It Tomorrow

Invite Feedback on Your Written Feedback

Try inviting feedback on your written feedback. First, prime students by telling them how interested you are in learning from their experiences of the written feedback you offered them recently. The more recent the better, although it does help if students have had opportunities to take up your written feedback before the exercise.

You can anchor the activity as a class by completing a T-chart similar to the one below. Let everyone know that the aim of the activity is to scribe and represent all the variations of their experiences with your written feedback from the last assignment.

Some of Us Found This Feedback Useful Because	Some of Us Didn't Find This Feedback as Useful Because

Before responses are scribed so that everyone can see them, invite students to first individually

- revisit the written feedback they received,
- refresh their memories about how they took up the feedback (or didn't), and
- note what they found useful and what they didn't find useful.

Then have students pair up and share their thoughts. Inevitably, as students discuss your written feedback with a partner, some will recall something helpful they want to add to the T-chart or something that they hadn't initially thought of on their own. This is one of the benefits of pair sharing. Finally, invite everyone to share out and scribe all student responses so that everyone can see them.

Look for patterns and discuss. One benefit of this activity is that students see how serious you are about learning to improve your written feedback practices. Another benefit is that students may see for themselves the range of experiences with typed or handwritten feedback in the class. Still another benefit is that students experience an opportunity to engage with the feedback (i.e., comments, suggestions, questions) they've received from you and also with feedback you gave to their classmates.

The most important benefit, of course, is what you learn from this activity. It gives you feedback on their experiences so you can learn and improve your practice.

Setting Goals and Monitoring Progress With Written Formative Feedback: Questions for Lesson Study and Professional Learning Communities

In this chapter, you read about different ways two science teachers in the same department—Mr. Roy and Ms. Marsalis—approached supporting written formative feedback loops and exchanges with their students. You read how Mr. Roy uses a progress guide anchored in the rubrics he uses for the Green Island design project (see Figure 8.5).

You also read how Ms. Marsalis felt puzzled and frustrated when two student groups responded quite differently to the formative feedback protocols she had put in place. One group revised by incorporating nearly all the next steps Ms. Marsalis had suggested; the other group revised their work but failed to take the next steps she had suggested.

Science, of course, is not the only subject area in which students benefit from formative feedback in the written modality. Members of your **professional learning community (PLC)** may teach social science, history, English language arts, mathematics, world languages, art, music, and physical education. No matter the subject area you teach, remind yourself of the salient details of Mr. Roy's and Ms. Marsalis's stories. Then, use the questions below to start a discussion that can help your PLC members think about the benefits of a progress guide for teacher use to support their written formative feedback loops/exchanges with students on a variety of media.

For a Department- or Subject-Specific PLC

1. For your subject area, what can be gleaned from Mr. Roy's and Ms. Marsalis's stories?

2. In what ways do their stories fail to resonate with what occurs in your subject area at your school? Is this significant? If so, why?

3. In your subject area, what role does giving students formative feedback in writing play? How is written formative feedback typically supported? What are the major constraints?

4. What do you think teachers in your subject area could do differently when it comes to supporting students in engaging in formative feedback loops that occur in the written modality?

5. Next steps: Consider and then share with the group how you will strive to change what you do regarding written formative feedback. Be specific. How could you begin using a progress guide for teacher use to better support the use of written feedback? How can

you align the progress guide for teacher use with a progress guide designed for student self-assessment? Is there another tool or procedure you currently use to communicate written comments/questions/notes to your students? Please share.

For PLCs Across Many Departments and Subject Disciplines

1. Tell us why having students engage in written formative feedback loops and exchanges in your subject matters. For whom does it matter? If you believe that having students engage in written formative feedback loops doesn't matter, please share more about why you feel this way. In your experience, does the most effective feedback draw from different modalities (e.g., spoken, nonverbal, etc.)? How?

2. Share a time in your life when written formative feedback you received or wrote to someone else made a significant impact. Was the experience based at the school, at another job, or in another setting? What about the experience could inform what you do with your own students in your subject area in terms of written formative feedback? Are there *do*'s and *don't*s you learned from those experiences that you can share with everyone?

3. Brainstorm what you would want new teachers to know about the value of supporting written formative feedback practices at your school, whether they teach in your subject area or not. Are any of these values or practices related to 21st century skills? Do written feedback exchanges connect to the aim of workplace or college readiness for your students? If so, how?

4. In your understanding of progress guides for teacher use in decision making and for student self-assessment, what are some of the ways information from both tools can be used to support student learning and differentiate formative feedback practices? What do you find appealing about this approach? What is puzzling? What might be daunting for the school as a whole if you all committed to developing progress guides?

5. Next steps: Consider and share with the group how you will strive to change what you do regarding written formative feedback. Be specific. How could you begin using progress guides for teacher use across different departments? Could students benefit from consistency in self-assessment routines using progress guides—across subject disciplines—on the field, in the art or music room, in the science lab, in the theater, and in other learning spaces? What is something you, your team, or your instructional coaches haven't thought of yet that might get students in the habit of offering and using written feedback based on students' interests?

Recap/Review

- Formative feedback in written modalities (whether written by hand or typed, recorded on a sticky note or digital comment) needs to be accompanied by spoken and nonverbal modalities.
- Supportive spoken conversations can help unpack written text, clarify meaning, and demystify what students are expected to do with the information.
- Concrete graphic organizers, clear procedures, and visible protocols ensure that written feedback is more likely to be incorporated in next drafts.
- Less is more. Prioritize what to communicate in writing to students. Suggestions for next steps are aided by shared progress guides aligned with learning targets.
- Plan to support students *before*, *during*, and *after* giving formative feedback in writing.
- When it comes to written feedback, anticipate challenges with academic language. Provide a glossary to accompany written comments as a reference.
- Always strive to convey warmth, respect, and encouragement in written formative feedback.
- Help students understand why a particular next step is important to take. One way to remember this is to think of all feedback as next steps feedback.
- It is a valuable exercise to have students reflect in writing on the process of giving and/or receiving written formative feedback, one that can help them deepen their metacognitive skills and support them in learning how to learn.

Ticket Out the Door

1. For better or worse, everyone who has taught (or learned) has experienced written feedback that was confusing, off-putting, or even offensive. Based on your experiences, what is important to address that we may have missed in this chapter?

2. Revisit Ms. Marsalis's story in the "Focus on Practice" section. Imagine you are assigned as Ms. Marsalis's instructional buddy (a more informal version of an instructional coach or induction mentor). How would you approach a feedback session with Ms. Marsalis to debrief possible next steps with the student presentations that lead up to the Green Island design project?

    a. Would you write notes/comments on her lesson/unit plan and then ask to talk about these written comments/suggestions?

    b. Would you talk first and then add your written comments/suggestions to the online Docs? (Please explain your approach and why you chose it).

    c. Would you take an entirely different approach? If so, please describe what you would do and explain why.

3. Pick one of the "Recap/Review" bullets. Share how it resonates with your experience as a teacher (or learner) who has felt empowered in a written feedback exchange.

CHAPTER 9

Spoken Feedback

> We will have to repent in this generation not merely for the hateful words and actions of the bad people but for the appalling silence of the good people.
>
> —Martin Luther King Jr. (1963)

Real, authentic turns of talk happen quickly. They can feel confusing, unanchored, and rushed. The clock is ticking, the **first draft** is due, everyone is trying to wrap up before the end of the week. We may feel the need to be silent, to just go along, to pretend we are listening to one another.

Feedback loops—no matter what the **directionality**, **configuration**, or **modality**—place high cognitive and affective demands on participants in a learning community. If we value deep engagement and deeper equity, we will need to break the silence around what we call "**binning for grading**" (which differs from **binning for feedback**). Numbers and formulae won't cut it for those interested in growth and change (Safir & Dugan, 2021). We need to slow down, prepare, and get ready to make **formative feedback** a companion to learning.

In schools that place formative feedback at the center of teaching and learning, we see **assessment for learning** opportunities that emphasize verbal communication skills. In a pioneering study of three high schools in New York City, Darling-Hammond and colleagues (1995) documented the role of spoken **feedback** as part and parcel to authentic assessment. Among those working on school reform since the 1990s, feedback has been an essential driver of **deeper learning** and the movement toward authentic assessment to improve equity and excellence in our educational systems.

Multiple researchers have observed the importance of spoken feedback loops in advancing equity. In relation to the development of listening skills, how we talk and listen is part and parcel to what makes **formative assessment** *formative*. Holmberg and Muwwakkil (2020) note:

> Extensive research in linguistics has shown that, in every language, these conversational dynamics are extraordinarily intricate and require people to make incredibly quick decisions and interpretations. In the cooperative, turn-taking world of social talk, meaning is often conveyed through actions that occur in milliseconds—yes, milliseconds. (p. 25)

So we have to prepare ourselves and our students for the twists and turns of spoken feedback routines, which always include how we listen and choose to speak to one another. It's important to remember how complex even simple conversation can be. They add,

> Conversations are inherently rapid and cooperative, requiring participants to know precisely when to take turns and how to interpret brief silences and extended pauses. . . . Even split-second variations in the length of time between turns can make the difference between being perceived as early (i.e., interrupting), on time, or late to respond. . . . In U.S. English, answers to questions typically start 150 milliseconds from the end of the question, which is roughly twice as fast as the blink of an eye. And when a response to a question starts noticeably later (such as approximately 600 milliseconds after the end of the question), people tend to make assumptions about the reasons for this delay. (Holmberg & Muwwakkil, 2020, p. 26)

While our students may not actually choose to interrupt the teacher or one another, the demands of spoken feedback require additional supports and **scaffolds** to remind everyone: We will need to signal ways for everyone to intermittently **pause**, to slow down to check for understanding, and to adjust for reception and uptake of feedback as needed.

The spoken modality is probably the one teachers rely on most for enacting formative feedback processes and practices. But just because we're engaged in it often doesn't mean we can't improve and rethink our purposes and aims in this familiar modality. The following guiding questions anchor our exploration of this topic.

Guiding Questions

1. Why plan, enact, and reflect on spoken modalities of formative feedback? For whose good is spoken feedback often most useful? What educational goals or purposes does spoken feedback serve?

2. How can we meet the challenges and opportunities that come with formative feedback in the spoken modality?

3. In what ways can spoken formative feedback be more like a back-and-forth conversation between the giver and recipient(s), where all participants exert influence?

4. What are ways that spoken formative feedback can be scaffolded and connected to other modalities (written and nonverbal) to strengthen feedback loops?

It is common in subject areas that emphasize physical techniques (ceramics, physical education, music, culinary arts, drama, and even science labs) for spoken words to accompany haptic/body-kinesthetic feedback. For example, a science teacher might say, "Hold the pipette vertically, like this," while re-angling the pipette the student is holding. Or the drama teacher might reposition a cape a student is wearing while simultaneously coaching, "During this particular line, if you start with the cape here and move it like so, that will make a difference for your character that the audience will notice." The physical education teacher may press into a student's badminton racket while coaching, "Note where your power on a backhand is going to have to come from. Do you feel that?" We will get to these nonverbal **moves** in Chapter 10.

For now, we will focus on speaking and listening aspects of formative feedback while keeping in mind that written cues and physical practices are equally important to ensure students can unpack and carry out next steps on a project, complex assignment, or performance task.

Most often, spoken feedback will appear as the primary processing tool for making sense of student responses: "What is next?" "What do I do now?" "I wrote that already!"

Figure 9.1 depicts the three main feedback focal points and their lenses in our framework for this book. This chapter is about the focal point *modality* and the second of the three lenses associated with it—spoken feedback. We will interchangeably refer to this lens as *spoken feedback* or *verbal feedback* and *oral feedback* approaches. Teachers who engage students in verbal formative feedback practices, protocols, and experiences will blend other modalities but will also examine the effectiveness of spoken modality with attention to particular needs of students.

Figure 9.1 Formative Feedback Framework

Contexts for Learning		
Face-to-Face	Blended	Distance Learning
Focal Point		
Directionality	**Configuration**	**Modality**
Lenses		
Teacher-driven	Whole class	Written
Peer-to-peer-driven	Small groups (2–4)	Spoken
Self-driven	Individual (1:1)	Nonverbal
Tasks, Projects, Activities	Learning Goals, Standards, Skills Rubrics, Progress Guides, "Next Steps" Organizers	

Defining Spoken Formative Feedback

The communication between participants in spoken formative feedback exchanges can be synchronous or asynchronous, in-person or remote. Asynchronous spoken formative feedback routines necessarily involve audio or video recordings and are less common than real-time dialogue, though smartphones, tablets, and laptops make such feedback more common than it once was. Engaging students in real-time formative feedback dialogues via streaming video is noteworthy and has many implications for practice. Teaching remotely—whether fully online or in blended settings—is now a set of skills that preservice and in-service teachers are increasingly experimenting with, and remote spoken feedback tools are part of the 21st century learning environment.

Traditionally, learning in school consists of students and teachers working together side by side, face-to-face in physical classrooms. Most of this chapter will address supporting sound formative feedback practices in this context. Nonetheless, we will examine explorations for spoken feedback loops and exchanges in different media with new technologies, in part, because schools and schooling are changing in the 21st century.

But first, let's look at what defines and distinguishes formative feedback in the spoken modality from other modalities.

FORMATIVE FEEDBACK IN THE SPOKEN MODALITY	
What It Is	**What It Isn't**
▸ qualitative observations, comments, and questions communicated by means of speech ▸ may occur synchronously or asynchronously (e.g., a recorded audio memo or a video clip) ▸ can be teacher-driven, peer-driven, or self-driven (e.g., audio memo to self) ▸ great for checking for understanding and adjusting feedback to learners' needs (strong potential for differentiating on the fly) ▸ great for dialogic feedback conversations, not only one-way monologues ▸ inherently complex ▸ a good way to augment/support focused written and haptic/body-kinesthetic feedback ▸ perceived by many students as of higher quality and more useful than written feedback	▸ Written comments repeated aloud ▸ praise. As Wiggins (2012) notes, effective feedback is "specific" ▸ quantitative scores or points ▸ a quick-fix solution when written feedback feels like it isn't working ▸ a common or comfortable experience for many students—and teachers—not accustomed to dialogic exchange ▸ all about what you say (versus what you hear and observe during the exchange) or what your students are hearing you say explicitly or implicitly ▸ intended to stand alone without progress guides, a glossary, exemplars, graphic organizers, visual aids, and so on ▸ a one-off. As Wiggins (2012) notes, effective feedback is "ongoing"

(Continued)

(Continued)

FORMATIVE FEEDBACK IN THE SPOKEN MODALITY	
What It Is	**What It Isn't**
• viewed by students as a sign of care and respect for their progress • an opportunity to listen and to observe carefully • prone to as many opportunities for miscommunication and misunderstanding as any other modality • while listening and/or talking, participants may jot notes or use visual scaffolds/graphic organizers	

> One of my favorite phrases to use with students is, "Tell me about what you've got going on here." And then I listen, really listen. That's what I base a lot of my spoken feedback on—what they've said about their own work-in-progress.
>
> —Celine, middle school art teacher

We invite you to get reflective as you plan for your next round of spoken formative feedback. Everyone gets better with intentional practice. Plan to improve. Choose an aspect to focus on first that seems most suitable for you and your students.

Table 9.1 presents three things to consider when planning for spoken formative feedback conversations:

- participants' experiences of auditory, affective, and/or **cognitive load**;
- the timing of the conversation in the phase of the work; and
- your effectiveness at eliciting understandings and misunderstandings.

It also lays out what you should "Ask Yourself" ahead of spoken formative feedback interactions, and it summarizes "Why It Matters." Finally, you'll find "Tips and To-Do's" that have worked for teachers.

Use the table to plan separately (or together as a team) for different subject matters in varied contexts. The goal is to start tapping into the power of the spoken modality when it comes to supporting formative feedback practices and routines in your classrooms.

Table 9.1 Planning for Formative Feedback in the Spoken Modality: What to Consider and Why It Matters

WHAT TO CONSIDER	ASK YOURSELF	WHY IT MATTERS	TIPS AND TO-DO'S
Participants' Experiences of Auditory, Affective, and/or Cognitive Load	What will I do to prevent students from being cognitively overwhelmed during the conversation? Are there routines and cues I can draw upon to support auditory processing? How can we manage emotional blockages and affective filters more compassionately and effectively?	Students can't take up feedback they don't really hear. Students whose affective filters rise no longer hear what we think is important to hear.	▸ Prioritize what is the most important feedback to focus the conversation on with the help of a progress guide for teacher use in differentiating initial drafts or first tries. ▸ Use a conversation protocol and/or a graphic organizer (including progress guide for student self-assessment). Encourage students to put content of the spoken conversation into their own words and to write/draw notes. ▸ Pause often enough and long enough. Create "How are you feeling right now?" routines for you and your students that aim to ensure this.
Timing in Phase of the Work, Learning, Project, or Performance	What difference does it make to students' engagement when our conversation occurs? Is the focus of the formative feedback conversation appropriate for this student at this time?	Students will often respond differently to your invitations to engage, depending on where they are in the learning process.	▸ Make use of a progress guide for teacher use to help you determine how appropriate the intended focus of the formative feedback conversation is for a particular student or group of students. ▸ Prime, prime, prime. Even during the conversation, prime. Aim to normalize students' experiences with the work and with the feedback process. ▸ Have a system for keeping track of the spoken feedback so that both you and your students can see how it changed over the course of the project. ▸ Affirm where they are and help them take their next step. Again, progress guides for teacher use and for student use can be tremendously helpful here.

(Continued)

(Continued)

WHAT TO CONSIDER	ASK YOURSELF	WHY IT MATTERS	TIPS AND TO-DO'S
Eliciting Understandings and Misunderstandings	How will I obtain evidence of what students understand and don't yet understand with respect to content, performance, and next steps? How can you effectively work to advance student learning if you haven't elicited understandings and misunderstandings?	The spoken modality is in many ways the best modality for discovering student understandings and misunderstandings because the capacity to clarify effectively is greater when the dialogue is in real time (audio recordings are not as advantageous in this regard).	• Check for understanding often. • Invite students to explain in their own words. • Teach students to offer their own understandings during a conversation before you ask them (or their classmate asks them). This fosters agency/autonomy, mutual respect, and collegiality. • Listen carefully and probe (gently). Be on the lookout for correct responses that students might anchor in incorrect reasoning.

Spoken formative feedback conversations that occur in classrooms, we've found, benefit when teachers plan to improvise. In many ways, this is what Table 9.1 stresses: Plan to improvise so that you can differentiate the formative feedback moves you make according to the principle of "kids first, then contexts and curriculum." Each young person is unique, each context is different, and each curriculum places special demands on what works. But one way to be an effective **formative assessor** is to stay flexible, consider options, and be ready to improvise when necessary (Duckor & Holmberg, 2017).

Have and use a scaffold, a protocol, or a routine that you and your students can count on. At the same time, be sure you observe carefully, listen actively, and pause respectfully so you can improvise artfully.

What the Research Tells Us

Educational researchers John Hattie and Shirley Clarke (2019) assure us that verbal feedback is the most potentially powerful feedback, especially when it occurs "in 'the golden moment' when the context is alive, the student is 'in flow' and the learning is gaining momentum'" (p. 82). They note that feedback exchanges during a lesson are more effective than "anything which happens after the lesson" (p. 123).

Research also tells us that timing matters across the board. In fact, everyone agrees that *when* we speak is as important as *how* and *what* we say in a feedback loop. In schools, classrooms, and learning environments where time is available for verbal/spoken feedback, students can immediately clarify, question, and seek more instruction on our feedback. We can deliver feedback, and most importantly, we can listen to how it sounds in real time with real young people.

Definition: Dialogic

[dahy-*uh*-loj-ik]

adjective

1. of, relating to, or characterized by dialogue
2. participating in dialogue

A dialogue, of course, is a conversation between two or more persons. It's an exchange of ideas or opinions on a particular issue, with a view to reaching agreement, resolving a problem, or communicating an idea.

That a feedback conversation includes turn-taking does not mean it is dialogic in the sense we intend here. Turn-taking is a start, but it's not enough.

To be dialogic, both participants need to actively listen to the other. They need to relate their contribution to the conversation to what the other person has said.

To be dialogic, a conversation needs to be taken in a direction by more than one participant. In the case of a teacher–student formative feedback conversation, the student needs to be able to take the conversation in a direction they want.

As you aim for more **dialogic** feedback conversations with your students, be on the lookout for

- turn-taking that's too fast—pauses are necessary to engage in complex thinking;
- side-stepping questions (your own side-stepping or the student's)—it's a sign that an internal agenda may be taking precedence over responding to the other; and
- moving too quickly past "I don't know"—frequently, a long enough pause is all it takes to move beyond "I don't know." Keep in mind that students not knowing *yet* is okay.

Rich Tasks at a Challenge Level Appropriate for the Student's Skill Level

We know that rich tasks—tasks that allow student choice and are more open ended and authentic—offer greater opportunities for meaningful verbal/oral formative feedback dialogue than narrower, more closed-ended tasks (Small & Lin, 2018). Rich tasks, projects, and assignments should also provide students with a challenge that is appropriate to their skill level: not too difficult as to be off-putting nor too easy without a path for transfer or extension. When students are engaged in such meaningful, authentic tasks, conversations with them about where they're headed and how they're getting there tend to come easily. There is a natural flow of conversation because everyone is interested in the outcome.

Dialogic-ness Means the Interaction Is Mutual

A significant value of the spoken modality over other modalities lies in its potential for **dialogic exchanges**. In this sense, *dialogic discourse* means how much back-and-forth—in a meaning-making way, not a strictly turn-taking way—is evolving in the conversation as it is unfolding (Alexander, 2006).

Too often, teachers do too much of the talking. In some studies, 90% or more of classroom time is spent listening to the instructor talk. We know from research that all students need to talk to learn (Bransford et al., 2000) and teachers need to listen carefully to what students are saying to discover what sense they're making of our attempts to communicate with them.

Researchers have also found that teachers don't pause long enough during writing conferences with students for students to actually generate content-specific language to use in their revisions (Schuldt, 2019). It can take quite a bit of time for students to come up with specific content, and we face competing demands on our time. Sometimes it is enough for students to know the direction they should take, even if they don't yet have specific, strong, contending possibilities in mind for how they will go in that direction.

Students Perceive Spoken Feedback More Positively Than Written Feedback

While there are always exceptions, when teachers communicate feedback through the spoken modality, students have more positive perceptions than when it is communicated in the written modality. While much of the research was conducted with college students (see, e.g., Agricola et al., 2020; Merry & Orsmond, 2008), smaller studies with secondary school students have reached similar conclusions (see, e.g., Van der Schaaf et al., 2011).

Keep the Ball in Their Court

When engaging students through the spoken modality, teachers need to put students' work front and center: Students need to be the ones talking, thinking, and articulating their meaning-making in the feedback process. Such moves to invite student talk might include a teacher saying,

- "Tell me what you're thinking right now."
- "Can you say back to me what I've just said but in your own words?"
- "So, what are you going to do next?"
- "I need to know what's puzzling you. It's okay if you feel stuck."
- "How would you explain it to a friend or someone younger than you?"

Even if your dialogue with students occurs via a streaming service, remember that the affordances of a spoken formative feedback conversation in real time are still the same: opportunities to check for understanding, course correct, and clarify foremost among them. Keep putting the ball back into the student's court. Keep having the student explain what sense they are making of your questions, your suggestions for next steps, and your explanations of the task, including what a quality performance looks like. To make the most of these conversations, teach your students to be both active listeners and active participants.

Essential Spoken Feedback Practices Supported by Research

Just-in-Time Spoken Feedback Is Key When There Is a Need to Intervene

- Set up regular routines in multiple configurations to maximize opportunities for spoken feedback when students need it most. Identify places in performance tasks, projects, or assignments where bottlenecks are likely to occur and be flexible when you see a need to intervene with spoken support and use verbal scaffolding in the conversation.

Align Comments, Questions, and Suggestions With Visible Scaffolds and Learning Goals

- Use a progress guide and/or right-sized rubric to align your spoken feedback with learning goals and success criteria along a continuum of next steps. Refer to a glossary of academic language terms (domain-specific and general) to help students define aloud. Help them make sense of what you mean by talking through your spoken and written comments, questions, and suggestions.

Invite Opportunities to Produce Academic Language in Discussion

- Examine registers and domain-specific language cues in your turns of talk (Zwiers, 2007, 2019a, 2019b). Surface academic language demands in the task, evaluation tools, and your own written and spoken comments for productive use in a dialogic exchange. By talking through feedback, students are acquiring and gaining facility with academic language while you are assessing progress informally. Have students use their own registers and voice to surface questions and seek clarifications.

Use Nonverbal Cues to Invite Conversations Where All Feel Safe to Speak and Listen

- There are easy-to-implement ways to encourage and sustain engagement in spoken modalities, which include sitting next to the student (as opposed to across from them), maintaining eye contact with the student, and using a soft and relaxed tone of voice.

Did You Know? Characteristics of Formative Assessors

Learning Pathways Videos

Formative assessors are flexible, are open to improvisation, and seek out teachable moments as they assess for learning during a lesson.

Formative assessors anchor their formative assessment practices in rich learning targets such as the habits of mind, **Common Core State Standards**, and 21st century collaboration skills.

Formative assessors see how assessment for learning directly supports building students' agency and understanding *during* the instructional cycle—not after, when it's too late to assist or make a difference.

They believe in the core principles of equity and continuous improvement in all forms of classroom assessment. Perhaps most importantly, formative assessors make visible moves that link good instruction and assessment practices seamlessly.

Formative assessment is deep equity in action.

Formative assessors know in their hearts that seeing students—their ideas, their beliefs, their opinions, their p-prims, and their misconceptions—as assets is the only authentic way forward. Good classroom teaching, like good classroom assessment, requires our commitment to bringing all this diverse "soft data" to light.

Students shine when *what they think* and *what they say* matters enough for adults to attend to their ideas with consideration and care.

Spoken Formative Feedback Practices that Align Purposes, Tasks, and Tools: The Case of Mr. Roy and the Green Island Design Project, Continued

In the following vignette, Mr. Roy provides further insights into the use of spoken formative feedback as part of the Green Island design project discussed in Chapter 8.

Mr. Roy, in His Own Words

"Checking in on each group's progress is one thing. But getting into deeper conversations with each group about subjects like the learning expectations and **standards** is another. It can suck up a lot of time. It's almost too obvious, but students really do need to speak to connect the concepts they're supposed to be learning with their own actual projects.

"This was a real *aha* moment in my teaching practice, which I can now see seven years into this profession. I need to listen to discover where my students' understanding is. Sometimes I can get this from hearing what they're saying to one another. More often, I'm the one asking questions, listening carefully, and getting them to elaborate. As I do this, I'm encouraging them to use **academic language** as we learned to call it in my teacher credential program. This doesn't mean a vocabulary review on the dry-erase board; it means working on using phrases and special ways scientists write and talk to one another.

"When it's the Green Island project they're doing, I'm encouraging them to use words like *infrastructure, blueprint, impact, biodiversity,* and so on in context. I also try to model the less-obvious ways scientists talk: I remind them of phrases like *In addition to, that is,* and *we can conclude from this.* I had to learn this science speak in college, but I try to give my students a head start.

"Physically going around the room to each of the groups is one way I'm able to keep track of who I've interacted with on a roster with my clipboard. But I've also learned that to be the most equitable I can with my feedback, I need to be strategic and disciplined, too. There is only so much time each period. When it is time for a quick conference or huddle, I use what I've written on my **progress guides** and sometimes the student's version of the progress guide, so that I am strategic with my spoken feedback."

Connecting My In-Class, Spoken Feedback to Written Feedback I've Already Shared

"Here's how I do that. For the Green Island design project, which takes about three weeks, I want to connect our in-person conversations with written feedback I've already given to them about their projects. This is to give my students the experience of coherence and alignment with the learning goals for the unit. For my students, who bring a variety of dispositions and expectations to the science classroom, this means letting them know that the next steps are important. Even making revisions matters. Again and again, I remind everyone: I'm here to answer questions and assist as a coach does on the field or on the court.

"Before we start talking, I remind them, 'If it was worth *my* writing the feedback on your Doc, it is worth *our* talking together about those comments during class time.' The same goes for any support your classmates or team gave you in the peer feedback session.

"At this midpoint in the Green Island design project, they've given themselves formative feedback on their drafts using their **self-assessment** progress guide (see Figure 8.6 in Chapter 8). And I've already read their next steps and responded in writing. So now, when I'm in class, I'm strategically checking on how they're handling their next steps.

"I have a general feedback strategy, but it also depends on the kids (i.e., their mood, feelings, and readiness to work). I tend to focus on a few aspects as I prep these talks in my mind. Before talking with the kids, I ask myself,

- Were there any inaccuracies or overlooked aspects from the self-assessment we did yesterday?
- Which students' drafts need triage and which ones require me to reteach a concept or demonstrate a skill?
- From my quick review of the progress guide results, where should I focus my verbal feedback today (e.g., in the middle or lower and upper ranges)?"

Connecting With at Least Two Kids at Each Level of the Progress Guide

"Before it's time for them to work in groups and for me to visit each group during the block, I pull out my analysis from my progress guide for teacher use for the Green Island design project, the one that shows me the trends in the class (Figure 8.5 in Chapter 8).

"I generally choose two students whose current work is at each level of performance and make sure I talk with those students one-on-one by the end of the period. I choose *two* students at each level so I can more easily see how different my conversations might be. I expect that conversation with a student whose work is at the topmost level will need extensions-type feedback while the conversation with a student whose work is at an emerging level will need re-engagement–type feedback. I also check if language status, special needs/supports, or an **individualized education plan** (**IEP**) can help me better understand where the work needs to go next. I believe in making sure my feedback takes the whole person into account.

"Since there are five levels of performance on the 'Understanding and Representing Island Infrastructure' progress guide (Figure 8.5), I set a goal of speaking with 10 students out of 37 during the block period. [**Block scheduling** is used at Mr. Roy's school.]"

Why I Focus on Talking With Students Whose Self-Assessments Were Inaccurate

"Among these 10 students are individuals whose self-assessments were inaccurate in noteworthy ways. The number of students this happens to be varies a great deal. For the Green Island design project, there were only three students. One of them was in the topmost assessment level based on our learning goals and success criteria.

"It's normal for students who are learning something to be inaccurate in their self-assessments. Part of my job is to help my students talk through these progress guides to reveal those gaps but, more importantly, my job is to offer a hand in learning what's next to get on track. I stress again and again—we are revising our work just as real scientists do.

"I find that in talking with my students, I learn a great deal about how they're understanding the language on the progress guide, what makes them tick, and how they see themselves as scientists. My mission isn't to get them to change their self-assessment immediately through magical student–teacher conversations; it's to discover what is going on with them and how I can learn from their experiences with the curriculum, project, and task before us."

Focus on Practice: Interview With High School Student Hazel

Most of us are familiar with the animated television specials starring the characters from the Peanuts cartoon. Adult speech in that series is a perfect *negative* example of teacher talk: All anyone under a certain age hears from adults is a muffled "mwah mwah mwah." Viewers can't make out the adult's words any more than Charlie Brown or Linus can.

Something similar can happen with formative feedback in the spoken modality. What gets said, especially when it's a teacher saying it, can sound like "mwah mwah mwah" to the student.

The following interview with a high schooler gives us an adolescent's perspective on what it's like to experience spoken formative feedback from a teacher. Note how the student's experience suggests areas of the formative feedback process that are ripe for improvement. Some are related to the actual spoken modality in the context of distance learning, others are larger in scope, such as the mindset a student (and teacher) brings to the conversation.

While reading this interview, simple fixes may spring to your mind. Note them, as well as anything else you pick up that may be harder to fix (e.g., increasing the amount of talk a student does during a feedback conversation or ensuring that the conversation is actually dialogic, not merely a vehicle for a student collecting "to-do's" from a teacher).

Hazel considers herself an achievement-oriented student but not a high-achieving one. She, like millions of other high school students, struggled during the pandemic. Learning loss was not foremost on her mind. She had more immediate concerns. How would she get to college when her grades had suffered? How could she figure out what to do with assignments as her teachers were adjusting to online and blended instructional and assessment settings? How could she maintain attention, listen well, and get clarification on next steps to improve those assignments as the world seemed to falter around her? The transcript has been edited for clarity.

Interview With Hazel: On Teacher–Student Conversations During the Pandemic

Interviewer: What would you tell a beginning teacher in order to get them to 80/20—where the student is doing 80% of the talking and the teacher is doing 20%—in a one-on-one feedback conversation over Zoom?

Hazel: It's *never* going to be 80/20 over Zoom.

Interviewer: You sound so sure about that.

Hazel: It's never going to be 80/20 in person, either.

Interviewer: Why not?

Hazel: Because half the time when a teacher is talking to me [in a one-on-one feedback conversation], my main concern is, "How do I remember what they're telling me?" If it's a lot at one time, I definitely can't remember it. I try to hang on to the three most achievable or important things. I let the rest wash over me.

Interviewer: If it's important and *new* to you . . . ?

Hazel:	Sometimes it's not new to me. It's like, "Oh, right! I didn't get to that yet!" Whether or not it's achievable matters most. If it's important, but not achievable, I'll let it go. I'll also let things go if they're achievable but not important enough. I'm trying to sort that out. Once I've got my list of three things, their words wash over me. The teacher is talking and I'm nodding my head saying, "Yes," and "Okay," but I'm repeating those three things over and over in my head. I'm just trying to remember them.
Interviewer:	Is it ever any different? When *you're* doing the talking? Besides saying "Yes," and "Okay"?
Hazel:	If it's "along-the-way" feedback. And the teacher is asking me, "Where are you going here?" And I'll be like, "I'm not sure yet." And they'll be like, "Because it looks to me like this is what you're intending, when you wrote here at the top of the paragraph." And they'll read to me a part of my paper.
Interviewer:	"Along-the-way" feedback?
Hazel:	Yes. That's like when, for example, you have two body paragraphs, your intro is kinda skimpy, and no conclusion.
Interviewer:	That's when you'll do some real talking?
Hazel:	Yes. Because we both don't know where the paper's going. I'm still trying to figure that out. It's like a real conversation. The teacher can't tell from my paper, so it's like they're trying to help me get possible directions for my paper from my mind.
Interviewer:	You're thinking on the spot.
Hazel:	I'm thinking on the spot. Sometimes I have an answer. Sometimes I don't. Along-the-way feedback is like a discussion of ideas and mapping out where you're going. It's like the teacher saying, "Your commentary kind of contradicts itself in these places, so I want you to take another look at that and fix it. Do you have any ideas right now?" They ask you a question and you have time to answer it in along-the-way feedback.
Interviewer:	How are these times—where you're talking—different from the times you're not talking? The times you're trying to remember the three most achievable and important things to do?

(Continued)

(Continued)

Hazel:	It's the timing. When there's a complete first draft or the project is almost done, it's totally different. Where you give them a complete first draft and they lightly grade it by the rubric.
Interviewer:	They actually give you a grade?
Hazel:	No. It's a pre-grading. They check off things like, "Yes, you did this on the rubric. Yes, you did this. This needs work." They don't go super into detail. They're going to say, "Yes, you have commentary," but they're not going to grade how good your commentary is. That's for you to decide. They're just checking, "Yes, you have commentary. And, yes, you have quotes." Stuff like that. It's like you're getting a fake grade, so you'll know how to improve it. They're not grading it too deeply, but they're checking for the elements and then saying, "If you did all these elements well, you'll get about this grade." If there are glaring errors or super obvious stuff, they'll say, maybe, "Fix it up," or "Here's a suggestion." But they're not asking questions.
Interviewer:	So the timing of your conversation with a teacher really matters.
Hazel:	Yes. But in any conversation, if they get carried away with trying to help you, it's hard. It's like, "Here's what you can do next. You can also do this and this and this and this!" And I'm like, "O-*kay*!" (*Hazel laughs.*)
Interviewer:	So if a teacher is listening, what advice would you give them to make feedback formative for you?
Hazel:	What do you mean by "formative for me"?
Interviewer:	You know. Like something you can use, learn from, get you to the next level?
Hazel:	Well . . . (*long pause*). Maybe they could ask me before I get into the conversation, "Did you have a chance to see my comments? Let's walk through each comment I made to make sure we understand this together." That way I can breathe, not panic, and know I'll remember what's next.

Scaffolds and Guided Practice for Individual Teachers

Supporting Students to Document Spoken Formative Feedback Conversations

Let's now return to Mr. Roy and explore how he helps all of his students by documenting spoken formative feedback conversations. Many students have an IEP and/or 504 plan at Mr. Roy's school, and he carefully considers how those accommodations require **differentiated formative feedback** since one size does not fit all the needs of his students. Yesenia is one such student who Mr. Roy is working with while he is learning to use different lenses to better differentiate feedback on her current classroom project. In what follows, we illustrate Mr. Roy's use of a **graphic organizer** (Figure 9.2) to document his supports/accommodations for Yesenia's work in his classroom.

Yesenia is one of four students in Mr. Roy's third period who has an IEP. She is also a designated **English learner**. According to the three stages of English language development described in California's **English language development standards**, Yesenia's English proficiency is "Expanding," the middle stage between "Emerging" and "Bridging."

At Yesenia's last IEP meeting, Yesenia's parents said they were thankful for the aides who were helping Yesenia, but they were concerned she was too dependent on them. Through a translator, they said, "We want Yesenia talking to her teachers herself. If she has a question, she can ask the teacher herself."

Mr. Roy took this concern to heart and developed the following graphic organizer/protocol not only for Yesenia, but for all his students with IEPs and for those with special needs, whether they are designated or not. The aim of this spoken feedback protocol is to support students in determining what they want to talk with Mr. Roy about and to document—in their own words—how Mr. Roy helps them. This approach would provide evidence for Yesenia's parents that she is in the process of doing what they wanted and hoped for. And he could use the protocol to keep a record with the paraprofessionals and others who supported Yesenia in her studies at the school.

Because Mr. Roy wants his students to develop a sense of *why* they're doing what they're doing (the relevance **habit of mind** discussed in Chapter 1), Mr. Roy included a place for students to explain "Why that next step?" on this graphic organizer.

Figure 9.2 Graphic Organizer for a Student to Document Their (Spoken) Formative Feedback Dialogue With a Teacher

Name: Yesenia	
Period: 3	
Learning Target/Skill: Understanding and Representing Island Infrastructure	
My question:	
Mr. Roy's response:	
Notes on next steps:	Why? (If you have more than one next step, circle *one* and explain why it's necessary.)

The strengths of using this or other similar graphic organizers/protocols for students to record the content of their feedback with teachers are numerous and include:

- Students know ahead of time what to expect in a conversation.
- It fosters student agency.
- It helps students and teachers negotiate language and meaning together.
- It keeps conversations on track with well-defined goals.

The spoken feedback protocol also gives everyone evidence of ongoing support with multiple snapshots of feedback-driven exchanges over time. When collected across a semester, these documents can be helpful when teachers, students, and parents are reflecting on what has been accomplished together (e.g., did the student's questions to the teacher change over time? Have the student's explanations for certain next steps become more sophisticated? Is the student showing evidence of growth in their ability to self-assess?).

Notice that the "Notes on next steps" section of the graphic organizer in Figure 9.2 doesn't communicate *who* comes up with the next steps. It may be Mr. Roy, it may be Yesenia, or it may be their dialogue together that determines Yesenia's next steps. However, as the process or exchange of information evolves, Mr. Roy feels that Yesenia is the one who needs to write the notes on her next steps. As she does this, it's an opportunity for Mr. Roy to check for understanding. It is also an opportunity for Yesenia to engage in productive uses of academic language as part of the project goals. Feedback—when done well—feeds many proverbial birds with one seed.

Try It Tomorrow

Vocaroo

Vocaroo is an online tool that allows users to record, send, and download voice messages. There are many solutions besides Vocaroo, including Rev, Telbee, Google Recorder, Voicecoach, VirtualSpeech, SpeakPipe, and Easy Voice Recorder. Some apps are proprietary and have a cost, others are offered for free. Your school district likely has a policy on app use and may offer other tech solutions for communicating information. We don't endorse these products—we only point to how they can, when used appropriately, change how feedback is produced and exchanged in the 21st century classroom.

You can consider using Vocaroo to give spoken formative feedback to students. Once you've recorded what you want to tell students, it's as easy as copying and pasting a URL into your message to the student. It's especially useful if your learning management system (LMS) doesn't already have the capability to record and easily share audio messages or if your LMS limits the length of the messages you can record. There's no fixed limit on the length of recording you can make with Vocaroo. But since playing the message/recording does rely on an uninterrupted internet connection, even brief internet connectivity issues can cause the recording to stop or fail.

No logging in or accounts are required. Recordings are available for approximately three months.

I teach sixth graders. The transition to middle school from their elementary schools is a big one. So is note-taking while listening. One thing I say often is, "It's okay to write down what I've told you. Writing it will help you remember." I model this all the time on shared sheet—writing down what they've said to me as they're saying it. I listen better when I do it. It's the same for them, too.

—Aaron, middle school math/science teacher

Setting Goals and Monitoring Progress With Spoken Formative Feedback: Questions for Lesson Study and Professional Learning Communities

Although this chapter gave examples from a science classroom and from a student–teacher writing conference held with face-to-face and online settings, formative feedback conversations in the spoken modality happen between students and teachers in a variety of subject areas in today's schools. No matter what you teach—and whether or not the members of your **professional learning community** (**PLC**) also teach your subject area—we invite you to use the questions below to discuss how students at your school and/or district can be helped by better implementation of formative feedback in the spoken modality.

For a Department- or Subject-Specific PLC

1. Mr. Roy prioritized having conversational check-ins with students whose self-assessments he viewed as inaccurate. What is useful about prioritizing this? Do you agree with it being prioritized? Why or why not?

2. Mr. Roy also prioritized checking in with students whose work on the Green Island design project spanned all the levels of the progress guide they were using at that point in the unit. What do you think Mr. Roy gains by talking with at least two different students whose work is at each level? What other way(s) could Mr. Roy have prioritized his check-ins?

3. Look again at the graphic organizer Mr. Roy developed for students to document spoken feedback dialogues (Figure 9.2). How useful would it be for your subject area? In which **unit of instruction** could you see yourself using something like it? With which projects, assignments, or performance tasks could you use spoken feedback? How might you revise Figure 9.2 for your students?

4. Can you be strategic with your spoken formative feedback dialogues *without* the help of tools and organizers such as progress guides for teacher use and/or student use? What makes you say so? Share an example.

5. In your estimation, what's the ratio between spoken and written formative feedback in your subject area? Is it 90/10, 80/20, 50/50, or some other ratio?

6. High school student Hazel asserted that the percent of student–teacher talk was never going to be 80/20 (where a student would do 80% and the teacher would do 20% of the talking) during a formative feedback conversation with a teacher. What do you make of that? What is worth noting about Hazel's experience with conversations about her work-in-progress? What about Hazel's experience applies most to students in your subject area?

7. Consider and then share as a group how you will strive to change what you do regarding spoken formative feedback. Be specific. What role might progress guides, graphic organizers, or **rubrics** play? What other visible structures and scaffolded systems to support spoken feedback exchanges could you employ? Please share your ideas.

For PLCs Across Many Departments and Subject Disciplines

1. Discuss the different ways Mr. Roy used the progress guide for teacher use to determine whose work was currently at which level of performance. Discuss how he used the student self-assessment version of the progress guides to prioritize which angles his spoken formative feedback conversations would take. Given the subject area you teach, can you be strategic with your spoken formative feedback dialogues *without* the help of tools? How so? Share an example with your colleagues.

2. A theme of this chapter is how formative feedback dialogues in the spoken modality relate to written formative feedback students may (or may not yet) have received. For the subject areas you typically teach, what is the most important takeaway in this chapter regarding the relationship between written and spoken feedback? Are there different ratios of feedback modality (spoken/written) in your subject as compared to others (e.g., in physical education and language arts)? Why? How might you address the gaps?

3. When it comes to making the content of spoken formative feedback more visible, students often benefit from using scaffolds and graphic organizers. Who also benefits from their use (e.g., parents/guardians, paraprofessionals, instructional aides, etc.)? Why is it important that many different people other than students are on the same page with feedback routines and protocols?

4. Does being mindful of the ratio of student–teacher talk during a formative feedback dialogue matter in your subject area? Why does it matter to you and/or your colleagues? If you think

about the big picture, what difference could moving the needle toward students talking more make in your subject area? What difference could it make in your school or district? How might you go about increasing student talk?

5. Consider and share with the group how you will strive to change what you currently do regarding spoken formative feedback. What assistance or coaching do you need to move to the next level? Be specific. What motivates and assists you in making changes with deeper feedback practices? Please share.

Recap/Review

- Invite students to use their voices and to trust that you are listening carefully to what they say while inviting them to do the same.

- Use your body language, tone of voice, and eye contact to set students at ease when talking and listening.

- In conversations about feedback, coach students and yourself to pause often enough and long enough during turns of talk.

- Supportive spoken conversations can help unpack written feedback, clarify its meaning, and help demystify what students are expected to do with next steps.

- Help students understand *why* a particular next step is important to take. Use words, images, metaphors, and similes to express and invite expression about next steps.

- Students build meaning from genuine back-and-forth dialogue during feedback conversations. They also perceive spoken feedback as more useful and of higher quality than written feedback (which they only sometimes or partially comprehend). So, check for understanding. Probe. Use the conversation to elicit understandings and misunderstandings of next steps.

- It's easy for students to experience auditory, affective, and cognitive overload during spoken formative feedback conversations. Conversation protocols can help. Use graphic organizers when possible.

- Spoken formative feedback is most powerful when you offer it as their learning is unfolding in a task, project, or performance. Timing matters in the feedback loops and exchanges. Identify touchpoints to check in on progress as a guide/coach.

Ticket Out the Door

1. For better or worse, everyone who has taught (or learned) has experienced spoken feedback that was confusing, off-putting, or even offensive. Based on your experiences, what is important to address about spoken feedback that we may have missed in this chapter?

2. What do you see as the most important benefit of spoken feedback for our students in extraordinary times?

3. In your own words, what makes a feedback conversation *dialogic* and why might it be good for students to experience dialogic formative conversations with adults and others, including peers, particularly in their middle and high school years?

4. Revisit the interview with Hazel, a high school student who offers some insight into what feedback by Zoom has looked and felt like. What aspect of Hazel's experience is likely to endure even in more ordinary times?

5. Pick one of the "Recap/Review" bullets. Share how it resonates with your experience as a teacher or learner.

CHAPTER 10

Nonverbal Feedback

> Skilled use of one's body has been important in the history of the species for thousands, if not millions, of years.
>
> —Gardner (2011, p. 219)

If asked to think of nonverbal **formative feedback** in school settings, many of us think first of music, art, and physical education teachers. We know that these teachers use nonverbal **feedback** to help students as they learn to act, sing, move, run, draw, sculpt, weave, and paint.

But all teachers—at some time or another—will use nonverbal feedback (also called *haptic* or *body-kinesthetic* feedback) to communicate learning goals. This **modality** helps us share information on next steps, close the gaps in current levels of performance toward the next level of progress, and broaden our own understanding of what makes formative feedback *formative*.

Humans use a variety of feedback modalities—spoken, written, and nonverbal—to communicate and exchange information. Our students rely on our skills with all of these myriad **formative assessment (FA) moves** to advance the work of learning. The intentional use of proximity, eye gaze, gestures, body position, movement, and facial expressions is key to communication. Even when our primary modality of communication with a student or students is written or spoken, we are engaged in nonverbal feedback routines. In this chapter, we explore how to marshal nonverbal feedback to augment our written or spoken feedback exchanges with greater clarity, intention, and care.

In classrooms where students are invited to learn by doing, as we saw in the chapters that explored math/science classrooms at Central Park East Secondary School (CPESS), myriad opportunities for the use of proximity, hand gestures, body positioning, and other moves will naturally appear. These nonverbal feedback **moves** are seamlessly integrated into feedback-rich dialogues and are interwoven into instruction across multiple subject disciplines and topic areas. The value of using gestures and body position when communicating verbal and written feedback, as teacher Debbie showed in Chapter 4, should not be underestimated.

When it comes to supporting feedback processes and cycles that occur in linguistically, culturally, and economically diverse classrooms, all educators need to focus on developing and sustaining the requisite skills and habits that support nonverbal formative feedback by all, for all. This chapter is about the key ideas underlying such nonverbal communication and about supporting communication in ways that go beyond spoken and written words. The following guiding questions anchor our explorations. As you read, keep in mind that nonverbal feedback cues and moves are potentially the most powerful modalities in our tool kit. They are too often overlooked or seen as outside the teaching methods and discipline of a traditional classroom teacher.

Guiding Questions

1. Why plan, enact, and reflect on nonverbal modalities of formative feedback? For whose good is nonverbal feedback offered and why does it matter? What educational goals or purposes does nonverbal feedback potentially serve?

2. How can nonverbal communication support students to re-engage the work, take up offered feedback, and revise?

3. What are ways that nonverbal formative feedback can be scaffolded and connected to other modalities (spoken and written) to strengthen feedback loops?

4. How can we learn to better use nonverbal feedback to engage, elicit, and help students extend their work/performance when they have such widely differing personalities, backgrounds, and needs?

These four questions will guide us with the last of the focal points we offer to better unpack and explore effective formative feedback practices. We should keep in mind that **directionality** and **configuration** matter for planning, enacting, and reflecting upon what works with formative feedback. How each of these lenses influences one another within and across subject matter matters, too.

Our exploration of the formative feedback framework (Figure 10.1) in this last chapter addresses the third lens associated with *modalities*: nonverbal formative feedback. Let's look at how the production and exchange of nonverbal feedback routines and moves in the modality lens can set students up for success in your classroom.

Figure 10.1 Formative Feedback Framework

Contexts for Learning		
Face-to-Face	Blended	Distance Learning
Focal Point		
Directionality	**Configuration**	**Modality**
Lenses		
Teacher-driven	Whole class	Written
Peer-to-peer-driven	Small groups (2–4)	Spoken
Self-driven	Individual (1:1)	Nonverbal
Learning Goals, Standards, Skills Tasks, Projects, Activities Rubrics, Progress Guides, "Next Steps" Organizers		

A quick note before we proceed: Many, if not most, **feedback loops** will embody elements of written, spoken, and nonverbal exchange. Real-world conversations about drafts of student performance tasks, projects, and assignments are inevitably multidimensional, multilayered conversations. Each conversation will and should feature multiple modalities. Teachers, instructional coaches, and paraprofessionals who engage students in nonverbal formative feedback practices and protocols will blend other modalities while holding space for students who appreciate the immediacy of gesture, movement, and physical cues.

Defining Nonverbal Formative Feedback

When we say *nonverbal formative feedback*, we are referring to physical actions, both subtle and obvious, intentional or unintentional, made in an attempt to engage others in a formative feedback dialogue. In this sense, the nonverbal formative feedback modality encompasses everything that does not fall specifically under the spoken and written formative feedback modalities.

Nonverbal formative feedback cues and moves comprise:

- Visual feedback that doesn't involve reading written words (e.g., seeing someone react expressively, such as making a surprised face, or observing someone model with their body a more effective technique or watching someone draw a sketch illustrating a key point).

- So-called haptic feedback in which one can physically feel forces that push back, offer tension, and suggest texture (e.g., in science labs where a joystick-type device pushes back on a student's hand as they manipulate it).

- Appropriate physical touch, such as when a special education teacher helps a student hold a pencil or guides the use of a mouse or when a physical education (PE) teacher repositions a racquet while a student is holding it.

- "Contactless contact," which can occur, for example, when a music teacher repositions a violin bow while a student is holding it, or in a shop class when students are encouraged to help each other to check the smoothness of a cut, or in an arts class where both student and teacher might need to check the hardness of clay.

Table 10.1 provides definitions of these as used in research studies featuring classroom teaching and learning scenarios.

Table 10.1 Nonverbal Immediacy Cues for Making Feedback Moves

	Nonverbal Immediacy Cues	
	Immediate	Nonimmediate
Proximity	Approaches audience	Keeps a distance, stays behind desk
Eye gaze	Frequent, prolonged	Infrequent, brief
Gestures	Uses hands and arms	Stiff, infrequent, or ineffective gesturing
Body position	Open, relaxed	Closed, formal
Movement	Moves around naturally	Rigid, stays in one place
Facial Expressions	Pleasant, smiles	Straight face, frowning, or lack of expression

Source: Adapted from Witt & Wheeless (2001).

The following table summarizes what we consider nonverbal forms of formative feedback and distinguishes these from other assessment practices.

NONVERBAL FORMATIVE FEEDBACK

What It Is	What It Isn't
- includes all feedback that is not spoken or written - visual feedback that includes physical demonstrations and/or drawings/illustrations (anything where words don't have to be read, sometimes called *nonprint texts*) - body language/movement while other modalities of communication are in use (e.g., facial expressions while speaking, hand gestures, etc.) - includes safe and appropriate physical touch relevant to the teaching and learning context - contactless contact through a mediating prop or device (e.g., adjusting a violin bow while a student is holding it) - sometimes ambiguous (micro-expressions or tells that suggest feelings and cognition are busy under the surface of the exchange) - a way to reinforce a verbal or written communication strategy - a way to modulate an unintended effect (e.g., by encouraging a student to breathe deeply if they show signs of anxiety) in a feedback exchange	- a fail-safe way to reach all students - any form of unsafe or inappropriate physical touch - only useful for special education contexts based on specific accommodations - easier to implement than other modalities - commonly understood across all cultural groups, genders, and individual humans (e.g., facial expressions do not necessarily reflect the same emotions across all cultures and backgrounds) - one-size-fits-all - only used by PE, art, or music teachers

> I'm 6 foot 4. I learned early on that if I wasn't careful in how and where I stood in the classroom when I paused to think for a moment about my feedback that students easily experienced my being near their desk as "awkward looming."
>
> —Eduardo, high school history and Spanish teacher

Table 10.2 presents four aspects to consider when planning for formative feedback interactions that you expect will feature nonverbal communication. The table tells why these aspects matter and provides tips and questions to guide your decisions as you plan so you and your students can connect more effectively around improving their performances.

When it comes to planning your nonverbal communication for formative feedback, it helps to ask yourself these questions before you start a unit:

- What's already in your personal toolkit of nonverbal cues and behaviors?
- How are you fostering connections with your students?
- How sensitive are you to the differences and similarities you and your students may have around nonverbal communication? Think, for instance, about comfort levels concerning personal space.
- How are you leveraging the strengths of nonverbal feedback moves with students who appreciate them?
- Are you planning to meet the challenges of the different settings and media in which formative feedback interactions will occur?
- Where is the place in the project, task, or assignment to bring nonverbal, spoken, and written modalities into focus for your students?

Sometimes it takes a little courage and personal reflection to explore these questions. Many of us probably didn't think that, as middle and high school teachers, we would have to spend time considering our posture, how we move our hands, or whether we could calm or support a student by the way *we* were breathing or gesturing. But we believe it's necessary to explore these considerations for the sake of good formative feedback and the sake of our students.

At the heart of Table 10.2 is a fundamental question: "How can I use my personal toolkit of nonverbal cues and behaviors to connect with students in ways that might catalyze their growth? How can I use those tools to foster their skills, connect to their **prior knowledge**, and support their emerging understandings in the subject area I teach?" Both the research and focus on practice sections that follow illustrate the different ways other practitioners have answered these questions for themselves.

Table 10.2 Planning for Nonverbal Formative Feedback: What to Consider and Why It Matters

WHAT TO CONSIDER	ASK YOURSELF	WHY IT MATTERS	TIPS AND TO-DO'S
Your Personal Toolkit of Nonverbal Cues and Behaviors	Which aspects of nonverbal communication do I already have awareness of (e.g., my posture, what my resting face conveys to people, how rapidly I tend to move my hands—if/when I move them)? How practiced am I at intentionally altering aspects of my nonverbal communication? What aspects of nonverbal communication would I like to bring to my awareness or use intentionally?	Before you can expand what's in your nonverbal formative feedback toolkit, you need an accurate inventory of what you're already doing. This is because it might make the most sense to focus on something you're already aware of (e.g., your proximity to a student) than to try changing something you have little/no awareness of (e.g., your rate of breathing). Bringing attention to an aspect of your practice uses cognitive resources. As humans, the level of cognitive/physical resources available for us does not remain constant. It is wise to respect our fluctuations and work within our limits.	▸ Make a T-chart with "What I Know I Can Do (Nonverbally)" on one side and "What I'd Like to Be Able to Do (Nonverbally)" on the other. Circle something on each side of the T-chart that seems within your reach for improvement. ▸ Try watching video recordings of yourself that capture your nonverbal communication. It's valuable feedback to have on how aspects of your nonverbal feedback may be coming across to others. It can be an uncomfortable, humbling, humorous, and fascinating process to view and hear how others see and hear you. ▸ Observe others in action (while watching your favorite program or a movie or in real life). See if there is something that you see someone else doing that you could incorporate

WHAT TO CONSIDER	ASK YOURSELF	WHY IT MATTERS	TIPS AND TO-DO'S
Connecting	How can the nonverbal tools available to me be used to help me connect while engaging students in a formative feedback dialogue? How can I elicit their thoughts/feelings and help them extend their work/performance/learning? How do I typically reassure students with and without words?	Students are more willing to revise when they feel a connection with the person supporting them. Nonverbal cues and behaviors can be marshaled to enhance connection between you and your students when you're in the tough or critical formative feedback part of your dialogue.	▸ During one-on-one formative feedback dialogues, try mirroring the student's body language to enhance connection/rapport. ▸ Just before what you think is going to be the toughest part of the conversation for your student(s), inhale and exhale with awareness. Soften your gaze.
Sensitivity to Differences and Similarities Related to Nonverbal Cues/Behaviors/ Actions, Including Personal Space	In what ways might differences and similarities in how we experience personal space and our bodies influence formative feedback conversations? How could paying attention to these differences and similarities inform how we coach ourselves before formative feedback conversations and how we coach our students to give each other peer-to-peer formative feedback? From the student's point of view, which nonverbal cues do they experience as germane and which do they experience as extraneous and distracting? Are there recognized and salient differences in nonverbal communication styles attributable to culture and gender that are relevant to my teaching context?	Students respond differently to our nonverbal communication during formative feedback conversations—for example, reaching over to point to specific content on a student's computer screen may feel like an invasion of personal space to one student but be unremarkable to another. When something you are doing nonverbally taxes a student's cognitive and emotional resources unnecessarily, they have fewer resources in that moment to draw upon for the work/problem solving at hand.	▸ Emphasize the concepts of cognitive load theory (including intrinsic load, germane load, and extraneous load) in your reflections on how you use nonverbal cues/behaviors during formative feedback interactions with students. ▸ Use the definitions, principles, and implications of cognitive load theory to inform how you strive to interact nonverbally with students. That is, consider what nonverbal actions might (or might not) be intrinsic to this formative feedback interaction. Which ones are germane? Which are extraneous? ▸ Ask permission: "Can I demonstrate for you? Can I use your [clay, racket, bow, mouse, etc.] to show you?"

(Continued)

(Continued)

WHAT TO CONSIDER	ASK YOURSELF	WHY IT MATTERS	TIPS AND TO-DO'S
Strengths and Challenges of the Setting in Which the Formative Feedback Interaction Will Occur (Classroom, Field, or Online, etc.)	Given the setting in which the formative feedback interaction will occur (crowded classroom, windy playing field, breakout room online, etc.), what do I have to watch out for and what can I use to good effect?	Some elements of the settings in which we work are within our sphere of influence (e.g., how to arrange the desks in our classroom), others are not/less so (e.g., the features available to us online). Students respond differently to different environments and mediums in which formative feedback interactions occur. To become more equitable in our practices, it behooves us to explore these differences.	▸ To the extent you can, ensure the physical space where formative feedback interactions will occur will support success when it comes to nonverbal communication (e.g., are you able to make eye contact? Do you have room to gesture freely?). ▸ Use the reaction features available via digital meeting platforms to reinforce spoken communication.

What the Research Tells Us

Howard Gardner, a Harvard psychologist and theorist of the notion of multiple intelligences, has devoted much effort to discussing what he calls *body-kinesthetic skills*. In *Frames of Mind* (2011), Gardner writes,

> Body-kinesthetic intelligence is necessary for *problem solving that requires the individual to use his or her physical body*, as would be necessary for performing a complex surgical procedure, executing a series of dance steps, or catching a fly ball. Some syndromes and brain traumas can disable a person's ability to use the physical body, leaving intelligence otherwise intact. Tool use among nonhuman animals and precursors to *Homo sapiens* demonstrate a clear evolutionary history. A developmental trajectory is clear as human *children develop fine and gross motor skills*. Dance can be thought of as a symbol system that communicates meaning through movement. . . . Musical intelligence generates the *set of skills* that allow

> musicians to play a tune by ear or to execute a phrase with sensitivity and grace . . . skill in the use of the body for functional or expressive purposes tends to go hand in hand with skill in the manipulation of objects. . . . *Skilled use of one's body* has been important in the history of the species for thousands, if not millions, of years. (pp. 218–219; emphasis added)

It makes sense that formative feedback will include some degree of touch, gesture, and body-kinesthetic movement (including the viewing of another's physical movements). Moreover, subject areas in our middle and high schools such as music, art, drama, and all manner of physical education must actively take up forms of nonwritten and nonverbal feedback to support students' learning.

When we say we all learn by doing, a corollary must follow that we all need feedback for doing. *Feedback-for-doing moves* model and support how to approach a performance task by intentionally focusing on all of the requisite physical skills and actions. These physical feedback processes and protocols, while often invisible and taken for granted, nonetheless require consideration of all available modalities. We may think "I teach history—not PE—so what do nonverbal feedback cues have to do with me or my lesson?" but there is much more to it.

Teachers who already teach by doing (i.e., mobilizing a wide range of nonverbal, tactile, and haptic moves) know that there is no other sensible way to teach or assess a complex skill set such as those required for singing, running, acting, drafting, sculpting, and so on. Being nonverbal is required.

Surprisingly, research on the actual development and articulation of skilled used of one's body in K–12 settings is thin and even thinner when it comes to the study of formative feedback's presumed role in supporting students' growth in body-kinesthetic skills development.

Most of what we know about body-kinesthetic feedback comes from the fields of physical education, music, science, and medical education. Research on the effects of combining haptic feedback with verbal feedback in physical education (known as *augmented* feedback) is promising. In gymnastics, it has been found that combining haptic feedback with verbal feedback significantly enhanced students' learning of a new skill on the parallel bars compared to students who received only verbal feedback from the same instructor (Frikha et al., 2019). Not only did the students' retention of the new skill significantly improve by objective indicators, but the students receiving the augmented feedback also perceived learning the skill as an easier, richer, and more engaging experience compared to the group that only received verbal feedback.

Though coaches, PE teachers, and parents involved in supporting school sports have long recognized that augmented feedback affects motor learning across a range of activities, the effects that each mode of feedback has on motor learning acquisition, retention, and perceived competence has rarely been studied.

The research we do have suggests that the importance of receiving tactile feedback as you learn depends on what you're learning. While learning motor skills, it is notably beneficial. But according to experts, for able-bodied students in science class, for example, the extent to which tactile feedback matters is not yet definitively known. Zacharia's (2015) review of the literature, in particular, noted inconsistent findings. New learning technologies, including virtual labs and so-called maker spaces, may or may not make good use of nonverbal communication techniques—it's too early to tell.

Communication research has provided consistent support for the finding of a positive relationship between nonverbal immediacy and student affective learning (Andersen, 1979; Andersen et al., 1981; Kelley & Gorham, 1988; Plax et al., 1986; Richmond et al., 1987). Of those engaged in the use of nonverbal immediacy routines in the classroom, researchers report an "increased student affect for the teacher" and "increased student affect for the subject matter" (McCroskey & Richmond, 1992, p. 116). The communication behaviors employed by teachers also play a strategic role in student learning outcomes. For example, nonverbal immediacy behaviors such as eye gaze, smiles, nods, relaxed body posture, forward leans, movement, and gestures have the effect of reducing physical and/or psychological distance between teacher and students and increase learning (Andersen, 1979; Christophel & Gorham, 1995; Hackman & Walker, 1990; Plax et al., 1986; Witt & Wheeless, 2001).

Not surprisingly, research has also found that what many teachers intuitively do to convey warmth, interest, and positivity while they're conversing with students also matters. During dialogue with students, nonverbal signals of openness, engagement, and high regard make a difference (Martin & Mottet, 2011). The research literature calls these *nonverbal immediacy behaviors.*

A teacher displaying nonverbal immediacy will

- sit next to the student (as opposed to across from them),
- smile frequently,
- lean forward in a relaxed fashion,
- maintain eye contact with the student,
- use a soft tone of voice, and
- gesture with their hands while asking a question.

Laura Martin and Timothy Mottet (2011) found that these behaviors positively impacted students' affect for the teacher, the writing conferences they were engaged in, and the students' writing processes, regardless of how demanding or sensitive the teacher's feedback was during the writing conference. The majority of the students in their study were Hispanic (96%) and most qualified for free or reduced lunch. Many were designated as **English learners (ELs)**.

In summary, what's important for teachers to take from the research is that combining different feedback "channels" benefits students' learning. For most students, making learning a haptic, auditory, and visual experience is more efficient than relying on one feedback channel alone (Sigrist et al., 2013).

Essential Nonverbal Feedback Practices Supported by Research

Use Proximity Intentionally to Bolster Communicative Connection

- Awareness of physical distance (proximity) between formative feedback participants is important. Students who feel too far away from the person interacting with them may feel reluctant to respond. At the same time, it's critical to observe signs that the distance may be perceived as too close for one or more of the participants. Zones of personal space (Hall, 1959) around individuals may differ between cultures (Beaulieu, 2004). Not only distance but orientation (the angle at which a person will position themselves in front of the other person) may differ as well. Avoid awkward looming near students who are seated.

Augment Nonverbal Feedback, Both in Real Time and After the Fact, With Other Feedback Modalities

- Combine nonverbal feedback messages with spoken and written feedback in ways that students will experience as coherent and aligned with the task/activity. Check that your body position (open and relaxed versus closed and tight), eye gaze, gestures, and physical movements (including hand gestures) authentically match what you're aiming to communicate in written or spoken words.

Leverage What You Know About Students' Energy and Comfort Zones With Nonverbal Communication Strategies

- See yourself as a conductor who can muster the energy, tempo, and dynamics of an orchestra through nonverbal behaviors. We suggest you pay close attention to and modify your posture, facial expressions, breathing, intensity of eye contact, hand and arm gestures, and your physical proximity (to the extent that these are within your control) in ways that make sense for your students and your past experiences with them. Play with how you might influence the energy and tempo around a feedback exchange using nonverbal as well as verbal techniques.

Focus on Practice: How Do Teachers Support/Give Nonverbal Feedback?

In the following exchange, we see Debbie (the teacher) and her high school students, Betty and Danni (introduced in Chapter 4), using all sorts of nonverbal communication cues.

In this episode, we see that teacher Debbie utilizes proximity without slipping into awkward looming; she uses her hands to communicate instructions and coax more **elaboration** in the writing. Danni, who is Betty's peer, uses her hands to undo a crumpled wad of paper to nonverbally communicate to her table partner, "Let's rescue this **first draft**."

> **WATCH THIS**
>
> **Graduation by Portfolio**
>
> Please use the QR code above and watch the video starting at 9:12. You can stop the video after 14:32.

Betty pulls back, runs her hand through her hair, takes a deep breath, and sighs aloud before uttering, "I just have to relax and try to explain myself."

Whether they seek clarification, confirmation, or support as they reformulate an idea, both students and the teacher use verbal and nonverbal signals to make sense of next steps.

How do teachers use nonverbal formative feedback to greater effect? Here are a few takeaways from this powerful video-based example (9:12–14:32) in its entirety:

1. **Hands-on learning:** Debbie offers physical ways for students to experience a phenomenon themselves. In the sound **exhibition** episode, we see and hear students in Debbie's class plucking strings, tuning instruments they have built, drumming, and even drawing sine waves over and over again.

2. **Nonverbal cuing:** Debbie masterfully gives nonverbal cues, mostly with her hands, arms, and facial expressions, that make it easier for students to understand and accept what she is saying. For example, when getting Betty and Danni to elaborate on their initial responses to one of her questions, Debbie rotates her hand in a circle to indicate the space within their instrument (a thumb piano). She continues in the video segment, using both of her hands to make a box shape directly in front of Betty and Danni while asking them, "Which makes the box vibrate, which makes what vibrate?"

3. **Proximity:** By moving nearer or farther away when communicating with students, as Debbie does, we can create a safe, professional space. Pulling in closer to a student while talking typically conveys the message, "I want you to listen even more carefully to this part of what I'm saying." As teachers move away from students, what is often reinforced is that the teacher is releasing the student to think about or work on the task on their own (or with their peers).

We suggest you strive—as Betty, Danni, and teacher Debbie have—to embrace cues and build up routines using the nonverbal feedback modality. A **cultural assets inventory**/framework can help you and your students examine how verbal, written, and nonverbal feedback looks and feels from different cultural perspectives (Borerro & Sanchez, 2017; Hollins, 2015; Ladson-Billings, 1995, 2014). Then, teachers and students can all work on a set of shared agreements for keeping feedback real, relevant, and safe in the classroom.

Placing nonverbal communication strategies and agreements on the proverbial table will help everyone to see that *how* we communicate feedback matters as much as *why* we do it.

> ## Did You Know?
>
> Total physical response (TPR) is a language teaching method developed by James Asher, who taught at San José State University for over 30 years. It is a method popularly used with beginning students of a second or third (or more) language.
>
> The TPR method prompts language learners to respond physically to commands in the target language. The physical movements that match the verbal commands are first modeled by the teacher. Once students have acquired the vocabulary necessary to understand a series of commands, the teacher delays modeling the command. The teacher eventually omits modeling the command altogether and simply prompts students to perform on their own.
>
> One of the principles behind the TPR method is the motor skills hypothesis: that memory is linked to movement and that what we learn with our bodies will be remembered longer. The idea is that students whose experience learning language with their entire bodies can acquire vocabulary and concepts faster and retain them longer than with written and spoken language alone. TPR enables teachers to assess students' comprehension of the target language without requiring verbal output from beginning-level students.

Focus on Practice: How Different Teachers Use Nonverbal Immediacy and Contactless Contact to Support Formative Feedback Dialogues and Student Learning

Physical Education: Mr. Lorenzo's Lesson on Putting Backspin on a Pickleball During a Larger Multi-Unit Semester on Racket Sports

For most of the 48 sophomores in Mr. Lorenzo's second period PE class, this is the fifth year they've played pickleball. Mr. Lorenzo happened to be teaching at the middle school most of them attended when they were sixth graders. He was the teacher who introduced pickleball to them.

Now, as 15- and 16-year-olds, their bodies are bigger, stronger, and more powerful. Many are noticeably more agile than they were as sixth graders. Their game play shows it.

Today, Mr. Lorenzo is introducing the idea of intentionally putting spin on the pickleball when returning an opponent's serve, also called a *backspin return*. Mr. Lorenzo begins by telling them, "Pickleball isn't all about power. It's also about control and strategy. One way to control where the ball is going after it bounces is to put spin on it. If you can control how the pickleball spins, then you can make it much harder for your opponent to get to the ball in time. So today, you're going to learn to put backspin on a ball."

At this point, the students aren't even holding pickleball paddles yet. Mr. Lorenzo tells them to spread out "so you have enough room to really swing your paddle arm around without hitting anyone. We're going to practice cutting or slicing before we get our paddles."

The students spread out in a semicircle around Mr. Lorenzo.

"Without our paddles, we're going to do the slicing or cutting motion. Like this." Mr. Lorenzo, a right-hander, demonstrates. "Try it!"

Students all around Mr. Lorenzo start imitating his cutting motion.

"Of course, if you're left-handed, it looks a bit different," Mr. Lorenzo looks around. "Anya and Beto," Mr. Lorenzo calls out, "you're left-handed! Come on up here and let's see the two of you cut with your left hands. Do it at regular speed, like you're really hitting a ball and putting backspin on it."

"Most of us are doing it with our right hands, right? Like this," Mr. Lorenzo cuts the air while holding an invisible pickleball paddle in his right hand. "But I want you to see how it looks for lefties, so you can see what's common. Take a look at their wrists and the inside of their forearms. See how the inside of their wrist and forearm points up? Thank you, Anya. Thank you, Beto." Anya and Beto return to their spots. "Everybody, touch the inside of your forearm with your own hand. It doesn't matter which one. Right here." Mr. Lorenzo pats the inside of his right forearm with his left hand. "Right here. Let me see you do that." Mr. Lorenzo checks to see that everyone is patting the right place on their arm. "Exactly. That's it!"

"Everyone, listen up. Here's the secret of backspin. It's going from this position—See where the inside of my forearm is?—to this position. And doing it in such a way that when your paddle hits the ball, it puts a spin on the ball—a backspin, like this." Mr. Lorenzo holds up a pickleball and rotates it. He grabs a paddle and demonstrates, at quarter speed, the paddle contacting the pickleball in such a way that it puts backspin on the ball. He then moves around the court and uses light taps (nonverbal gestures combined with appropriate touch) to double check on grip, forearm extension, and swing. Students expect this one-on-one attention as Mr. Lorenzo publicly provides it to all his students.

Physical Education: Ms. Pena's Lesson on Changing Direction During a Mini-Unit on Soccer, Which Follows the Larger Unit of Field-Based Games

PE teacher Ms. Pena has 32 seventh graders warmed up and on the field, ready to continue their soccer unit. About half the students are experienced soccer players. The rest have only played when required to for PE class.

The cardiovascular fitness levels of the students vary widely: Some can run all period long; others get winded running a short distance. Today, Ms. Pena will be asking her students to focus on calling for the ball with their body movement, not their voices. She wants her students to be ready and able to change direction on their feet quickly.

Ms. Pena knows even the most agile, coordinated students in the class will be able to move more quickly when they are centered and have a good awareness of where they're initiating a change in direction from. Are they leading from their head? Does a direction change come from their core/center?

For her other students, Ms. Pena knows that their experience of "centeredness"—where the centers of their bodies are and what it feels like as they initiate a change in direction to call for the ball—will make a big difference in how quickly they move and how safely they play.

"The aim of this next activity is to increase your awareness of where you move from when you change directions during soccer play," Ms. Pena tells everyone. "It's a partner activity. Partner up with someone you are comfortable working with. You are going to lightly—very lightly—try to keep physical contact with your partner as you both move while you do this activity."

Ms. Pena looks to see how many eyes are on her for this next part. "Here is where the contact is going to be." Ms. Pena touches the space on her abdomen below her sternum but above her navel. "You're going to keep this light contact, very light contact, with your knuckles. Not with a fist, but with a claw hand, so the palm of your hand faces down toward the grass. Like this." Ms. Pena demonstrates. "Everybody make a claw hand. Let me see. Face it down. Put it out where I can see it. I'm going to check."

Ms. Pena checks the claw hands of her students. She adjusts a few and continues, "Now listen up. You are going to be the one to put one or two knuckles of your partner's claw hand on your center. Right here." Ms. Pena demonstrates. "It's at the bottom of your rib cage and above your belly button, right in the center."

"Now let's line up, each partner facing one another, across from each other. Space out as partners so you have room to move sideways. You won't move yet, only when I tell you to." The students line up in pairs, facing one another. "Now it's a bit like a dance. You're going to move together when I say. Your goal is to keep light contact. If you're the one with your partner's knuckles on your center, your job is to feel that space in your body right behind it: that space in you that's right behind where their knuckles are touching your shirt. *That* is where you want to be moving from when you change direction! I want you to really feel that. And keep your attention there as you move. We're going to move first like a dance. Remember our dance unit? In a box: back, left, forward, right. And keep contact the whole time. Now we're going to try it. Ready?"

Ms. Pena sees the knuckles of 16 claw hands touch the shirts of 16 students who have placed their partner's knuckles on their centers. Keeping everyone safe and engaged in appropriate haptic/body-kinesthetic feedback routines during this **peer assessment** is critical. She walks over to different pairs on the floor and puts pressure on a few of the knuckles. With a gentle gesture she says, "Feel that contact! Light contact. Keep it going as I give the next directions. Wait for my command. This line is going to step forward, and this line is going to step back in order to keep light contact. Light contact! Take a step back. Now another step. Now ready? Feel that space. Feel where you're moving from. Now everyone toward the school. Three steps toward the school. Keep that light contact! Feel where it is that you're moving *from*!"

Ms. Pena moves around the field and uses body-kinesthetic "*Show me*'s" (a form of contactless contact) to double-check the students' posture and contact points. Students are shown how to provide nonverbal feedback in their small groups as Ms. Pena demonstrates what is appropriate. Before moving into groups, Ms. Pena picks a student partner and together they simulate the contactless contact procedure as a team in front of the whole class on the field. Everyone can see them modeling these particular feedback moves. Everyone can ask questions about what is appropriate and what is not. By making it fun and focused on the upcoming peer assessment activity (giving and taking contactless contact feedback), Ms. Pena and her student team member show how to give nonverbal feedback as they get ready to break into small-group configurations.

Music Education: Mrs. Dennison's Lesson on Breathing, Posture, and the Use of Diaphragm in Choir

In intermediate choir, Mrs. Dennison tells all 42 of her students, "I want you to focus on being on the note. Remember what I've said before? I want you to keep the vowels going as long as possible."

Mrs. Dennison spreads her two hands wide apart, visually suggesting the length of the note and the passage of time with her hand motions. Then she takes her right hand to the top of her head, pinches her thumb and index fingers together as if she were holding a string, splays out the remaining three fingers of her right hand, and pulls upward. This is a cue

Mrs. Dennison has used countless times before, which signals, "Posture! Stand up tall! Tighten up your core." She models with hand movements and facial gestures without speaking a second time.

"I want to hear your voices. I want your sound coming out from here," exclaims Mrs. Dennison in her stage director's voice. As she says this, she puts one hand in front of her face. The palm of her hand is facing the tip of her nose, nearly touching it, and her fingers reach above her eyebrows.

"No spreading your *Es*!" Mrs. Dennison calls out. Then she dramatically makes a wide, tight-but-open-mouthed smile in front of everyone. "Instead," Mrs. Dennison takes both her hands and points them to her face, pantomiming the mouth shape she wants to see, "this! Draw out those vowels. Keep them going as long as possible. Look to my conducting for when to end the word." Mrs. Dennison looks over to Mr. Arnot, the accompanist at the piano.

"Okay, from the top," she tells everyone. The students hold the *E* sound in the word, stretching it out as long as they can. As they do this, Mrs. Dennison's right hand is sliding away from her body toward them. The choir doesn't start the "-ching" sound in the word *reaching* until all four fingers of Mrs. Dennison's right hand suddenly change direction and move sharply back toward her own body. That's the signal.

The mix of verbal and nonverbal feedback in this class is key to communicating information. Soon, the choir will perform *The Lion King* at their community theater. Day in and day out, Mrs. Dennison's combinations of nonverbal feedback provide the students with the next steps they need. She is simultaneously their leader/conductor who is also a guide on the side when it comes to gesture, eye contact, and physical demonstration. This use of nonverbal feedback with her music students is why everyone refers to her as an outstanding instructor at the school. Little do people know, Mrs. Dennison is not only an outstanding veteran teacher, but she is also a **formative assessor** who is expert in her craft—the craft of giving nonverbal feedback along with the spoken feedback to make just-in-time adjustments with her students.

Quick Check: Which Nonverbal Moves Did These Teachers Make?

Mr. Lorenzo   Ms. Pena   Mrs. Dennison

Scaffolds and Guided Practice for Individual Teachers

Self-Assess

As human beings, we have evolved to participate and communicate in complex social networks. Classroom learning spaces—whether in person or virtual—are one setting our students regularly experience where nonverbal communication plays an important role in their lives. Nonverbal communication may not get the recognition it is due in the **assessment for learning** research. It's time to look into the potential upsides of the artful use of nonverbal feedback with projects, assignments, and all manner of performance tasks across many subjects we teach in schools. We can improve our nonverbal formative feedback practices together. One way to begin the exploration of this modality is to self-assess.

Using the following organizer, take a moment to self-assess and see where you are in terms of using nonverbal cues and behavior during formative feedback-driven exchanges and conversations.

Instructions: Put a check mark by the **SOLO taxonomy** level that best describes the current state of your instructional practices as a teacher who can marshal different aspects of nonverbal cues and behavior in ways that help you connect with students during formative feedback interactions.

SOLO LEVEL	DESCRIPTION	PUT A ✓ MARK
Extended Abstract	I adjust my nonverbal cues and behaviors to student needs, preferences, and comfort zones. Based upon observations I make, I adjust what I'm doing with my proximity, eye gaze, gestures, body position, movement, and/or facial expressions with the aim of improving the dialogic quality of the interaction. I reflect regularly on the nonverbal aspects of my formative feedback practices in terms of their relationship to socio-cultural, linguistic, and other key dimensions of communication.	
Relational	I talk about body language and nonverbal communication with my students. We don't necessarily talk about it during formative feedback interactions, although sometimes that happens. We talk about nonverbal cues and behaviors because it's a critical element of active listening and of communicating respect and caring for one another sometimes called *21st century skills*. I sometimes compare and contrast how different teachers in different subjects use this kind of nonverbal feedback with different topics.	

SOLO LEVEL	DESCRIPTION	PUT A ✓ MARK
Multi-structural	I am intentional in how I use my nonverbal cues and I aim to influence the energy of a formative feedback interaction with my body-kinesthetic skills (e.g., nonverbal immediacy cues in my classroom or other learning spaces).	
	I try to influence the tempo, pace, cadence, and dynamism of our feedback exchanges with nonverbal moves to augment my students' sense of connection to the task or topic.	
Unistructural	I am aware of tendencies and/or habits I have concerning my posture, my facial expressions, my eye contact, my hand and arm gestures, and my body position, specifically in relation to the student(s) I am interacting with during a formative feedback dialogue.	
Pre-structural	I have yet to try out being intentional with nonverbal cues (e.g., my body proximity) during a formative feedback dialogue.	
	Nonverbal feedback feels like something only a PE, art, or music teacher can or should do.	

Reflect

Now reflect on how you assessed your practice. What would it take to improve? Take a minute or two to think, then write in the following blank space one thing you could try this week to further your nonverbal formative feedback and/or add to your personal toolkit of nonverbal cues and behaviors.

One next step:

If you're already at the topmost level, what could you do to learn from others in another subject discipline or classroom context or professional setting to improve your practice further?

Try It Tomorrow

Go Slow-Mo With Your Nonverbals

Shift into slow-motion temporarily with the nonverbal cues you already control and then observe what happens next.

By working from your present strengths, you're likely to experience more success with this exercise. For example, if you're already aware of how you open up your body posture at the beginning of a formative feedback conversation, focus on doing that—but (in your mind) do it in slow motion (first).

If you're good at, for instance, using a "thinking face" when it's a student's time to think (e.g., by looking up with your eyes and resting your chin in your hand), do that, but in a slower, more drawn-out way than you usually do.

The point of this exercise is to

1. be explicit with yourself about what you're already intentionally controlling and focusing on during your next formative feedback interaction,
2. slow down what you intentionally do while communicating nonverbally,
3. pay close attention to what happens next, and
4. learn from what you have noticed.

The premise is that entering the temporary slow-motion state (in your mind or in practice) will allow and facilitate your ability to pay closer attention to your students' responses. You will likely observe aspects of your students' experience with the feedback exchange that you haven't noticed before.

When I'm teaching, I can get really excited. I naturally move pretty quickly anyhow, but when I get going, I move even faster. Moving quickly isn't conducive to encouraging deep, reflective thought in students. So I've learned to intentionally slow my physical movements down. It makes a difference.

—Miles, biology and chemistry teacher

Setting Goals and Monitoring Progress With Nonverbal Formative Feedback: Questions for Lesson Study and Professional Learning Communities

When you work with students, you will find that different approaches to formative feedback may work for different students in unexpected ways. Students bring various cultural, linguistic, and community-based **assets** to the classroom. Teachers may find it difficult to bring these student assets to the foreground for a variety of reasons. The goal is to get out of our own way. Let's start by reflecting upon our feedback routines and practices with culturally and linguistically diverse students.

Imagine your school has recently engaged with an instructional coach/facilitator who is committed to culturally responsive teaching and anti-racist assessment practices. Your facilitator sees the power of formative feedback to deepen equity for traditionally underserved and minority students in the district. She has worked in high school reform in new urban high schools for over three decades.

During a **professional learning community** (**PLC**) meeting, a slide is displayed that says, "Our feedback must care for the mind, heart, and body. But it must also show our students the way to grow, beyond our spoken words and written comments."

Discuss:

- Do you agree with this?

- If so, why? What, in your teaching experience, supports using different modes of feedback, particularly proximity, gestures, body position, movement, and facial expressions?

- Why does communicating feedback with our bodies matter? What, in your teaching experience, tells you written and spoken words aren't always enough?

- What are the implications of moving "beyond our spoken words and written comments" and trying new forms of nonverbal feedback? What are the implications for our students? What are the implications for our school community?

Now, take time in your PLC session to unpack which nonverbal feedback moves (e.g., from Table 10.1) you can leverage in teams or as individuals starting on Monday. Before closing the session, formulate a plan together to generate new strategies to achieve an aim/element that you all agree is important over the semester. If you can, commit yourselves to lesson and unit planning that includes:

1. a SMART (specific, measurable, achievable, realistic, and timely) goal,
2. a specific next step (e.g., "Use more inviting hand gestures"),
3. a deadline for when you will have enacted this next step, and
4. how you will hold each other accountable for that deadline.

Recap/Review

- Equity demands we approach feedback strategies and tactics in the nonverbal modality with care. How students perceive and respond to nonverbal formative feedback—what they do or don't do in response to it—is a critical aspect of good formative feedback practice.
- Invite students to use their hands, their gestures, and their bodies to express feedback.
- Use your own body language, tone of voice, and eye contact to set students at ease.
- Coach students and yourself to pause often enough and long enough during turns of talk in conversations as feedback unfolds.
- Use nonverbal feedback moves. Proximity, eye gaze, gestures, body position, movement, and facial expressions can be marshaled for good effect when engaging students in written or spoken feedback modalities.
- Help students understand why a particular next step is important to take. Use words, images, metaphors, and similes to verbally express and invite nonverbal expressions about those next steps.
- It's easy for students to experience cognitive overload as they engage with spoken and written formative feedback, so use nonverbal and unspoken feedback cues to influence the energy, tempo, and cadence of conversations while focusing on the task, assignment, or project.
- If you can give students nonverbal formative feedback as an accompaniment to spoken and written modalities when their learning is unfolding, that's when feedback is the most potentially powerful.

Ticket Out the Door

1. Please share at least three ways you currently use nonverbal feedback (e.g., proximity, eye gaze, gestures, body position, movement, facial expressions, etc.) to augment your feedback practices.

2. Based on your experience, what is important to address about the nonverbal/body-kinesthetic modality that we may have missed in this chapter?

3. What do you see as the most important opportunity/challenge when engaging in nonverbal/body-kinesthetic–oriented feedback?

4. Pick one of the "Recap/Review" bullets. Share how it resonates with your experience as a teacher or learner.

Optional Self-Assessment: Focus on Nonverbal Feedback

You have now read the chapters on different modalities of formative feedback. Let's reflect and self-assess. Take a moment to consider what you've experienced and what you value about nonverbal/body-kinesthetic feedback. Try to consider not only what you value but also what your students have appreciated and gained from formative feedback exchanges conducted asynchronously and in real time.

1. Describe a time when a nonverbal/body-kinesthetic feedback practice really worked for a student you've been working hard to reach. Which combinations made a difference for you and your student? (Please explain why.)

2. My favorite way of having students experience my nonverbal feedback is . . . (Please share.)

3. Complete the following **sentence starters**: My go-to methods for nonverbal feedback routines include a variety of moves.

   a. When using proximity, I tend to . . .

   b. When using hand gestures, I tend to . . .

   c. When using body position or movement, I tend to . . .

   d. When using facial expressions, I tend to . . .

4. Complete the following sentence starter: For my students, the hardest thing about the nonverbal modality of formative feedback is . . .

5. Making connections exercise: Draw a line from the "Primary Goals for a Feedback Cycle" in your subject area listed in the first column to "Best Nonverbal Routine" to achieve those goals in the second column. (Note: You may have more than one line for each.)

PRIMARY GOALS FOR A FEEDBACK CYCLE	BEST NONVERBAL ROUTINE
1. To be able to check for students' understanding	Proximity
2. To demonstrate a skill or action related to a performance task	Hand Gesture
3. To build relationship by communicating warmth, respect, and encouragement	Body Position
4. To power through the process as efficiently as possible	Eye Movement
5. To foster dialogue about the revision process	Physical Touch

Self-Study Checklist

Learning objectives and goals anchor each of the chapters. These objectives and goals can be used as a checklist to ensure you meet your personal and professional goals for each chapter. Take a moment to decide how you want to focus your work with the formative feedback framework and what you would like to cover in depth.

Chapter 1: On the Role of Learning Goals, Tasks, and Cycles of Feedback for Continuous Improvement

Learning Objectives and Goals

Upon completing this chapter, I will be able to

- ❑ identify important aspects of purpose-driven feedback and why learning goals matter for guiding formative feedback;
- ❑ understand and list qualities of purpose-driven feedback;
- ❑ explain why purpose-driven feedback must be visible to teachers, students, parents, and others; and
- ❑ apply specific schematic representations (e.g., taxonomies) for defining learning goals to feedback cycles and routines.

Chapter 2: Teacher-Driven Feedback

Learning Objectives and Goals

Upon completing this chapter, I will be able to

- ❑ identify important aspects of teacher-driven feedback and why they matter for planning a lesson and/or unit;

(Continued)

(*Continued*)

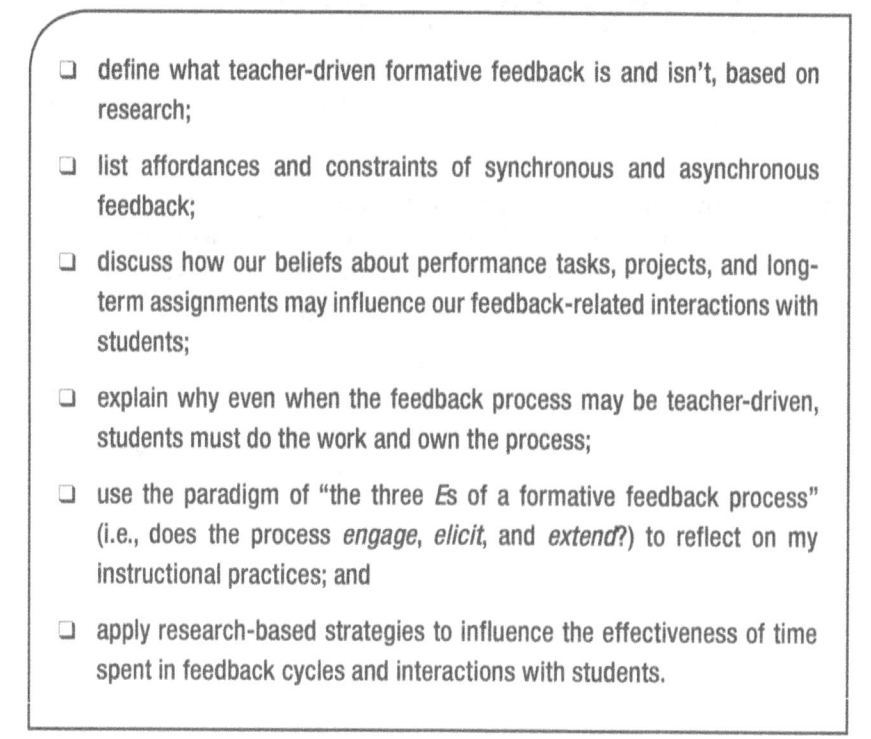

- ❏ define what teacher-driven formative feedback is and isn't, based on research;
- ❏ list affordances and constraints of synchronous and asynchronous feedback;
- ❏ discuss how our beliefs about performance tasks, projects, and long-term assignments may influence our feedback-related interactions with students;
- ❏ explain why even when the feedback process may be teacher-driven, students must do the work and own the process;
- ❏ use the paradigm of "the three *E*s of a formative feedback process" (i.e., does the process *engage*, *elicit*, and *extend*?) to reflect on my instructional practices; and
- ❏ apply research-based strategies to influence the effectiveness of time spent in feedback cycles and interactions with students.

Chapter 3: Peer-to-Peer-Driven Feedback

Learning Objectives and Goals

Upon completing this chapter, I will be able to

- ❏ identify a variety of ways to make the peer-to-peer feedback process interactive;
- ❏ define what peer-to-peer formative feedback is and isn't, based on research;
- ❏ describe how to use a progress guide to support peer-to-peer feedback protocols and processes;
- ❏ apply/tailor a peer-to-peer scaffold to support feedback exchanges for students; and
- ❏ explain feedback goals and purposes for peer-to-peer interactions with tasks, projects, and long-term assignments.

Chapter 4: Self-Driven Feedback

Learning Objectives and Goals

Upon completing this chapter, I will be able to

- ❏ identify a variety of ways in which the self-driven feedback process is based in learning goals and success criteria;
- ❏ define what self-driven formative feedback is and isn't, based on research;
- ❏ distinguish between general self-regulatory skills and content-specific forms of self-assessment based on a project, task, or long-term assignment;
- ❏ explain how self-assessment, self-driven formative feedback, and self-regulation of learning relate to one another; and
- ❏ apply the concept of a progress guide anchored in clear learning goals to help tailor students' feedback to themselves so that it is relevant and task related.

Chapter 5: Feedback With the Whole Class

Learning Objectives and Goals

Upon completing this chapter, I will be able to

- ❏ identify what is most salient/important when it comes to whole-class formative feedback—that is, that whole-class formative feedback processes/interactions should:
  - ❏ apply to all students,
  - ❏ involve checking for understanding and responding appropriately to gaps in understanding as appropriate, and

(Continued)

(Continued)

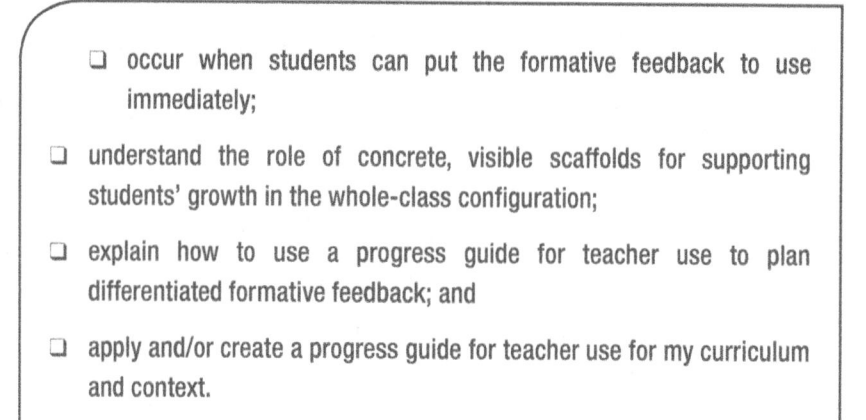

- occur when students can put the formative feedback to use immediately;
- understand the role of concrete, visible scaffolds for supporting students' growth in the whole-class configuration;
- explain how to use a progress guide for teacher use to plan differentiated formative feedback; and
- apply and/or create a progress guide for teacher use for my curriculum and context.

Chapter 6: Feedback With Small Groups

Learning Objectives and Goals

Upon completing this chapter, I will be able to

- describe ways teacher and student self-assessment progress guides can be used to support peer feedback sessions that occur in small-group configuration;
- understand how the lenses of content focus and process focus can inform how teachers support small-group formative feedback interactions;
- explain how small-group configurations often influence students' experiences of formative feedback interactions; and
- create scaffolds, protocols, and routines that will support students through three phases of formative feedback interactions with small groups: before, during, and after formative feedback.

Chapter 7: Feedback With Individuals

Learning Objectives and Goals

Upon completing this chapter, I will be able to

- ❑ identify strategies that help with planning, monitoring, and maximizing a student's individual experience with formative feedback exchanges of information;

- ❑ understand how planning for and carrying out one-on-one conversations with students can benefit other configurations (whole class and small groups);

- ❑ describe communication repair strategies to try before, during, and after individual formative feedback dialogues;

- ❑ explain how an equitable classroom depends on having a diverse set of tools for engaging, eliciting, and extending formative feedback dialogues with students; and

- ❑ apply the concept and tools from progress guides for student self-assessment and teacher use to support individual/one-on-one formative feedback conversations.

Chapter 8: Written Feedback

Learning Objectives and Goals

Upon completing this chapter, I will be able to

- ❑ identify the strengths and challenges of written forms of formative feedback in synchronous and asynchronous settings;

- ❑ describe ways to support students who are learning to engage written comments, questions, notations, and so on before, during, and (if necessary) after a formative feedback cycle;

(Continued)

(Continued)

- ❑ explain how the context of the written modality (e.g., online, in-person, synchronous, asynchronous) can influence students' experiences of formative feedback and reduce/increase chances of incorporation of feedback into the next draft of the performance task, project, or assignment; and
- ❑ create protocols, reminders, and routines that will support students in taking up written feedback while ensuring other modalities (spoken and nonverbal) are available to augment interactions.

Chapter 9: Spoken Feedback

Learning Objectives and Goals

Upon completing this chapter, I will be able to

- ❑ identify the strengths and challenges of spoken forms of formative feedback in synchronous, asynchronous, in-person, and remote settings;
- ❑ describe ways to support students who are learning to engage spoken feedback before, during, and after a formative feedback cycle;
- ❑ explain how the spoken modality can influence students' experiences of formative feedback and reduce/increase chances of incorporation of feedback into next drafts; and
- ❑ apply, revise, and/or create protocols, reminders, and routines that will support students in taking up spoken feedback while ensuring other modalities are available to augment interactions.

Chapter 10: Nonverbal Feedback

Learning Objectives and Goals

Upon completing this chapter, I will be able to

- ❏ identify the strengths and challenges of nonverbal forms of formative feedback in synchronous, asynchronous, in-person, and remote settings;

- ❏ understand how planning for and reflecting on nonverbal formative feedback can benefit students with widely differing personalities, backgrounds, and needs;

- ❏ describe ways to support students who are learning to engage with nonverbal feedback before, during, and after a formative feedback cycle;

- ❏ explain how the context in which nonverbal feedback and communication occurs (e.g., online, in-person, synchronous, or asynchronous) can influence students' experiences of formative feedback and reduce/increase chances of incorporation of feedback into the next draft of a performance task, project, or assignment; and

- ❏ create protocols, reminders, and routines that will support students in taking up nonverbal feedback while ensuring other modalities are available to augment interactions.

Available for download at **resources.corwin.com/ContinuousImprovement**

Glossary

Academic language (AL): The oral, written, auditory and visual language that helps students meet the demands of school environments. While academic language (AL) includes discipline-specific vocabulary, grammar, and punctuation and applications of rhetorical conventions and devices (e.g., in lab reports, essays, blogs, and oral presentations) that are typical for a content area, it also encompasses knowledge about how language is used in different ways according to the purposes of the communication, the relationship between speakers, and the context and is connected to particular identities and social roles. AL demands are frequently contrasted with "conversational" or "social" language students need to acquire so they can successfully navigate school assignments, lesson expectations, and the norms of different subject disciplines.

Advisory: An advisory is a regularly scheduled period, typically during the school day, when teachers meet with small groups of students for the purpose of advising them on academic, social, emotional, and other needs related to the school, family, and/or community. Many advisories cover topics related to homework, college preparation, work–life balance, and future planning issues. Van Ryzin (2010) and others have documented how advisories build positive mentor relationships between students and teachers.

Answer key: When dealing with traditional quiz and test data, many teachers use an answer key. The answer key determines how to bin correct and incorrect responses. Answer keys generally rely on dichotomous bins (such as *correct* or *incorrect*), with corresponding numbers such as *0* or *1*. By using this binning tool, teachers can quickly and efficiently evaluate student achievement on a set of items/questions/tasks. See **assessment of learning**.

Assessment for learning (AfL): The purpose of assessment for learning is typically formative. It usually occurs during a lesson and within an instructional cycle or unit. AfL is meant to size up a learner's current knowledge/skills and add feedback to directly augment the learning process. AfL relies less on points, grades, or scores and more on direct communication and feedback aimed at improving performance.

Assessment of learning: The purpose of assessment of learning is largely summative. It typically occurs at the end of an instructional cycle or unit. Assessment of learning is meant to determine what knowledge/skills have been achieved by students at the end of the week, semester, or academic year. Assessments of learning are often accompanied by grades. See also **binning for grading**.

Asset(s): An asset-based approach to learning focuses on students' strengths, including their previous experiences and backgrounds, which can be woven into a lesson or unit of instruction. It views diversity in thought, culture, and dispositions as positive assets to be leveraged for assessment and deeper learning during instruction. Teachers and students alike are valued for what they bring to the project, performance task, and/or long-term assignment rather than being characterized by what they may lack or some preconceived deficit.

At-promise: An assets-based term to characterize the learner who is considered at risk of not earning a high school diploma for a variety of reasons, including irregular attendance, a past record of academic underachievement, perceived low motivation, economic disadvantage, or low scores on math or English standardized tests. The term *at promise* (in contrast to *at risk*) puts the focus on the opportunity to learn gap rather than the so-called achievement gap. See **assets**.

Big idea(s): Big ideas are introduced, anchored, and revisited recursively through an essential question that serves to shape the way students learn to think critically for themselves during a unit or course. A big idea encompasses the ideas students will be grappling with through discussions, written responses, and ongoing investigations and research—all of which might culminate in a paper, presentation, or some appropriate project or artifact. See also **essential question**.

Bin(s): A bin is a figurative term for a schematic container we use to process information about student learning. Bins, like schema, are what we use to assimilate and accommodate student responses. Bins may hold collections of student responses that we've schematized over years of teaching experience. Bins allow us to make sense of and form judgments about the meaning of student responses in a lesson or across a unit. In the classroom assessment domain, bins may be as simple as *correct*, *incorrect*, *incomplete*, and *not attempted*, or bins may be much more nuanced, such as bins that hold all the responses that suggest students subscribe to common misconceptions (e.g., that all hollow things float). See also **learning progressions** and **schema**.

Binning: Binning is noticing patterns in student responses, categorizing them along learning trajectories, and using them to inform next steps. The purposes for creating and using different bins vary depending on subject content, skill development, and contexts for learning. Bins created to facilitate the process of providing formative feedback (binning for feedback) differ from bins created to differentiate summative evaluations of student performance (binning for grading), which often employ the *A*, *B*, *C*, *D*, and *F* grading bins. See *Module 8 on Binning* from the CCEE Learning Path Series.

Binning for feedback: Binning for feedback (Duckor & Holmberg, 2017) is an orientation toward assessment for learning. Binning student work involves categorizing, evaluating, and judging that work according to "bins" (progress levels) using a progress guide. These non-graded bins involve verbal representations gathered from qualitative descriptors, which are then assigned to each student's response. The focus of binning—whether driven by teachers, peers, or individual self-assessment—is to identify where one is and which next steps can be taken to improve performance. The act of binning for feedback is inherently formative. See **assessment for learning** and **formative assessment**.

Binning for grading: Binning for grading (Duckor & Holmberg, 2017) is an orientation toward assessment of learning. Binning student work involves categorizing, evaluating, and judging that work according to predetermined bins such as the *A–F* grading scale. These graded bins involve numerical representations gathered from point values assigned to each student's response. Numerical values may or may not be generated from a rubric or scoring guide. The act of binning for grading is inherently summative in nature. See **answer key**.

Block schedule/scheduling: A block schedule is a system for scheduling how long and how frequently classes in a middle or high school meet. With block scheduling, a traditional daily schedule of six or seven 50-minute class periods is replaced by longer class periods that meet fewer times each day and week. Block periods are often between 75 and 120 minutes long.

Bouncing: Bouncing is sampling a variety of student responses intentionally and systematically to better map the terrain of student thinking. Bouncing involves sampling student responses systematically to broaden participation, manage flow of conversation, and gather more soft data for instructional use. It is one of the essential assessment for learning moves first coined in the seven formative assessment moves framework (Duckor, 2014). See *Module 6 on Bouncing* from the CCEE Learning Path Series.

California Common Core State Standards: The California Standards for all public school students (from kindergarten through Grade 12) that have been adopted by the State Board of Education. These standards are drawn from the Common Core State Standards (CCSS) initiative.

California content standards: Content standards are designed to encourage the achievement of every student by defining the knowledge, concepts, and skills that students should acquire at each grade level. The 12 content standards adopted by the California State Board of Education are arts, career technical education, computer science, English language arts, English language development, health education, history/social science, mathematics, physical education, school library, science, and world languages. California has also adopted the Next Generation Science Standards (NGSS) and the Common Core Standards, both of which have been developed by national consortia.

Cognitive load: Cognitive load encompasses a learner's capacity for processing information as students learn, retain, and store information and build mental models in different domains of knowledge. A learner's capacity for information processing is conditioned by three potential sources of cognitive load: **intrinsic load**, **extraneous load**, and **germane load**. In the context of formative assessment, *intrinsic load* refers to the number of elements that the brain processes simultaneously in working memory for schema construction to address a prompt/task. If we pose questions with many prior-knowledge elements, students will naturally slow down, require more search-and-retrieval time, and need to tee up a response. *Extraneous load* in formative assessment refers to questioning techniques that require learners to engage their working memory in information processing not necessarily tied to the learning target(s). Often unintentionally mixed in with a question or prompt, illegible writing on a dry-erase board, small font on a presentation slide, rapidity of appearance and disappearance of text in a chat—even the tone of delivery of a question—can inadvertently overload students and lead to off-target responses. In the context of formative assessment, *germane load* refers to cognitive processes embedded in our questioning strategies that prime on-target responses to questions. Metaphors, analogies, and symbols—visual and auditory representations and elaborations—that help students build schema and conceptual understanding tied to the learning targets make up germane cognitive load. A challenge is knowing our students well enough to decide which analogies or scaffolds, for example, will guide them rather than distract or confuse them as they work to cognitively process information in our checks for understanding.

Configuration/Configurations: This dimension of feedback refers to the primary mode of organization and arrangement teachers use to check for understanding during a lesson and across a unit. Formative feedback relies on the use of multiple configurations—whole class, small groups, one-on-one/individual—to engage students while gathering information about their current level of understanding and engaging in next steps to support the improvement of practice. The term *configurations* also refers to the cross-cutting patterns of groupings of students in a learning environment. In most lessons, one can distinguish three basic types of learning configurations: a whole class (typically 16–40+ students), a small group (3–5 students), and one-on-one. Formative assessment moves must take into account the affordances and constraints associated with each learning configuration to maximize the effectiveness of any checks for understanding.

Constructivist learning theory: Constructivist learning theory posits that learners actively construct knowledge and make meaning based on their individual or social experiences. The belief that knowledge must be actively constructed by a person stands in contrast to the belief that knowledge can be transmitted to a person (informally known as the "banking" or "sit and get" model of learning). Constructivist learning theories recognize that learners are not blank slates, that prior knowledge always influences the formation of new knowledge, and that learning is an active process. See **prior knowledge**.

Continuous improvement: There are myriad ways to define continuous improvement. Fullan and associates (2018) have written extensively about continuous improvement systems and leadership approaches for deeper learning. Park and colleagues (2013) frame continuous quality improvement as the act of integrating quality improvement into the daily work of individuals in a system. Others note that continuous school improvement is a cyclical process intended to help groups of people in a system—from a class to a school district or even a network of many districts—set goals, identify ways to improve, and evaluate change in a continuous feedback loop. Duckor and Holmberg (2017) offer a formative assessment moves-based framework for continuous improvement at the level of daily classroom assessment practices that mirror the larger goals of school improvement and reform.

Criterion-referenced: Well-designed analytic rubrics typically use criterion-referenced performance categories that are based on content standards and/or a well-defined taxonomy of skills. The alignment of standards-based performance categories, for example, ensures that the performance task is representative of a more general set of skills and proficiencies and not too task-specific. When evaluating student performances, the classroom assessor must think carefully about these bins (performance categories) to ensure they represent learning targets and goals across the unit and course objectives.

Cultural assets inventory: A cultural inventory is a listing of a community's cultural assets or resources. A cultural inventory can be used as a resource for schools, cultural organizations, and others seeking to better understand a community or identify specific cultural resources within that community.

Deeper learning: Deeper learning is a pedagogical stance toward the curriculum. Relevance, rigor, and real-world experiences are essential to deeper learning outcomes. Deeper learning can be used as a lens to guide the development, planning, enactment, and reflection on what makes a good lesson. Deeper learning can utilize active learning principles and education technology to teach skills such as the importance of mastering specific content, learning to effectively communicate both orally and in writing, boosting problem-solving and critical-thinking skills, learning to collaborate with others, monitoring and directing one's own learning, and the promotion of the habits of mind. (See **habits of mind**.)

Depth of knowledge (DOK): The depth of knowledge (DOK) taxonomy is a general theoretical framework used in assessment contexts to describe, characterize, or hierarchically organize student responses to tasks related to cognition. The model designates how deeply students must know, understand, and be aware of what they are learning in order to attain and explain answers, outcomes, results, and solutions. It also designates how extensively students are expected to transfer and use what they have learned in different academic and real-world contexts. There are four DOK levels: Level 1 focuses on recall and reproduction of data, definitions, details, facts, information, and procedures (knowledge acquisition). Level 2 involves the use of academic concepts and cognitive skills to answer questions, address problems, accomplish tasks, and analyze texts and topics (knowledge application). Level 3 requires students to think strategically and reasonably about how and why concepts, ideas, operations, and procedures can be used to attain and explain answers, conclusions, decisions, outcomes, reasons, and results (knowledge analysis). When demonstrating DOK Level 4 cognition, students think extensively about what else can be done, how else learning can be used, and how the student could personally use what they have learned in different academic and real-world contexts (knowledge augmentation).

Dialogic: The adjective *dialogic* refers to the back-and-forth, exchange-based, conversational nature of human interactions of two or more people. Dialogic teaching is a pedagogical approach that attempts to use the power of talk to further students' thinking, learning, and problem solving. The amount and kinds of talk that occur in classroom communities influence student learning in various important ways. Researchers have explored how dialogic teaching functions in terms of the issue of discourse form and function and the role of classroom culture in supporting norms for interactions.

Dialogic exchange(s): The key concept of dialogic exchange refers to extended verbal sharing, during which the educator and students ask questions, listen to each other, and share their points of view, all in an attempt to build a joint understanding. Actions include scaffolding questions and modeling through language, scaffolding thought processes that catalyze deeper thinking, and scaffolding educational dialogue that includes joint sharing and elaborating.

Differentiated formative feedback: Formative feedback that is tailored to assist an individual student or group of students (whose work, responses, or performances share key characteristics relevant to improving performance related to a specific learning target) can be said to be differentiated feedback. Feedback can be differentiated by level of performance, such as when a teacher uses a progress guide to help determine what formative feedback to offer students whose work/response/performance is binned into the same bin or category. Formative feedback may also be differentiated—within a bin—according to students' needs, individual context, and personal preferences. For example, the teacher may adjust how and what formative feedback to provide to two students whose responses belong to the same bin because the students got there for very different reasons and because sometimes students require quite different next steps. Formative assessors recognize that some students can take relatively big next steps independently while other students benefit from taking (or need to take) many smaller next steps with support.

Directionality/Directionalities: This dimension of feedback refers to the primary mode of direct action and agency teachers use to check for understanding at a given time during a lesson and across a unit. Formative feedback relies on the use of multiple agents—teacher, peer, and self—to engage students while gathering information about their current level of understanding and promoting the taking of next steps to support the improvement of practice. Formative assessment moves must take into account the affordances and constraints associated with each agency (who is giving feedback to whom) to maximize the effectiveness of any checks for understanding.

Elaboration: Elaboration, in the general sense, is the expansion of an initial statement or idea. Elaboration involves enhancing the original idea or statement with additional, related information generated by students. Teachers have many purposes for seeking student elaboration on so-called first draft responses. From a cognitive learning perspective, elaboration strengthens ties to long-term memory by inviting associations such as analogies, particular details, even imagery and sound with a concept or skill. The act of elaboration—while checking for understanding—helps students to build and strengthen connections between their prior knowledge and new classroom learning experiences. Formative assessors make posing, pausing, and probing moves—with requests for visual and verbal elaboration from students—to evaluate the depth and breadth of current levels of understanding. As teachers assess initial responses by probing on first drafts, they can identify a zone of proximal development and better determine which supports and scaffolds (if any) are needed.

English language development standard(s): States typically adopt standards specifically aimed to help English learners engage with and master their state's content standards and clarify what knowledge, skills, and abilities are needed for them to do this and become college and career ready. For example, the state of California has adopted English Language Development Standards that align with the **California Common Core State Standards** for English language arts and literacy in history/social studies, science, and technical subjects (CA CCSS for ELA/Literacy). However, the California English Language Development Standards do not repeat the CA CCSS for ELA/Literacy nor do they represent English language arts content at lower levels of achievement or rigor. They are designed to provide challenging content in English language development so English learners gain proficiency in a range of rigorous academic English language skills.

English learner (EL): Also refers to an English language learner (ELL). Many recognize the affirming connotations of terms such as *emergent bilingual students* or *emergent multilingual learners*. We use *ELs* since that is the terminology most commonly recognized across school systems, accountability frameworks, policy documents, and recent K–12 education literatures. We avoid using formerly common but deficit-oriented terms such as *limited English proficient* (*LEP*). See **assets**.

Entrance ticket(s): An entrance ticket is a formative assessment tool used to activate students' prior knowledge and check for understanding at the beginning of class, hence the moniker *entrance*. The name *entrance ticket* refers to when this assessment activity is deployed (i.e., at the beginning of a lesson). The intent varies, but many teachers use these entrance tickets in so-called flipped lessons to informally assess the current levels of student understanding before launching the lesson. Progress guides and other purpose-driven feedback tools can be used as entrance or exit tickets. See **exit ticket**.

Essential question (EQ): Essential questions are designed to invite inquiry. EQs do not yield a single answer, as a standard quiz or test questions typically do. Instead, EQs tend to elicit different plausible responses about which knowledgeable people may disagree. Wiggins and McTighe (1998) state that EQs get at and help learners uncover the heart of a subject or a curriculum; they are neither trivial nor do they lead to a single correct answer. EQs promote inquiry within and across units of a subject.

Exemplar(s): Sadler (1987) defines *exemplars* as key examples chosen by a teacher that are typical of designated levels of quality or competence. These carefully chosen exemplars convey a clear picture about the meaning of levels of quality—for example, from "Needs Improvement" to "Advanced"—so that students better understand what is required to achieve a particular level of performance on a scoring guide. Key to formative assessment is the use of these exemplars in non-graded settings. See also **moderation**.

Exhibition(s): An exhibition is a demonstration of learning that is both a learning experience in itself and a means of evaluating academic progress and achievement. Educators use many different terms to refer to this general concept: *capstone project, learning demonstration, culminating exhibition*, and so on. Exhibitions often encompass a wide variety of forms demonstrating learning: oral presentations; video documentaries; physical products such as models, sculptures, or robots; and portfolios of work samples that students collect over time.

Exit ticket(s): An exit ticket is a formative assessment tool used to check student understanding and to offer students opportunities to communicate where they may be stuck, need assistance, and so on. The name *exit ticket* refers to when this assessment activity is deployed (i.e., toward the end of a lesson, immediately before students exit class). The intent varies, but many teachers use these exit tickets to informally assess the current levels of student understanding in order to better plan for the next lesson. Progress guides and other purpose-driven feedback tools can be used as exit or entrance tickets. See **entrance ticket**.

Extant: Extant literature/music refers to text/music that has survived from the past to the present time as opposed to lost work.

Extraneous load: The term *cognitive load* is associated with information processing theories of learning. *Extraneous load* refers to the way the instructional (and assessment) tasks are organized and presented to the learner. Extraneous load can be reduced by appropriately designing assessment items, tasks, and materials that focus the learner on relevant, useful information or procedures.

Feedback: Hattie and Timperley (2007) note that feedback is "information provided by an agent (e.g., teacher, peer, book, parent, self, experience) regarding aspects of one's performance or understanding. A teacher or parent can provide corrective information, a peer can provide an alternative strategy, a book can provide information to clarify ideas, a parent can provide encouragement, and a learner can look up the answer to evaluate the correctness of a response" (p. 81). There are many qualities and purposes of feedback in classroom assessment. Feedback is a key practice in assessment for learning. See **formative feedback**.

Feedback loop(s): Formative feedback is the exchange of information aimed at a task, project, or process that occurs in an assessment cycle (*loops*, as we call them). These feedback loops can occur during the learning cycle and provide the learner with information regarding aspects of the learner's performance or understanding that requires, for example, augmentation and improvement. Formative feedback in these loops or turns of talk can come from teachers, peers, and students themselves. Typically, the feedback loop includes written, oral, and/or nonverbal/body-kinesthetic modalities. Formative feedback loops can also occur in different configurations, including whole class, small group, or one-on-one. The aim of formative feedback loops as part of a classroom assessment cycle is improvement before the end of the instructional cycle so that the learner has the opportunity to revise and improve the task, project, or assignment.

First draft(s): The initial response to a question, prompt, or task is what we refer to as a first draft response. These first draft responses may be on or off topic. They may include body gestures, initial statements, unorthodox comments, scattered utterances, even "I don't know" or "Who cares?" The goal of the formative assessor is to move these initial responses along, to help them take shape in written and verbal forms, and to create multiple drafts (if necessary) until students are ready to stand by their answers. All teachers in every subject who assess for learning are focused on developing their students' responses into the best ones possible at any given point in time. See **soft data**.

Fishbowl: Fishbowling is a strategy for organizing medium- to large-group in-person, classroom-based discussions. In professional development settings, teachers form two groups: an inner circle, which is the fishbowl, and an outer circle. Typically, the inner circle of teachers is significantly smaller in number than the outer circle. The strategy sets up a situation for those in the outer circle to observe those in the fishbowl as they discuss a problem of practice. When working on supporting a focal student that represents challenges and opportunities for the school community to improve, the teachers in the fishbowl may be tasked with trying to present a case. The case is intended to help the group offer observations, feedback, and next steps on improving relationships and supports for students.

Focal/focus student: A student that for some length of time receives focused attention during lesson planning, enactment, and reflection by the teacher for the purpose of benefiting not only that student but other students who may also share similar assets and needs. By focusing on and learning from a single case, a teacher can explore the extent to which generalizations that might benefit classmates are relevant. In the context of Teacher Performance Assessment (TPA) licensure, a focal student is often a student with learning challenges (e.g., identified disability or individualized education plan goal[s]). Focal students may also include those who have a 504 plan or who need greater instructional challenges as part of a Gifted and Talented Education (GATE) designation.

Formative assessment(s): Formative assessment is an assessment process used by teachers and students during instruction to provide feedback for adjusting ongoing teaching and learning with the goal of improving students' achievement of intended instructional outcomes.

Formative assessment move(s): The formative assessment (FA) moves framework focuses on assessment for learning aimed at deeper learning. It introduces seven high-leverage, research-based moves: priming, posing, pausing, probing, bouncing, tagging, and binning. See *Module 1 Introduction* from the CCEE Learning Path Series.

Formative assessor(s): A person who is committed to the process of formative assessment and seeks to integrate moves, strategies, and tactics in every lesson and across each unit of instruction to enact deeper assessment for learning practices in a learning environment. Formative feedback routines, practices, and protocols are a major part of the formative assessor's toolkit.

Formative feedback: The production and exchange of information aimed at a task, project, or process that occurs in an assessment cycle. This feedback occurs during the learning cycle and provides the learner with information regarding aspects of the learner's performance or understanding that requires, for example, augmentation and improvement. The three main dimensions of formative feedback are directionality, configuration, and modality. The directionality dimension of formative feedback is generated by teachers, peers, and/or students for themselves. The configuration dimension of formative feedback is situated in whole-class, small-group, and/or one-on-one settings. The modality configuration of formative feedback is exchanged in written, spoken, and/or nonverbal modes.

Formative feedback loop(s): Formative feedback is the exchange of information aimed at a task, project, or process that occurs in an assessment cycle (many intersecting *loops*, as we call them). These feedback loops can occur during the learning cycle and provide the learner with information regarding aspects of the learner's performance or understanding that requires, for example, augmentation and improvement. Formative feedback in these loops or turns of talk can come from teachers, peers, and students themselves. Typically, the feedback loop includes written, spoken, and/or nonverbal modalities. Formative feedback loops can also occur in different configurations, including whole class, small group, or one-on-one. The aim of formative feedback loops as part of a classroom assessment cycle is improvement before the end of the instructional cycle so that the learner has the opportunity to revise and improve the task, project, or assignment.

Germane load: Germane load refers to the parts of our assessment strategies that support student processing and allow each student to better understand the question, task, or prompt. The distinctive characteristic of germane load is that, unlike intrinsic load or extraneous load, it has a positive relationship with learning because it enhances the use of cognitive resources toward schema acquisition rather than to other off-target mental activities/processes not aligned with the learning target(s).

Grading: Grading is a way for teachers to summatively evaluate individual students' performances. Grading is used to communicate achievement. Grading leads to letter grades (e.g., *A, B, C, D, F*) or pass/fail marks. There are different methods for calculating grades. See **binning for grading**.

Graphic organizer(s): A graphic organizer is a tool students use to represent information visually in order to assist in meaning making. Teachers provide graphic organizers to help deepen students' understanding of subject content. Graphic organizers include T-charts, concept maps, Venn diagrams, and diagrams and charts that highlight causes and effects, the nature of relationships (e.g., hierarchy), and sequences.

Habit(s) of mind: The habits of mind, cast as essential questions, formed the cornerstone of the curriculum and essential schoolwide learning goals at Central Park East Secondary School (CPESS) in East Harlem, New York. Through the cognitive lens of the five habits of mind, all the teachers at CPESS sought to develop interdisciplinary curricula to better foster their students' curiosity, intellectual engagement, and academic mastery in preparation for college.

The five habits of mind are evidence, perspective, connection, supposition, and relevance, as highlighted by the following questions:

- How do we know what we know? (Evidence)
- From whose point of view is this being presented? (Perspective)
- How is this event or work connected to others? What causes what? (Connection)
- What if things were different? (Supposition)
- Who cares? Why is this important? (Relevance)

Teachers can embed these cross-cutting questions and concepts (which are aligned to California's Common Core Standards) into the curriculum while promoting healthy skepticism and deeper thinking.

Higher-order question(s): Higher-order questions are designed to prompt students to engage in higher-order or critical-thinking skills as defined by various taxonomies of learning, such as Benjamin Bloom's (1956) taxonomy of educational objectives: the classification of educational goals. Higher-order thinking skills include analysis, synthesis, evaluation, interpretation, transfer, prediction, and creation. Lower-order questions target thinking skills that require recall. These types of questions require students to recall and remember, for example, definitions, dates, events, names, formulae, rules, symbols, and so forth. Some refer to this type/level of question as eliciting declarative knowledge. Lower-order questions are typically drawn from the lowest levels in Bloom's and Webb's taxonomies.

Individualized education plan (IEP): An individualized education plan (IEP) is a written document required for each public school student who receives special education and related services. A main purpose of the IEP is to facilitate communication between teachers, parents, school administrators, related services personnel, and students to work together to improve educational results for students with specific needs. An IEP states how a student is currently doing in school (i.e., current performance) and articulates annual goals.

Intrinsic load: Intrinsic load refers to the number of elements that the brain processes simultaneously in working memory for schema construction to address a prompt/task. If we pose questions with many prior-knowledge elements, students will naturally slow down, require more search-and-retrieval time, and need to tee up a response.

Learning criteria: The design of an analytic rubric has two major features: a set of criteria/skill indicators and corresponding descriptions of four to five expected levels of performance for each indicator. In the science lab rubric example, there are four criteria: hypothesis and research questions, lab setup and procedures, evidence and data collection, and analysis of results and conclusion. See **criterion-referenced**.

Learning progression(s): Learning progressions describe a trajectory of learning within a content domain that spans a much longer period of time than a lesson or single unit of instruction. The trajectory may provide a multi-year image of students' successively more sophisticated performance levels, for example, in addressing the big idea of "Why things sink and float" in physics. Heritage (2008) notes that a progression of learning in a domain can provide the big picture of what is to be learned, support instructional planning, and act as a touchstone for formative assessment.

Learning target(s): Learning targets are what teachers intend for students to learn by the end of a class, unit, project, or course. They are concrete goals written in student-friendly language. They clearly describe what students should learn, how deeply they should learn it, and what they should be able to do to demonstrate they have learned it. When students share in learning targets and understand well from the beginning of a lesson or unit what it is they are attempting to learn and how they will demonstrate what they have learned, they can better—and more intentionally—expend their energy and effort. Shared learning targets can help students develop and improve self-regulation.

Lesson plan(s): A lesson plan is a written document that describes key aspects of how a teacher intends to orchestrate and support students' learning experiences within a defined period of time. The format of a lesson plan depends on overall teaching aims, assumptions about learning theory, and factors related to students' needs, the curriculum, and the content of any unit. Formative assessors will embed many checks for understanding across a lesson, from opening to close. These checks may include describing plans for use of specific formative assessment tools (e.g., word web, do now, quick write, turn and talk, exit ticket). To deepen feedback practices in terms of protocols, processes, and use of tools such as progress guides, lesson and unit plans assist in backward planning and design. A set of lesson plans can embed the feedback moves and cycles intended to support projects, performance tasks, and assignments.

Lifelong learning: Lifelong learning encompasses all the learning activities people engage in throughout their lives to improve knowledge, skills, competencies, and understanding. Unlike compulsory schooling, lifelong learning is voluntary. It can occur in informal and formal settings. Many progressive educators see the goal of democratic education as going beyond schooling and compliance; they have called for the development of lifelong learners who live in an open society that encourages intellectual growth, continuous inquiry, and the cultivation of authentic dispositions toward learning. See also **continuous improvement**.

Mental model(s): A mental model is an internal representation about the way things work in the external world. (Note: A mental model may be about the internal processes of others.) People rely on mental models to understand and interact with systems in the world, partly in order to not have to figure things out from scratch every time they encounter a new situation or problem.

Metacognitive skill(s): Metacognitive skills have to do with thinking about one's thinking. Metacognitive skills allow learners to organize, guide, evaluate, and influence their own thought processes related to learning and problem solving.

Misconception(s): Cognitive scientists and educational researchers note that when teachers provide instruction on concepts in various subjects, students already have some prior knowledge, experiences, and beliefs about a topic. Student knowledge, however, can be erroneous, illogical, or misinformed (Lucariello & Naff, 2010). Experts call these erroneous understandings *alternative conceptions* or *misconceptions* or *intuitive theories*. Misconceptions, not unlike p-prims and preconceptions, are an expected feature of learning. Every student who is a novice learning to apply knowledge to a new subject discipline or complex topic is expected to bring some misconceptions while working to better understand the project, task, or assignment. Feedback is part of how we learn to rethink our misconceptions. See **p-prims** and **preconceptions**.

Modality/Modalities: This dimension of feedback refers to the primary mode of communication teachers use to check for understanding during a lesson and across a unit. Formative feedback relies on the use of multiple modalities—spoken, written, and nonverbal/body-kinesthetic—to engage students while gathering information about their current level of understanding and engaging in next steps to support the improvement of practice. Formative assessment moves must take into account the affordances and constraints associated with these modes of communication to maximize the effectiveness of information exchange directed at a project, performance task, and/or long-term assignment.

Moderation: Moderation may be conducted by groups of teachers or by students. Moderation occurs after participants have scored samples of anonymous students' work using a scoring guide. The purpose of moderation is for participants to reach agreement about which score is most appropriate for a work sample in cases where they have initially disagreed about which score, according to the guide, it should receive. During moderation, student participants are expected to explain and justify each score they have given to a sample of work. One benefit of moderation is that as participants discuss and elaborate on their reasons for a particular score, they reveal their understanding of the topic. Through this peer-to-peer assessment process, students also come to understand the assessment criteria more clearly and are better positioned to revise based on exemplars.

Move(s): The language of assessment moves draws upon the knowledge and skills teachers and students use to assess for learning. A moves-based framework in formative assessment, for example, puts a premium on action and reaction during teaching and learning exchanges (Duckor & Holmberg, 2017). Feedback moves, in particular, are high-leverage instructional actions that simultaneously serve to position learners for taking up, offering, and exchanging information about a project, task, or long-term assignment.

Next Generation Science Standards (NGSS): The NGSS are K–12 science content standards that articulate the expectations for what students should know and be able to do. They were developed by educators across the United States to create a set of research-based, up-to-date K–12 science standards. The standards accommodate educators by flexibly designing classroom learning experiences that will stimulate students' interests in science and prepare them for college, careers, and citizenship.

Opportunity gap(s): Closely related to the achievement gap and the learning gap, this term refers to the ways in which race, ethnicity, socioeconomic status, English proficiency, community wealth, familial situations, or other factors contribute to or perpetuate lower educational aspirations, achievement, and attainment for certain groups of students. Generally speaking, *opportunity gap* refers to inputs—the unequal or inequitable distribution of resources and opportunities—while *achievement gap* refers to outputs—the unequal or inequitable distribution of educational results and benefits. *Learning gap* refers to the relative performance of individual students—the disparity between what a student has actually learned and what students are expected to learn at a particular age or grade level (Great Schools Partnership, 2013). See *Module 9 on Closing Opportunity Gaps* from the CCEE Learning Path Series.

Pausing: Pausing is one of the essential assessment for learning moves first coined in the seven formative assessment moves framework (Duckor, 2014). Pausing refers to providing students adequate time to think and respond as individuals or in groups. Pausing involves supporting all students in thinking aloud and using speaking and listening skills related to academic language and wait time and think time procedures after powerful questions and rich tasks to encourage more student responses. In the context of formative assessment practices, *wait time* refers to the pausing moves, routines, and/or scaffolds a teacher initiates to assist students with engaging questions posed in a lesson. Wait time supports will differ according to students' needs in relation to each question (its level of difficulty, for example). Questions call for different types and amounts of wait time. See *Module 4 on Pausing* from the CCEE Learning Path Series.

Peak-end effect: The notion of the peak-end effect comes from the field of cognitive psychology. It refers to a phenomenon related to how people tend to evaluate remembered experiences. To what extent—and why—do they associate pain or pleasure with past experiences? It turns out that when people form retrospective evaluations of an experience, their judgments and memories are based predominantly on how they felt during the most intense moment (the peak) of the experience and how they felt when the experience ended (the end). They tend to neglect, for example, how long the experience was. The peak and end are much more salient and important to how they remember and evaluate the experience than the duration of the experience.

Peer assessment: Peer assessment describes the act of student (peer-based) evaluation of other students. When students are asked to peer assess, they are being invited to evaluate others' own responses, task performances, and projects. There are likely other benefits to peer assessment related to collaboration and other 21st century skills. Gallery walks, writing circles, spot and lift, and other team-based share outs are all examples of peer-to-peer feedback activities. Feedback from peers can be given anonymously or face-to-face, depending on the classroom learning environment and other goals. From the formative assessor's point of view, the goal of peer assessment is to generate feedback that is useful for revision processes to improve performance. See also **binning for feedback**.

Performance assessment: A performance assessment is any assessment event, task, or project that occurs over multiple days or weeks. Typical performance assessments include language arts essays, science labs, history posters and research projects, works of art, musical performances, physical education games, world language projects, structured dialogues, and so forth. Performance assessments are often contrasted to traditional test, quiz, and homework items/questions because they involve the creation of student work products. Advocates for performance assessment describe these assessment tasks/projects as more authentic, real world, and relevant to the lives of students. From the formative assessor's point of view, a quality performance assessment aimed at deeper learning will generate cycles of feedback that lead to productive, visible revisions to improve the final work product for summative evaluation.

Pivotal point: Similar to a hinge point, this is a moment in the instructional cycle that usually occurs in a lesson segment, marking the point when the teacher has gathered sufficient soft data to infer that students will need support. In formative feedback turns of talk, these moments appear as clarifications, transitions, and/or reteaching and recovery of a lesson segment.

Posing: Posing is one of the essential assessment for learning moves first coined in the seven formative assessment moves framework (Duckor, 2014). Posing refers to asking questions while checking for understanding to size up the learner's needs in the lesson and across the unit. These questions, prompts, and tasks are posed in relation to learning targets within a lesson and across the curriculum to elicit habits of mind. See *Module 3 on Posing* from the CCEE Learning Path Series.

P-prim(s): P-prim is an abbreviation for *phenomenological primitive* developed from diSessa's (1983) research on learning. P-prims are intuitive ideas about a particular phenomenon based on everyday experiences (e.g., things with sharp edges will sink). P-prims represent less-sophisticated understandings than experts' more robust, systematic ideas (sometimes called *mental models*) of a particular phenomenon or topic/subject under study. All students have preconceptions and p-prims related to each subject that are likely to surface during projects and performance tasks. Checking for p-prims, preconceptions, and misconceptions during multiple feedback cycles invites students to discover and unpack novice ways of thinking about the work and the first draft responses. See **assets** and **mental model**.

Preconception(s): Not unlike p-prims and so-called misconceptions, preconceptions are an expected feature of learning. A schema is a cognitive framework or concept that helps organize and interpret information. All learners in any topic or subject matter are likely to have preconceptions as part of their interpretive frameworks. These schemas (even the preconceptions themselves) represent less-sophisticated understandings of a phenomenon. These preconceptions can be labeled naive or nascent. Checking for p-prims, preconceptions, and misconceptions invites the discovery of novice thinking in a lesson using an assets-based model of learning. Every student who is a novice is learning to apply knowledge (preconceptions are a form of knowledge) to a new subject discipline or complex topic. While working to better understand the project, task, or assignment, feedback is part of how we learn to rethink our preconceptions. See **p-prims** and **learning progressions**.

Priming: Priming is one of the essential moves coined in the seven formative assessment moves framework (Duckor, 2014). Priming refers to preparing the groundwork for assessment for learning. It includes establishing and maintaining norms and working to acculturate students to assessing their own and each other's work publicly. By building on assets and background knowledge of students, priming moves sustain and support a formative assessment–rich, equitable classroom culture where everyone feels safe and respected as they share first draft responses. See *Module 2 on Priming* from the CCEE Learning Path Series.

Priming agreement(s): Priming agreements in the formative assessment moves framework (Duckor & Holmberg, 2017) serve to bolster classroom assessment procedures and support practices that embody the values and beliefs necessary for a formative assessment–rich culture to flourish. These agreements are not contracts or bills of rights/responsibilities. They include cues, sentence starters, mottos, and simple reminders for use by students during a formative feedback exchange.

Prior knowledge: Prior knowledge encompasses all the knowledge, skills, and experiences a student brings to a learning situation. Prior knowledge has long been considered the most important factor influencing learning and is considered key to closing the student achievement/opportunity gap. Similar to constructivists, formative assessors will work strategically to make students' prior knowledge visible for a variety of reasons. Perhaps the most important reason to elicit, honor, and examine students' prior knowledge is for teachers to use this information to inform their decision making about the planning and support of learning situations that are likely to be optimal situations for particular students to actively construct knowledge and skills on the basis of their prior knowledge. See **constructivist learning theory**.

Probing: Probing is one of the essential moves coined in the seven formative assessment moves framework (Duckor, 2014). Probing refers to asking follow-up questions that use information from actual student responses. This move deepens learning and helps teachers to identify zones of proximal development. By asking for elaboration, students also make connections and work toward higher-order thinking skills while the teacher can assess how much scaffolding and assistance is needed to reach beyond surface understanding. See *Module 5 on Probing* from the CCEE Learning Path Series.

Professional learning community (PLC): Professional learning communities (PLCs) involve teacher-led collaboration at a school site. PLCs often involve a group of educators that meet regularly, share expertise, and work collaboratively on a focus topic for an academic year. Topics can include the collaborative improvement of teaching skills, classroom-based assessment practices, and the use of different supports for the academic and socio-emotional performance of students.

Progress guide(s): A progress guide is a supplement to a rubric (Duckor & Holmberg, 2017). It is a feedback-oriented binning strategy that articulates a single strand/criteria of an analytic rubric. Progress guides are designed for rapid, focused uses of teacher and student time to generate next steps. They can be used for peer- and self-assessment in addition to teacher-driven assessment for learning. The formative assessor uses these guides to mark progress, identify waypoints, and deliver targeted, skills-based feedback that students use to revise their work and performances before the final version of the performance, assignment, or project is collected. Progress guides do not include numbers, points, or scores. Compare, for example, to a **scoring guide**.

Project-based learning (PBL): Project-based learning is a teaching method in which students learn by actively engaging in real-world projects, by solving complex problems in situated contexts over extended periods of time, and by doing so in ways that are personally meaningful.

Prompt(s): A prompt is a question, phrase, word, brief passage, image, or performance cue intended to catalyze a response in students. *Assessments*, by definition, seek to elicit student responses to a stimulus. Prompts are used in large-scale testing and classroom assessment practice. Student responses to a prompt can be carefully observed and interpreted in order to draw inferences about what students currently know and can do in a subject domain. The degree to which a prompt targets what is intended to be assessed and the degree to which the method of interpreting the responses makes sense for the context directly impacts the validity of the inferences that can be drawn. See also **stimulus**.

Register(s): A register is a variety of a language used for a specific purpose and audience in a particular social setting. Throughout the day, people may use several different registers of language, depending on context. Consider three ways of saying essentially the same thing, depending on the relationship between the speakers and the circumstance: (1) *I would appreciate it if you would please pass that to me.* (2) *Please hand that to me.* (3) *Give me that!* According to the California Department of Education, register also refers to variation in the vocabulary, grammar, and discourse of a language to meet the expectations of a particular context. A context can be defined by numerous elements, such as audience, task, purpose, setting, social relationship, and mode of communication (written versus spoken). Specific examples of contextual variables are the nature of the communicative activity (e.g., talking with someone about a movie, persuading someone in a debate, or writing a science report), the nature of the relationship between the language users in the activity (e.g., friend to friend, expert to learner), the subject matter and topic (e.g., photosynthesis in science, the Civil War in history), and the medium through which a message is conveyed (e.g., a text message versus an essay). See also **academic language**.

Rubric(s): A rubric is an evaluation tool that can help teachers and students bin performances. Rubrics may be holistic or analytic. Analytic rubrics use four to six criteria and performance levels to define successful performance. Well-designed analytic rubrics define four to five performance levels with clear, well-defined, and student-friendly descriptions that avoid using deficit language or potentially hurtful labels. See **learning criteria** and **exemplar**.

Running record(s): A running record is a type of observational note taking and informal record keeping; it involves an observer writing down "everything" that is happening during a lesson. Running records are commonly used in early childhood education and reading instruction. In the seven formative assessment moves framework, the action of tagging serves to create a running record of a classroom's responses in order to publicly represent variation in student thinking. These records can be documented through various media (e.g., downloading a Zoom chat, taking pictures from a dry-erase board, or saving comments on Google Docs). These soft data records can be collected for later analysis and evaluation. See **soft data**.

Scaffold(s)/scaffolding: Scaffolding is temporary guidance or assistance provided to a student by a teacher, another adult, or a more capable peer that enables the student to perform a task they otherwise would not be able to do alone, with the goal of fostering the student's capacity to perform the task on their own later on. Though Vygotsky himself does not use the term *scaffolding*, the educational meaning of the term relates closely to his concept of the zone of proximal development. See also **zone of proximal development**.

Schema: Theorist Jean Piaget introduced the term *schema*, and its use was popularized through his work. In constructivist learning theory, a schema is both the category of knowledge as well as the process of acquiring that knowledge. Students and teachers are constantly adapting to the environment as they take in new information and learn new things. A schema is a general idea about something. Its plural form is *schemata*. Through a process of assimilation and accommodation, schemata are constructed and reconstructed in learning experiences. In order to uncover schemata in a lesson, teachers can activate prior knowledge with brainstorm/**word web**/concept-mapping routines. These routines allow for linking new information to old information and connecting different schemata to each other within or across a unit. See **bin(s)**.

Scoring guide(s): A scoring guide is an evaluation tool. Scoring guides are less cognitively and linguistically complex than the analytic rubric; therefore, they may be employed as a more student-friendly binning strategy. Scoring guides can be used by teachers and by students for peer and self-assessment. Scoring guides tend to contain less verbiage and dysfunctional detail that might overwhelm students, including English learners and students with special needs. Unlike progress guides, scoring guides may not be aligned with rubrics. Scoring guides, as the name implies, typically include numbers, points, or scores. See **moderation**.

Scribe/Scribing: A scribe may be the teacher of the class or one or more students who are striving to accurately and faithfully represent what students are saying publicly as everyone is responding to a prompt. The act of scribing involves actively listening to a variety of student responses and writing or typing these responses such that they are visible to all in the learning community. A scribe may or may not probe on individual responses while recording them. Key to the practice of (re)presenting student ideas is (de)scribing without evaluation or judgment. Scribes serve as record keepers who help gather students' responses without bias. See **tagging**.

Self-assessment: Self-assessment describes the act of student ("self") evaluation. When students are asked to self-assess, they are being invited to evaluate their own responses, task performances, and projects. Some suggest there are metacognitive benefits to self-assessment, such as helping students to make plans, monitor, and evaluate their work. From the formative assessor's point of view, the goal of self-assessment is to generate feedback that is useful for revision processes to improve performance. See also **binning for feedback**.

Sentence starter(s): A sentence starter is a technique to help students formulate a response to a question, prompt, or task. Sentence starters provide a scaffold/frame for students to express their thoughts in writing or when speaking. Sentence starters can be used to assist students to focus and organize their thoughts to increase germane load. Sentence starters are a common strategy for scaffolding students' first draft responses and help to support academic language production in a lesson.

Soft data: The term *soft data* encompasses all the utterances (including student questions), writings, drawings, diagrams, physical actions, and even silences generated by students that are often difficult to quantify and that teachers frequently depend upon to make instructional decisions. Soft data is generated on the fly during a lesson and can be used as a benchmark for setting up the next lesson. Soft data may be intentionally and systematically elicited through carefully planned questions, tasks, exit ticket prompts, and activities. Screen capture, photos, and other media can aid in documenting learnings while the teacher checks for understanding. Soft data can be collected by students while they scribe ("tag") for other students in whole-class, small-group, or one-on-one configurations. These running records of soft data allow for informal pre/post comparisons in a unit to examine progress, for example, with a word web or concept map. See **running record**.

SOLO taxonomy: The SOLO taxonomy (Biggs & Collis, 1982) is a general theoretical framework used in assessment contexts to describe, characterize, or hierarchically organize student responses to tasks related to cognition. As learning progresses, it becomes more complex. SOLO, which stands for the *structure of the observed learning outcome*, is a means of classifying learning outcomes in terms of their complexity, enabling us to assess students' work in terms of its quality, not how many bits of this and that they have mastered so far. Biggs writes, "At first we pick up only one or few aspects of the task (unistructural), then several aspects but they are unrelated (multi-structural), then we learn how to integrate them into a whole (relational), and finally, we are able to generalize that whole to as yet untaught applications (extended abstract)."

Standard(s): Standards aim to succinctly describe what students should know and be able to do. Standards are usually authored by content experts and educators and adopted by state and local boards of education.

Stimulus: In the context of a formative feedback loop, a stimulus is a thoughtfully chosen question, phrase, word, brief passage, image, or performance cue intended to catalyze a response in students so that these responses—individually and as a set—may be examined, analyzed, and evaluated. See also **prompt**.

Tagging: Tagging is one of the essential assessment for learning moves. First coined in the seven formative assessment moves framework (Duckor, 2014), tagging refers to publicly representing variation in student thinking by creating a snapshot or a running record of a class's responses. It aids in describing and recording student responses without judgment and making public how students with different styles and needs approach learning in real time. Student scribes can assist teachers in tagging, which leads to more agency and efficacy and better communication in the classroom learning environment. See *Module 7 on Tagging* from the CCEE Learning Path Series. See **soft data**.

Think time: Think time is the time teachers intentionally offer students to support cognitive processing of questions, directions, explanations, and other visual, aural, and sensory inputs during a lesson. It includes routines, scaffolds, and norms related to pausing moves. Teachers also need adequate think time to support their on-the-fly decision making regarding soft data during lessons.

Unit(s) of instruction: A well-defined portion of a course or instructional program that centers on an overarching topic, theme, or big idea. A unit is often marked by a culminating assessment event such as a test, project, or performance task. Units typically encompass many lessons across several weeks.

Wait time: Wait time describes the time between when a teacher stops speaking (such as when a teacher poses a question to a student, group of students, or whole class) and when a student responds. Wait time also describes the time between when a student speaks and the teacher responds or the time between when a student speaks, pauses, and speaks again.

Word web: Word webs belong to the same family of graphic organizers known as *mind maps* and *concept maps*. The content (i.e., student responses) of a word web is organized around a central idea or topic. Related ideas radiate out from this central idea or topic, which may actually be a phrase or image. When a whole class works to create a word web, students' knowledge, beliefs, and opinions associated with the idea or topic under consideration are made visible for the entire learning community. See **graphic organizer** and **soft data**.

Zone of proximal development (ZPD): Vygotsky coined the term *zone of proximal development* (*ZPD*) to describe the distance between the actual developmental level as determined by independent problem solving and the level of potential development as determined through problem solving under adult guidance or in collaboration with more capable peers. We refer to ZPD as what students can do with assistance from others until the point of release of scaffolds and supports, which characterizes the movement toward independence or mastery of the concept or task. Well-designed rubrics, progress guides, and other formative assessment binning-for-feedback tools can assist students in examining gaps and next steps in current performance in order to make progress with guidance.

References

Admiraal, W., Huisman, B., & Pili, O. (2015). Assessment in massive open online courses. *Electronic Journal of e-Learning, 13*, 207–216.

Agricola, B. T., Prins, F. J., & Sluijsmans, D. (2020). Impact of feedback request forms and verbal feedback on higher education students' feedback perception, self-efficacy, and motivation. *Assessment in Education: Principles, Policy & Practice, 27*(1), 6–25.

Airasian, P. W., Cruikshank, K. A., Mayer, R. E., Pintrich, P. R., Raths, J., & Wittrock, M. C. (2001). *A taxonomy for learning, teaching and assessing: A revision of Bloom's taxonomy of educational objectives* (Complete ed., L. W. Anderson & D. R. Krathwohl, Eds.). Longman.

Alaoutinen, S. (2012). Evaluating the effect of learning style and student background on self-assessment accuracy. *Computer Science Education, 22*, 175–198.

Alexander, R. J. (2006). *Towards dialogic teaching: Rethinking classroom talk*. Dialogos.

Allal, L. (2019). Assessment and the co-regulation of learning in the classroom. *Assessment in Education: Principles, Policy & Practice, 27*(4), 332–349.

Alonzo, A. C., & Gotwals, A. W. (Eds.). (2012). *Learning progressions in science: Current challenges and future directions*. Sense.

American Educational Research Association (AERA), American Psychological Association (APA), & National Council on Measurement in Education (NCME). (2014). *Standards for educational and psychological testing*. American Educational Research Association.

Andersen, J. F. (1979). Teacher immediacy as a predictor of teacher effectiveness. In D. Nimmo (Ed.), *Communication yearbook* (pp. 543–559). Transaction Books.

Andersen, J. F., Norton, R. W., & Nussbaum, J. F. (1981). Three investigations exploring relationships between perceived teacher communication behaviors and student learning. *Communication Education, 30*, 377–392.

Anderson, L. W., & Krathwohl, D. R. (Eds.), Airasian, P. W., Cruikshank, K. A., Mayer, R. E., Pintrich, P. R., Raths, J., & Wittrock, M. C. (2001). *A taxonomy for learning, teaching and assessing: A revision of Bloom's taxonomy of educational objectives* (Complete ed.). Longman.

Andrade, H. G., & Boulay, B. A. (2003). Gender and the role of rubric-referenced self-assessment in learning to write. *The Journal of Educational Research, 97*(1), 21–30.

Andrade, H. L. (2000). Using rubrics to promote thinking and learning. *Educational Leadership, 57*(5), 13–18.

Andrade, H. L. (2010). Students as the definitive source of formative assessment: Academic self-assessment and the self-regulation of learning. In H. Andrade & G. Cizek (Eds.), *Handbook of formative assessment* (pp. 90–105). Routledge.

Andrade, H. L. (2018). Feedback in the context of self-assessment. In A. A. Lipnevich & J. K. Smith (Eds.), *The Cambridge handbook of instructional feedback* (pp. 145–168). Cambridge University Press.

Andrade, H. L., Brookhart, S. M., & Yu, E. C. (2021). Classroom assessment as co-regulated learning: A systematic review. *Frontiers in Education, 6*, 751168.

Andrade, H. L., Du, Y., & Wang, X. (2008). Putting rubrics to the test: The effect of a model, criteria generation, and rubric-referenced self-assessment on elementary school students' writing. *Educational Measurement: Issues and Practice, 27*(2), 3–13.

Andrade, H. L., & Heritage, M. (2017). *Using formative assessment to enhance learning, achievement, and academic self-regulation* (1st ed.). Routledge.

Andrade, H. L., & Valtcheva, A. (2009). Promoting learning and achievement through self-assessment. *Theory Into Practice, 48*, 12–19.

Apple, M. W. (2011). *Education and power* (1st ed.). Routledge.

August, D. (2018). Educating English language learners: A review of the latest research. *American Educator, 42*(3), 4.

Baxter, P., & Norman, G. (2011). Self-assessment or self deception? A lack of association between nursing students' self-assessment and performance. *Journal of Advanced Nursing, 67*, 2406–2413.

Beaulieu, C. (2004). Intercultural study of personal space: A case study. *Journal of Applied Social Psychology, 34*(4), 794–805.

Bensman, D. (2000). *Central Park East and its graduates: Learning by heart.* Teachers College Press.

Biggs, J., & Collis, K. (1982). *A system for evaluating learning outcomes: The SOLO taxonomy.* Academic Press.

Black, P., Harrison, C., Lee, C., Marshall, B., & Wiliam, D. (2003). *Assessment for learning: Putting it into practice.* Open University Press.

Bloom, B. S., Engelhart, M. D., Furst, E. J., Hill, W. H., & Krathwohl, D. R. (1956). *Taxonomy of educational objectives handbook I: The cognitive domain.* David McKay.

Boekaerts, M. (1999). Self-regulated learning: Where we are today. *International Journal of Educational Research, 31*, 445–457.

Boon, S. I. (2016). Increasing the uptake of peer feedback in primary school writing: Findings from an action research enquiry. *Education 3-13, 44*(2), 212–225.

Borrero, N., & Sanchez, G. (2017). Enacting culturally relevant pedagogy: Asset mapping in urban classrooms. *Teaching Education, 28*(3), 279–295.

Bourke, R. (2016). Liberating the learner through self-assessment. *Cambridge Journal of Education, 46*(1), 97–111.

Brandmo, C., Panadero, E., & Hopfenbeck, T. N. (2020). Bridging classroom assessment and self-regulated learning. *Assessment in Education: Principles, Policy & Practice, 27*(4), 319–331.

Bransford, J. D., Brown, A. L., & Cocking, R. R. (2000). *How people learn* (Vol. 11). National Academy Press.

Brookhart, S. M. (2007). Expanding views about formative classroom assessment: A review of the literature. In J. H. McMillan (Ed.), *Formative classroom assessment: Theory into practice* (pp. 43–62). Teachers College Press.

Brookhart, S. M. (2017). *How to give effective feedback to your students.* ASCD.

Brown, A. L., & Campione, J. C. (1996). Psychological theory and the design of innovative learning environments: On procedures, principles, and systems. In L. Schauble & R. Glaser (Eds.), *Innovations for learning: New environments for education* (pp. 289–325). Lawrence Erlbaum Associates.

Brown, A. L., & Campione, J. C. (1998). Designing a community of young learners: Theoretical and practical lessons. In N. Lambert & B. McCombs (Eds.), *How students learn: Reforming schools through learner-centered education* (pp. 153–186). American Psychological Association.

Brown, A. L., Campione, J. C., Webber, L. S., & McGilly, K. (1992). Interactive learning environments: A new look at assessment and instruction. In B. R. Gifford & M. C. O'Connor (Eds.), *Changing assessments* (pp. 121–212). Kluwer Academic.

Brown, G. T., & Harris, L. R. (2013). Student self-assessment. In J. H. McMillan (Ed.), *SAGE handbook of research on classroom assessment* (pp. 367–393). SAGE.

Bruno, I., & Santos, L. (2010). Written comments as a form of feedback. *Studies in Educational Evaluation, 36*(3), 111–120.

Burns, M. (2010). Snapshots of student misunderstandings. *Educational Leadership, 67*(5), 18–22.

Butler, R. (1987). Task-involving and ego-involving properties of evaluation: Effects of different feedback conditions on motivational perceptions, interest, and performance. *Journal of Educational Psychology, 79*(4), 474–482.

California Collaborative for Educational Excellence (CCEE). (2019). *CCEE pilot partner continuous improvement: Resources for LEA's continuous improvement effort, September 2017–June 2019.* Author.

Carless, D. (2019). Feedback loops and the longer-term: Towards feedback spirals. *Assessment & Evaluation in Higher Education, 44*(5), 705–714.

Chan, M. (2020). A multilevel SEM study of classroom talk on cooperative learning and academic achievement: Does cooperative scaffolding matter? *International Journal of Educational Research, 101*, 101564.

Christophel, D. M., & Gorham, J. (1995). A test–retest analysis of student motivation, teacher immediacy, and perceived sources of motivation and demotivation in college classes. *Communication Education, 44*, 292–316.

Claesgens, J., Scalise, K., Wilson, M., & Stacy, A. (2009). Mapping student understanding in chemistry: The perspectives of chemists. *Science Education, 93*(1), 56–85.

Coburn, C. E. (2003). Rethinking scale: Moving beyond numbers to deep and lasting change. *Educational Researcher, 32*(6), 3–12.

Cohen, E. G., & Lotan, R. A. (Eds.). (1997). *Working for equity in heterogeneous classrooms: Sociological theory in practice.* Teachers College Press.

Cohen, E. G., Lotan, R. A., & Leechor, C. (1989). Can classrooms learn? *Sociology of Education, 62*, 75–94.

Cohen, E. G., Lotan, R. A., Scarloss, B. A., & Arellano, A. R. (1999). Complex instruction: Equity in cooperative learning classrooms. *Theory Into Practice, 38*(2), 80–86.

Cowie, B. (2005a). Pupil commentary on assessment for learning. *Curriculum Journal, 16*(2), 137–151.

Cowie, B. (2005b). Student commentary on classroom assessment in science: A sociocultural interpretation. *International Journal of Science Education, 27*(2), 199–214.

Cuban, L. (1990). Reforming again, again, and again. *Educational Researcher, 19*(1), 3–13.

Darling-Hammond, L. (1996). The right to learn and the advancement of teaching: Research, policy, and practice for democratic education. *Educational Researcher, 25*(6), 5–17.

Darling-Hammond, L. (1997). *The right to learn: A blueprint for creating schools that work.* Jossey-Bass.

Darling-Hammond, L. (2006). Securing the right to learn: Policy and practice for powerful teaching and learning. *Educational Researcher, 35*(7), 13–24.

Darling-Hammond, L., & Adamson, F. (2014). *Beyond the bubble test: How performance assessments support 21st century learning.* Jossey-Bass & Pfeiffer Imprints, Wiley.

Darling-Hammond, L., Ancess, J., & Falk, B. (1995). *Authentic assessment in action: Studies of schools and students at work.* Teachers College Press.

Darling-Hammond, L., Flook, L., Cook-Harvey, C., Barron, B., & Osher, D. (2020). Implications for educational practice of the science of learning and development. *Applied Developmental Science, 24*(2), 97–140.

De Graz, L., Valcke, M., & Roozen, I. (2012). How effective are self- and peer assessment of oral presentation skills compared with teachers' assessments? *Active Learning in Higher Education, 13*, 129–142.

Dewey, J. (1900/1990). *The school and society.* University of Chicago Press.

Dewey, J. (1902). *The child and the curriculum.* University of Chicago Press.

Dewey, J. (1903). Democracy in education. *The Elementary School Teacher, 4*(4), 193–204.

Dewey, J. (1910). *How we think.* D. C. Heath & Co. Publishers.

Dewey, J. (1916). *Democracy and education.* Macmillan.

Dewey, J. (1920). *Reconstruction in philosophy.* H. Holt and Company.

Dewey, J. (1923). *Democracy and education: An introduction to the philosophy of education.* Macmillan.

Dewey, J. (1933). How we think: A restatement of the relation of reflective thinking to the educative process. In J. Boydston (Ed.), *The later works of John Dewey* (Vol. 8, pp. 105–352). Southern Illinois University Press.

Dewey, J. (1938). Experience and education. In J. Boydston (Ed.), *The later works of John Dewey* (Vol. 13, pp. 1–62). Southern Illinois University Press.

Dignath, C., Büttner, G., & Langfeldt, H. (2008). How can primary school students learn self-regulated learning strategies most effectively? A meta-analysis on self-regulation training programmes. *Educational Research Review, 3*(2), 101–129.

diSessa, A. (1983). Phenomenology and the evolution of intuition. In D. Gentner & A. L. Stevens (Eds.), *Mental models* (pp. 15–33). Erlbaum.

Duckor, B. (2014). Formative assessment in seven good moves. *Educational Leadership*, *71*(6), 28–32.

Duckor, B., & Holmberg, C. (2017). *Mastering formative assessment moves: 7 high-leverage practices to advance student learning*. ASCD.

Duckor, B., & Holmberg, C. (2021a). *Assessment for learning to support student achievement: Module 1 on introduction to FA moves framework*. California Collaborative for Educational Excellence.

Duckor, B., & Holmberg, C. (2021b). *Assessment for learning to support student achievement: Module 2 on priming*. California Collaborative for Educational Excellence.

Duckor, B., & Holmberg, C. (2021c). *Assessment for learning to support student achievement: Module 3 on posing*. California Collaborative for Educational Excellence.

Duckor, B., & Holmberg, C. (2021d). *Assessment for learning to support student achievement: Module 4 on pausing*. California Collaborative for Educational Excellence.

Duckor, B., & Holmberg, C. (2021e). *Assessment for learning to support student achievement: Module 5 on probing*. California Collaborative for Educational Excellence.

Duckor, B., & Holmberg, C. (2021f). *Assessment for learning to support student achievement: Module 6 on bouncing*. California Collaborative for Educational Excellence.

Duckor, B., & Holmberg, C. (2021g). *Assessment for learning to support student achievement: Module 7 on tagging*. California Collaborative for Educational Excellence.

Duckor, B., & Holmberg, C. (2021h). *Assessment for learning to support student achievement: Module 8 on binning*. California Collaborative for Educational Excellence.

Duckor, B., & Holmberg, C. (2021i). *Assessment for learning to support student achievement: Module 9 on closing opportunity gaps with the FA moves framework*. California Collaborative for Educational Excellence.

Duckor, B. & Holmberg, C. (2022). *Differentiated formative feedback for all: Learning from secondary math and science teachers about deep equity during a pandemic* [Monograph]. *CCTE Fall Research Monograph*. California Council for Teacher Education.

Duckor, B., Holmberg, C., & Rossi Becker, J. (2017). Making moves: Formative assessment in mathematics. *Mathematics Teaching in the Middle School*, *22*(6), 334–342.

Duckor, B., Holmberg, C., & Rossi Becker, B. (2018). Focusing on moves-based formative assessment to increase equity of voice and academic language use in middle school mathematics: A case for video-based professional development. In S. B. Martens & M. M. Caskey (Eds.), *The handbook of research in middle level education: Preparing middle level educators for 21st century schools: Enduring beliefs, changing times, evolving practices* (pp. 335–363). Information Age.

Duckor, B., & Perlstein, D. (2014). Assessing habits of mind: Teaching to the test at Central Park East Secondary School. *Teachers College Record*, *116*(2), 1–33.

Duncan, R. G., & Hmelo-Silver, C. E. (2009). Learning progressions: Aligning curriculum, instruction, and assessment. *Journal of Research in Science Teaching*, *46*, 606–609.

Ferguson, P. (2011). Student perceptions of quality feedback in teacher education. *Assessment & Evaluation in Higher Education*, *36*(1), 51–62.

Filius, R. M., de Kleijn, R. A., Uijl, S. G., Prins, F. J., van Rijen, H. V., & Grobbee, D. E. (2018). Strengthening dialogic peer feedback aiming for deep learning in SPOCs. *Computers & Education*, *125*, 86–100.

Foner, P. S. (Ed.). (1949). *The freedom to learn. W.E.B. Du Bois speaks*. Pathfinder.

Frikha, M., Chaâri, N., Elghoul, Y., Mohamed-Ali, H. H., & Zinkovsky, A. V. (2019). Effects of combined versus singular verbal or haptic feedback on acquisition, retention, difficulty, and competence perceptions in motor learning. *Perceptual and Motor Skills*, *126*(4), 713–732.

Fullan, M., & Quinn, J. (2015). *Coherence: The right drivers in action for schools, districts, and systems*. Corwin.

Fullan, M., Quinn, J., & McEachen, J. (2018). *Deep learning: Engage the world change the world*. Corwin.

Fullan, M., & Rincón-Gallardo, S. (2017). *California's golden opportunity: Taking stock: Leadership from the middle*. Retrieved from https://michaelfullan.ca/wp-content/uploads/2017/09/17_Californias-Golden-Opportunity-Taking-Stock-FinalAug31.pdf

Furger, R. C., Hernández, L. E., & Darling-Hammond, L. (2019). *The California way: The Golden State's quest to build an equitable and excellent education system*. Learning Policy Institute.

Gallimore, R., & Tharp, R. (1990). Teaching mind in society: Teaching, schooling, and literate discourse. In L. C. Moll (Ed.), *Vygotsky and education: Instructional implications and applications of sociohistorical psychology* (pp. 175–205). Cambridge University Press.

Gan, M. J., & Hattie, J. (2014). Prompting secondary students' use of criteria, feedback specificity and feedback levels during an investigative task. *Instructional Science, 42*(6), 861–878.

Gardner, H. E. (2011). *Frames of mind: The theory of multiple intelligences* (3rd ed.). Basic Books.

Gaynor, P. (1981). The effect of feedback delay on retention of computer-based mathematical material. *Journal of Computer-Based Instruction, 8*(2), 28–32.

Gielen, S., Dochy, F., Onghena, P., Struyven, K., & Smeets, S. (2011). Goals of peer assessment and their associated quality concepts. *Studies in Higher Education, 36*(6), 719–735.

Gielen, S., Peeters, E., Dochy, F., Onghena, P., & Struyven, K. (2010). Improving the effectiveness of peer feedback for learning. *Learning and Instruction, 20*(4), 304–315.

Gillies, R. M. (2008). The effects of cooperative learning on junior high school students' behaviours, discourse and learning during a science-based learning activity. *School Psychology International, 29*(3), 328–347.

Gillies, R. M., & Ashman, A. (1998). Behavior and interactions of children in cooperative groups in lower and middle elementary grades. *Journal of Educational Psychology, 90*, 746–757.

Glover, C., & Brown, E. (2006). Written feedback for students: Too much, too detailed or too incomprehensible to be effective? *Bioscience Education, 7*(1), 1–16.

Gold, J. (Producer & Director), & Lanzoni, M. (Ed.). (1993). *Graduation by portfolio: Central Park East Secondary School* [Video]. 29th Street Video.

Goldstein, L. (2006). Feedback and revision in second language writing: Contextual, teacher and student variables. In K. Hyland & F. Hyland (Eds.), *Feedback in second language writing: Contexts and issues* (pp. 185–205). Cambridge University Press.

Graham, S. (2018). Instructional feedback in writing. In A. A. Lipnevich & J. K. Smith (Eds.), *The Cambridge handbook of instructional feedback* (pp. 145–168). Cambridge University Press.

Great Schools Partnership. (2013). *Opportunity gap*. Retrieved from https://www.edglossary.org/opportunity-gap/

Guha, R., Wagner, T., Darling-Hammond, L., Taylor, T., & Curtis, D. (2018). *The promise of performance assessments: Innovations in high school learning and college admission*. Learning Policy Institute.

Guskey, T. R. (2019). Grades versus comments: Research on student feedback. *Phi Delta Kappan, 101*(3), 42–47.

Hacker, D. J., Bol, L., Horgan, D. D., & Rakow, E. A. (2000). Test prediction and performance in a classroom context. *Journal of Educational Psychology, 92*, 160–170.

Hackman, M. Z., & Walker, K. B. (1990). Instructional communication in the televised classroom: The effects of system design and teacher immediacy on student learning and satisfaction. *Communication Education, 39*, 196–206.

Hall, E. T. (1959). *The silent language*. Anchor Books.

Harris, L., Irving, S., & Peterson, E. (2008, December). *Secondary teachers' conceptions of the purpose of assessment and feedback* [Conference presentation]. Annual Conference of the Australian Association for Research in Education, Brisbane, Australia.

Hattie, J., & Clarke, S. (2019). *Visible learning feedback.* Routledge.

Hattie, J., & Timperley, H. (2007). The power of feedback. *Review of Educational Research, 77*(1), 81–112.

Hattie, J., & Zierer, K. (2018). *10 mindframes for visible learning: Teaching for success.* Corwin.

Havnes, A., Smith, K., Dysthe, O., & Ludvigsen, K. (2012). Formative assessment and feedback: Making learning visible. *Studies in Educational Evaluation, 38*(1), 21–27.

Heritage, M. (2008). *Learning progressions: Supporting instruction and formative assessment.* Council of Chief State School Officers. Retrieved from http://www.ccsso.org/Documents/2008/Learning_Progressions_Supporting_2008.pdf

Heritage, M. (2016). Assessment for learning: Co-regulation in and as student–teacher interaction. In D. Laveault & L. Allal (Eds.), *Assessment for learning: Meeting the challenge of implementation* (pp. 327–343). Springer.

Heritage, M., & Wylie, E. C. (2020). *Formative assessment in the disciplines: Framing a continuum of professional learning.* Harvard Education Press.

Higgins, R., Hartley, P., & Skelton, A. (2001). Getting the message across: The problem of communicating assessment feedback. *Teaching in Higher Education, 6*(2), 269–274.

Higgins, R., Hartley, P., & Skelton, A. (2002). The conscientious consumer: Reconsidering the role of assessment feedback in student learning. *Studies in Higher Education, 27*(1), 53–64.

Hollins, E. (2015). *Culture in school learning: Revealing the deep meaning* (3rd ed.). Routledge.

Holmberg, C., & Duckor, B. (2018). Reframing classroom assessment. *California English, 23*(2), 6–9.

Holmberg, C., & Muwwakkil, J. (2020). Conversation in the classroom. *Phi Delta Kappan, 101*(5), 25–29.

Hoogerheide, V., Vink, M., Finn, B., Raes, A. K., & Paas, F. (2018). How to bring the news... peak-end effects in children's affective responses to peer assessments of their social behavior. *Cognition and Emotion, 32*(5), 1114–1121.

Hounsell, D., McCune, V., Hounsell, J., & Litjens, J. (2008). The quality of guidance and feedback to students. *Higher Education Research and Development, 27*(1), 55–67.

Hoy, A. W., & Davis, H. A. (2006). Teacher self-efficacy and its influence on the achievement of adolescents. In F. Pajares & T. Urdan (Eds.), *Adolescence and education: Self-efficacy beliefs of adolescents* (Vol. 5, pp. 117–137). Information Age.

Hyatt, D. F. (2005). "Yes, a very good point!": A critical genre analysis of a corpus of feedback commentaries on Master of Education assignments. *Teaching in Higher Education, 10*(3), 339–353.

Hyland, K. (2013). Student perceptions of hidden messages in teacher written feedback. *Studies in Educational Evaluation, 39*(3), 180–187.

Institute for Manufacturing (IfM). (2016). *Just-in-time manufacturing.* Retrieved from https://www.ifm.eng.cam.ac.uk/research/dstools/jit-just-in-time-manufacturing/

Jansen, R. S., van Leeuwen, A., Janssen, J., Jak, S., & Kester, L. (2019). Self-regulated learning partially mediates the effect of self-regulated learning interventions on achievement in higher education: A meta-analysis. *Educational Research Review, 28*, 100292.

Kablan, Z. (2014). Comparison of individual answer and group answer with and without structured peer assessment. *Research in Science & Technological Education, 32*(3), 251–262.

Kahneman, D., Fredrickson, D. L., Schreiber, C. A., & Redelmeier, D. A. (1993). When more pain is preferred to less: Adding a better end. *Psychological Science, 4*, 401–405.

Kelley, D. H., & Gorham, J. (1988). Effects of immediacy on recall of information. *Communication Education, 37*, 198–207.

Kilpatrick, W. H. (1918). The project method. *Teachers College Record, 19*(4), 319–335.

King, M. L., Jr. (1963). *Letter from Birmingham City Jail.* Retrieved from https://www

.africa.upenn.edu/Articles_Gen/Letter_Birmingham.html

Kingston, N., & Nash, B. (2011). Formative assessment: A meta-analysis and a call for research. *Educational Measurement: Issues and Practice, 30*(4), 28–37.

Kliebard, H. M. (2004). *The struggle for the American curriculum, 1893–1958* (3rd ed.). Routledge.

Knoll, M. (1995). The project method—Its origin and international influence. In H. Rohrs & V. Lenhart (Eds.), *Progressive education across the continents* (pp. 307–318). Peter Lang.

Ladson-Billings, G. (1995). Toward a theory of culturally relevant pedagogy. *American Educational Research Journal, 32*(3), 465–491.

Ladson-Billings, G. (2014). Culturally relevant pedagogy 2.0: a.k.a. the remix. *Harvard Educational Review, 84*(1), 74–84.

Lee, H., Chung, H. Q., Zhang, Y., Abedi, J., & Warschauer, M. (2020). The effectiveness and features of formative assessment in US K–12 education: A systematic review. *Applied Measurement in Education, 33*(2), 124–140.

Lew, M. D. N., Alwis, W. A. M., & Schmidt, H. G. (2010). Accuracy of students' self-assessment and their beliefs about its utility. *Assessment & Evaluation in Higher Education, 35*, 135–156.

Li, L., Liu, X., & Steckelberg, A. L. (2010). Assessor or assessee: How student learning improves by giving and receiving peer feedback. *British Journal of Educational Technology, 41*(3), 525–536.

Lieberman, A., Falk, B., & Alexander, B. (2007). A culture in the making: Leadership in learner-centered schools. In A. Danzig, K. Borman, B. Jones, & W. Wright (Eds.), *Learner-centered leadership: Research, policy, and practice* (pp. 21–42). Routledge.

Lin, T-J., Jadallah, M., Anderson, R. C., Baker, A. R., Nguyen-Jahiel, K., Kim, I-H., Kuo, L-J., Miller, B. W., Dong, T., & Wu, X. (2015). Less is more: Teachers' influence during peer collaboration. *Journal of Educational Psychology, 107*(2), 609–629.

Lortie, D. (1975). *Schoolteacher: A sociological study*. University of Chicago Press.

Lucariello, J., & Naff, D. (2010). *How do I get my students over their alternative conceptions (misconceptions) for learning?* American Psychological Association. Retrieved from http://www.apa.org/education/k12/misconceptions.aspx

Lui, A. M., & Andrade, H. L. (2022). The next black box of formative assessment: A model of the internal mechanisms of feedback processing. *Frontiers in Education, 7*, 751548.

Martin, L., & Mottet, T. P. (2011). The effect of instructor nonverbal immediacy behaviors and feedback sensitivity on Hispanic students' affective learning outcomes in ninth-grade writing conferences. *Communication Education, 60*(1), 1–19.

Mason, B. J., & Bruning, R. (2001). *Providing feedback in a computer-based instruction: What the research tells us*. Center for Instructional Innovation, University of Nebraska-Lincoln.

McCroskey, J. C., & Richmond, V. P. (1992). Increasing teacher influence through immediacy. In V. P. Richmond & J. C. McCroskey (Eds.), *Power in the classroom: Communication, control, and concern* (pp. 101–121). Routledge.

Meier, D. (1995). *The power of their ideas: Lessons for America from a small school in Harlem*. Beacon.

Meier, D., & Schwartz, P. (1995). Central Park East Secondary School: The hard part is making it happen. In M. Apple & J. Beane (Eds.), *Democratic schools* (pp. 26–40). ASCD.

Merry, S., & Orsmond, P. (2008). Students' attitudes to and usage of academic feedback provided via audio files. *Bioscience Education, 11*(1), 1–11.

Murray, J., Gasson, N. R., & Smith, J. K. (2018). Toward a taxonomy of written feedback messages. In A. A. Lipnevich & J. K. Smith (Eds.), *The Cambridge handbook of instructional feedback* (pp. 79–96). Cambridge University Press.

National Research Council (NRC). (2001). *Knowing what students know: The science and design of educational assessment* (Committee on the Foundations of Assessment, J. Pellegrino, N. Chudowsky, & R. Glaser, Eds.). National Academies Press.

National Research Council (NRC). (2012). *Education for life and work: Developing transferable knowledge and skills in the 21st century*. National Academies Press.

National Science Teaching Association. (2022). *How to design a performance task*. Author.

Newmann, F. M. (1996). *Authentic achievement: Restructuring schools for intellectual quality*. Jossey-Bass.

Nielsen, K. (2014). Self-assessment methods in writing instruction: A conceptual framework, successful practices and essential strategies. *Journal of Research in Reading, 37*, 1–16.

Nitko, A. J., & Brookhart, S. M. (2019). *Educational assessment of students* (8th ed.). Pearson Merrill Prentice Hall.

Nottingham, J., & Nottingham, J. (2017). *Challenging learning through feedback: How to get the type, tone, and quality of feedback right every time*. Corwin.

Page, E. B. (1958). Teacher comments and student performance: A seventy-four classroom experiment in school motivation. *Journal of Educational Psychology, 49*(2), 173–181.

Pajares, M. F. (1992). Teachers' beliefs and educational research: Cleaning up a messy construct. *Review of Educational Research, 62*(3), 307–332.

Palladino, J., & Shepard, L. (2022). Authentic assessment embedded in project-based learning. In A. York, K. Welner, & L. M. Kelley (Eds.), *Schools of opportunity*. Teachers College Press.

Panadero, E., Brown, G. T. L., & Strijbos, J. W. (2016). The future of student self-assessment: A review of known unknowns and potential directions. *Educational Psychology Review, 28*, 803–830.

Panadero, E., Jonsson, A., & Botella, B. (2017). Effects of self-assessment on self-regulated learning and self-efficacy: Four meta-analyses. *Educational Research Review, 22*, 74–98.

Panadero, E., Jonsson, A., & Strijbos, J-W. (2016). Scaffolding self-regulated learning through self-assessment and peer assessment: Guidelines for classroom implementation. In D. Laveault & L. Allal (Eds.), *Assessment for learning: Meeting the challenge of implementation* (pp. 311–326). Springer International.

Panadero, E., Tapia, J. A., & Huertas, J. A. (2012). Rubrics and self-assessment scripts effects on self-regulation, learning and self-efficacy in secondary education. *Learning and Individual Differences, 22*(6), 806–813.

Park, S., Hironaka, S., Carver, P., & Nordstrum, L. (2013). *Continuous improvement in education: Advancing teaching—improving learning*. Carnegie Foundation for the Advancement of Teaching.

PBL Works. (2022). *What is PBL?* Retrieved from https://www.pblworks.org/what-is-pbl

Pellegrino, J. (2017). Teaching, learning and assessing 21st century skills. In S. Guerriero (Ed.), *Pedagogical knowledge and the changing nature of the teaching profession* (pp. 223–251). OECD Publishing.

Pintrich, P. R. (2000). The role of goal orientation in self-regulated learning. In M. Boekaerts, P. Pintrich, & M. Zeidner (Eds.), *Handbook of self-regulation* (pp. 452–502). Academic Press.

Plax, T. G., Kearney, P., McCroskey, J. C., & Richmond, V. P. (1986). Power in the classroom VI: Verbal control strategies, nonverbal immediacy, and affective learning. *Communication Education, 35*, 43–55.

Popham, W. J. (1997). What's wrong—and what's right—with rubrics. *Educational Leadership, 55*(2), 72.

Popham, W. J. (2007). All about accountability/grain size: The unresolved riddle. *Educational Leadership, 64*(4), 80–81.

Price, M., Handley, K., Millar, J., & O'Donovan, B. (2010). Feedback: All that effort, but what is the effect? *Assessment & Evaluation in Higher Education, 35*(3), 277–289.

Quinn, J., McEachen, J., Fullan, M., Gardner, M., & Drummy, M. (2019). *Dive into deep learning: Tools for engagement*. Corwin.

Ramaprasad, A. (1983). On the definition of feedback. *Behavioral Science, 28*(1), 4–13.

Ravitch, D. (2001). *Left back: A century of battles over school reform*. Simon and Schuster.

Resnick, L. B., & Resnick, D. P. (1992). Assessing the thinking curriculum: New tools for educational reform. In B. R. Gifford & M. C. Connor (Eds.), *Changing assessments: Alternative views of aptitude, achievement, and instruction* (pp. 37–75). Kluwer Academic.

Richmond, V. P., Gorham, J., & McCroskey, J. C. (1987). The relationship between selected immediacy behaviors and cognitive learning. In M. McLaughlin (Ed.), *Communication yearbook* (Vol. 10, pp. 574–590). SAGE.

Roberts, L., & Sipusic, M. (Director). (1999). *Moderation in all things: A class act* [Film]. Berkeley Evaluation and Assessment Center, Graduate School of Education, University of California, Berkeley.

Roberts, L., Wilson, M., & Draney, K. (1997). The SEPUP assessment system: An overview. (BEAR report series. SA-97-1). Berkeley, CA: University of California.

Roper, W. J. (1977). Feedback in computer assisted instruction. *Programmed Learning and Educational Technology, 14*(1), 43–49.

Rothman, R. (1995). *Measuring up: Standards, assessment, and school reform.* Jossey-Bass.

Rotsaert, T., Panadero, E., Schellens, T., & Raes, A. (2018). "Now you know what you're doing right and wrong!" Peer feedback quality in synchronous peer assessment in secondary education. *European Journal of Psychology of Education, 33*(2), 255–275.

Rowe, A. (2011). The personal dimension in teaching: Why students value feedback. *International Journal of Educational Management, 25*(4), 343–360.

Ruiz-Primo, M. A., & Li, M. (2013). Examining formative feedback in the classroom context: New research perspectives. In J. H. McMillan (Ed.), *Handbook of research on classroom assessment* (pp. 215–232). SAGE.

Sadler, D. R. (1987). Specifying and promulgating achievement standards. *Oxford Review of Education, 13*(2), 191–209.

Sadler, D. R. (1989). Formative assessment and the design of instructional systems. *Instructional Science, 18*, 119–144.

Sadler, D. R. (2010). Beyond feedback: Developing student capability in complex appraisal. *Assessment & Evaluation in Higher Education, 35*, 535–550.

Safir, S., & Dugan, J. (2021). *Street data: A next-generation model for equity, pedagogy, and school transformation.* Corwin.

Schuldt, L. C. (2019). Feedback in action: Examining teachers' oral feedback to elementary writers. *Teaching and Teacher Education, 83*, 64–76.

Shepard, L. A. (2000). The role of assessment in a learning culture. *Educational Researcher, 29*(7), 4–14.

Shepard, L. A. (2005). Linking formative assessment to scaffolding. *Educational Leadership, 63*(3), 66–70.

Shepard, L. A., Penuel, W. R., & Davidson, K. L. (2017). Design principles for new systems of assessment. *Phi Delta Kappan, 98*(6), 47–52.

Shulman, L. (1986). Those who understand: Knowledge growth in teaching. *Educational Researcher, 15*(2), 4–14.

Shulman, L. (1987). Knowledge and teaching: Foundations of the new reform. *Harvard Educational Review, 57*(1), 1–23.

Shute, V. J. (2008). Focus on formative feedback. *Review of Educational Research, 78*(1), 153–189.

Sigrist, R., Rauter, G., Riener, R., & Wolf, P. (2013). Augmented visual, auditory, haptic, and multimodal feedback in motor learning: A review. *Psychonomic Bulletin & Review, 20*, 21–53.

Sizer, T. R. (1996). *Horace's hope: What works for the American high school.* Houghton Mifflin.

Sizer, T. R. (2013). *Places for learning, places for joy: Speculations on American school reform.* Harvard University Press.

Skipper, Y., & Douglas, K. (2012). Is no praise good praise? Effects of positive feedback on children's and university students' responses to subsequent failures. *British Journal of Educational Psychology, 82*(2), 327–339.

Small, M., & Lin, A. (2018). Instructional feedback in mathematics. In A. A. Lipnevich & J. K. Smith (Eds.), *The Cambridge handbook of instructional feedback* (pp. 79–96). Cambridge University Press.

Soderstrom, N. C., & Bjork, R. A. (2015). Learning versus performance: An integrative review. *Perspective Psychological Science, 10*(2), 176–199.

Stoll, L., & Schultz, S. E. (2019). How to design a performance task. *Science Scope, 42*(7), 40–45.

Tan, K., & Wong, H. M. (2018). Assessment feedback in primary schools in Singapore and beyond. In A. Lipnevich & J. Smith (Eds.), *The Cambridge handbook of instructional feedback* (pp. 123–144). Cambridge University Press.

Tevis, W. (1983). *The queen's gambit.* Vintage.

Tharp, R. G., & Gallimore, R. (1991). *Rousing minds to life: Teaching, learning, and schooling in social context.* Cambridge University Press.

Tobin, K. (1980). The effect of an extended teacher wait-time on science achievement. *Journal of Research in Science Teaching, 17*(5), 469–475.

Tobin, K. (1986). Effects of teacher wait time on discourse characteristics in mathematics and language arts classes. *American Educational Research Journal, 23*(2), 191–200.

Tobin, K. (1987). The role of wait time in higher cognitive level learning. *Review of Educational Research, 57*(1), 69–95.

Topping, K. J. (2010). Peers as a source of formative assessment. In H. L. Andrade & G. J. Cizek (Eds.), *Handbook of formative assessment* (pp. 61–74). Routledge.

Torrance, H. (1995a). The role of assessment in educational reform. In H. Torrance (Ed.), *Evaluating authentic assessment* (pp. 144–156). Open University Press.

Torrance, H. (1995b). Teacher involvement in new approaches to assessment. In H. Torrance (Ed.), *Evaluating authentic assessment* (pp. 44–56). Open University Press.

Tyack, D. B. (1974). *The one best system: A history of American urban education* (Vol. 95). Harvard University Press.

Tyack, D. B., & Cuban, L. (1995). *Tinkering toward utopia: A century of public school reform.* Harvard University Press.

Underwood, J., & Tregidgo, A. (2006). Improving student writing through effective feedback: Best practices and recommendations. *Journal of Teaching Writing, 22,* 73–98.

Van der Schaaf, M. F., Baartman, L. K. J., Prins, F. J., Oosterbaan, A., & Schaap, H. (2011). Feedback dialogues that stimulate students' reflective thinking. *Scandinavian Journal of Educational Research, 57*(3), 227–245.

Van Helvoort, A. A. J. (2012). How adult students in information studies use a scoring rubric for the development of their literacy skills. *Journal of Academic Librarianship, 38,* 165–171.

Van Ryzin, M. (2010). Secondary school advisors as mentors and secondary attachment figures. *Journal of Community Psychology, 38*(2), 131–154.

Vygotsky, L. S. (1978). *Mind in society: The development of higher psychological processes.* Harvard University Press.

Waks, L. J. (1997). The project method in postindustrial education. *Journal of Curriculum Studies, 29*(4), 391–406.

Walqui, A., & Heritage, M. (2018). Meaningful classroom talk: Supporting English learners' oral language development. *American Educator, 42*(3), 18.

Weaver, M. R. (2006). Do students value feedback? Student perceptions of tutors' written responses. *Assessment & Evaluation in Higher Education, 31*(3), 379–394.

Whitaker, J. A. (2011). High school band students' and directors' perceptions of verbal and nonverbal teaching behaviors. *Journal of Research in Music Education, 59,* 290–309.

Wiggins, G. (1993a). Assessment: Authenticity, context, and validity. *Phi Delta Kappan, 75*(3), 200–214.

Wiggins, G. (1993b). *Educative assessment: Designing assessments to inform and improve student performance.* Jossey-Bass.

Wiggins, G. (2012). Seven keys to effective feedback. *Educational Leadership, 70*(1), 11–16.

Wiggins, G., & McTighe, J. (1998). Backward design. In G. Wiggins & J. McTighe (Eds.), *Understanding by design* (pp. 13–34). ASCD.

Wiggins, G. P., & McTighe, J. (2005). *Understanding by design* (2nd ed.). ASCD.

Wiliam, D. (2018). Feedback: At the heart of—but definitely not all of—formative assessment. In A. A. Lipnevich & J. K. Smith (Eds.), *The Cambridge handbook of instructional feedback* (pp. 3–28). Cambridge University Press.

Wilson, M. (2005). *Constructing measures.* Lawrence Erlbaum Associates.

Wilson, M. (2009). Measuring progressions: Assessment structures underlying a learning progression. *Journal of Research in Science Teaching, 46,* 716–730.

Wilson, M., & Sloane, K. (2000). From principles to practice: An embedded assessment system. *Applied Measurement in Education, 13*(2), 181–208.

Wisniewski, B., Zierer, K., & Hattie, J. (2020). The power of feedback revisited: A meta-analysis of educational feedback research. *Frontiers in Psychology, 10,* 3087.

Witt, P. L., & Wheeless, L. R. (2001). An experimental study of teachers' verbal and nonverbal immediacy and students' affective and cognitive learning. *Communication Education, 50*(4), 327–342.

Wong, H. M. (2017). Implementing self-assessment in Singapore primary schools: Effects on students' perceptions of self-assessment. *Pedagogies: An International Journal, 12*(4), 391–409.

Wong, H. M., Safii, L., & Kwek, D. (2019). *Seeing self-assessment and teacher feedback through students' lenses: Implementation of self-assessment and investigation of feedback in lower primary classrooms* (NIE Research Brief Series No. 19–014). National Institute of Education.

Wulf, S. (1997, October 27). Teach our children well (it can be done). *Time.* Retrieved from http://www.cnn.com/ALLPOLITICS/1997/10/20/time/special.teaching.html

Yeager, D. S., Purdie-Vaughns, V., Garcia, J., Apfel, N., Brzustoski, P., Master, A., Hessert, W. T., Williams, M. E., & Cohen, G. L. (2013). Breaking the cycle of mistrust: Wise interventions to provide critical feedback across the racial divide. *Journal of Experimental Psychology: General, 143*(2), 804–824.

Zacharia, Z. C. (2015). Examining whether touch sensory feedback is necessary for science learning through experimentation: A literature review of two different lines of research across K–16. *Educational Research Review, 16,* 116–137.

Zwiers, J. (2007). *Building academic language: Essential practices for content classrooms.* Jossey Bass.

Zwiers, J. (2019a). *The communication effect: How to enhance learning by building ideas and bridging information gaps.* Corwin.

Zwiers, J. (2019b). *Next steps with academic conversations: New ideas for improving learning with classroom talk.* Stenhouse.

Index

Academic language
  self-driven feedback and, 87
  sentence starters for, 71–72
  spoken feedback and, 260, 261
  whole class feedback and, 132, 142
  written feedback and, 226
Affective learning, 284
AfL (assessment for learning), 4, 27, 152–153
All Things in Moderation, 72–74
Ancess, J., 133
Andrade, H. L., 84
Answer keys, scoring guides compared with, 69–70
Asher, James, 287
Assessment activities, 9, 18. *See also* Self-assessment for students; Self-assessment for teachers
Assessment for learning (AfL), 4, 27, 152–153
Asynchronous versus synchronous contexts, 51–54, 217–218, 242–243
Audio messaging, 103, 189, 269
Augmented feedback, 283
Authenticity, 157–158

Back-of-the-envelope method, 139–140
Backward design, 20
Binning for feedback, 130–132, 138–139, 178f, 191
Black, P., 127
Bloom's taxonomy, 13
Body-kinesthetic feedback. *See* Nonverbal feedback
Body-kinesthetic skills, 282–283
Botella, B., 83
Bouncing, 178f
Brandmo, C., 83–84
Brown, A. L., 190

Campione, J. C., 190
Central Park East Secondary School (CPESS), 92–97
Checking in, 188
Clarke, Shirley, 256
Coaching, 44, 92, 94
Cognitive load, 214, 255t, 281t
Cohen, E. G., 152

Collaboration, reminders about, 118
Configurations
  challenges and opportunities with, 145–146
  defined, 122, 180
  in framework, 123t
  reflection on, 209–210
  See also Individual feedback; Small group feedback; Whole class feedback
Contactless contact, 277, 290. *See also* Nonverbal feedback
Conversations, complexity of, 250–251
Co-regulation, 84, 95, 152
Cowie, B., 187
CPESS (Central Park East Secondary School), 92–97
Crosscutting concepts, 10
Cultural differences in feedback, 286–287
Culture of questioning, 153

Darling-Hammond, Linda, 4, 133
Debriefing, 167, 168f
Deep equity. *See* Equity
Deep learning, 44–45, 68, 250
Democracy, 19
Depth of knowledge (DOK), 13–14
Dessert projects versus main course projects, 19
Dewey, John, 19
Dialogic, defined, 257
Dialogue, defined, 257
Differentiation
  equity and, 120–121
  graphic organizers for, 267–269, 268t
  individual feedback and, 182–183, 185, 205–206
  spoken feedback and, 256
Directionality, 38, 39–40. *See also* Peer-to-peer-driven feedback; Self-driven feedback; Teacher-driven feedback
Discourse analysis, 109–116
DuBois, W. E. B., 3
Duckor, B., 92

Education standards, 9–10
80/20 rule, 52

334

Eliciting information. *See* Three Es of feedback
Emotional flooding, 243
Engagement. *See* Three Es of feedback
English learners (ELs)
    graphic organizers for, 267–269, 268t
    peer-to-peer-driven feedback and, 68, 71–72
    progress guides benefitting, 22
    total physical response and, 287
Equity
    differentiated feedback and, 120–121
    feedback and, 20
    fishbowl and, 105
    individual feedback and, 189
    small group feedback and, 151–152
Essential questions (EQs), habits of mind as, 11
Exemplars, 69, 71, 88t
Exhibitions, 12
Exit tickets, 133, 171, 171f
Extant texts, 216
Extending performance. *See* Three Es of feedback

Falk, B., 133
Feedback
    overview, 31
    cultural differences in, 286–287
    cycles of, 23–28
    importance of, 2–4
    as information exchange, 18
    learning goals and, 8–17
    performance tasks and, 20
    rich, meaningful tasks, 17–20
    See also Formative feedback; Progress guides; *specific configurations, directionalities, and modalities*
Feedback loops
    demands of, 250
    individual feedback and, 177–179, 178f, 188–189
    intersection of during shared project, 25–28, 26f
    multiple modalities and, 276
    peak-end-effect and, 188–189
Feedback parameters, systems thinking and, 17
Feedback-for-doing, 283
Feed-forward feedback, 226–227
First drafts, defined, 26
Fishbowl, equity and, 105
Flip, 77
Formative assessment moves
    overview, 177–178, 178f

    binning for feedback, 130–132, 138–139, 178f, 191
    bouncing, 178f
    pausing, 178f, 251, 257, 258
    probing, 177, 178f, 243–244
    tagging, 178f
    See also Priming
Formative assessors, characteristics of, 260
Formative feedback
    continuous improvement and, 5–6
    data-driven mindset and, 5
    defined, 119
    dialogic approach to analyzing, 110–116
    factors to encourage listening, 144
    importance of, 2–4
    purpose-driven feedback, 7–8
    See also Progress guides; *specific configurations, directionalities, and modalities*
Formative feedback (FF) framework, overview, 6–7, 7f
Formative Feedback Process Model, 25–28, 26f
Frames of Mind (Gardner), 282–283
Freedom to learn, 3, 28

Gardner, Howard, 282–283
Google Docs, 47, 103
Grades, feedback and, 45
Gradual release, 44
Graduation by Portfolio, 11, 95, 97, 104–105, 286
Grain size, 16
Graphic organizers
    for differentiation, 267–269, 268t
    small group feedback and, 157, 169f
    SOLO taxonomy and, 16
Group creation, 154, 157
Group interaction focus, 155, 157–158

Habits of heart, 93
Habits of mind, 5, 11–12, 229. *See also* Self-driven feedback
Haptic feedback. *See* Nonverbal feedback
Hattie, John, 256
Holmberg, C., 250–251
Hopfenbeck, T. N., 83–84

I Do, We Do, You Do, 103
Individual feedback
    overview, 176, 179–181, 181f, 209
    defined, 181–182
    differentiation and, 182–183, 185, 205–206

example of, 198–201
importance of, 204
initiation of, 195–197, 196f
mental model for, 196–197, 196f
misunderstandings or confusion with, 179–180, 187–188
planning for, 183–185t, 183–186, 194
professional learning communities and, 205–208
progress guides for student use, 193–195, 194f
progress guides for teacher use, 190–193, 191–192f
reflection on, 203
relationships as important to, 202
research about, 186–189
scaffolds and guided practice for, 202–204
self-study checklist for, 303
three Es of feedback, 176–179
ticket out the door, 209
Instructional design, backward design for, 20

Jonsson, A., 83
Just-in-time feedback, 23–24

Language
impact of, 118
subject specialties and, 87
tone and, 54, 57, 225–226, 243
total physical response for learners of, 287
See also English learners (ELs)
Learning goals
overview, 2–4, 31
dimensions of, 13
establishing, 8–17
purpose-driven feedback goals, 8–11
SOLO taxonomy and, 14–17, 16f
ticket out the door, 31–33
Learning progressions, 28
Lifelong learning, feedback and, 3
Long-term cycles of feedback, 24–25

Main course projects versus dessert projects, 19
McTighe, J., 20
Metacognitive skills, 188
Minority students, mistrust and, 45–46
Mistrust, feedback and, 45–46
Modalities, 215, 218–219. See also Nonverbal feedback; Spoken feedback; Written feedback
Modeling, 157–158

Moderation process, 72–74
Motor skills hypothesis, 287
Muwwakkil, J., 250–251

National Science Teaching Association, 18
Nonprint texts, 278
Nonverbal communication, 115
Nonverbal feedback
overview, 274–276, 276f, 296
contactless contact, 277, 290
defined, 276–278, 277t
examples of, 287–291
how to give, 285–287
planning for, 279, 280–282t
professional learning communities and, 295–296
research about, 282–285
scaffolds and guided practice for, 292–294
self-assessment for, 292–293, 297–298
self-study checklist for, 305
slow-motion with, 294
spoken feedback and, 252, 283, 285
ticket out the door, 297
Non-verbal immediacy behaviors, 284
Nonverbal immediacy cues, 277t
Norms, 145, 159, 169–172, 171f
Note-taking, 269

One-on-one feedback. See Individual feedback
Oral feedback. See Spoken feedback

Panadero, E., 83–84
Parent engagement, progress guides for, 103
Pausing, 178f, 251, 257, 258
PBL-Works, 19
Peak-end-effect, 188–189
Pedagogical content knowledge (PCK), 49–51
Peer-to-peer-driven feedback
overview, 60–62, 62t, 79
criteria for success and, 127
defined, 62–64
moderation process, 72–74
planning for, 64–66t, 64–67
preparation for success with, 70–74
primary goal for, 74–75
professional learning communities and, 78
reflection on, 76–77
research about, 67–70
scaffolds and guided practice for, 66t, 67, 74–77
scoring guides and, 68–70, 72–74

self-assessment and, 65t, 67, 114
self-driven feedback and, 95–96
self-study checklist for, 300
ticket out the door, 79
Perlstein, D., 92
Physical proximity, 285
Pivotal points, 199
Popham, W. J., 16
Portfolios, 12
Posing, 178f
Praise, observational statements versus, 186, 189, 214
Priming
  defined, 56, 178f
  individual feedback and, 195–196, 204
  revision and, 27
  self-assessment progress guides for, 195–196
  self-driven feedback and, 87t
  teacher-driven feedback and, 56
  whole class feedback and, 119
  written feedback and, 242
Probing, 177, 178f, 243–244
Professional learning communities (PLCs)
  individual feedback and, 205–208
  nonverbal feedback and, 295–296
  peer-to-peer-driven feedback and, 78
  self-driven feedback and, 104–107
  small group feedback and, 173
  spoken feedback and, 270–272
  teacher-driven feedback and, 57–58
  whole class feedback and, 140–142
  written feedback and, 246–247
Progress guides
  overview, 21–22, 31
  binning for feedback with, 130–132, 138–139, 191
  defined, 98
  designing, 136–138
  differentiated feedback and, 120–121
  example of, 21f
  individual feedback, student use, 193–196, 194f
  individual feedback, teacher use, 190–193, 191–192f
  key features of, 101f, 193
  purposes of, 138, 154
  revision of, 97, 101–102
  role in Formative Feedback Process Model, 27–28
  rubrics and, 96–98, 227–234, 229–231f, 233f, 235f

self-regulation and, 97–103, 100–101f
small group feedback, student use, 153–158, 155–156f
for student self-assessment, 193–196, 194f, 234, 235f, 262
suggestions for creation and use of, 100–103
using to inform spoken feedback, 261–263
whole class feedback, student use, 129, 132, 134
whole class feedback, teacher use, 119–121, 120f, 126, 129–132, 131–132f
written feedback, student use, 234, 235f
written feedback, teacher use, 232–234, 233f
Project-based collaboration tools, 172
Project-based learning (PBL), rich, meaningful tasks and, 18–19
Prompts, asynchronous feedback and, 54
Purpose-driven feedback, 8–11, 30, 129, 299

Ramaprasad, A., 17
Remote learning, 40, 148
Respect, 197, 225–226
Review, ask, to-do model, 196–197, 196f
Revision
  importance of, 49, 167
  priming for, 27
  of progress guides, 97, 101–102
  resistance to, 212
  respect and, 197
Rich, meaningful tasks, 17–20, 258
Right to learn, 4, 30
Rubrics
  feedback not limited by, 48–49
  importance of, 170
  problems with, 21
  progress guides and, 96–98, 227–234, 229–231f, 233f, 235f
  scoring guides compared with, 70

Scaffolding, 15, 66t, 67
Schemas, defined, 13
Schooling, purposes of, 31–33
Science Education for Public Understanding Project (SEPUP), 72
Scoring guides, 68–70, 72–74, 85. *See also* Progress guides
Self-assessment for students
  criteria for success and, 127
  defined, 83
  inaccuracy in student perception of, 263

as necessary for self-driven feedback, 85–86, 99
nonverbal feedback and, 292–293, 297–298
peer assessment and, 65t, 67
peer-to-peer-driven feedback and, 65t, 67, 114
priming and, 195–196
progress guides for, 193–196, 194f, 234, 235f, 262
questions to ask about, 96
relationship with self-driven feedback and self-regulated learning, 83–84, 83f
research about, 89–91
using to inform spoken feedback, 262

Self-assessment for teachers
directionality, 39–40
individual feedback, 202–203, 206–208
instructional and assessment practices, 28–30
modalities, 218–219
nonverbal feedback, 292–293, 297–298
small group feedback, 175

Self-driven feedback
overview, 80–82, 82f, 107
calling attention to process and, 88t, 89
defined, 83–86, 83f
example of, 91–97
peer-to-peer-driven feedback and, 95–96
planning for, 86–89, 87–88t
professional learning communities and, 104–107
relationship with self-assessment and self-regulated learning, 83–84, 83f
research about, 89–91
scaffolds and guided practice for, 97–103, 100–101f
self-assessment as necessary but not sufficient for, 85–86, 99
self-study checklist for, 301
ticket out the door, 108

Self-regulation
overview, 83–84
attempts to get evidence of, 85
co-regulation and, 84, 95
dialogic approach to analyzing, 110–116
example of, 91–97
progress guides for, 97–103, 100–101f
relationship with self-driven feedback and self-assessment, 83–84, 83f

Self-study checklist, 299–305
Short-turn cycles of feedback, 23–24
Sizer, Theodore, 189

Small group feedback
overview, 144–147, 147f, 174
creation of groups, 154, 157
defined, 147–148
enactment of formative feedback and, 166, 166–167f
example dialogue with, 159–162
goals for, 158
interaction focus and, 155, 157–158
norms for, 145, 159, 169–172, 171f
peer dynamics and, 145, 151–152, 172
phases of feedback with, 162–169, 165–169f
planning for, 148–151, 149–150t, 168–169, 169f
post-formative feedback and, 167, 168f
pre-formative feedback and, 164, 165f
professional learning communities and, 173
progress guides for student use, 153–154
progress guides for teacher use, 154–158, 155–156f
reflection on, 171, 171f
research about, 151–153
scaffolds and guided practice for, 162–163
self-study checklist for, 302
ticket out the door, 174–175

SOLO taxonomy, 14–17, 16f, 202–203, 292–293

Spoken feedback
overview, 250–252, 252f, 272
defined, 253–254
differentiation and, 256
nonverbal feedback and, 252, 283, 285
planning for, 254, 255–256t, 256
professional learning communities and, 270–272
progress guides to inform, 261–263
research about, 256–260
scaffolds and guided practice for, 267–269, 268t
self-study checklist for, 304
student interview about, 263–266
ticket out the door, 273
voice recording tools for, 269
writing down, 267–269, 268t
written feedback and, 216, 258, 262

Status problems in small groups, 151–152
Student engagement. *See* Three Es of feedback
Students, 45–46, 47. *See also* Peer-to-peer-driven feedback; Self-assessment for students; Self-driven feedback; Self-regulation

Students with special needs, 22, 267–269, 268t. *See also* Differentiation; English learners (ELs)
Surface learning, feedback and, 44
Synchronous versus asynchronous contexts, 51–54, 217–218, 242–243

Tagging, 178f
Tasks, rich and meaningful, 17–20
Teacher-driven feedback
   overview, 36–37, 38t, 58
   defined, 38–39
   medium of feedback and, 47
   pedagogical content knowledge and, 49–51
   planning for, 41–42t, 41–43
   practice and, 48–49
   professional learning communities and, 57–58
   research about, 43–47
   scaffolds and guided practice for, 55–57
   self-assessment for, 39–40
   self-study checklist for, 299–300
   synchronous versus asynchronous contexts, 51–54
   three Es of feedback, 41–42t, 41–43, 55–57
   ticket out the door, 59
   tone and, 54, 57
Think time, 202
Three Es of feedback
   individual feedback and, 176–179
   pedagogical content knowledge and, 50–51
   teacher-driven feedback and, 41–42t, 41–43, 55–57
   whole class feedback and, 125–126t
Tincture of time, 204
Tips to try
   audio messaging, 103
   binning for feedback, 138
   feedback on feedback, 245
   Flip, 77
   Google Docs, 103
   positive comments with audio or voice feedback, 189
   priming, 56, 204
   reflection prompts, 239
   slow-motion with nonverbals, 294
   student response to feedback, 46
   student self-assessment progress guide check boxes, 102
   tincture of time, 204

Trello, 172
Vocaroo, 269
voice typing, 56–57
Tone, 54, 57, 225–226, 243
Topping, K. J., 67
Total physical response (TPR), 287
Transfer of learning, feedback and, 44
Trello, 172
Trust, 45–46, 188
Try it tomorrow. *See* Tips to try

Van der Schaaf, M. F., 213
Venting, 112
Verbal feedback. *See* Spoken feedback
Video feedback, 189
Vinh, Kim, 48–49
Virtual learning, 40, 148
Visual collaboration platforms, 172
Vocaroo, 269
Voice recording tools, 103, 269
Voice typing, 56–57
Voxer, 103
Vygotsky, Lev, 69

Webb's depth of knowledge (DOK), 13–14
Whole class feedback
   overview, 118–119, 123f, 142
   back-of-the-envelope method, 139–140
   binning for feedback, 130–132, 138–139
   checking for understanding about, 121, 124
   defined, 123–124
   differentiation of feedback, 129–132, 130–132f
   example of, 133–136
   planning for, 124–127, 125–126f
   professional learning communities and, 140–142
   progress guides for student use, 129, 132, 134
   progress guides for teacher use, 119–121, 120f, 126, 129–132, 131–132f
   research about, 127–129
   scaffolds and guided practice for, 136–140
   self-study checklist for, 301–302
   ticket out the door, 143
   when to use, 121, 133
Wiggins, G. P., 20
Wise feedback, 188
Wisniewski, B., 128
Written feedback
   overview, 212–216, 216f, 248

addressing challenges with, 236–239
asynchronous versus synchronous contexts, 217–218, 242–243
defined, 216–217
feedback on, 245
feed-forward feedback, 226–227
improving quality of, 240–241
intentionality about, 213–214
intersection with other modalities, 213, 214, 215, 224, 240–241
misunderstandings or confusion with, 224–225, 244
planning for, 219, 220–224t, 224
probing and, 243–244
professional learning communities and, 246–247
progress guides for student use, 234, 235f
progress guides for teacher use, 232–234, 233f
research about, 225–227
rubrics, augmenting with progress guides, 227–234, 229–231f, 233f, 235f
scaffolds and guided practice for, 241–245
self-study checklist for, 303–304
spoken feedback and, 216, 258, 262
student reflection on, 239, 243
ticket out the door, 248–249
tone and, 225–226, 243

Yeager, David Scott, 45–46

Zones of proximal development (ZPD), 15, 69, 126, 182

Solutions YOU WANT | Experts YOU TRUST | Results YOU NEED

INSTITUTES
Corwin Institutes provide regional and virtual events where educators collaborate with peers and learn from industry experts. Prepare to be recharged and motivated!

corwin.com/institutes

ON-SITE PROFESSIONAL LEARNING
Corwin on-site PD is delivered through high-energy keynotes, practical workshops, and custom coaching services designed to support knowledge development and implementation.

www.corwin.com/pd

VIRTUAL PROFESSIONAL LEARNING
Our virtual PD combines live expert facilitation with the flexibility of anytime, anywhere professional learning. See the power of intentionally designed virtual PD.

www.corwin.com/virtualworkshops

CORWIN ONLINE
Online learning designed to engage, inform, challenge, and inspire. Our courses offer practical, classroom-focused instruction that will meet your continuing education needs and enhance your practice.

www.corwinonline.com

Visit www.corwin.com

CORWIN

CORWIN
A SAGE Publishing Company

Helping educators make the greatest impact

CORWIN HAS ONE MISSION: to enhance education through intentional professional learning.

We build long-term relationships with our authors, educators, clients, and associations who partner with us to develop and continuously improve the best evidence-based practices that establish and support lifelong learning.